HUME'S 'A TREATISE OF HUMAN NATURE'

AF167661

David Hume's *A Treatise of Human Nature* (1739–40) presents the most important account of skepticism in the history of modern philosophy. In this lucid and thorough introduction to the work, John P. Wright examines the development of Hume's ideas in the *Treatise*, their relation to eighteenth-century theories of the imagination and passions, and the reception they received when Hume published the *Treatise*. He explains Hume's arguments concerning the inability of reason to establish the basic beliefs which underlie science and morals, as well as his arguments showing why we are nevertheless psychologically compelled to accept such beliefs. The book will be a valuable guide for those seeking to understand the nature of modern skepticism and its connection with the founding of the human sciences during the Enlightenment.

JOHN P. WRIGHT is Professor of Philosophy at Central Michigan University, and was Visiting Professor in Philosophy at the University of Edinburgh from 2004 to 2007. He is the author of *The Sceptical Realism of David Hume* (1983), and co-editor of *Hume and Hume's Connexions* (1994) and *Psyche and Soma: Physicians and Metaphysicians on the Mind-Body Problem from Antiquity to Enlightenment* (2000).

CAMBRIDGE INTRODUCTIONS TO KEY PHILOSOPHICAL TEXTS

This new series offers introductory textbooks on what are considered to be the most important texts of Western philosophy. Each book guides the reader through the main themes and arguments of the work in question, while also paying attention to its historical context and its philosophical legacy. No philosophical background knowledge is assumed, and the books will be well suited to introductory university level courses.

Titles published in the series:

DESCARTES'S *MEDITATIONS* by Catherine Wilson

WITTGENSTEIN'S *PHILOSOPHICAL INVESTIGATIONS* by David G. Stern

WITTGENSTEIN'S *TRACTATUS* by Alfred Nordmann

ARISTOTLE'S *NICOMACHEAN ETHICS* by Michael Pakaluk

SPINOZA'S *ETHICS* by Steven Nadler

KANT'S *CRITIQUE OF PURE REASON* by Jill Vance Buroker

HEIDEGGER'S *BEING AND TIME* by Paul Gorner

KANT'S *GROUNDWORK OF THE METAPHYSICS OF MORALS* by Sally Sedgwick

HEGEL'S *PHENOMENOLOGY OF SPIRIT* by Larry Krasnoff

NIETZSCHE'S *ON THE GENEALOGY OF MORALITY* by Laurence J. Hatab

RAWLS'S *A THEORY OF JUSTICE* by Jon Mandle

HUME'S *A TREATISE OF HUMAN NATURE* by John P. Wright

HUME'S 'A TREATISE OF HUMAN NATURE'

An Introduction

JOHN P. WRIGHT

Central Michigan University

CAMBRIDGE
UNIVERSITY PRESS

CAMBRIDGE
UNIVERSITY PRESS

University Printing House, Cambridge CB2 8BS, United Kingdom

One Liberty Plaza, 20th Floor, New York, NY 10006, USA

477 Williamstown Road, Port Melbourne, VIC 3207, Australia

314-321, 3rd Floor, Plot 3, Splendor Forum, Jasola District Centre, New Delhi - 110025, India

79 Anson Road, #06-04/06, Singapore 079906

Cambridge University Press is part of the University of Cambridge.

It furthers the University's mission by disseminating knowledge in the pursuit of education, learning and research at the highest international levels of excellence.

www.cambridge.org
Information on this title: www.cambridge.org/9780521541589

First published 2009

A catalogue record for this publication is available from the British Library

Library of Congress Cataloging in Publication data
Wright, John P.
Hume's "A Treatise of Human Nature" : an introduction / John P. Wright.
p. cm. (Cambridge introductions to key philosophical texts).
ISBN 978-0-521-83376-9 (hardback)
1. Hume, David, 1711–1776. A Treatise of Human Nature. 2. Knowledge, Theory of.
3. Emotions (Philosophy) 4. Ethics. 5. Skepticism. 6. Reason. 7. Philosophical anthropology. I. Title.
B1489.W75 2009
128–dc22
2009027848

ISBN 978-0-521-83376-9 Hardback
ISBN 978-0-521-54158-9 Paperback

To the late John W. Yolton, teacher and friend,
who taught me to love both philosophy and its history,
and to appreciate the difference

Contents

Preface

There is no better example of the *baroque* style of writing in philosophy than David Hume's *A Treatise of Human Nature*. Like the Hall of Mirrors at Versailles, a Handel Oratorio, or Lord Shaftesbury's *Characteristics of Men, Manners, Opinions, Times*, it is characterized by complexity, grandeur, and expansiveness. Published in three separate volumes in 1739 and 1740, it well represents the age in which it was written. Indeed, there is a striking contrast between the *Treatise* and the core writings of Hume's later philosophy – his *Enquiry Concerning Human Understanding* and his *Enquiry Concerning the Principles of Morals*, first published in 1748 and 1752 respectively – where, as he said, he cast his earlier ideas anew. By comparison with the *Treatise*, these philosophical writings are simple and elegant. There is a reason for this. Hume was profoundly disappointed by the reception of the *Treatise*, and judged that its failure lay more in the manner than the matter. He decided that "by care and art, and the avoiding of all unnecessary detail" he could throw more light on the subjects he dealt with in the earlier book.[1]

Nevertheless, it is this irregular pearl, *A Treatise of Human Nature*, which has come to be regarded as Hume's great philosophical masterpiece and, indeed, among the greatest philosophical books ever written. It is a book which every serious student of philosophy is expected to read, and the philosophical struggles of its author, dramatically described in the famous skeptical Conclusion to Book I, have come to represent the philosophical enterprise itself. Yet, as might be expected from a book of its reach and complexity, it has spawned vastly differing interpretations. Very different philosophical

[1] EHU 1.17

schools have claimed Hume as one of their own – positivism, naturalism, skepticism, empiricism, and phenomenology – to name a few. Competing interpretations of Hume's analysis of causality regard him variously as a regularity theorist, a quasi-realist, and a skeptical realist. In recent years his ethical theory has been considered a work in virtue ethics, focusing on the evaluation of human character. But in earlier years he was regarded as an emotivist or a proto-utilitarian – theories generally considered as exclusive of each other and certainly of virtue ethics. These varying interpretations are evidence, if nothing else, of the seminal nature of this famous book.

At the same time, they present a particular problem for a scholar who seeks to introduce the *Treatise* to those who are just beginning to study it. An attempt to take the reader through the scholarly literature comparing one interpretation with another one runs the risk of convincing her that the *Treatise* is so unclear that, in the words of one commentator, one can "find all philosophies in Hume, or, by setting up one statement against another, none at all."[2] On the other hand, by presenting a single interpretation and disregarding all others one runs the risk of oversimplifying his doctrines and leaving the reader with little appreciation of the richness of the philosophical ideas he struggled with. In this book, I have attempted a middle course, presenting a unified interpretation of the *Treatise* while at the same time indicating how my interpretation differs from those of other commentators on his philosophy. The main lines of this interpretation were first put forward in my book *The Sceptical Realism of David Hume* (1983), and developed in subsequent articles. They are based, above all, on a consideration of the relation of Hume's views to the philosophers he identified as his predecessors, both in the text of the *Treatise* and in his contemporary correspondence.

I open the book with a chapter discussing Hume's intellectual development as he was writing the *Treatise* – a subject which has been the study of much careful scholarship in recent years. This scholarship challenges assumptions which are often repeated from one book on Hume's philosophy to another. In this chapter, I attempt to use this recent scholarship to throw light on the ways in which Hume's

---

[2] Editor's Introduction, David Hume, *Enquiries Concerning Human Understanding and Concerning the Principles of Morals*, ed. L. A. Selby-Bigge, 3rd edn., revised by P. H. Nidditch (Oxford: Clarendon Press, 1975), p. vii.

personal and intellectual struggles while he was writing the *Treatise* influenced his conclusions about skepticism and human nature. Throughout the book I draw links back to this biographical study.

In Chapter 2, "First principles," I stress the centrality of the principle of association of ideas throughout the *Treatise*, and argue that it is rooted in the standard eighteenth-century theory of the imagination. I contend that Hume's experimental method, modeled on that of natural scientists such as Bacon and Boyle, involved a careful use of mechanical hypotheses, and that the Cartesian theory of the imagination provided Hume with a hypothesis concerning the workings of the brain in associating perceptions. He presupposes this model in explaining the transfer of force and vivacity from impressions to ideas, as well as in explaining what commentators call his *copy principle*. I also argue that his account of the origin of ideas plays a *skeptical* role in his philosophy, leading him to acknowledge the limits and imperfections of our clear and distinct impression-derived ideas. Throughout this chapter I stress Hume's engagement with Cartesian science and philosophy.

I introduce my discussion of Hume's theory of causation in Chapter 3 by distinguishing those epistemological features of Hume's theory about which scholars agree from those questions concerning the ontology of causation about which there is sharp disagreement. I begin my exposition by explaining his distinction between knowledge and probability, and stress the importance of the *insight ideal* of knowledge in understanding his claim that we have no knowledge of causality. In presenting his accounts of both the causal maxim and of inductive inference I argue that his aim is to show that reason and insight cannot by themselves provide a basis for our inferences, and that these inferences have their source in the mechanical processes of imagination as altered by experience. I show that Hume provides a systematic critique of Locke's views on probability and causal inference. It is especially in Hume's account of the causes of the *belief* in what is probable that his mechanical model of association becomes crucial. He argues that after experience the impression *determines* the mind to conceive of the idea in a certain way, and that it is this determination or new impression which then becomes the source of the idea of a necessary connection between cause and effect. Finally, I lay out and discuss the texts which have led to opposing interpretations of his view of the ontology of causation – the regularity theory, quasi-realism and skeptical realism. I defend the last of these interpretations: Hume's account is *skeptical* in the sense that it denies the adequacy of our actual ideas of cause and effect, and *realist* in the sense that it postulates the existence of an unknown necessary connection in which we naturally believe.

In chapter 4, "Skepticism," I discuss Hume's extensive account of this theme in Part 4 of Book 1. I lay out each of the skeptical topics which he deals with – skepticism concerning reason, the senses, material substrata, and personal identity. In relation to the first two topics Hume argues that the doubts which reason and philosophy create *in theory* cannot be maintained *in practice*. He explains the natural processes of imagination which do not allow reason to undermine our belief. I stress that Hume's skepticism with regard to the senses arises from experiments which show that our sensory perceptions are mind or brain dependent. His task is then to explain how we come to believe that they continue to exist while unperceived. His core explanation of the belief in the independent existence of the objects of our senses, as well as material substrata and personal identity is based on what I call the *identity substitution principle* – a principle of the association of ideas which causes us to mistake other relations for numerical identity. I also argue that his deepest form of skepticism is cognitive – based on the obscurity of the basic suppositions which we naturally make about reality, including the belief that the objects of our senses continue to exist while unperceived. In this way the skepticism of the *Treatise* is linked to ancient academic skepticism – though he explicitly makes that connection only in his first *Enquiry*. I also discuss the sources of the total skepticism which marks the Conclusion to Book 1 of the *Treatise*: his escape from this total skepticism is not based on reason, but on the passions – particularly those of curiosity and ambition. It is passions rather than reason which provide the motivation for us to pursue science.

In Chapter 5, I return to Hume's account of causality – this time to discuss his explanation of human action in Book 2 of the *Treatise*. In his discussion "Of liberty and necessity" he stresses that we have exactly the same basis for ascribing necessity to the human will as to external objects – namely the regularity of our experience and our natural tendency to infer effects from their causes and causes from their effects. He argues that our actions are determined by circumstance, motive and character – and that there is no more chance or "indifference" in human action than in physical causes. In practice we all assume the truth of determinism, and yet we have a subjective feeling of liberty when reflecting on our own actions. Hume holds that whatever our philosophical principles we all naturally adopt the spectator's point of view in ascertaining the causes of human actions. While he appeals to his "two definitions of cause" (as involving mere regularity and predictability) in order to disarm his libertarian opponents, he attributes a real ontological necessity to the human will, as well as to physical events.

Hume's accounts of the causes of our passions and of sympathy (i.e. empathy) are discussed in Chapter 6. I begin by explaining his distinction between direct and indirect passions, and the decisive role of association of ideas in creating the latter. The parallels with the mechanisms Hume postulated in his account of inductive inference in Book 1 are explained – especially in relation to his account of sympathy. The transfer of psychic energy in all these cases is controlled by the natural relations of ideas. In the case of sympathy the *idea* of the other person's feelings is transformed into an *impression*, which allows us to enter into her feelings, and distinguish them from our own. I discuss the limits of Hume's mechanistic explanation of sympathy, and the puzzle as to why he does not think he must explain our belief in other minds in Book 2, as he did our belief in external objects in Book 1. I also discuss his account of the person as it relates to the passions, and also the question whether the Book 2 conception of self is consistent with that of Book 1.

Chapter 7 is focused on Hume's theory of motivation, including his claim that reason can never motivate us, and that what is mistaken for reason by Platonic philosophers who describe morality in terms of a war between reason and passion is a *calm passion*. I return to earlier discussions in the book of just what Hume means by 'reason' – a central problem for interpreters of the *Treatise*. I contend that Hume's conception of a calm passion is closely tied to his account of the development of character – a link which becomes crucial in his own account of morality in Book 3. In crucial cases calm passions are not instinctive: they are the result of custom and habit. I show that Hume follows Joseph Butler in claiming that when a passion gains strength through custom it also loses emotional intensity. Hume holds with Butler that what is key to moral motivation is a natural development through custom and habit of certain calm passions.

In Chapter 8, I discuss those features of Hume's moral philosophy which derive largely from the philosophy of Francis Hutcheson – his attack on moral rationalism and his view that moral judgment is based in sentiment and not reason. I begin with a caution about Hume's use of the expression "moral sense," a term he borrows from Hutcheson and Shaftesbury. I explain the conception of a moral sense in Hutcheson's philosophy and his reduction of all virtues to that of benevolence. I describe Hume's main arguments, largely based on those of Hutcheson, against the view that morality is based on reason. I comment extensively on Hume's claim, also borrowed from Hutcheson, that virtue and vice do not lie in the agent or her actions but are to be found in a feeling of the spectator in responding to them. We should take seriously Hume's analogy between moral feeling and secondary qualities – an analogy he draws out in later writings. For Hume, there is a radical distinction between fact and value. Unlike Hutcheson, who held that we have strong evidence from the design of the creation that its creator shares our judgments concerning moral value, Hume held that morality concerns "only human Nature & human Life."

In Chapter 9, I discuss Hume's own moral theory and argue that it provides a solution to the controversy between Hutcheson and Bernard Mandeville regarding the artificiality or naturalness of virtue. I argue that we can trace a development in Hume's account of moral approval from his discussion of our natural uncultivated ideas of morality at the beginning of Part 2 of Book 3 of the *Treatise* to the view that most virtues are judged on the basis of their utility in Part 3. I describe his theory of the development of the artificial virtue of justice, showing how he explains the origin of the conventions of property without any formal social contact, and the subsequent moral judgments of those who follow and fail to follow these conventions. I discuss the role of sympathy and custom in his account of moral judgment and moral motivation. Hume argues that moral judgment is based on our genuine sympathy with others and so rejects Mandeville's view that our moral judgments are based simply on indoctrination and self-interest. But he also rejects Hutcheson's view that our moral judgments are based on an innate moral sense which approves of moral virtues apart from their consequences.

In 1776, the year of Hume's death, Jeremy Bentham, the founder of utilitarianism, wrote in his *Fragment on Government* that when he read Book 3 of the *Treatise*, particularly Hume's account of justice, he felt as though "scales had fallen from ... [his] eyes" and he first "learned to call the cause of the People the cause of Virtue."[3] He stated that what he found there "demonstrated, after a few exceptions made, with the strongest force of evidence" that "the foundations of all *virtue* are laid in *utility*." He added that he could see no "need ... for the exceptions." Some years later, in a letter discussing the principle of utility, or greatest happiness principle, Bentham wrote that the main difference between him and Hume was that "the use he made of it, was to *account* for that which *is*, [whereas] I ... shew what *ought to be*."[4]

Hume was not a "philosophical utilitarian" – in spite of his important role in developing that philosophy.[5] As he clearly stated in a letter to Hutcheson as he was revising Book 3 for the press, his aim was to describe and explain the principles of morals on which people operate, not to be a moralist.[6] Hume argues that we base most moral judgments on a consideration of the utility of the characters and actions we are evaluating. However, his own study of morals is fundamentally not normative: he is *not* telling people how they *ought to act* but explaining to them how they come to make the normative moral judgments they actually make.

A similar point may be made about Hume's epistemology and metaphysics. A major goal of Book 1 of the *Treatise* is to explain the origin of our common-sense beliefs, such as the belief in the existence of an external world. Hume held that such beliefs are so firmly implanted in our nature that we cannot doubt them. Indeed, he asserts that our survival depends upon our acceptance of them, and that they must be taken for granted in our reasoning – including

---

[3] Jeremy Bentham, *A Fragment on Government*, in *The Works of Jeremy Bentham*, John Bowring (ed.), Vols. 1–10 (New York: Russell and Russell, 1962), Vol. I, p. 149, note H.
[4] Bentham to Étienne Dumont, 6 September, 1822, in Catherine Fuller (ed.), *The Correspondence of Jeremy Bentham* (Oxford: Clarendon Press, 2000), Vol. XI, p. 149.
[5] Stephen Darwall, "Hume and the Invention of Utilitarianism," in M. A. Stewart and J. P. Wright (eds.), *Hume and Hume's Connexions* (Edinburgh University Press, 1994), pp. 58–82.
[6] Chapter 1, pp. 33–4 below.

the investigation into their causes. Some have concluded from this that Hume's philosophy is fundamentally the same as that of his successors of the Scottish School of Common Sense who argued that we are justified in accepting such common-sense beliefs.[7] But while the *Treatise* played a decisive role in the development of the views of Thomas Reid and other writers of the Scottish School – Reid told Hume that he would "always avow my self your Disciple in Metaphysics"[8] – Hume's aim is to explain and describe the *content* of these beliefs, not justify them. He argues that a scientific study of their sources reveals that these common sense beliefs contain a fundamental incoherence. This is precisely what Reid denied.[9] Thus while Hume no more doubts the existence of an external world than his Scottish successors, his account of the nature of the belief is skeptical in a way that theirs is not.

I do not want to deny that Hume gives us interesting hints regarding both epistemic and moral justification – and that good scholarly work has been done drawing out those hints.[10] But I do want to argue that the dominant thrust of Hume's philosophy is descriptive and not normative, and that his conclusions are fundamentally skeptical. In my earlier book on Hume I coined the expression "skeptical realism" to characterize his philosophy. This still seems to me to be the best way to describe his basic philosophical principles. He assumes that there is a world independent of us which we can but

---

[7] Norman Kemp Smith, *The Philosophy of David Hume: A Critical Study of its Origins and Central Doctrines* (London: Macmillan, 1941), pp. 3ff. Kemp Smith writes in his Preface of Hume's "non-sceptical, realist teaching." See esp. pp. 150–1 below for my criticism of Kemp Smith's interpretation of Hume's view on the belief in the existence of the external world.

[8] Thomas Reid to David Hume, 18 March 1783, in Thomas Reid, *An Inquiry into the Human Mind on the Principles of Common Sense*, ed. Derek R. Brookes (Edinburgh University Press, 1997), pp. 264–5. I have discussed the relation of Hume's philosophy to that of Reid in a number of articles listed in the bibliography.

[9] On Reid's and Hume's different conceptions of common-sense belief see my "Reid's Answer to Hume's Scepticism: Turning Science into Common Sense," in E. Mazza and E. Ronchetti (eds.), *Instruction and Amusement: Le ragioni dell'Illuminismo brittanico* (Padua: Il Poligrafo, 2005), pp. 143–63.

[10] See Louis Loeb, *Stability and Justification in Hume's Treatise* (Oxford: Clarendon Press, 2002). Loeb argues that Hume could have avoided skepticism by more consistently applying the principles he develops in Part 3 of Book 1 of the *Treatise*. On the historical background of Hume's discussion of epistemic justification in *Treatise* 1.4.2 see my *Sceptical Realism of David Hume*, (Manchester University Press and University of Minnesota Press, 1983), pp. 74–6.

imperfectly cognize. He argues that while we naturally suppose both the existence and basic characteristics of such a world, we do not understand its nature through our cognitive faculties. Moreover, he holds that experimental science builds on these natural suppositions of common sense by way of hypotheses that are constantly open to revision by experience. I regard my own task as a historian of philosophy as one of recovering the basic principles and presuppositions of his philosophy as revealed in his most seminal writing – that is *A Treatise of Human Nature.*

Acknowledgments

This project has received generous support from my home university, Central Michigan University, and from Edinburgh University, where I was Visiting Professor in the School of Philosophy, Psychology and Language Sciences from 2004 to 2007. My trips to Edinburgh, particularly through the winter of 2005 when I taught a postgraduate class, and in the spring of 2006 when I gave a public lecture, were invaluable in the writing of the book. Students and colleagues at both universities have patiently listened and commented as I tried different ways of explaining the fundamental ideas of Hume's *Treatise*.

The project has gone forward with the strong encouragement of Sandy Stewart, Peter Kail, Galen Strawson, and Luigi Turco. They have read and offered useful comments on draft chapters of the book. So have Annette Baier, James Buickerood, Dorothy Coleman, Gary Fuller, Michael Gill, Peter Millican, Robert Stecker, and Stephen Wright. Sue Ann Martin has read through and commented on drafts of every chapter of the book. The book has also benefited from the judicious and insightful comments of an anonymous press referee. The encouragement and patience of Hilary Gaskin has been invaluable throughout the project.

Abbreviations

Clarendon Critical Edition by the same editor (Oxford: Clarendon Press, 2000); references are made to section and paragraph number.

EPM   *Enquiry Concerning the Principles of Morals*, ed. Tom L. Beauchamp (Oxford University Press, 1998), or the Clarendon Critical Edition by the same editor (Oxford: Clarendon Press, 1998); references are made to section and paragraph number.

Essays   *Essays Moral, Political, and Literary*, ed. E. F. Millar (Indianapolis: Liberty Classics, rev. edn., 1987).

HL   *The Letters of David Hume*, ed. J. Y. T. Greig, 2 vols. (Oxford University Press, 1932); this collection is referred to by the volume and page number.

WORKS BY OTHER WRITERS

CSM   René Descartes, *The Philosophical Writings of Descartes*, trans. John Cottingham, Robert Stoothoff, Dugald Murdoch, and Anthony Kenny, 3 vols. (Cambridge University Press, 1985–1991); this collection is referred to by the volume and page number.

Essay on the Passions   Francis Hutcheson, *An Essay on the Nature and Conduct of the Passions and Affections, with Illustrations on the Moral Sense*, ed. Aaron Garrett (Indianapolis: Liberty Fund, 2002).

Inquiry into Beauty and Virtue   Francis Hutcheson, *An Inquiry into the Original of Our Ideas of Beauty and Virtue*, ed. Wolfgang Leidhold (Indianapolis: Liberty Fund, 2004).

ECHU   John Locke, *An Essay Concerning Human Understanding*, ed. P. H. Nidditch (Oxford University Press, 1975); this book is referred to by book, chapter, and section number.

Principles   George Berkeley, *A Treatise concerning the Principles of Human Knowledge*, in *The Works of George Berkeley, Bishop of Cloyne*, Vol. II, eds. A. A. Luce and T. E. Jessop (London: Nelson, 1949).

Search   Nicolas Malebranche, *The Search After Truth*, trans. Thomas M. Lennon and Paul J. Olscamp (Cambridge University Press, 1997).

CHAPTER I

The author and the book

I. REFLECTIONS ON THE ROAD FROM LONDON TO BRISTOL

The state of mind of the twenty-two-year-old David Hume as he was jostled up and down in the stagecoach traveling the rough road from London to Bristol in March of 1734 is not difficult to imagine. He had plenty of time on the fifteen-hour-long journey to reflect back on his young life and think about what the future might bring. He must have felt some sadness, having left his family and friends back in Scotland a few weeks earlier. At the same time, Hume was on his way to take up a position with a sugar merchant in Bristol and would have felt the excitement of a young man on a new adventure, traveling alone far from home for the first time in his life. Nevertheless, this was not the life that he had set out for himself five years earlier, and it was with some regrets that he had made this decision. The truth of the matter was that he had made himself ill by the studious way of life that he had adopted, and he had decided to set aside his books and writing for a time until he recovered his health. He believed that this would be best accomplished through an "active" life in business. Thus he was heading toward the major port city of western England to take up a position with a "considerable Trader" to whom he had been recommended.[1]

David Hume was not from a very wealthy family and, being a second son, was expected to earn his own living. His father had died in 1713 when he was two years old, and the family estate at Ninewells, in the Scottish borders overlooking England, had been

---

[1] To [Dr. George Cheyne], March or April 1734, HL I, 12–18, esp. p. 18. Hereafter referred to as 'Letter to a Physician.'

inherited by his elder brother John. His mother was (to use his own words) "a woman of singular Merit, who ... devoted herself entirely to the rearing and educating of her Children";[2] yet her patience must have been tried when her brilliant and industrious second son, who had been studying to become a lawyer like her late husband, gave up that practical pursuit at the age of eighteen to become "a Scholar & Philosopher" (HL I, 13). More frustrating still, both for himself and for those who cared for him, must have been his illness, which began shortly after he committed himself to the life of scholarship. Was it a relief or simply a worry when he finally decided shortly before his twenty-third birthday, to seek a career in business?

No doubt, Hume himself had strongly felt the need to leave home and seek his fortune abroad. Even after he had published *A Treatise of Human Nature* he hesitated to return home because he could not "over-come a certain Shamefacedness" at appearing among his friends and family without yet having "a Settlement."[3] In his *Treatise* he wrote about "men of good families, but narrow circumstances" who "leave their friends and country, and rather seek their livelihood by mean and mechanical employments among strangers, than among those, who are acquainted with their birth and education" (T2.1.11.14–15: 322).[4] He wrote about the shame we feel when we adopt menial employment among those "who are both related to us by blood, and contiguous in place." We feel the contempt of our family when they are close by, and we are motivated to relieve our discomfort by moving away. When we are among strangers "no body will suspect from what family we are sprung," and our own inadequate situation "will by that means sit more easy upon us."

But Hume would have had other reasons to leave home than his shame at not having gainful employment equal to his station and education. He lived in a complex social network in which certain religious beliefs and attitudes were expected, especially of educated people. Hume would have been under special scrutiny having declared his intention to become a philosopher, particularly a moral

---

[2] "My Own Life," HL I, 1–7, esp. p. 1.

[3] Hume to Henry Home, December 2, 1737, in *New Letters of David Hume*, eds. R. Klibansky and E. C. Mossner (Oxford: Clarendon Press, 1954), p. 2. Henceforth referred to as NHL.

[4] Of course, Hume was not seeking "mechanical employments" in Bristol; nevertheless his general psychological point about shame and friends and family clearly applied to his own situation.

philosopher. His uncle was the minister of the local Presbyterian church in the village of Chirnside and was probably involved in the prosecution of a local farmer named William Dudgeon, who had published a controversial book entitled *The State of the Moral World Consider'd* in 1732, two years before Hume left Scotland.[5] The charges laid against Dudgeon in the local Presbytery were taken all the way to the Commission of the General Assembly of the Church of Scotland before being dropped. Dudgeon was accused of denying human freedom and making God the author of all evil in the world. While ultimately no action was taken, the charge was still being considered at the time when Hume left Scotland. Hume may have known Dudgeon, and certainly would have known the controversy about his writings.

Hume's own views on religion were not orthodox, even at this early period of his life. He struggled with the question of the truth of religion after he left the College of Edinburgh at the age of fourteen or fifteen. In his logic and metaphysics class at college he had been taught that the study of both the powers of the human mind and the works of the natural world would make him appreciate the gifts of divine providence, and thereby teach him his duties "towards God, self, and other humans."[6] He learned that the study of philosophy supplemented scriptural revelation. But a few years later, after giving up his law studies and devoting his life to scholarship, he began a notebook in which he anxiously considered various arguments for the existence of God.[7] He studied the arguments of the greatest English philosophers of the late seventeenth and early eighteenth centuries, John Locke and Samuel Clarke.[8] In his *Essay Concerning*

---

[5] Paul Russell, "Dudgeon, William," in *The Dictionary of Eighteenth-Century British Philosophers*, eds. J. W. Yolton, J. V. Price, and J. Stephens (Bristol: Thoemmes Press, 1999). Also, James McCosh, *The Scottish Philosophy* (New York, 1885), pp. 111–13. McCosh mistakenly calls Dudgeon "David Dudgeon."

[6] M. A. Stewart, "Hume's Intellectual Development, 1711–1752," in *Impressions of Hume*, eds. M. Frasca-Spada and P. J. E. Kail (Oxford: Clarendon Press, 2005), pp. 11–58, esp. p. 11. These words are translated by Stewart from a transcription of the logic lectures of Colin Drummond, the year before Hume took the course. He took it in 1723, when he was 12.

[7] Hume to Gilbert Elliot, March 1751, HL I, 154.

[8] James Boswell, "An Account of my last Interview with David Hume, Esq.," in *Dialogues Concerning Natural Religion*, ed. N. K. Smith, 2nd edn. (Edinburgh: Nelson, 1947), pp. 76–9: "He said he never entertained any belief in Religion since he began to read Locke and Clarke."

Human Understanding Locke had claimed to demonstrate the existence of God, beginning with our self-evident knowledge of our own existence.[9] He also appealed to a causal principle which he considered to be self-evident, namely that "*nothing can no more produce any real Being, than it can be equal to two right Angles.*" From these premises Locke inferred that "from Eternity there has been something," and that this eternal Being must contain more power and knowledge than any other being. This argument was discussed at length in Samuel Clarke's *A Demonstration of the Being and Attributes of God.*[10] In addition, Clarke argued that one can infer the wisdom of such a being by observing the order and harmony of the natural world. Hume found that the more he worked on these arguments the more his own "doubts stole in, dissipated, return'd, were again dissipated, return'd again."[11] He may have already begun to realize the devastating effect on these arguments of his discovery that knowledge of any cause and effect can only be derived from experience. In any case, the upshot of his reflections was that he had lost his faith by the time he completed his notebook on religion at the age of twenty.

The discussion of such metaphysical issues probably began among a group of friends with whom Hume met during the winters he spent in Edinburgh after he left college. Most important among these friends was Henry Home, a lawyer, about fifteen years older than Hume. Home was already a published author in 1728, and he was probably a mentor to Hume in his adolescence. Hume was later to tell Home that he was "the best Friend, in every respect, I ever possest."[12] In 1723, Henry Home had carried on a correspondence with Samuel Clarke about his philosophical writings on religion. He had a lifelong interest in the concept of power or force, both in the natural and moral worlds, and he is reported to have said that his reading Locke's chapter on "power" in the *Essay* "crucified" him.[13] Home also had a correspondence at this time with Andrew Baxter, a local Scottish defender of Clarke's philosophy. Baxter later published

[9] ECHU 4.10.2–6.
[10] Samuel Clarke, *A Demonstration of the Being and Attributes of God and Other Writings*, ed. E. Vailati (Cambridge University Press, 1998). These were Clarke's Boyle Lectures, first published in 1705.
[11] Hume to Gilbert Elliot, March 1751, HL I, 154.
[12] Hume to Henry Home, 13–15 June 1745, NHL, 17.
[13] Ian Ross, *Lord Kames and the Scotland of his Day* (Oxford: Clarendon Press, 1972), p. 60.

a book in which he denied that matter has any power or force of its own, and he argued that the only power in the universe belongs to immaterial beings.[14] Home, on the other hand, contended that matter was "active," a view which, according to Baxter, undermined the foundations of the Newtonian philosophy, and its fundamental concept of "inertia." These philosophical disputes would no doubt have been discussed by Henry Home and the young men surrounding him, including David Hume. It is striking that Home, Baxter and Dudgeon, who were thinking and writing about these metaphysical issues while Hume was growing up, all lived within a few miles of his family home at Ninewells.

2. STOIC REFLECTIONS, A "NEW SCENE OF THOUGHT" AND THE "DISEASE OF THE LEARNED"

Is it possible that Hume's religious doubts put a strain on him which caused his illness? That was not the way he himself saw his difficulties. Rather he came to conclude that the nervous disorder which began to trouble him when he was eighteen was brought on by an excessive use of reason, an attempt to use it to suppress his passions, and his inactive, isolated, studious way of life. According to his own account, when he was sixteen years old he had found his spiritual centre through "Philosophy and general Learning,"[15] rather than religion. He immersed himself in classical writers of philosophy and poetry, perhaps following the advice he had read in Lord Shaftesbury's *Characteristics of Men, Manners, Opinions, Times*, a book which he acquired at fifteen.[16] He became especially preoccupied with books on morality written by Seneca, Cicero, and Plutarch[17] and from them he learned Stoic techniques for becoming indifferent to one's passions and living one's life totally in accord

---

[14] Andrew Baxter, *An Enquiry into the Nature of the Human Soul* (London, 1733).

[15] "My Own Life," HL I, 1.

[16] D. F. Norton and M. Norton, *The David Hume Library* (Edinburgh Bibliographical Society, 1996), p. 16. Hume's copy of this multi-volume work was published in 1723.

[17] Letter to a Physician, HL I, 14. On Hume and Stoicism in Scotland, see M. A. Stewart, "The Stoic Legacy in the Early Scottish Enlightenment," in *Atoms, 'Pneuma', and Tranquility; Epicurean and Stoic Themes in European Thought*, ed. M. J. Osler (Cambridge University Press, 1991), pp. 273–96.

with reason. One book he studied with particular care was Cicero's *Tusculan Disputations*,[18] where it was argued that the soul is never cured of its unhappiness "without philosophy."[19] Hume concluded that the "Greatness & Elevation of the Soul is to be found in Study and contemplation, [and] that this can alone teach us to look down upon humane Accidents." Following the advice of the Stoics he constructed a set of principles in order to strengthen his character. These included "Reflections against Death, & Poverty, & Shame, & Pain, & all the other Calamities of Life."[20] He probably wrote down rules like the following: "*You should always have before your eyes death, disease, poverty, blindness, exile, calumny, and infamy, as ills which are incident to human nature. If any one of these ills falls to your lot, you will bear it the better when you have reckoned upon it.*"[21] Or, reflecting on the vicious things people often say or do to one another, he might have copied the following maxim from Plutarch's essay "On the Control of Anger": "*Let not the injuries or violence of men ... ever discompose you by anger or hatred. Would you be angry at the ape for its malice, or the tyger for its ferocity?*" Such Stoic reflections were of some use to him for a couple of years, but in 1729, after he had made his decision to devote himself entirely to philosophy and had begun to write his book in earnest, he realized that they had backfired. He discovered "by Experience" that these attempts to eliminate his feelings had ruined his health.[22] He concluded that while such principles may indeed have some use for a person leading "an active Life," they were worse than useless for someone like himself who was leading an isolated and sedentary existence.

Hume came to conclude not only that the Stoics' cure was worse than the disease, but that they had misidentified the source of the disease itself. In the remarkable Letter to a Physician, which he composed just before he set off from London to Bristol in 1734, he

---

[18] Hume to Michael Ramsay, 4 July 1727, HL I, 9–11, esp. p. 10.

[19] Cicero, *Tusculan Disputations*, III, VI, trans. J. E. King (London: Heinemann, 1966), pp. 240–1. Compare Hume's Letter to Michael Ramsay, 2 July 1727, HL I, 9–11, esp. p. 10 where he says that he is reading both philosophy and poetry, "for what will more surely engrave upon my mind a Tusculan Dispute of Cicero's de aegritudine lenienda [on the relief of distress] than an Eclogue or Georgick of Virgils."

[20] Letter to a Physician, HL I, 13–14.

[21] This and the following rule are taken from Hume's essay "The Sceptic," which was first published in 1742 (*Essays*, pp. 159–80, esp. pp. 172–6).

[22] Letter to a Physician, HL I, 14–15.

attributed his nervous disorder to his total unwavering devotion to philosophy and the life of reason. He remembered how in 1729, at the age of eighteen, after he had decided to set aside his law books and devote himself totally to his philosophical studies, "there seemed to be open'd up to [him] a new Scene of Thought, which transported [him] beyond Measure, & made [him] with an Ardor natural to young men, throw up every other Pleasure or Business to apply entirely to it."[23] Unfortunately after a few months of intense philosophical studies he started to develop physical symptoms such as "Scurvy Spots on his fingers," and was warned by the local doctor that he consulted that he was in danger of developing "Vapors" – what today would be called depression. Hume's energy dissipated and he found it difficult to concentrate or continue with the kind of enthusiasm required by his studies. When he went back to the doctor the next year, he was told that he had "fairly got the Disease of the Learned," a kind of depression caused by intense study. Finally, after admitting to himself that he had "a Disease, to which any one may be subject" he was relieved. He started taking the "Anti-hysterick Pills" prescribed by his doctor, developed a regular exercise routine, and left off his studies before he completely fatigued himself. While he was not cured, at least his condition grew no worse. Indeed, in the summer of 1731, he suddenly gained an enormous amount of weight so that from a tall skinny young man, who people thought subject to tuberculosis, he suddenly grew into a "sturdy robust healthful-like fellow." His family thought he had made a complete recovery – though he continued to suffer from symptoms such as a palpitation of the heart, perhaps caused by anxiety, and excessive wind in his stomach (HL I, 14–16).

The conclusions Hume drew from his Stoic attempts to control his passions through reason and his subsequent illness were important for the philosophy he was developing. A stress on the limits of reason forms a basic part of the skepticism that pervades his whole

---

[23] *Ibid.*, HL I, 13–14. The speculation that this seeming "new Scene of Thought" prefigured the main themes of Book 1 of the *Treatise* was made by Norman Kemp Smith in his well-known 1941 book, *The Philosophy of David Hume* (London: Macmillan, 1941), p. 17. But this speculation is unsupported by any surviving documents, and does not take into account indications of major changes in the direction of Hume's thought in the next decade before the *Treatise* was published; see my "Kemp Smith and the Two Kinds of Naturalism in Hume's Philosophy," in *New Essays on David Hume*, eds. E. Ronchetti and E. Mazza (Milan: FrancoAngeli, 2007), pp. 17–36.

philosophy. When he began writing in earnest at the age of eighteen, he set out to pursue the scientific study of "human Nature" which, he concluded, had not been successfully carried out by the ancient moralists he had been reading (HL I, 16). He wrote that their moral philosophy, like their natural philosophy, depended "more upon Invention than Experience." They relied upon "Fancy in erecting Schemes of Virtue & of Happiness" rather than investigating the actual nature of human beings through observation and experience, and thus drew incorrect conclusions about the road to human happiness and the true source of morality.

Moreover, Hume's own experience of living too much in his head had convinced him of the close relation of the mind and the body, and particularly of the effect of the former on the latter. He believed that the intense thinking he was doing and his passionate devotion to the philosophic life had served to "discompose the Fabric of the Nerves and Brain" (HL I, 17). He compared his own condition to that which is described in "the Writings of the French Mysticks & ... [religious] Fanatics" who complain of "a Coldness and Desertion of the Spirit." He was no doubt thinking about what the mystics call the "dark night of the soul."[24] Their "kind of Devotion" requires "the Force of Passion" which, in turn, is dependent on its physical correlate "the Animal Spirits" (HL I, 17). Hume thought that the enthusiasm of both mystical exercises and his own intense philosophical reflections affected these nervous fluids, and caused a loss of mental energy from which it was very difficult to recover. "More than any thing" it was his reading of Stoic books on morality which caused him "to waste [his] Spirits & bring on ... this Distemper" (HL I, 14–15).

The analysis of his nervous disorder which Hume adopts in his Letter to a Physician seems to be based on a book by philosopher/physician Bernard Mandeville which was revised and republished in 1730. In his *Treatise of the Hypochondriack and Hysterick Diseases. In Three Dialogues*, the physician who represents Mandeville's views identifies the cause of these diseases as "the Waste" or "Deficiency" of animal spirits, or nervous fluids.[25] One main cause of this loss

---

[24] Evelyn Underhill, *Mysticism*, 3rd edn. (London: Methuen, 1912), esp. p. 455.

[25] Bernard Mandeville, *Treatise of the Hypochondriack and Hysterick Diseases. In Three Dialogues*, 3rd edn. (London, 1730), pp. 212, 215. In the course of this dialogue between a physician

of animal spirits, according to Mandeville, is excessive thinking (pp. 216ff.). This loss of nervous energy results in digestive disorders as well as other physical and psychological symptoms. Mandeville argues that there is a limited quantity of neural energy available to carry out the various functions attributed to the animal spirits, and that their overuse in the performance of one function will result in dysfunction of another. He wrote that persons who suffer from the symptoms he describes are "oftner Men of Learning, than not; insomuch, that the *Passio Hypochondriaca* in High-Dutch is call'd *Der Gelahrten Krankheydt*, the Disease of the Learned" (p. 106).

A central aim of Mandeville's book is to argue for the importance of the union of mind and body in explaining the chronic diseases he is writing about. In the first edition of the book (1711), he seems to have felt compelled to adopt Cartesian dualism: "We all agree," he wrote, "some few Atheists excepted, that matter it self can never think."[26] But in the 1730 edition which Hume probably read, Mandeville dropped this claim. Here he writes of "how absolutely necessary the Brain is, in the Act of Thinking" and that it is "contradictory to human Reason, that any Part of Man should continue to think, when his body is dead and motionless." The mind cannot act independently of the body, and "Thinking only consists *in a various Disposition of Images received before*"; these images arise through the operation of the animal spirits on the brain.[27]

As we shall see, this claim about thinking depending on images in the brain would not have been lost on Hume as he developed his science of human nature in the *Treatise*.[28] Nor would Mandeville's claim that there is a limited quantity of mental energy or animal spirits which, when overused in one operation of the mind/body complex, results in a loss of function in other operations.[29]

---

and his patient, Mandeville identifies himself as the physician. This third edition of 1730 and the second edition of the same year are heavily revised from the first edition which was published in 1711 under the title given in the next footnote.

[26] Bernard Mandeville, *A Treatise of the Hypochondriak and Hysterick Passions, Vulgarly call'd the HYPO in MEN and VAPOURS in WOMEN* (London, 1711), p. 124.

[27] See pages 159–60 of the 1730 third edition.   [28] Chapter 2, pp. 52–3 and 70.

[29] Chapter 4, pp. 135–6.

3. FORMAL EDUCATION AND SELF-EDUCATION

Certainly, Hume was still concerned about his precarious health as he rode the stagecoach to Bristol in 1734. He was thinking that he had "not come out of the Cloud so well as [the mystics whom he had been reading] commonly tell us they have done" and he still despaired "of ever recovering" (HL I, 17). But, in spite of his worries, Hume was also tremendously proud of the achievements of his young life and would have reflected on them with some satisfaction. He had been sent to the College of Edinburgh in 1721 at the age of ten along with his brother Joseph, who was a couple of years older, and did well. He remembered his formal studies there as "extending little further than the Languages" (HL I, 13). He signed the matriculation book for the class in Greek in 1722 and certainly also took courses in Latin. He also studied some philosophy in school: he probably took the Logic and Metaphysics course when he was twelve, and we know he took Robert Steuart's course in natural philosophy (what we would now call physics) when he was thirteen and an extramural mathematics class when he was fifteen.[30] As we shall see in Chapter 2, Steuart's course in natural philosophy was particularly relevant to Hume's claim in the *Treatise* to found his science of human nature on the same methods which had previously been applied in the natural sciences.[31]

But Hume's serious education probably began after he left school at age fourteen. He was basically self-educated. He later remarked to a friend that "there is nothing to be learnt from a Professor, which is not to be met with in Books, & there is nothing requir'd in order to reap all possible Advantages from them, but an Order & Choice in reading them."[32] He seems to have begun such a program of systematic reading in philosophy and poetry at the age of fifteen, while his family thought he was preparing himself for a career in law. While they thought he was reading "Voet and Vinnius [Roman writers on jurisprudence], Cicero and Virgil were the Authors [he] was secretly

---

[30] See Stewart, "Hume's Intellectual Development," pp. 11–25.

[31] See Chapter 2, pp. 44–7. On Hume's course in natural philosophy and its relevance to his claims about experimental method see Michael Barfoot, "Hume and the Culture of Science in the Early Eighteenth Century," in *Studies in the Philosophy of the Scottish Enlightenment*, ed. M. A. Stewart (Oxford: Clarendon Press, 1990), pp. 151–90.

[32] Hume to James Birch, May 18, 1735, in E. C. Mossner, "Hume at La Flèche, 1735: an unpublished Letter," The University of Texas, *Studies in English*, 37, 1958, pp. 30–3.

devouring."[33] But Hume was not just reading ancient authors such as Cicero, Virgil, Seneca, and Plutarch. We know, as mentioned before, that he obtained a copy of Shaftesbury's fashionable *Characteristics* in 1726 when he was sixteen. And, it would be surprising if, shortly after they appeared, he had not read the first books of Shaftesbury's most important defender, namely Francis Hutcheson, whose *Inquiry into the Original of our Ideas of Beauty and Virtue* and his *Reflections on Laughter and Remarks on the Fable of the Bees* were published respectively in 1725 and 1726. And given his strong interests not only in moral philosophy, but also in the theory of the passions on which both Shaftesbury and Hutcheson thought it must be based, Hume would surely have carefully studied Hutcheson's *Essay on the Nature and Conduct of the Passions, with Illustrations on the Moral Sense* when it appeared in 1728 – after Hutcheson had moved back to Scotland from Dublin and had become Professor of Moral Philosophy at the University of Glasgow. And as we noted before, by 1729 Hume was also probably reading Locke and Clarke and becoming convinced that their arguments for the existence of God were unsound. From a letter written when he was twenty-one (1732) we have evidence that he was reading the great French skeptic Pierre Bayle,[34] perhaps considering his discussions of the ineffectiveness of Christian teachings on moral behavior. He was almost certainly reading the philosophical (as well as medical) writings of Mandeville, who developed Bayle's ideas on morality and religion, and who attacked the views of Shaftesbury and Hutcheson on the naturalness of virtue.[35]

4. HUME'S EARLY WRITING

Some idea of Hume's philosophical commitments and ability as a writer around the time of the Letter to a Physician may be drawn from an essay he never published, but which has survived in manuscript. This essay, entitled "An Historical Essay on Chivalry and modern Honour," was probably written one or two years before the letter.[36] It

---

[33] "My own Life," HL I, 1. [34] Hume to Michael Ramsay, March 1732, HL I, 11–12.
[35] Chapter 9, pp. 259ff.
[36] On the dating of the essay see M. A. Stewart, "The Dating of Hume's Manuscripts," in *The Scottish Enlightenment: Essays in Reinterpretation*, ed. Paul Wood (University of Rochester

shows that at this time, Hume adopted rather uncritically the view of Shaftesbury and Hutcheson that virtue is natural. In the essay, Hume discusses the perversion of the passions and manners adopted by the barbarians who conquered the Christianized later Roman Empire, and who formed the basis of the culture of medieval Europe. He contrasts the naturalness of the values of courage and generosity represented in the epics of Homer with those represented in medieval romances. These latter values are perverse, and involve a distortion of natural passions by the imagination or fancy. The knight-errant of medieval romance distorts natural human values. His courage is mixed with a false politeness, and his generosity with unnatural submissiveness. He "salutes you before he cuts your Throat, & a plain Man who understood nothing of the Mystery wou'd take him for a treacherous Ruffian, & think that like Judas he was betraying with a Kiss, while he is showing his generous Calmness & amicable Courage" (16). Moreover, he comes to worship his mistress "as a God or Saint," and "by a curious Reversement [i.e. reversal] of the Order of Nature" makes women superior to men. Every passion and custom is exaggerated and perverted: romantic love makes chastity, which is necessary to some extent in any human society, "an extravagant Point of Honour" among women and even requires it of men.[37]

In the Essay on Chivalry, Hume compares the distorted Christian virtues adopted by the barbarians with those of philosophers who form "Rules of Conduct" different from those "which are set to us by Nature" (3). Both monks and philosophers set themselves apart from the society of other men, the first becoming hermits, and the second acting as if they were superior and "different Beings from the rest of Mankind." In the essay, Hume lays out the difference between what is natural and artificial in human passions, manners, and artistic productions and clearly expresses his belief in the superiority of what is natural – a view he was to modify before he published his *Treatise*.

Press, 2000), pp. 267–314, esp. pp. 270–6; see also my transcription and discussion of the essay in "Hume on the Origin of 'Modern Honour': a study in Hume's Philosophical Development," in *Philosophy and Religion in Enlightenment Britain*, ed. Ruth Savage (Oxford University Press, forthcoming). The manuscript is to be found today in the National Library of Scotland (NLS ms. 23159, 89–96). I refer to it by paragraph numbers.

[37] Hume's conventional attitudes about relations between men and women (in this case what is euphemistically called "the double standard") come through loud and clear in the essay.

While the views on the naturalness of virtue in "An Historical Essay on Chivalry and modern Honour" uncritically reflect those of Shaftesbury and Hutcheson, the essay also shows the influence of Mandeville. There are echoes of Mandeville's *Enquiry into the Origin of Honour and the Usefulness of Christianity in War* (1732), where he argued that modern honor was "an Invention of Politicians, to keep Men close to their Promises and Engagements, when all other Ties" such as the Christian religion "prov'd insufficient for that Purpose" (p. 30). Hume echoes Mandeville's general view that "all ideas of Merit naturally descend from the Governors of the Nation" and that at the beginning of society the virtue of courage will "be sure of the Approbation of all Politicians ... who principally reap Advantage by it" (p. 7). It appears that Hume is just beginning to imbibe the writings of Mandeville at this time, though his basic moral philosophy still remains that of Shaftesbury and Hutcheson.

The Essay on Chivalry gives us some idea of the quality of his writing at this time – seven or so years before the publication of the first two books of the *Treatise*. The writing in the Essay is somewhat strained, and does not show the confidence of the writer of the *Treatise*. It certainly does not show the careful balancing of ideas which marks Hume's published writing, both in the *Treatise* and the popular essays published in 1741–2. There is reason to think that his writing style, as well as his ideas, underwent a major transformation over the next few years. This is confirmed by what Hume says about his dissatisfaction with his writing in the Letter to a Physician, probably written about two years after the Essay on Chivalry.

Hume's first unsuccessful attempts to write on some of the topics dealt with in his *Treatise* began in 1727 when he was sixteen: in his first surviving letter to his friend Michael Ramsay, he writes that the best he is able to do is write some notes on "a passion," an explanation of "a Phenomenon in the mind," or "a remark upon an Author ... [that he has] been reading."[38] He told Ramsay that none of these were worth anything to anybody, even himself. But by 1734, he has clearly come a long way in his writing. He tells the physician that he has many notes in which "there is nothing contain'd but [his] own Inventions," and that he has "collected the rude Materials for many

---

[38] Hume to Michael Ramsay, 2 July 1727, HL I, 9–11, esp. p. 9.

Volumes" (Letter to a Physician, HL, I, 16). He also states that he is
still very dissatisfied with his writing. Given his illness, he thinks,
he has "no Hopes of delivering [his] Opinions with such Elegance
& Neatness" that he would gain recognition in the world, and he is
determined to "live & dye in Obscurity than produce them maim'd
and imperfect" (p. 17).

How *did* Hume ever learn to be the great writer he became? It
was obviously a gradual process over many years. First and foremost,
he seems to have loved books from an early age. In the Letter to a
Physician he writes that "From my earliest Infancy, I found alwise
[always] a strong Inclination to Books & Letters" (HL I, 13). In his
autobiography he calls his "passion for Literature ... the ruling Passion
of [his] Life, and the great Source of [his] Enjoyments."[39] In fact, in
the Letter to a Physician, he made the astonishing claim that he had
read "most of the celebrated Books in Latin, French & English" (as
well as learning Italian) over the past five years (HL, I, 16). He had
done this in spite of the "cruel Incumbrance" of his disease, which
made it difficult for him "to follow out any Train of Thought, by
one continued Stretch of View, but by repeated Interruptions, & by
refreshing my Eye from Time to Time upon other Objects."

It seems likely that shortly after he acquired Shaftesbury's
Characteristicks of Men, Manners, Opinions, Times when he was sixteen he would have eagerly read Treatise III, which was entitled
Soliloquy: or, Advice to an Author. Here Shaftesbury stresses the
importance of solitude for a life of writing and it is not surprising that
we find Hume commenting to Michael Ramsay in 1727 that he lives
"like a King pretty much by my self."[40] Shaftesbury states that one
who wishes to understand the characters of men "must of necessity
know his own."[41] No doubt already very thoughtful and reflective,
Hume would have been very receptive to Shaftesbury's advice to divide himself into two persons by means of a dialogue with himself – a
soliloquy. Shaftesbury goes so far as to call this "Doctrine of *Two
Persons* in one individual *Self*" "the chief Principle of Philosophy."
The writer becomes "Pupil and Preceptor. He teaches and learns."

[39] "My Own Life," HL I, 1.
[40] Hume to Michael Ramsay, 4 July 1727, HL I, 10.
[41] Shaftesbury Anthony, Third Earl of Shaftesbury, *Characteristicks of Men, Manners, Opinions,
      Times*, 3 vols. (London, 1732; reprinted by the Liberty Fund, 2001), Vol. I, p. 117.

The injunction of the Oracle at Delphi to "know thyself" becomes in Shaftesbury's hands the injunction to "Divide your-self, or Be Two" (p. 107). He makes the image of the mirror central in his discussion of what is necessary to become a writer.[42] The whole discussion is prefaced by an engraving showing on the left a young man holding a mirror up to his own face with healthy birds flying around; when he sets the mirror down on the right side, the healthy birds of nature are replaced by monstrous winged creatures. The image is particularly fitting for writing about the passions, a task which Hume, following Shaftesbury, considered central for moral philosophy. Like Shaftesbury, Hume also considered the development of the skill of carrying on a dialogue with oneself a central step for becoming a writer and a student of human nature. In these early years, Hume seems not to have taken in Shaftesbury's further advice to seek out company to make observations on human nature; and it was only later on, after experiencing the negative effects of his solitary way of life, that he realized that not only his own health, but the study of human nature suffered by living such an introspective life.[43]

5. BRISTOL AND THE ADVICE OF THE PHYSICIAN

When Hume got off the stagecoach in the bustling port city of Bristol in that March day in 1734, he was still brimming over with confidence in the philosophical opinions he had formed. It is therefore not surprising that his respite from his studies and writing through a career in business was of short duration, only three or four months. He was later to write that he found the "more active Scene of Life" in Bristol "totally unsuitable to [him]."[44] Unfortunately, we know next to nothing of Hume's life in Bristol and how he fared as a clerk in the office of the sugar merchant. There is an anecdote that he fell out with his employer because he insisted on correcting the style and grammar of his letters, but there is no firm documentation backing

---

[42] *Ibid.*, Vol. I, pp. 97, 122; see Isabel Rivers, *Reason, Grace, and Sentiment, II* (Cambridge University Press, 2000), pp. 109–10. On the usefulness of the image of the mirror for explaining the act of creativity in writing see Margaret Atwood, *Negotiating with the Dead* (Cambridge University Press, 2002), Chapter 2.

[43] On introspection and Hume's inductive method see Chapter 2, pp. 45–6.

[44] "My Own Life," HL I, 1–2.

this up.[45] He did make at least one close friend in Bristol, namely James Birch, a younger man who was also of a scholarly disposition. Hume was later to encourage Birch to join him in France.[46] He also made friends with John Peach, a linen draper, and this intellectual friendship is said to have lasted into the 1750s when he sent Peach drafts of his *History of England* for comment.

During the few months he spent in Bristol, or perhaps even before reaching Bristol, Hume might have consulted face to face with the physician to whom he wrote from London before getting on the stagecoach. That physician may well have been Dr. George Cheyne[47] who fits Hume's description of his correspondent as an eminent Scotsman, "a skilful Physician, a man of Letters, of Wit, of Good Sense, & of great Humanity" (HL I, p. 12). Cheyne practiced medicine in Bath, only twelve miles from Bristol on the London road. It is very possible that Cheyne's "Fame pointed [him] ... out as the properest Person to resolve [Hume's] Doubts ..." about whether and how his disorder could be cured (p. 18). The previous year, 1733, Cheyne had published a discussion of vapors and related disorders in his popular and celebrated book, *The English Malady*.[48] In reading it, Hume's eye may have been caught by "The Case of the Author" where Cheyne described how he himself had "passed [his] *Youth* in close study, and almost constant Application to the *abstracted Sciences*... wherein [his] chief pleasure consisted" (p. 325). Cheyne notes that in his youth he practiced "great *Temperance* and [led] a *sedentary Life*" and only fell sick when he fell into a way of life that was less than temperate. This, of course, was no part of Hume's own disease. But earlier in the book Cheyne gave a description of the disease of learned and studious people which did closely fit Hume's own situation. Cheyne describes how the organs of the mind are "worn and spoil'd" in "the Arts of

[45] See J. Latimer, *Annals of Bristol in the Eighteenth Century* (Bristol, 1893), pp. 189–90. Cf. E. C. Mossner, *The Life of David Hume*, revised edition (Oxford: Clarendon Press, 1980), p. 90.

[46] Hume to James Birch, 12 September 1734, HL I, 22–23; cf. the letter to Birch referred to in note 32, above.

[47] See my "Dr. George Cheyne, Chevalier Ramsay, and Hume's Letter to a Physician," *Hume Studies*, April 2003, pp. 125–41.

[48] George Cheyne, *The English Malady: or, a Treatise of Nervous Diseases of all Kinds, as Spleen, Vapours, Lowness of Spirits, Hypochondriacal, and Hysterical Distempers, & c.* (London and Bath, 1733), p. 325; cf. John Hill Burton, *Life and Correspondence of David Hume*, 2 vols. (Edinburgh, 1846), pp. 44–5.

Ingenuity, Invention, Study, Learning and all the contemplative and sedentary Professions" (p. 54). Excessive mental activities "deaden the whole *System*, and lay a Foundation for the Diseases of Lowness and Weakness." (Hume echoes this language when he writes that it is "a Weakness rather than a Lowness of Spirits which troubles me" [HL I, 17]). Cheyne stressed the influence of the mind on the body and that "the Works of *Imagination* and *Memory*, of *Study*, *Thinking*, and *Reflecting* . . . must necessarily require bodily Organs."

Cheyne had been a student at Marischal College, Aberdeen in the late 1680s and had become a protégé of a famous Edinburgh medical professor Archibald Pitcairne in the 1690s. Pitcairne was an early Newtonian and applied Newtonian principles to medicine. When Cheyne went to London in the first decade of the eighteenth century, he became involved with the circle of scientists around Newton and was elected a fellow of the Royal Society in 1702. He published a book on calculus in 1703 and the *Philosophical Principles of Natural Religion* in 1705: in this latter book, he argued that the principles of the Newtonian philosophy support the belief in a providential Deity. Hume appears to have gone back to this book some years later in formulating his discussion of the argument from design in Part II of his *Dialogues Concerning Natural Religion*: Hume's character Cleanthes echoes Cheyne's claim that by "nature" he understands "this vast, if not infinite, *Machine* of the *Universe* . . . consisting of an infinite Number of lesser *Machines*"; and Cheyne's claim that analogy provides a secure basis in drawing an inference from part to whole could have provided a basis for the subsequent criticisms of that claim by Hume's skeptic, Philo.[49]

If Hume did consult Cheyne, how would he have answered the questions Hume put at the end of his Letter to a Physician? Had he known other scholars "affected in this manner"? Could he hope for a recovery? How long would it take? And had he taken the right steps to recover? The answer Cheyne would have given to each of these questions would surely have been 'yes.' We possess copies of an extensive correspondence which Cheyne carried on with the printer and novelist Samuel Richardson beginning around the time Hume

---

[49] Cheyne, *Philosophical Principles of Natural Religion*, 5th edn. (London, 1736), pp. 2 and 5. Compare *Dialogues*, 2.5 & 2.20, and see Robert Hurlbutt, *Hume, Newton, and the Design Argument* (Lincoln: University of Nebraska Press, 1965), p. 141.

went to Bristol. Like Hume, Richardson complained how "close Application sinks [his] spirits often."[50] Richardson also complained of some of the same physical ailments as troubled Hume. Hume also asked the physician whether he could "ever hope for a Recovery" so that he could once again be able to "endure the Fatigue of deep & abstruse thinking." If Cheyne met Hume, he would surely have talked to him and encouraged a positive attitude toward his recovery. Cheyne wrote to Richardson encouraging him to come to Bath to "converse honestly and freely" in order to make him "more alive, active, and gay than I am myself." Conversation between patient and doctor formed a great part of eighteenth-century medicine, and it might be argued that it anticipated what in the twentieth century came to be known as the "talking cure." Hume already knew that it was "a Symptom of this Distemper to delight in complaining & talking of itself," and may have been convinced that talking his problems through with an experienced writer and physician would form part of the cure (HL I, 18). As to Hume's question whether his present course of action was the correct one, Cheyne probably would have encouraged Hume to continue his present plan and be patient. To Richardson he wrote that "all Chronical Cases require ... Time, Patience and Perseverance ..." Cheyne may have added his standard rules of regimen which included primarily recommendations for exercise, fresh air, and eating "the lightest and least of any Kind of Food" (p. 49).

Cheyne may have provided Hume with a link to the person who served as a kind of mentor when he went to France, namely Cheyne's friend Andrew Michael Ramsay, commonly known as the Chevalier Ramsay. Cheyne's connections with Chevalier Ramsay dated from the first decade of the eighteenth century, when they were both involved with a group of writers and thinkers – mainly Scottish Episcopalians – interested in a quietist form of mysticism. Given Hume's interest in metaphysics and his reflections on the similarity between his own state of mind and that of mystics in the letter, Chevalier Ramsay may have seemed to Cheyne an obvious person to put Hume in contact with. In fact, as we shall see, in spite of deep philosophical differences

---

[50] George Cheyne to Samuel Richardson, December 21, 1734, in Charles Mullett, *The Letters of Doctor George Cheyne to Samuel Richardson (1733–1743)* (Columbia, Missouri: University of Missouri Press, 1943), pp. 31–2.

between them, Ramsay proved extremely helpful to Hume during his time in France. Hume probably left Bristol for Paris in July, 1734 with a letter of introduction to Ramsay.

6. HUME'S "RETREAT" IN FRANCE AND THE WRITING OF THE *TREATISE*

In "My Own Life," the short autobiography Hume wrote at the end of his life, he stated that he went to France in order to carry on his studies in a "Country Retreat" where he could live frugally and independently, apparently on a small stipend which he received from his parents' estate. But his first residence in France, after spending a few weeks in Paris, was the university and cathedral town of Reims, about a hundred miles east of Paris; it was not a "Country Retreat." The letters he wrote when he first arrived indicate that he met the wealthy people in town and attended parties that they gave in his honor.[51] His lifestyle appears to have been anything but cheap. It was only after eight months that he moved to the "Country Retreat" of La Flèche where he could indeed live inexpensively. But if that was his main concern why didn't he find a rural setting in England, or indeed, back in Scotland?

Whatever his original reasons for going to France, Hume seems to have found the road to health and concentration there by learning to lead a more balanced life than he had in Scotland. Besides its having been a time of enormous creative output – in "My Own Life" he stated that it was in France that he "composed [his] *Treatise of Human Nature*"[52] – it also seems to have been a time when Hume learned to find some balance between reason and the passions, between a life of solitary study and a life socializing with other people.[53] In his *Treatise* he wrote that the mind naturally seeks out other people and in this way is cured of the "deepest melancholy and despair" (T2.2.4.4: 352). Through company and conversation "the whole man acquires a vigour, which he cannot command in his solitary and calm moments."

---

[51] Hume to James Birch, 12 September 1734, HL I, 22–3.
[52] "My Own Life," HL I, 2.
[53] When he was in La Flèche he spent more than one half of each day studying and writing, but also some substantial time each day conversing and socializing; see Mossner, "Hume at La Flèche," pp. 30–3.

We regain psychic energy by way of "a rational and thinking Being like ourselves, who communicates to us ... his inmost sentiments and affections; and lets us see, in the very instant of their production, all the emotions, which are caused by any object." Hume argued that through the mechanism of sympathy, we enter into the emotions of others, and the lethargy caused by philosophical reflections is dissipated. It appears to have been in France where he learned to find a cure for what, in the Conclusion to Book 1 of his *Treatise* he called "philosophical melancholy and delirium" (T1.4.7.9: 269).

What better place to learn about the importance of social relations for leading a healthy intellectual life? Hume was later to write that, above all other peoples, the French have "perfected that art, the most useful and agreeable of any, l'Art de Vivre, the art of society and conversation." He developed a deep admiration for French culture during his time in France. While "the English are, perhaps, greater philosophers," and other modern nations may have excelled the French in particular arts, "the French are the only people except the Greeks, who have been at once philosophers, poets, orators, historians, painters, architects, sculptors, and musicians."[54] They have "carried the arts and sciences as near to perfection as any other nation."

Chevalier Ramsay seems to have played an important role in Hume's life during his time in France. When Hume first arrived in Paris from England he was received "with all imaginable Kindness" by the Chevalier.[55] He probably spent a few weeks having discussions with him and visiting the sights of Paris.[56] The two clearly got along very well at the beginning. Under the Chevalier's auspices, Hume traveled to Reims, where he originally planned to settle: he carried to Reims letters of introduction from Ramsay "to two of the best Families in Town" and also to a man who Ramsay identified as "one of the most learned in France."[57] Hume hoped to have conversations with the latter and use his "fine library." It is also very likely that it was with the help of Ramsay that eight months later Hume moved

[54] "Of Civil Liberty," *Essays*, pp. 90–1.
[55] Hume to James Birch, 12 September 1734, HL I, 22.
[56] My speculation is based on Hume's advice to James Birch referred to in note 32 above.
[57] The learned man was probably Lesvesque de Pouilly, who had adopted a moral philosophy very like that of Francis Hutcheson.

to La Flèche and made contact with the Jesuits at the college there.[58] Finally, just before leaving France, Hume wrote to his friend Michael that he is "oblig'd to put all [his] papers in the Chevalier's hands."[59]

In his earliest surviving letter to Michael from France, Hume reports a conversation he had with the Chevalier Ramsay about French and English manners; it gives us insight into Hume's own thinking processes and the way they proceeded from his conversations with others. The Chevalier had advised him to carefully observe and imitate French manners, claiming that while the English had more genuine feelings of politeness, "the French certainly have a better way of expressing it."[60] Hume turned this claim over in his mind, and after observing French manners for a few weeks, decided that he believed "just the Contrary." He concluded that the exaggerated expressions of politeness among the French actually come to soften their manners and make them more genuinely inclined to be helpful to others. He notes that French servants who use exaggerated expressions of politeness to each other, as well as to their masters, don't quarrel with each other like English servants. He even comments that Catholic ceremonies such as "Sprinkling, Kneeling, Crossing &c" insensibly soften men's passions and improve their behavior toward each other. While he does not use the word here, it is clear that he is thinking about the influence of what he called "*active* habits" and the way they change both feelings and actions, a principle he appealed to in Book 2 of *A Treatise of Human Nature* (T2.3.5.5: 424).[61]

It is likely that Hume and the Chevalier Ramsay also had conversations about more abstract philosophical issues, and that Hume listened to the older philosopher's advice and opinions and sifted them through in his own mind before coming to his own conclusions. Ramsay may have encouraged Hume to study the metaphysics and epistemology of Nicolas Malebranche, who he considered

---

[58] At the time that Hume made this move Ramsay clearly had Jesuit connections. In the next year, he published an article in the Jesuit *Journal de Trévoux*; see his "Le Psychomètre ou Réflexions sur les différens caracteres de l'Esprit par un Mylord Anglois" *Mémoires pour l'Histoire des Sciences & des beaux Arts*, April, 1735.

[59] Hume to Michael Ramsay, August 31, 1737, in Tadeusz Kozanecki, "Dawida Hume'a Nieznane Listy W Zbiorach Muzeum Czartoryskich (Polska)," *Archiwum Historii Filozofii Spolecznej*, Vol. IX, 1963, pp. 127–41, esp. pp. 133–4; see also Richard Popkin, "So Hume did Read Berkeley," *Journal of Philosophy*, 61 (1964), 773–8.

[60] Hume to Michael Ramsay, 12 September 1734, HL 19–21.

[61] See Chapter 7, pp. 229ff.

"the most subtle, logical and systematic genius which any nation had produced,"[62] advice that Hume seems to have taken to heart. Not that Ramsay himself agreed with Malebranche's best known theses, such as "occasionalism" or the "vision of all things in God." In fact, as Hume was later to do, Ramsay opposed Malebranche's view that denied all power and force to finite beings, and lodged it in the Supreme Being. Ramsay thought that this view was similar to Spinozism, a philosophy which he bitterly opposed throughout his philosophical writings. According to Ramsay, the conclusions of both Malebranche and Spinoza with regard to force or power were based on the observation that "we have no clear and perfect idea of force" – Malebranche in matter, and Spinoza in the first being (p. 711). But Ramsay argued that "both had forgotten a first principle of logic which teaches that to see clearly [to have a clear idea] is a reason to affirm, but that not to see clearly [not to have a clear idea] is never a reason to deny."[63] This is a principle that Hume was himself to incorporate into his own critique of Malebranche's occasionalism in Book 1 of his *Treatise* (T1.3.14.10: 160). Just because we don't have a clear idea of the power or force in nature, that does not mean it does not exist.[64]

Another important idea that Hume appears to have taken directly from Chevalier Ramsay was the division of human reason into three kinds, "*that from knowledge, from proofs, and from probabilities*" (T1.3.11.2: 124). What was original in Ramsay's distinction was the category of "proofs" which encompassed arguments from experience "which are entirely free from doubt and uncertainty." Ramsay introduced this distinction in the 1732 edition of his *Voyages de Cyrus* as a way of attacking extreme or Pyrrhonian skepticism: "Scepticism arises from the failure to distinguish between a demonstration, a proof and a probability."[65] Ramsay went on to say that a "demonstration supposes that the contradictory idea is impossible; a proof of fact is where all reasons lead us to believe, without there being any

---

[62] See Ramsay, "Le Psychomètre," (note 63), p. 710.
[63] Compare A. M. Ramsay, *Philosophical Principles of Natural and Revealed Religion* ..., 2 vols. (Glasgow: Foulis, 1748–9), Vol. II, pp. 265–6.
[64] See Chapter 3 §9, pp. 126–8ff.
[65] A. M. Ramsay, *Les Voyages de Cyrus*, 2 vols. (Amsterdam, 1732), Vol. II, p. 22, note b. This note appears neither in the 1730 edition of the *Voyages* bought by the Faculty of Advocates Library in 1732, nor in the English translation of 1730 (called the fourth edition).

pretext for doubt. A probability is where the reasons for belief are stronger than those for doubting." Ramsay tied up the appeal to facts in proofs with "continuous uniformity, and the constant relation of our sentiments" (p. 23), an idea developed by Hume in his discussion of the sources of our belief in cause and effect in Part 3 of Book 1 of the *Treatise*.

Chevalier Ramsay seems, like his friend Cheyne, an unlikely person for David Hume to have attached himself to. He was born in Ayrshire in 1686 and studied philosophy and theology at Edinburgh and Glasgow. Like Hume, he went through a religious crisis in his youth, but it led him to a deep interest in mysticism and mathematics, rather than unbelief. It was these interests which led Ramsay first to London where he studied with a Newtonian mathematician, then to Holland, and finally to France where he became secretary to the famous Archbishop Fénelon, under whose guidance he converted to Catholicism. Ramsay became Fénelon's editor, and ultimately his biographer. He was awarded the title of Chevalier by the Duc d'Orléans, Regent of France. He also became tutor to a number of wealthy families including that of the exiled James III, pretender to the English throne, and was for a short time tutor to Charles Edward Stuart (Bonnie Prince Charlie) and his brother. The Chevalier was a "prime architect" of French Catholic Freemasonry,[66] and an advocate of religious toleration. He returned to England for a short period in 1729–30 where he received an honorary doctorate from the University of Oxford and was admitted into the Horn Lodge of freemasons in London. By the time Hume met him in 1734, Chevalier Ramsay was a renowned and celebrated author. His popular philosophical novel, *Travels of Cyrus*, was first published in 1727 and went through a number of subsequent editions. Ramsay died in 1742. His posthumous *Metaphysical Principles of Natural and Revealed Religion* was published in Scotland in 1748–49 with the help of Francis Hutcheson (before his own death in 1746) and Dr. John Stevenson.

What would Hume have made of Ramsay's mystical religion – his belief in the pure disinterested love of God – the main theme of the quietist mysticism that he shared with George Cheyne and

---

[66] Margaret Jacob, *The Radical Enlightenment: Pantheists, Freemasons, and Republicans* (London: George Allen and Unwin, 1981), p. 257.

Archbishop Fénélon? Perhaps Hume avoided such topics in his conversations with the Chevalier; or perhaps he listened politely while the Chevalier discussed his views. In any case, Hume was interested in the psychological cause of such mystical beliefs. He later sought to explain how talk of the mystical love of God appears intelligible to mystics, even though it seems nonsensical for most other people.[67] He thought that through association of ideas, mystics become convinced of the genuineness of the feelings on which such an idea is based. Hume's explanation is tied up with the theory of abstraction which he develops at the beginning of Book 1 of the *Treatise*. Mystics form a general idea of love based on feelings of ordinary sexual love, and then lose sight of the origin of their idea. There is reason to think that Hume would not have belittled the mystical beliefs of the Chevalier; as a student of human nature he tried to explain them.

Nevertheless, Ramsay recognized that Hume had beliefs fundamentally different from his own, and there was something of a falling out between the two men during Hume's stay in France. Though he felt obliged to leave his papers with Ramsay before he left France, Hume expected nothing but negative criticism from him. He wrote to his friend Michael that though the Chevalier is "Freethinker enough not to be shockt with my Liberty, yet he is so wielded to whymsical Systems, & is so little of a Philosopher, that I expect nothing but Cavilling from him."[68] The Chevalier for his part considered Hume to be "full of himself," and to have lacked "a sufficient Stock of solid Learning," "noble Sentiments," and the "Geometrical attention, penetration and Justness, necessary to make a True Metaphysician."[69] Writing to Dr. John Stevenson, five years after Hume left France, the Chevalier describes him as having a "heart too dissipated with material objects & spiritual Self-Idolatry to pierce into the sacred recesses of divine Truths." One has a clear sense of two characters unable to fully appreciate the other's genius, and perhaps somewhat threatened by it.

---

[67] Hume to Joseph Spence, 15 October 1754, HL I, p. 201; compare his explanation with his discussion "Of Abstract Ideas" in *Treatise*, T1.1.7.

[68] Hume to Michael Ramsay, August 31, 1737.

[69] Chevalier Ramsay to Dr. John Stevenson, August, 1742, cited in Mossner, *Life of David Hume*, pp. 94–5.

At the same time, it is interesting to note that when, much later, Hume came to comment in print on the Chevalier's character and views, his remarks were objective and appreciative. He describes him as a person who had so much "humanity" that he "rebelled against the doctrines of eternal reprobation and predestination."[70] Hume notes that in spite of the fact that he was an orthodox Christian in other respects and "that his reason never found any difficulty, in the doctrines which freethinkers scruple the most, [namely] the trinity, incarnation, and satisfaction," Ramsay could not bring himself to believe that any beings were condemned to eternal damnation. In spite of his Christianity, Ramsay believed in "the eternal salvation and conversion of all men, beasts and devils." Hume's account of Ramsay's religious beliefs illustrates a major theme of the *Treatise*, namely that human beliefs are generally based on the passions, and not on reason.

Hume tells us in "My Own Life" that he wrote most of his *Treatise* at La Flèche, where he lived for more than two years. The town had much natural beauty, and offered Hume a serene place to study and write. He described it as a "well-built small Town, very pleasantly situated, on the Banks of a River ... in one of the finest Provinces of France."[71] He described the people as "extremely civil, & sociable." But clearly La Flèche also offered much more than a serene and pleasant place to live: its major attraction was the famous Jesuit College of Henri IV, where Descartes had gone to school a century earlier. Hume described it as "a College of a hundred Jesuits, which is esteem'd the most magnificent both for Buildings & Gardens of any belonging to that Order in France or even in Europe." It is likely that Hume would have had access to the substantial library at the College, and he certainly had conversations with the learned men who taught there. He was later to tell a friend that he first thought of his famous argument against the credibility of miracles when "walking in the cloisters" of the College.[72] He was "engaged in a conversation with a Jesuit of some parts and learning who was relating to [him], and

---

[70] *The Natural History of Religion*, Sect. 13, in *A Dissertation on the Passions and The Natural History of Religion*, ed. Tom L. Beauchamp (Oxford: Clarendon Press, 2007), pp. 79–80, n. 87.
[71] Hume to James Birch, May 18, 1735.
[72] Hume to the Rev. George Campbell, 7 June 1762, HL I, 361.

urging some nonsensical miracle performed in their convent" when the "argument immediately occurred to [him]." When he gave the argument to his "companion" he was very troubled by it, and finally responded that Hume's argument undermined the credibility of "the Gospel as the Catholic miracles" – an answer which very much satisfied Hume. When he published the argument some years later, it was correctly seen by many of his Protestant critics as an attack on the foundations of all revealed religion.

What would Hume have gained intellectually from discussing philosophy with the learned Jesuits at La Flèche? During the first third of the eighteenth century Cartesian natural philosophy held sway in France and it was only about the time that Hume arrived that real enthusiasm for Newtonianism began. The year before Hume went to France Voltaire published his famous *Letters concerning the English Nation* based on his own stay in England a few years earlier; Voltaire stated that "a Frenchman who arrives in *London*, will find Philosophy, like everything else, very much chang'd there."[73] Presumably the same was true of a Scotsman who arrived in Paris! Voltaire contrasted Newtonian with Cartesian science, favoring the former, for which he became a major advocate on his return to France. He also praised the English philosopher John Locke, who he described as the wisest, most methodical and precise logician who ever lived.[74] Voltaire compared the philosophical views of Locke with those of Descartes – particularly stressing Locke's view that God may be able to create matter that can think, as opposed to creating a separate thinking soul as Descartes had maintained. According to Voltaire, "very few People in England read *Descartes*, whose Works indeed are now useless." But this was not true in France, and debates about the truth or falsity of Cartesian physics and philosophy would have been very much alive during Hume's time at La Flèche.

Like Voltaire and other thinkers of the Enlightenment,[75] Hume was to declare publicly that the roots of his own philosophy were English rather than French. As we shall see, in the Introduction to *A Treatise*

[73] Voltaire, Letter XIV "On Descartes & Newton," in *Letters concerning the English nation,*, ed. Nicholas Cronk (Oxford University Press, 1994), p. 61.
[74] *Ibid.*, Letter XIII, "On Mr. Locke," p. 54.
[75] See Peter Gay, *The Enlightenment: an Interpretation*, 2 vols (London: Weidenfeld and Nicolson, 1973), Vol. I, p. 11.

of Human Nature he names Francis Bacon and John Locke, among a number of other thinkers, mostly English, who first introduced the experimental method of reasoning into philosophy.[76] (The exceptions were Bernard Mandeville, who was born in the Netherlands, and Hume's fellow countryman Francis Hutcheson.) Hume does not mention in his Introduction the revolutionary ideas of Descartes, Malebranche, or even Pierre Bayle (who adopted a kind of skeptical Cartesianism), who many scholars recognize as having at least equal influence on Enlightenment thought as Bacon, Locke and Newton.

And yet there is good reason to believe that Hume was heavily influenced by his study of Cartesian philosophy during his time in France. In 1737, just before returning to England with the manuscript of his *Treatise*, Hume wrote to Michael Ramsay recommending four books to read in order to "easily comprehend the metaphysical Parts of my Reasoning."[77] These included Nicolas Malebranche's *Search after Truth*, George Berkeley's *Principles of Human Knowledge*, and "the more metaphysical articles" of Pierre Bayle's *Dictionnaire Historique et Critique* "such as those [of] Zeno and Spinoza." Hume added that "Des-Cartes Meditations woud also be useful but [I] don't know if you will find it easily among your Acquaintances." These writings played an important role in Book 1 of the *Treatise* which, since there is no mention of its topics before Hume left for France, may well have been substantially written during his time there. Of course, as with almost everything Hume wrote, his absorption of the thought of these philosophers is complex and highly original. He is sharply critical of many of their conclusions, while accepting their more radical premises. But this is no different than Hume's treatment of English thinkers such as John Locke, or his own compatriot Francis Hutcheson. Still, it is a reasonable hypothesis that in order to become the original and independent thinker he became, Hume needed to leave behind for a few years the British philosophical views he had imbibed earlier, and mine the depths of French philosophy.

It is unfortunate that we do not possess a better record of Hume's life during his three-year stay in France while he was writing the *Treatise*. What we do believe, based on his own recollection in "My Own Life," is that he arrived back in England in the summer of 1737

---

[76] Chapter 2, pp. 43–4.   [77] Hume to Michael Ramsay, August 31, 1737; see note 59.

with the first two books of *A Treatise of Human Nature* substantially written. He also probably had preliminary drafts of some of the literary and political essays he was to publish in the early 1740s.

7. HUME IN LONDON: REVISION AND PUBLICATION OF BOOKS 1 AND 2

When Hume arrived in London in early September of 1737, he began immediately to approach printers; however, he did not sign a contract for publication of the first two books of the *Treatise* for another year. He spent much of that time editing his work. When he wrote to Henry Home in December of 1737, he told him that he had spent the last three months since he arrived in London improving his "style and diction" and, more significantly, "castrating [his] work, that is, cutting off its noble parts" in order that "it shall give as little offence [to religious people] as possible."[78] He mentions in the letter that he had once thought of publishing his argument showing the lack of credibility of miracles as part of the *Treatise*, but had thought better of it. He removed other sections which might offend religious sensibilities. These may have included discussions in which he showed the unsoundness of philosophical arguments for the immortality of the soul, the belief in an afterlife, and the existence of God.

In cutting out these discussions, Hume was particularly concerned about the judgment of Joseph Butler, a famous contemporary philosopher who was also a clergyman. Hume admired Butler's writings on moral philosophy, which he may have read before he left for France.[79] Butler had argued against the view that human beings always act out of self-interest, pointing out that even such passions as ambition or revenge do not have the self for their object. Nor do they arise from desire for pleasure. These were arguments which Hume himself endorsed.[80] It is also likely that he read Butler's *Analogy of Religion*, published in 1736, while he was in France. In

---

[78]   Hume to Henry Home, 2 December 1737, HL, I, pp. 23–5.
[79]   Joseph Butler, *Fifteen Sermons Preached at the Rolls Chapel*, in *The Works of Joseph Butler*, edited by W. E. Gladstone; with a new introduction by R. G. Frey, Vol. II (Bristol, England: Thoemmes Press, 1995). The sermons were published in 1726.
[80]   In a note to the first two editions of his *Enquiry Concerning Human Understanding* Hume wrote that Butler first taught that passions "commonly esteem'd selfish, carry the Mind

that work Butler argued that experience in this life gives evidence that there is an afterlife in which the good are rewarded and the evil punished. This was a view with which Hume disagreed. But in arguing for his conclusion, Butler endorsed a number of views about the nature and importance of probabilistic reasoning with which Hume could agree.[81]

Hume considered asking Butler to read the *Treatise* before it was published and to that end he called on him in March of 1738 with a letter of introduction from Henry Home, who had met him previously. Unfortunately, Butler was out of town. Hume did send him a copy of the first two books of the *Treatise* after they were published in January of 1739; but he did not feel it was right to deliver them in person since Butler had been made a bishop in the meantime. Butler was later to recommend some of Hume's popular essays to other people.

The reason Hume gives for taking out the offending passages in his letter to Home is particularly interesting, and bears thinking about. He tells him that he has "resolv'd not to be an enthusiast in philosophy, while [he] was blaming other enthusiasms" – those in religion and politics. The word "enthusiast" in Hume's day had many of the same connotations as the word "fanatic" in ours. We all know what it is to be fanatical in religion or politics from reading and watching the daily news, if not from the study of history. But how can one be a fanatic in one's attachment to truth? Perhaps it was this thought that later led Hume to write that "there is no enthusiasm among philosophers," that is, those who seek for truth.[82] In any case, his remark in his letter to Henry Home suggests that he did not endorse dogmatic unbelief. It is true that circumstances were to lead Hume to change his mind about publishing skeptical essays and dialogues which argued that religion has no rational foundation.[83] In his later writings he was also to discuss the immoral consequences of religious

beyond Self, directly to the Object" (*Enquiry Concerning Human Understanding: A Critical Edition*, edited by Tom L. Beauchamp (Oxford: Clarendon Press, 2000), pp. 232–3.

[81] See Chapter 3, pp. 98–9 and Chapter 7, pp. 229ff.

[82] His stated reason was that the theories of philosophers have no effect on ordinary people (EHU 11.29).

[83] See my "The Treatise: Composition, Reception and Response," in *The Blackwell Guide to Hume's Treatise of Human Nature* ed. Saul Traiger (Oxford: Blackwell, 2006), pp. 5–25, esp. pp. 10–14.

extremism, and why he thought religion itself had the psychological tendency to lead people to hypocrisy and immorality.[84] At the same time, he seems to have thought that some form of public foundation of religion was necessary in order to avoid factionalism.[85] And either from prudence or from some other motive, like other skeptics of the day (e.g. Pierre Bayle), Hume left open the possibility that his own attack on the rationality of religion would be regarded as supporting fideism – the view that religion depends on a leap of faith.[86]

Are we to conclude from Hume's discussion of "castrating" his work that the *Treatise* is without any negative implications for religion? I think that would be a mistake. He did leave in passages which undermine Christian dogma about the positive effects of belief in an afterlife (T1.3.9.14–15). Without question, Hume laid down in his *Treatise* the foundations for his later critique of rational religion. His analysis of the ideas of causality and substance, his account of the foundations of belief in unperceived objects, his general account of the limits of reason – all these have important implications for religion and served as the basis for his later explicit critiques of philosophical arguments supporting it. Not to mention the fact that simply by writing a book on philosophy in which there are no proofs for the existence of God, Hume's philosophy would have been seen as suspect by pious philosophers. Moreover, by laying down secular psychological explanations of the foundations of morality and political society, Hume was challenging popular theologically based theories of his own day – including those of John Locke.

Throughout the next year and a quarter, both before and after the publication of the first two books of the *Treatise*, Hume was deeply anxious about the response of his readers. Writing to Henry Home in March of 1738, nine months before publication, he says that thinking about the possible reactions to the book "sometimes . . .

---

[84] See his *Dialogues* 12.17, his *Natural History of Religion*, Sect. 14, and numerous passages in his *History of England*.

[85] M. A. Stewart, "Religion and Rational Theology," in *The Cambridge Companion to the Scottish Enlightenment*, ed. A. Broadie (Cambridge University Press, 2003), pp. 31–59, esp. pp. 47–8.

[86] Hume was interpreted as a fideist by the German philosopher Hamann: see Richard Popkin, "Hume and Kierkegaard," *Journal of Religion*, 31 (1951), 274–81 and Manfred Kuehn, "Kant's Critique of Hume's Theory of Faith," in *Hume and Hume's Connexions*, eds. M. A. Stewart and John P. Wright (Edinburgh University Press, 1994), pp. 239–55. On the fideist tradition see Terence Penelhum, *God and Skepticism* (Dordrecht: D. Reidel, 1983).

elevates [him] above the clouds; at other times, it depresses [him] with doubts and fears."[87] He says that he wants to spend some "philosophical evenings" with Home so he can get his judgment, both positive and negative, of the ideas of the book. Right after the book was published, he wrote to Home that he was worried that reactions of readers would be long in coming because those who "reflect on such abstract subjects, are commonly full of prejudices; and those who are unprejudiced are unacquainted with metaphysical reasonings."[88] In fact, he needed only one good "judge" who would take the trouble to carefully read through "a book ... that does not come recommended by some great name or authority." He hoped that Home could find one, though he was also concerned about a negative judgment from such a person. But while he wondered about the reactions of his readers, at this time his own confidence in the importance of what he had written was not in doubt: he writes that his "principles" are so different from the prevailing ones that were they to take hold "they would produce almost a total alteration in philosophy."

However, six months later, after he had returned to Scotland and the book sales were "indifferent," he doubted that he had really made "new discoveries."[89] He reflected that he might well be disappointed, like other "projectors" (i.e. speculators): like them, he would soon have other projects, and his disappointment would pass. Indeed, Hume had a number of projects to work on while he was awaiting readers' reactions to the first two Books of the *Treatise*, and he pursued these as soon as he returned to Ninewells. In the first place, he still had to prepare the third Book of the *Treatise*, "Of Morals," for publication. As we shall see, this was a task that probably proved much greater than he first thought: Book 3 was not published for another year and a half, in November of 1740. Secondly, he set out to explain in succinct form "the Chief Argument" of Book 1 of the *Treatise*; this was published as *An Abstract of a Book lately published; entituled A Treatise of Human Nature ...* early in 1740. Finally, he began sending various popular essays to Henry Home for comment, essays which would later be published in his *Essays, Moral, Political, and Literary*.

---

[87] Hume to Henry Home, 4 March 1737/8, HL I, 23–5.
[88] Hume to Henry Home, 13 February 1739, HL I, 26–7.
[89] Hume to Henry Home, 1 June 1739, HL I, 30–31.

8. RETURN TO SCOTLAND: HUTCHESON'S CRITICISMS
AND THE REVISION OF BOOK 3

Henry Home did in fact find an excellent "judge" who took the trouble to read the first two books of the *Treatise*, even though the author was totally unknown. That person was Francis Hutcheson, Professor of Moral Philosophy at the University of Glasgow, to whom Home sent a copy of the first two books of the *Treatise* shortly after they were published in January of 1739. Hutcheson's initial response to the first two books of Hume's *Treatise* was very positive. He had read through them by April of 1739, and wrote back to Home that he "was every where surprised with a great acuteness of thought and reasoning in a mind wholly disengaged from the prejudices of the Learned as well as those of the Vulgar."[90] He appreciated the skepticism of the anonymous author, saying that he himself in recent years had begun to despair "of Certainty in the most important subjects" and thought that one must be "satisfied with a sort of Probable knowledge which to an honest mind will be sufficient for the Conduct of Life." Hutcheson acknowledged that he hadn't worked on such topics for a long time, but promised to think more about them during the summer vacation and send any comments that occurred to him to the author via Home. He also expressed a desire to meet the author.

This letter encouraged Hume to send Hutcheson a copy of the manuscript of Book 3 of the *Treatise*, which dealt directly with Hutcheson's main interest, namely moral philosophy. What ensued was probably the most high-powered philosophical exchange of Hume's career. The two met in person at least once in late 1739 or early 1740. While we have only Hume's side of the correspondence between them, it is clear that the discussions with Hutcheson led Hume to make a number of revisions in his manuscript. Indeed it is possible that the final structure of Book 3 was a result of his exchanges with Hutcheson.[91] That is not to say that the relationship between

[90] Francis Hutcheson to Henry Home, April, 1739, in Ian Ross, "Hutcheson on Hume's *Treatise*: An Unnoticed Letter," *Journal of the History of Philosophy*, 4 (1966), 69–72.
[91] See James Moore, "Hume and Hutcheson," in *Hume and Hume's Connexions*, eds. M. A. Stewart and John P. Wright (Edinburgh University Press, 1994), pp. 23–57.

the two ended harmoniously or that they reached agreement on the basic issues in moral philosophy that divided them.

It is to Hutcheson's great credit that, in spite of the fact that he was a renowned author and professor, and that much of Hume's moral theory was critical of his own, he was extremely helpful to him. At Hume's request, in March of 1740, Hutcheson sent a copy of Hume's *Abstract* to his friend William Smith in Amsterdam. Smith was the editor of the *Bibliothèque Raisonée*, a journal that specialized in reviewing new books: the review that appeared a few months later consisted largely of a translation of the *Abstract* into French.[92] Hume also sought out Hutcheson's help with the publication of Book 3 of the *Treatise*: Hutcheson almost certainly sent a letter recommending publication of the book to his own London publisher, Thomas Longman.[93]

Hume very much appreciated Hutcheson's generosity, but this did not stop him from forcefully answering his criticisms, which in turn deeply challenged the fundamentals of Hutcheson's own moral philosophy. Hume's commitment to the truth of his own views seems to have overcome his own prudence, and he seems to have been impervious to the older philosopher's sensibilities, especially those regarding religion. We shall examine in detail the clash between their philosophical ideas about moral philosophy in Chapter 9. For now, let us consider just a few points that bring out the depth of their differences with regard to morals and religion.

Hutcheson, a rousing and inspiring classroom teacher of moral philosophy, told Hume that his writing lacked a "Warmth in the Cause of Virtue."[94] In other words, Hutcheson objected that Hume's writing on morals did not encourage its readers to become virtuous. Hume's answer in his letter of September 1739 is that he is writing a scientific ('metaphysical') work explaining how and why people make the moral evaluations that they do make; he is not writing as a moralist who tries to change people's behavior. Hume uses the

---

[92] See Hume to Francis Hutcheson, 4 March 1740, HL I, 36–8; M. A. Stewart and James Moore, "William Smith (1698–1741) and the Dissenters' Book Trade," *Bulletin of the Presbyterian Historical Society of Ireland*, 22 (1993), 20–7; John W. Yolton, "Hume's *Abstract* in the *Bibliothèque Raisonée*," *Journal of the History of Ideas*, 40 (1979), 157–8.

[93] See Hume's letter to Hutcheson of 4 March, 1740 and 16 March 1740, HL I, 38–40.

[94] Hume to Francis Hutcheson, 17 September 1739, HL I, 32–5.

analogy of the "anatomist" and "painter" to explain the necessity of separating these two tasks: an anatomist can be of use to a painter in showing the nature of human muscles, but as soon as the flesh is put over the anatomy and it becomes beautiful and pleasing, one is no longer able to identify the parts underneath that cause movement. Therefore he "cannot easily conceive" the two tasks of anatomy and painting "united in the same Work." Nevertheless, Hume told Hutcheson that he would make a new effort to see if he could "make the Moralist & Metaphysician agree a little better."

Hutcheson was also concerned about certain passages that he thought "defective in Point of Prudence" because they would offend religious people.[95] Hume says he will follow Hutcheson's advice and remove these passages; so once again he set about "castrating" his writing. But he also tells Hutcheson that he thinks him "a little too delicate" and that "except a Man be in Orders, or be immediately concern'd in the Instruction of Youth" he does "not think his Character depends upon his philosophical Speculations." Since Hume was neither a teacher nor a clergyman he did not think he needed to be concerned. This response of Hume came back to haunt him five years later when he sought a teaching position, and Hutcheson opposed his candidacy for the Edinburgh Chair of Moral Philosophy.[96]

After making extensive revisions to Book 3, Hume wrote to Hutcheson on March 4, 1740 asking for his help finding a publisher. He assured Hutcheson that the revisions he had made left nothing to which religious people should take offence, though he adds that "the Clergy … [are] always Enemys to Innovations in Philosophy."[97] Hume sent Hutcheson his altered Conclusion which, he claimed, would show even "the strictest & most rigid" persons the "Soundness of [his] Morals." In it he argued that his own system of *sympathy* shows how our happiness depends upon the approval of others of our virtuous characters. He also claimed that his system was superior to

[95] *Ibid.* p. 34.
[96] See Richard B. Sher, "Professors of Virtue: The Edinburgh Chair," in *Studies in the History of the Scottish Enlightenment*, ed. M. A. Stewart (Oxford: Clarendon Press, 1990), pp. 87–126; Roger Emerson, "The 'Affair' at Edinburgh and the 'Project' at Glasgow," in *Hume and Hume's Connexions*, eds. M. A. Stewart and John P. Wright (Edinburgh University Press, 1994), pp. 1–22; and M. A. Stewart, *The Kirk and the Infidel* (Lancaster, England, 1994).
[97] HL I, 36–8.

the system of those who depend on "original instincts of the human mind" (T3.3.6.3: 619). We shall see in Chapter 9 that this is clearly a reference to Hutcheson's own theory of moral sense. Moreover, while reaffirming his original claim to Hutcheson that "anatomy" and "painting" cannot be combined in one work, Hume argues that the anatomy of human nature that *he* has provided will be useful to the painter. The latter must base his exhortations to virtue on facts about human nature (T3.3.6.6: 620).

Did Hume think that Hutcheson would be won over to his own philosophy? Or that Hutcheson's philosophical and religious beliefs were closer to his than they actually were? What one modern commentator has called the "air of jocularity directed against the clergy"[98] with which Hume carried on his correspondence with Hutcheson is very puzzling. Hutcheson was a licensed minister of the Presbyterian Church, and leader in the attack on rigid Calvinism that led to moderation in the Church of Scotland in the latter half of the eighteenth century.

Hume certainly followed Hutcheson philosophically in arguing that moral distinctions are based on feeling or sentiment rather than reason. He adopted Hutcheson's arguments against the rationalist theory of ethics of Clarke, Malebranche and others.[99] He also developed an analogy used by Hutcheson, comparing vice and virtue to "*Colours, Sounds, Tastes, Smells, Pleasure, Pain,*" arguing that like these latter "*sensible Ideas*" the moral perceptions are not "Images of any like *external Quality*."[100] They do not resemble anything external to us. But in a letter to Hutcheson, just before sending the final book of the *Treatise* to the printer, Hume asked Hutcheson about the prudence of leaving in the passage where he drew the analogy.[101] Hume asked, "Is not this laid a little [too stro]ng?" He then went on to say that he regretted having to conclude that since, according to both their philosophies, "Morality … is determin'd merely by Sentiment, it regards only human Nature & human Life." If morality were

[98] Stewart, *The Kirk and the Infidel*, p. 13.
[99] See Chapter 8, pp. 235ff.
[100] Francis Hutcheson, *An Essay on the Nature and Conduct of the Passions and Affections, with Illustrations on the Moral Sense*, ed. Aaron Garrett (Indianapolis: Liberty Fund, 2004), p. 177; see Chapter 8, p. 228ff.
[101] Hume to Hutcheson, 16 March 1740, HL I, 38–40.

determined by reason it would apply to all "rational Beings"; but since it is only apprehended by feelings built into human nature how can we ascribe it "to superior Beings"?[102] Hume's clear implication is that God is indifferent to what we human beings call morality. We do not know exactly how Hutcheson answered Hume, though we will speculate on Hutcheson's answer in the Conclusion to Chapter 8.[103] But we do know that Hume left the passage in question in his published work.

The third Book of *A Treatise of Human Nature* was published in London in November of 1740 by Hutcheson's publisher, Longman.

9. THE 'FAILURE' OF THE *TREATISE* AND THE TASK OF A MODERN READER

At the age of twenty-nine years, David Hume had completed publication of what has come to be considered one of the greatest classics in the history of philosophy. The journey that our young philosopher began at the age of eighteen would seem to have ended in resounding success eleven years later. However, this was not the view of the first reviewers of the book nor, more importantly, of the author himself.

The first review, which appeared in *The History of the Works of the Learned* in late 1739 was, as Hume described it in a letter to Hutcheson, "somewhat abusive."[104] The review began by objecting that Hume denied the freedom of the will. The reviewer went on to complain of the author's pretentiousness in refuting authors such as Locke and Clarke, his excessive use of the first person singular, and the obscurity of his arguments. The final paragraph is complimentary in a rather backhanded way: the book "bears ... incontestable Marks of a great Capacity" and "a soaring Genius, but young, and not yet thoroughly practised." The reviewer says that after the author has matured, the book may be regarded like "the *Juvenile* Works of *Milton*" or the first paintings of a genius like Raphael.

---

[102] Hutcheson had been accused of heresy in the Glasgow Presbytery in 1737 partly on the ground that we can have knowledge of good and evil without knowledge of God; see J. Y. T. Greig's note to Hume's letter to Hutcheson, HL I, 40.

[103] See pp. 255ff.

[104] Hume to Hutcheson, 16 March 1740, HL I, 38. For the review in *The History of the Works of the Learned*, November and December 1739 see James Fieser (ed.), *Early Responses to Hume's Metaphysical and Epistemological Writings*, Vol. I, Eighteenth-Century Responses (Bristol: Thoemmes Press, 2000), pp. 1–40.

The three paragraphs added to a translation of the *Abstract* in the *Bibliothèque Raisonée* in the spring of 1740 were similarly critical in content and tone.[105] The reviewer noted the extreme Pyrrhonian skepticism that marks the *Treatise*, the inconsistencies of many propositions in the book, the dangerous results for religion that can be inferred from its principles, and the dogmatism with which the author "dares to substitute his speculations for the opinions of the greatest philosophers." The reviewer says he had never encountered "a more dogmatic Pyrrhonism." He ends the review by saying that far better work can be expected once age "has matured his taste and given him time to think anew" on the subjects he has dealt with in the *Treatise*. Other reviews appeared in the *Gottingische Zeitungen* (January, 1740) and the *Nouvelle Bibliothèque* (July and September, 1740): they have few critical comments and, as was not unusual at the time, consist mostly of quotations from the book. The response to Book 3 of the *Treatise* was, if possible, more disappointing: only one short review appeared in the *Bibliothèque Raisonée* which identified Hume as a follower of the moral sense theory of Hutcheson, as well as a follower of the infamous Thomas Hobbes in his theory of justice.

Hume wrote in "My Own Life" that there was never a "literary Attempt ... more unfortunate than my Treatise of human Nature. It fell *dead-born from the Press*; without reaching such distinction as even to excite a Murmur among the Zealots."[106] This was not entirely accurate, as we have just seen: the reviews constitute at least a "murmur" from those who suspected Hume of impiety. But what seems to have particularly affected Hume was the stress on his youth in the two first reviews. He wrote to Hutcheson shortly after the first review appeared that though he now thinks he was foolish to try to publish so many new ideas at his age, he thinks he can "plead as [his] Excuse that very Circumstance of Youth, which may be urg'd against [him]."[107] He also thinks that the *Treatise* will "be more useful in furnishing Hints & exciting People's Curiosity than as containing any Principles that will augment the Stock of Knowledge." In fact, the

---

[105] Review of the *Treatise*, Books I and II, *Bibliothèque Raisonée des ouvrages des savans de l'Europe* , April–June 1740. The review has been translated by David F. Norton and Mary Norton and published in Fieser, *Early Responses*, Vol. I, pp. 44–63.

[106] "My Own Life," HL I, p. 2.

[107] Hume to Hutcheson, 16 March 1740, HL, I, pp. 38–40.

stress on his youth and his claims to make so many new discoveries became a constant refrain whenever Hume discussed the *Treatise* in later life. When he wrote to his friend Gilbert Elliott in 1751 advising him not to read the *Treatise*, he told him that he was influenced by "the Heat of Youth & Invention to publish too precipitately."[108] Writing to a critic, Professor John Stewart, three years later, says he is particularly troubled by "the positive Air, which prevails in the [the *Treatise*] ... which may be imputed to the Ardor of Youth."[109] And in the famous advertisement, written at the end of his life, in which he publicly disowned the *Treatise*, he objected to critics who directed their criticisms "at that *juvenile* work, which the author never acknowledged."[110] So finally, for the author himself, like the first reviewers, the *Treatise* ended up being a juvenile piece of writing!

So, do we disregard the *Treatise* as its author requested and assume, as he tells us to do, that everything worth saving in the book has been "cast ... anew" in his later philosophical writings including *The Enquiry Concerning Human Understanding*, *The Enquiry Concerning the Principles of Morals* and *The Dissertation on the Passions*?[111] This does not seem satisfactory. Some of the most intriguing discussions of the *Treatise* were never incorporated in his *Enquiries*, and yet have been important in subsequent philosophy. These include the sections of the *Treatise* on personal identity (T1.4.6), on the immateriality of the soul (T1.4.5), and on the causal maxim (T1.3.3). Other key sections, including those on the causes of our belief in an external world (T1.4.2), on abstract ideas (T1.1.7), on our ideas of space and time (T1.2), and on the principles of probabilistic reasoning (T1.3.11–12) are drastically cut in his later *Enquiry Concerning Human Understanding*. Even though Hume's views in these sections

---

[108] Hume to Gilbert Elliot, March or April 1751, HL I, 158.

[109] Hume to John Stewart, February 1754, HL I, 187.

[110] EHU, unnumbered, p. 1. Hume sent the advertisement to his publisher Strahan in 1775 to be affixed to the second volume of his *Essays and Treatises on Several Subjects* which contained his two *Enquiries*, his *Dissertation on the Passions*, and his *Natural History of Religion*; see Hume to William Strahan, 26 October 1775, HL II, 301.

[111] *Ibid.* For an attempt at a systematic comparison of the contents of the *Treatise* with those of the two *Enquiries* and the *Dissertation on the Passions* see the tables prepared by L. A. Selby-Bigge following his Introduction to David Hume, *Enquiries Concerning Human Understanding and Concerning the Principles of Morals*, ed. L. A. Selby-Bigge, 3rd edn., revised by P. H. Nidditch (Oxford: Clarendon Press, 1975). Some of these comparisons need to be treated with some degree of skepticism.

are highly controversial, they continue to form the basis for contemporary philosophical discussion. The central distinction of Book 3 of the *Treatise* between natural and artificial virtues, introduced in Section 1 of Part 2, is completely dropped in the *Enquiry Concerning the Principles of Morals*. Further, in the *Enquiries*, Hume never mentions the overall project that he announces at the beginning of the *Treatise*, that of providing a new foundation for the sciences, based on a new science of human nature. And he cuts back on his discussion of the central metaphysical principle on which that science was supposed to be based, namely the principle of association of ideas and the related principle of association of impressions. At the same time, it is arguable that those principles are presupposed in his later writing as well as the earlier, especially in his theory of belief, the indirect passions, sympathy, and his theory of moral judgment. Isn't it to the *Treatise* that we must look to find the fundamental nature of the psychological assumptions on which his philosophical conclusions are founded?

So we should not follow Hume's advice and disregard the *Treatise*. But what do we do with his claim in the advertisement to his later writings that "some negligences" in his reasoning in the *Treatise* and "more in the expression" are there corrected (EHU, p. 1)? Unfortunately, except for a few points mentioned in the Appendix that he added to Book 3, Hume never tells us what these negligences were. The task left for a serious reader of Hume's *Treatise* is a daunting and challenging one. There is no doubt that it is not an easy book to read. Do we use the later philosophical writings such as his *Enquiry Concerning Human Understanding* and his *Enquiry Concerning the Principles of Morals* to illuminate our interpretation of the *Treatise*? This seems like a sensible interpretive policy where the topics of the books overlap, and I have followed it. But what of the doctrines only discussed in the earlier book, which he did not repeat in the later books, such as those put forward in his sections on space and time, and on the immateriality of the soul? Should we consider these as "negligences" in his earlier reasoning? I believe that this material is too suggestive and philosophically exciting to be discarded, and in Chapter 2 I have drawn on it to develop an interpretation of the basic philosophical principles of the *Treatise*.

CHAPTER 2

First principles

The scope of the book published by David Hume in 1739–40 is quite mind-boggling. He says in the Introduction to the *Treatise* that he is proposing "a compleat system of the sciences, built on a foundation almost entirely new" (TI 5–6: xv–xvi). This foundation consists in "the principles of human nature" which he sets out to explain. Not only does Hume propose to provide a unity to the natural and social sciences including "Mathematics, Natural Philosophy ... Natural Religion ... *Logic, Morals, Criticism* and *Politics*," but he also proposes to do so by establishing an entirely new science which will be the basis for this unity. It is no small wonder that the first reviewers of the *Treatise* called its author pretentious, and that he himself subsequently came to believe that his first publication was overly ambitious.

In order to get some idea of Hume's project we need to understand the nature of this foundational science which he is inventing – what in the Introduction he calls the "the science of man" (TI 7: xvi) or the science of human nature. The principles of human nature are also called "principles of the soul" – the psyche (TI 9: xvii). It is a science of what we today would call psychology, although that term did not come into general use until long after Hume wrote. In the body of the *Treatise* he discusses different powers of the soul or mind, such as the senses, reason, imagination, and the passions. The imagination plays a particularly prominent role in the *Treatise*, as do the passions – the first in Book 1, "*Of the Understanding*" and the second in Book 2, "*Of the Passions*." Hume's foundational science is above all a science which explores the powers of imagination and the passions which underlie human thought and behavior.

Hume's project invites comparison with another remarkably ambitious philosophical project – namely, that of Descartes, whose *Meditations on First Philosophy* was published just less than 100 years earlier. I do not think that it is an accident that Hume uses the same metaphor as Descartes, namely that of building on a new foundation. Indeed, as we have seen, the *Meditations* was one of four books which Hume encouraged his friend Michael Ramsay to read to better understand his metaphysical reasoning.[1] Like Hume later, Descartes sought to "start again right from the foundations" in order to establish something "in the sciences that was stable and likely to last" (CSM II, 12). While, as we shall see later in this chapter, Hume took up important ideas from Descartes and from Cartesian science, there are fundamental differences in the foundations of the sciences which each of them sought to establish.

I. HUME'S FOUNDATIONAL PROJECT: CONTRAST WITH THAT OF DESCARTES

First, there is reason to think that Hume rejected the central principle on which Descartes sought to found the sciences. Descartes formulated that principle at the beginning of his third *Meditation* where he laid down "a general rule that whatever I perceive very clearly and distinctly is true" (CSM II, 24). He wrote that "we cannot have knowledge of things except by the ideas we conceive of them," and that "whatever conflicts with these ideas is absolutely impossible and involves a contradiction."[2] He went on to examine our clear and distinct ideas of the mind, of God, and of matter in order to establish the foundation for the mechanistic conception of nature of which he was a leading proponent.

Now, it is true that Hume's foundational project, his "logic," also involved an examination of "the nature of our ideas" (TI 5: xv). A major part of that project, which he carried out in Book 1 of the *Treatise*, involved determining the nature and origin of our ideas of space and time, of causality, of matter, body, and soul. In Part 2 of Book 1, Hume writes of "an establish'd maxim in metaphysics,

---

[1] Chapter 1 §6, p. 27.   [2] Letter to Gibieuf, 19 January 1642, in CSM III, p. 202.

That whatever the mind clearly conceives includes the idea of possible existence" (T1.2.2.8: 32). Later he puts the principle in even more Cartesian terms: "Whatever can be conceiv'd by a clear and distinct idea necessarily implies the possibility of existence" (T1.2.4.11: 43). He also uses an example from Descartes' *Meditations* to illustrate the corollary of the principle: "We can form no idea of a mountain without a valley, and therefore regard it as impossible" (T1.2.2.8: 32; cf. CSM II, 46).

Yet, there is good reason to think that this part of Hume's project leads to *skepticism* – not to knowledge and certainty, as it did for Descartes. The examination of our clear and distinct ideas leads Hume to a recognition of the limits of our knowledge and understanding of reality. In the Conclusion to the first book of the *Treatise*, Hume attributes the paradoxes we run into when we attempt to understand causality to the "deficiency in our ideas" and our ignorance "of the ultimate principle" which binds cause and effect together (T1.4.7.6: 267). In his *Abstract*, he states that the *skepticism* which pervades the philosophy of Book 1 of the *Treatise* has its source in the discovery of "the imperfections and narrow limits of human understanding" (A27: 657). For Hume, unlike Descartes, the study of the nature of our ideas leads us to the acknowledgment that we have little understanding of reality.

Secondly, the principles of human nature on which Hume seeks to found the sciences are much broader than those officially endorsed by Descartes. The natural principles of imagination on which Hume seeks to found our basic beliefs, such as those in absolute space, in objective causes, in objects independent of our minds, and in a single identical self which lasts throughout our lives involve obscure and confused ideas. Moreover, these natural principles which Hume postulates involve feelings, as well as ideas. Hume famously argues that *belief* is a *feeling* based on the force and vivacity of ideas, rather than an intellectual act of reason.[3]

Thirdly, Descartes and Hume have diametrically opposed attitudes to skepticism. Descartes begins his *Meditations* by claiming that one needs "once in the course of [one's] life, to demolish everything completely and start again right from the foundations if [one] wanted

---

[3] Chapter 3 §5, pp. 107ff.

to establish anything at all in the sciences that was stable and likely to last" (CSM II, 12). Descartes' skepticism is a preliminary to the study of the sciences. It was what Hume later called "a scepticism, *antecedent* to all study and philosophy" (EHU 12.3). Once Descartes establishes the sciences on a secure foundation of clear and distinct ideas, doubt and uncertainty disappear.

According to Hume, on the other hand, philosophy can never provide a cure to skepticism. Indeed, Hume's skepticism is the inevitable result of philosophical enquiry. It is a skepticism which is "*consequent* to science and enquiry" (EHU 12.5).[4] He argues that reasoning and science can *in principle* undermine all natural judgments, and that the only cure can come from certain non-rational qualities of the imagination and from the passions.[5] "Philosophy," writes Hume, "wou'd render us *Pyrrhonian*, were not nature too strong for it" (A27: 657).

2. HUME'S CONCEPTION OF PHILOSOPHY AND ITS METHODS

Perhaps nothing makes clearer the differences between the foundations for the sciences laid by Hume and Descartes than their different claims concerning the *method* of discovering those foundations. Descartes sought to build the foundation of the sciences on "demonstration," or absolutely certain knowledge.[6] He begins by rejecting as "false everything that is merely probable" (CSM I, 115; cf. II, 15). Hume, on the other hand, sought to develop that part of logic which deals with probabilities (A4: 646–7). He ends up limiting the sphere of demonstrative knowledge to a very narrow range of truths, to those of pure mathematics.[7] Descartes, on the contrary, sought to extend the deductive methods of mathematics to establish knowledge concerning the basic nature of reality.

In the subtitle and Introduction to the *Treatise*, Hume announces that he is attempting to apply to "MORAL SUBJECTS" the

---

[4] Chapter 4 §2 i), pp. 137ff.   [5] Chapter 4, esp. §6, pp. 166ff.
[6] The subtitle of the *Meditations* announces that in it "are *demonstrated* the existence of God and the distinction between the human soul and the body" (CSM II, p. 12; my emphasis).
[7] T1.3.1.3–5: 70–1; see Chapter 3 §1, pp. 82–5ff.

"experimental Method of Reasoning" which has so successfully been applied in the natural sciences. He notes that just about the same amount of time has passed between the introduction of the experimental method into the natural sciences by Francis Bacon and the writings of some recent "philosophers in *England*, who have begun to put the science of man on a new footing" as between Thales and Socrates (TI 7: xvi–xvii). Among the recent innovators in the science of man he includes John Locke, Lord Shaftesbury, Bernard Mandeville, Francis Hutcheson and Joseph Butler. He implies that he himself is following on and advancing their first steps in applying the experimental method to the sciences of man.

In identifying Francis Bacon, Lord Chancellor to James I, as the "father of experimental physicks," Hume is clearly appealing to the chauvinism of his English readers (A2: 646). He was later to acknowledge that Bacon only "pointed out at a distance the road to true philosophy," while his contemporary Galileo not only "pointed it out to others" but also made "considerable advances in it."[8] Bacon was celebrated as the founder of the experimental method adopted by the Royal Society of London at the time of the Restoration – the method practiced by such celebrated scientists as Robert Boyle and Robert Hooke. Bacon had argued that observation and experiment were a prerequisite for the construction of scientific theory. Hume's own careful recording of large numbers of observations, particularly in Book 2 of the *Treatise*, reflects his use of a Baconian inductive methodology. So does his use of experience to find the most general principles which explain the phenomena. He writes in his Introduction that "we must endeavour to render all our principles as universal as possible, by tracing up our experiments to the utmost, and explaining all effects from the simplest and fewest causes" (TI 8: xvii; cf. A1: 646).

Hume also asserts that in order to determine the "powers and qualities" of the mind one must perform "careful and exact experiments"

---

[8] David Hume, *The History of England from the Invasion of Julius Caesar to the Revolution of 1688*, 6 vols. (Liberty Classics: Indianapolis, 1983), Vol. V, pp. 153–4. While today we seldom think of Bacon as a physicist in his own right as Hume did in the *Treatise*, recent studies have stressed the importance of the actual scientific experiments he carried out and reported; see Lisa Jardine's introduction to Francis Bacon, *The New Organon*, eds. Lisa Jardine and Michael Silverthorne (Cambridge University Press, 2000).

and observe "those particular effects, which result from its different circumstances and situations" (TI 8: xvii). He rarely performed a scientific experiment in our sense of the word – that is, an actual manipulation of prior circumstances to see what effects would result. Rather he isolated certain factors in thought, and considered the difference made in real life situations as these factors vary. He performed what we might call 'thought experiments.' This is well illustrated in a section of Book 2 entitled "*Experiments to confirm this system*" (T2.2.2: 332–47) where he asks his reader to consider a number of situations which confirm his hypothesis of the causes of the "indirect passions."

It is sometimes said that Hume's science of the human mind "involves an introspective study of one's own conscious states."[9] However, in the Introduction to the *Treatise* Hume explicitly rejects introspection – that is, the direct observation of the contents of his own consciousness – as the method of his science of human nature. Hume writes:

When I am at a loss to know the effects of one body upon another in any situation, I need only put them in that situation, and observe what results from it. But should I endeavour to clear up after the same manner any doubt in moral philosophy, by placing myself in the same case with that which I consider, 'tis evident this reflection and premeditation would so disturb the operation of my natural principles, as must render it impossible to form any just conclusion from the phænomenon. We must therefore glean up our experiments in this science from a cautious observation of human life, and take them as they appear in the common course of the world, by men's behaviour in company, in affairs, and in their pleasures.(TI 10: xix)

Unlike the natural sciences, where one can set up certain antecedent conditions and then directly observe the results, in the science of human nature one's attempt to set up the antecedent conditions to study one's own mind would interfere with what one wants to study. Instead of introspection we must generalize from observations of human behavior – including social relationships, business, and enjoyments. Hume's science of human nature is in principle based

---

[9] George Dicker, *Hume's Epistemology and Metaphysics: An Introduction* (London: Routledge, 1998), p. 2.

on data collected from the point of view of a spectator on human behavior.[10] We shall see that Hume's distrust of introspection takes on particular significance when he argues against the freedom of the will in Book 2 of the *Treatise*.[11]

Finally, in describing Hume's philosophical method we need to consider his ambivalent attitude toward hypotheses.[12] In his *Abstract* he says that in the *Treatise* he has written "with contempt of hypotheses," and he praises those recent moral philosophers (Locke, etc.) who have "banished them from moral philosophy" (A2: 646). But his own philosophy is full of hypotheses. Throughout the *Treatise* he refers to "my hypothesis" or "our hypothesis."[13] He characterizes philosophy as a "science [which] can only be admitted to explain the phænomena" by means of a "hypothesis" (T2.1.11.8: 319–20). His hypotheses include those concerning the cause of inductive reasoning and belief in Book 1, and of the indirect passions and sympathy in Book 2. In Book 3, he puts forward and defends his own hypothesis that our sense of morals can only be explained by sympathy, and not by an instinctive "moral sense" as Hutcheson had claimed.

What Hume does reject in the Introduction to the *Treatise* is "any hypothesis, that pretends to discover the ultimate original qualities of human nature" (TI 8: xvii). His rejection of such a hypothesis is tied up with his belief that "the essence of the mind [is] ... equally unknown to us with that of external bodies," and that one should not impose one's "conjectures and hypotheses on the world for the most certain principles" (TI 8–9: xvii–xviii). He states that after we have completed our investigations we must be "satisfy'd in the main of our ignorance, and perceive that we can give no reason for our

---

[10] Of course, on Hume's view, our ability to sympathize with others allows us to "enter into" their thoughts and feelings, so that a study of their behavior does not limit us to their outward actions; see Chapter 6 §9, pp. 207ff.

[11] Chapter 5 §1, pp. 170ff. & §2, pp. 173ff.

[12] Referring to Hume's attitude toward hypotheses, Mike Barfoot wrote that "Hume displayed the same Janus-faced attitude evident in the period at large: he simultaneously endorsed their elimination from philosophy generally, while reserving a use for them in favoured instances." (M. Barfoot, "Hume and the Culture of Science in the Early Eighteenth Century," in *Studies in the Philosophy of the Scottish Enlightenment*, ed. M. A. Stewart (Oxford: Clarendon Press, 1990), pp. 151–90, esp. p. 161.

[13] See T1.3.7.5n: 96; T1.3.8.14: 105; T1.3.9.2&10: 107&112; T1.4.1.8–9: 183–4; T2.1.3.7: 282; T2.1.12.1&9: 324&328; T2.2.2.12&13: 337–8; T2.2.5.14: 362; T2.2.9.16&19: 387&388; T3.3.1.25: 589; T3.3.5.5: 616; T3.3.6.1: 618.

most general and most refin'd principles, beside our experience of their reality." In the Conclusion to Book 1, after escaping from total skepticism, he writes of avoiding "hypotheses embrac'd merely for being specious and agreeable" (T1.4.7.14: 272–3). At the same time, he recommends that we follow his speculations with an "easy disposition," distrusting "his philosophical doubts, as well as . . . his philosophical convictions." As we shall see in §3 below, when he considers it appropriate he speculates concerning the physical underpinnings of his basic psychological principles. Such speculations and hypotheses are justified by appeals to experience, and are open to revision by further scientific investigation.

Hume's experimental method, like that of Francis Bacon himself and of members of the Royal Society such as Robert Boyle and Robert Hooke is *inductive*. That is to say he brings forward observations and experiments to support and refine a certain theory. In the case of Boyle and Hooke it was a theory of atoms or corpuscles which combine in a purely mechanical way to form natural substances. Our task in the next two sections is to explain the nature of the theory which Hume sought to support and refine through observation and experiment.[14]

3. THE ASSOCIATION OF IDEAS

The principle which runs through and unifies the hypotheses which Hume puts forward in the *Treatise* is that of the association of ideas. About a year after the publication of Books 1 and 2 of the *Treatise*, as he was preparing Book 3 for the press, Hume wrote in his *Abstract* that

thro' this whole book, there are great pretensions to new discoveries in philosophy; but if any thing can intitle the author to so glorious a name as that of an *inventor*, 'tis the use he makes of the principle of association of ideas, which enters into most of his philosophy. Our imagination has a great authority over our ideas; and there are no ideas that are different from each other, which it cannot separate, and join, and compose into all the varieties of fiction. But notwithstanding the empire of the imagination, there is a

---

[14] Michael Barfoot has shown that the experimental part of the course in natural philosophy which Hume took in his final year of college emphasized Boyle's work in hydrostatics and pneumatics ("Hume and the Culture of Science," p. 163.)

secret tie or union among particular ideas, which causes the mind to conjoin them more frequently together, and makes the one, upon its appearance, introduce the other ... (A35: 661–2)

Hume notes here that the imagination can separate ideas as they are reproduced in memory, and reassemble them in "all the varieties of fiction." Nevertheless, he argues, there is a regular order in the way our ideas are reassembled. In our speech, in our writing, and even in our daydreams our ideas tend to follow one another in a regular way. In the *Treatise* he notes that complex ideas in unrelated languages tend to correspond very closely to one another as a result of the ways in which ideas naturally order themselves in our imaginations.[15] He postulates three principles on which the reordering of ideas in the imagination are based: *resemblance, contiguity* and *causation*. One looks at a picture and thinks of the person whom it is supposed to represent (resemblance); one thinks of the town in which one lives and one's mind naturally turns to the thoughts of a neighboring town (contiguity); and when one thinks of the son one's thoughts often naturally turn to the father (causation).

Hume does not claim to be the first to identify the association of ideas.[16] Scholars trace the first clear formulation of the association of ideas to Aristotle's "On Memory and Reminiscence" where, in discussing recollection, he noted that one thought succeeds another which *resembles* it, which is *contiguous* to it, or which is *contrary* to it.[17] Aristotle argued that these principles are to be found not only when we are intentionally trying to recall a certain idea, but also in the spontaneous flow of thought. It is likely that Hume knew of this discussion in Aristotle.[18]

The actual expression "association of ideas" was coined by John Locke, who added a chapter entitled "Of the Association of Ideas" to the fourth edition of the *Essay Concerning Human Understanding*

---

[15] T1.1.4.1: 10–11.
[16] He does, however, claim in his first *Enquiry* to have been the first to have made a complete enumeration of its principles (EHU 3.2).
[17] Howard C. Warren, *A History of the Association Psychology* (New York: Scribner's, 1921), pp. 23–8; see Aristotle, "De Memoria et Reminiscentia," in *The Basic Works of Aristotle*, ed. Richard McKeon (New York: Random House, 1941), pp. 607–17, esp. 612–3, 451^{b}18–452^{a}5.
[18] He argues in the first *Enquiry* that (Aristotle's) associational principle of contrariety is not fundamental, and can be explained as a mixture of the principles of resemblance and causation (EHU 3.16n6).

published in 1700. Locke considered only one kind of association of ideas, that which arises from "Chance or Custom" (ECHU 2.33.5). He contrasted this connection of ideas with the "natural" connections of ideas discovered by reason.[19] Associations of ideas account for what we recognize to be "really Extravagant in the Opinions, Reasonings, and Actions of other Men," but are unable to recognize in ourselves (2.33.1). They cause a "sort of Madness" to which all of us are subject in some part of our thinking and acting (2.33.3–4). Their occasional cause is generally the indoctrination we receive as children: Locke gives the example of a child who has been frequently told stories "of *Goblins* and *Sprights*" which come out when it is dark, and who, as a result, will always associate the appearance of darkness with those "frightful *Ideas*" (ECHU 2.33.10). His central concern in writing the chapter on association was to account for religious and political fanaticism, as well as other kinds of irrationality.[20] The expression "association of ideas" always has a negative connotation in Locke's writing.

Francis Hutcheson applied Locke's account of association of ideas in a systematic way to moral philosophy, arguing in his *Essay on the Nature and Conduct of the Passions and Affections with Illustrations on the Moral Sense* that the association of ideas is the source of perverted values.[21] He wrote that "the common Effect of . . . *Associations* of Ideas is . . . that they raise the Passions into an extravagant Degree, beyond the proportion of real Good in the Object" (*Essay on the Passions*, p. 69). Even the best of passions may lead us into "pernicious Actions" when led by "*confused Sensations*, and *fantastick Associations* of Ideas which attend them" (pp. 110–11). Hutcheson held that what we morally approve of is *natural* and *original*.[22] It is

---

[19] See Chapter 3 §4, pp. 103–4.

[20] T2.33.15. I discuss the origins of Locke's chapter in my "Association, Madness and the Measures of Probability in Locke and Hume," in *Psychology and Literature in the Eighteenth Century*, ed. Christopher Fox (New York: AMS Press, 1987), pp. 103–27. The religious and political implications of Locke's theory are clearly recognized in the article on "Association of Ideas" in Ephraim Chambers, *Cyclopædia; or, An Universal Dictionary of Arts and Sciences. . .*, 2 vols. (London, 1728).

[21] See Michael B. Gill, "Nature and Association in the Moral Theory of Francis Hutcheson," *History of Philosophy Quarterly*, Vol. XII, no. 3, July 1995, 23–48. Also my "Hume on the Origin of 'Modern Honour': a study in Hume's Philosophical Development," in Ruth Savage (ed.), *Philosophy and Religion in Enlightenment Britain* (Oxford University Press, forthcoming).

[22] On Hutcheson's moral theory see Chapter 8 §1, pp. 236ff. & §10, pp. 255ff.

a state of the passions and their corresponding actions which exists prior to any change made by "Custom, Habits or Association of Ideas, or other preternatural Causes" (p. 131). It is true that, unlike Locke, Hutcheson allowed that association plays *some* positive role in our mental lives. He wrote that "should any one be surprized" at "how much *Corruption* of Affections is owing to [the association of ideas], it may help to ... consider 'that all our *Language* and much of our *Memory* Depends on it'" (*Essay on the Passions*, p. 21). Nevertheless, this concession is made in a context where Hutcheson alerts his reader to the dangers of association, and argues "that it is ... in our power by vigorous *Attention* ... to prevent *these Associations*."[23]

This negative view of the association of ideas is modified in Hume's philosophy. Associations of ideas, including those which arise from custom or habit are themselves considered "*natural* relation[s]," and are contrasted with relations merely known through reason – that is, "*philosophical* relation[s]."[24] In Book 1 of the *Treatise*, Hume argues that the association of ideas is the basis for our inductive inferences, the belief in causation, in an external world, in material substances, and in personal identity. In Book 2, the association of ideas generates the indirect passions of pride, shame, esteem and contempt. It is also the source of our sympathy with others, and allows us to enter into their feelings. In Book 3, he argues that sympathy is the basis for our moral judgments.

Hume summarizes the role of association in his *Abstract* where he writes that the three principles of association of ideas which he has identified

are the only links that bind the parts of the universe together, or connect us with any person or object exterior to ourselves. For as it is by means of thought only that any thing operates upon our passions, and as these are the only ties of our thoughts, they are really *to us* the cement of the universe, and all the operations of the mind must, in a great measure, depend on them. (A33: 662)

---

[23] Another writer of the day who appealed to association of ideas in connection with moral philosophy was John Gay. While he opposed Hutcheson's moral sense theory, he agrees with him on the negative effects of association of ideas on moral judgment and action; see his "Preliminary Dissertation Concerning the Virtue and Morality," prefaced to William King's *An Essay on the Origin of Evil* (London, 1731), Section III, pp. xxxiii–xxxv.

[24] T1.3.6.16:94; cf. T1.3.14.31: 170.

The claim that our connection with other persons or objects external to ourselves is through the association of ideas is tied here to the claim that it is "by means of thought only that any thing operates on the passions." Hume's thesis is that mental energy or force and vivacity is transferred from one perception to another via the associational links, generating belief in unobserved objects, the indirect passions, and sympathy with other human beings. To appreciate this thesis regarding the transfer of energy we need to understand the causal model of mental operations which underlie his theory of the imagination.

4. CAUSES OF ASSOCIATION: IMAGINATION, BRAIN TRACES, AND THE MIND/BODY UNION

In his influential book *The Philosophy of David Hume: A Critical Study of its Origins and Central Doctrines*, Norman Kemp Smith argued that Hume's theory of association incorporated "a statics and dynamics of the mind, modelled on the pattern of the Newtonian physics."[25] Kemp Smith drew on the fact that Hume characterizes the association of ideas as "a kind of ATTRACTION, which in the mental world will be found to have as extraordinary effects as in the natural, and to show itself in as many and as various forms" (T1.1.4.6: 12–13).[26] He claimed that Hume attempted to develop a Newtonian mechanistic psychology "with the various 'perceptions' treated as 'simples', and with association as the sole agency through which they are 'combined'" (p. 550). This analogy with universal attraction fits Hume's account of the formation of complex ideas (T1.1.4.7: 13). However, the function of association in Hume's psychology far outruns this combining function and, as we shall see in a moment, there is no evidence to support the claim that he ever adopted a Newtonian model of the way the mind works.

In fact, Hume's appeal to the analogy with universal attraction at T1.1.4.6 is merely *methodological*. First, he implies that just as universal attraction was used in the natural science of his day to explain

---

[25] See esp. pp. 71–6. For a systematic criticism of Kemp Smith's view on this topic, see my "Kemp Smith and the Two Kinds of Naturalism in Hume's Philosophy".

[26] He uses the term "attraction" again at T2.1.4.3: 283 and T2.1.5.10: 289 where he discusses the association of impressions.

such diverse phenomena as the movement of planets around the sun, the fall of bodies on the earth, the tides, and chemical affinities, so he is using the principle of association to explain diverse phenomena of the human mind including those of understanding, the passions, and morals. Second, Hume goes on to imply that just as Newton did not dogmatically put forward a cause for universal gravitation,[27] so he himself argues that the causes of association "are mostly unknown, and must be resolv'd into *original* qualities of human nature, which [he does not] pretend to explain" (T1.1.4.6: 13). He writes of being contented with establishing a "doctrine upon a sufficient number of experiments" when "farther examination would lead ... into obscure and uncertain speculations."

However, in Part 2 of Book 1, Hume writes that he "must here have recourse" to a hypothesis regarding these causes "in order to account for the mistakes that arise from these relations" (T1.2.5.20: 60–1). While he says that he avoided speculating on the causes of association in the first place because of his "first maxim, that we must in the end rest contented with experience,"[28] he now states that he has an explanation to offer which is "specious and plausible."[29] He is clearly putting forward a hypothesis here with some caution, but we should take it as showing the general kind of cause which underlies his account of the association of ideas.

According to the explanation which he puts forward, when the mind seeks to recollect a certain idea "it dispatches the [animal] spirits into that region of the brain, in which the idea is plac'd." Under ideal conditions "these spirits always excite the idea, when they run precisely into the proper traces, and rummage that cell, which belongs to the idea." But, in the cases he is discussing, where the mind systematically makes a mistake, the motion of the animal spirits "naturally turns a little to one side [and] ... falling into the

---

[27] Hume does not mention Newton by name here or elsewhere in the *Treatise*. He only mentions "the Newtonian philosophy" in the Appendix where he is discussing belief in absolute space. On Hume and Newton see my *Sceptical Realism of David Hume*, esp. pp. 161–74 & 195–200.

[28] Compare TI 8: vii where Hume writes that "we cannot go beyond experience".

[29] Hume's linking of these two terms shows that he is using the word 'specious' in its primary eighteenth-century usage to mean 'having a fair appearance'. 'Specious' in this context does not have the negative connotation that this word generally has today, meaning that the fair appearance is misleading.

contiguous [brain] traces, present[s] other related ideas in lieu of that, which the mind desir'd at first to survey." This substitution is commonly due to *resemblance*. The mind makes use of the related resembling idea without any awareness of the change, "as if it were the same with what we demanded." This disposes us to "confound these ideas" and to form a judgment based on the substitution of the one idea for the other (T1.2.5.21: 61).

The immediate context of this causal explanation is his account of why we believe in absolute space in spite of the contrary evidence of our impression-derived idea of space. Hume refers back to this psychophysiological explanation when he accounts for the common sense belief in the external world in Part 4 of Book 1 (T1.4.2.32n: 202). It is the basis for his *identity substitution* principle, a principle which he uses not only to explain belief in the external world, but also that of material substances, and personal identity.[30]

The account of the causes of association which Hume lays out here is Cartesian, not Newtonian. Indeed a Newtonian model of the causes of association was developed around the same time by David Hartley, but not published until ten years after Hume's *Treatise*.[31] The Cartesian model of psychophysiology which Hume appeals to here lies in the background of his appeal to the principles of the imagination throughout the *Treatise*, and would have been familiar to his eighteenth-century readers.[32] In his article on "Imagination" in his

---

[30] Chapter 4 §2, pp. 146ff.; §3, pp. 156ff.; and §4, pp. 158–66.

[31] It is generally recognized by historians of psychology that it was David Hartley who, in his *Observations on Man, his Frame, his Duty, and his Expectations* (London, 1749), developed a theory of association of ideas based on the physiological theory suggested by Newton. In the General Scholium to his *Principia*, Newton speculated that nervous energy was transferred through the brain and nervous system by way of vibrations of "a certain most subtle spirit which pervades and lies hid in all gross bodies" (*Sir Isaac Newton's Mathematical Principles of Natural Philosophy and his System of the World*, trans. by Andrew Motte (1729), revised by Florian Cajori, 2 vols. (New York: Greenwood Press, 1969), Vol. II, p. 547.) It is remarkable that in the paragraph before he makes this claim, Newton states that he will "frame no hypotheses" concerning the cause of gravitation. It is generally recognized by Newton scholars that in later writings he went on to frame many hypotheses which stimulated much scientific investigation in the eighteenth century. Hume himself refers approvingly to the hypothesis Newton put forward in his *Opticks* to explain universal gravitation, namely that of "an ethereal active fluid" (EHU 7.25n16).

[32] The specific explanation Hume gives in Part 2 may well derive from Joseph Addison's *Spectator Papers*. In Spectator No. 417, Addison puts forward what he calls a "Cartesian" explanation of "the pleasures of the imagination." Hume quotes another paper (No. 412) in

Cyclopædia: or Dictionary of the Arts and Sciences of 1728, Ephraim Chambers defines *imagination* as "a Power or faculty of the Soul, by which it conceives, and forms Ideas of Things, by means of certain Traces and Impressions that had before been made in the Fibres of the Brain by Sensation."[33] In order "to give a more distinct idea of the faculty of *Imagination*," Chambers goes on to summarize the main ideas of Book 2 of Nicolas Malebranche's *Search after Truth*, which was entitled "Of the Imagination."

Malebranche's *Search* was the first of the four books which Hume directed his friend Michael Ramsay to read in order to understand his metaphysics.[34] In Book 2 of the *Search*, Malebranche argues that there is "a natural and mutual correspondence of the soul's thoughts [or ideas] with ... brain traces, and of the soul's emotions with the movements of the animal spirits" (*Search*, 102). These "natural" connections are supplemented by connections which result from experience and from the voluntary actions of men – particularly in attaching certain sounds or letters as the signs of objects. Most relevant to Hume's account of the associations of ideas is what Malebranche calls "the reciprocal connection" between brain traces, and thus between their corresponding ideas (101 and 105–7). Many of these connections are due to "the *identity* of the times at which [the traces] were imprinted in the brain" which makes them "all to rise again together" when we reflect on them (106). The reason is that "the animal spirits, finding the path of all the traces made at the same time half open, continue on them, since it is easier for them to travel those paths than through other parts of the brain." Malebranche writes further that habit and repetition strengthen these connections, as well as those between their corresponding ideas. He uses the metaphor of an engraving to explain the role of repetition in opening up the pathways of the brain. We "imagine things more strongly in proportion as these traces are deeper and

---

this series in introducing his theory of the double relations of impressions and ideas at the beginning of Book 2 (T1.2.1.4.5: 284); see Joseph Addison, *The Spectator*, Vol. III, ed. Donald F. Bond (Oxford: Clarendon Press, 1965), No 412, p. 536. While the theory of animal spirits was criticized on the basis of an experiment by Newtonians such as George Cheyne (*The English Malady*, pp. 79ff.), it still represented the standard theory of nervous energy in the mid-eighteenth century, supported by the foremost physiologist of the period, Albrecht von Haller (*First Lines of Physiology*, ed. Wm. Cullen (Edinburgh, 1786), p.223, § 383).

[33] Chambers, *Cyclopædia*, Vol. II, p. 375; cf. *Search*, pp. 87–8.　　[34] Chapter 1 §6, p. 27.

better engraved, and ... when the spirits have passed through these traces many times, they enter there more easily [*avec plus de facilité*] than other places nearby ..." (134).[35] For Malebranche, the ease or facility which results from habit is a result of the engraving of pathways between brain traces.

Malebranche's reference to the *ease* or *facility* of the links between brain traces is particularly relevant to the principles which Hume goes on to develop in the *Treatise*. A major function of the natural relations or associations of ideas is to provide a conduit or passage through which feelings or passions are transferred from the idea of one object to that of another. Hume writes that "the very essence" of the three relations of association which he has identified "consists in their producing an *easy transition* of ideas" (T1.4.6.16: 260; my emphasis). This phrase, "easy transition," occurs over and over again throughout the *Treatise* to describe the function of the natural or associational relations of ideas.[36] A related word he uses is *facility*. He writes that the "facility of transition" is essential to natural relations of ideas (T1.3.8.3: 99). It is this ease or facility of transition which allows the imagination to affect the passions. Hume writes that "an easy transition of ideas ... can never be ... useful to the passions, but by forwarding the transition betwixt some related impressions" (T2.1.9.5: 305). Further, the "easy transition or passage of the imagination" brought about through the association of ideas plays a fundamental role in the systematic confusions of ideas which result in our beliefs in an external world and personal identity.[37]

The importance of Malebranche's theory of the imagination in early eighteenth-century writings on operations of the mind should not be underestimated. Even Locke turned to Malebranche's theory when he put forward a hypothesis to account for the associations of ideas caused by custom and habit.[38] In so doing he set aside the resolution he made at the beginning of his *Essay Concerning*

---

[35] Malebranche also argues that ideas are connected when they resemble one another (*Search*, 134–5).

[36] T1.3.8.5: 100; T1.3.9.9: 110; T1.3.9.16: 116; T1.3.10.4: 120; T1.4.4.3: 220; T2.1.5.9: 283; T2.1.5.9: 289; T2.1.9.11: 290; T2.1.9.5: 306; T2.2.8.20: 380; etc.

[37] T1.4.2.35: 204; T1.4.6.7: 255; T1.4.7.21: 262.

[38] On the evidence for this claim, see my "Association, Madness and the Measures of Probability in Locke and Hume," esp. pp. 111–15.

Human Understanding not "at present [to] meddle with the Physical Consideration of the Mind" (ECHU 1.1.2). In the new chapter on association added to the fourth edition he writes that

> Custom settles habits of Thinking in the Understanding, as well as of Determining in the Will, and of Motions in the Body; all which seems to be but Trains of Motion in the Animal Spirits, which once set a going continue on in the same steps they have been used to, which by oftener treading are worn into a smooth path, and the Motion in it becomes easy and as it were Natural. (ECHU 1.33.6)

As with Malebranche, repetition opens up a pathway which in turn causes one to think of two ideas together, and results in an *easy motion* of the nervous fluids from the traces of one idea to those of another which frequently appears along with it. We shall see the relevance of Locke's causal explanation of association when we turn to Hume's account of the causes of belief in Chapter 3.[39]

Malebranche stressed the significance of the examination of these relations for the development of the human sciences. He wrote that a study of "the mutual connection of the [brain] traces and consequently of the ideas with one another" has great "importance in morality, politics, and generally in all the sciences having some relation to man" (*Search*, 105–6). In the Preface to his *Search after Truth*, Malebranche stated that "of all the human sciences, the science of man is the most worthy" of study and yet it is scarcely studied (*Search*, xxv). There is reason to think that in developing "the science of man" in his *Treatise*, Hume saw himself as carrying out this study of the relations of the imagination proposed by Malebranche.

In spite of his extensive description of the psychophysiology of the imagination, Malebranche was a dualist who held that mind and body are distinct substances. In fact, he denied that there is any genuine causal link between the physical events in the brain and the corresponding thoughts in the mind.[40] He argued that God is the only source of force and power, and that there are no finite causes either of matter or mind. This view is known as *occasionalism*. Malebranche

---

[39] §5 ii), p. 110.   [40] *Search*, 446–52, 657 ff.

held that on the occasion of the physical events in the brain God creates a corresponding thought in the mind. God constantly acts according to universal psycho-physical laws which account for this correspondence.[41]

There is little doubt that Hume rejected occasionalism, though there is some dispute among scholars as to how far he went in this rejection. I argue in Chapter 3 that Hume not only rejected Malebranche's view concerning God's sole agency, but also his view that there are *only* regular conjunctions of objects in the universe itself. Hume argues that we are so constituted that regular conjunctions make us suppose genuine power and a real necessary connection between cause and effect.[42]

In concluding his discussion "Of the immateriality of the soul" in Part 4 of Book 1, Hume writes that since "every one may perceive, that the different dispositions of his body change his thoughts and sentiments" that "we may certainly conclude, that motion may be, and actually is, the cause of thought and perception" (T1.4.5.30: 248). He then poses a "dilemma" – either to deny that anything can really cause anything else except where one can perceive the necessary connection between them, or "to maintain, that all objects, which we find constantly conjoin'd, are upon that account to be regarded as causes and effects" (T1.4.5.31: 248–9). He rejects the first horn of the dilemma on the ground that it would lead to the conclusion that "there is no such thing in the universe as a cause or productive principle, not even the deity himself" (T1.4.5.31: 248). In arguing for the second horn, he concludes that "all objects, which are to be found constantly conjoin'd, are upon that account only to be regarded as causes and effects," and that since "any thing may be the cause or effect of any thing" this "evidently gives the advantage to the materialists above their antagonists" (T1.4.5.32: 249–50). In rejecting occasionalism, he argues that the facts favor materialism – that is, the necessary connection of "motion" with "thought and sentiment" (T1.4.5.33: 250).

---

[41] For a lucid account of Malebranche's philosophy and its influence on a number of British thinkers including Hume, see Charles McCracken, *Malebranche and British Philosophy* (Oxford: Clarendon Press, 1983).

[42] Chapter 3, pp. 122–6.

5. PERCEPTIONS AND EXTERNAL OBJECTS: HUME'S INDIRECT REALISM

Hume introduces the term 'perceptions' on the first line of the first page of Book 1 of the *Treatise*, but makes no attempt to define it before going on to discuss the different kinds of perceptions. This has, I believe, often led to misunderstandings of his account of the relation of perceptions to external objects.[43] In his *Abstract* he tells us that "he calls *a perception* whatever can be *present* to the mind, whether we employ our senses, or are actuated with a passion, or exercise our thought and reflection" (A5: 647). The idea of *presence to* or *presence with* the mind is also important in his characterization of a perception in his discussion "Of existence and external existence" at the end of Part 2 of Book 1:

> 'tis universally allow'd by philosophers, and is besides pretty obvious of itself, that nothing is ever really *present with the mind* but its perceptions … and that external objects become known to us only by those perceptions they occasion. To hate, to love, to think, to feel, to see; all this nothing but to perceive. (T1.2.6.7: 67; my emphasis)

Here the *presence* of perceptions is implicitly contrasted with the *absence* of external objects.[44] In this passage, Hume sets out the relation of the perceptions to external objects both epistemologically and causally. He says that external objects "become known" only by means of the perceptions, and that the external objects "occasion" the perceptions – a cautious way of saying they cause the perceptions.[45] Hume adopts what philosophers today call *indirect realism*.

---

[43] Hume has been interpreted as a 'phenomenalist' who attempts to show how our conception of the external world is constructed out of perceptions. The most interesting attempt to interpret Hume this way is in H. H. Price, *Hume's Theory of the External World* (Oxford: Clarendon Press, 1940). Price recognized that he was presenting a reconstruction of Hume's views, but many of his followers are not so explicit. The basis for this idea that Hume constructs the idea of external object out of perceptions is his account of the common sense belief in T1.4.2; see Chapter 4 §2, esp. pp. 146ff.

[44] John Yolton stressed Hume's use of the expression of *presence to mind* in his *Perceptual Acquaintance from Descartes to Reid* (Minneapolis: University of Minnesota Press, 1984), Chapter 8. Unlike Yolton, I take Hume's use of this expression always to signal the indirect realism of philosophers, a view whose truth he thinks can be established on the basis of a few simple experiments; see Chapter 4 §2 i), pp. 137ff.

[45] The theory that material objects merely *occasion* our sensory perceptions was put forward by Malebranche. Hume says at T1.3.5.2: 84 that it is impossible to decide "with certainty" between three theories of the immediate cause of sensory perceptions – those which Malebranche had set out in Book 3 of the *Search after Truth* (pp. 220–35). It is important

One might be tempted to think that Hume comes to take back the distinction between perceptions and external objects in the next paragraph where he writes that

Since nothing is ever present to mind but perceptions, and since all ideas are deriv'd from something antecedently present to the mind; it follows, that 'tis impossible for us so much as to conceive or form any idea of any thing specifically different from ideas and impressions. (T1.2.6.8: 67)

However, we need to pay attention to what Hume means by the phrase "specifically different" in this passage. It means different in *kind* or *nature*. He is saying that we cannot conceive or form an idea of anything of a different kind or different nature than a perception. When we think of an external object we think of it as being *just like* a perception. (This is a function of his *copy principle*, to which we shall turn in §8.) When I think that the table in the corner of the room exists independently of my perceptions of it, I think of it as being an external object which is just like my perception – brown, rectangular and with four legs. Hume says that we generally think that the object has "different relations, connexions and durations" than the perception. The table perception goes out of existence when I shut my eyes; but, of course, the real table which I think of as being just like my perception goes on existing in relation to the other objects in the room.

Indeed, Hume's comments on the relation of the perception to the external object in the section "Of existence and external existence" go further than that. He goes on to say that however much we may have to *conceive* of the external objects as being just like our perceptions they can still be *"suppos'd specifically* different," and that we can "form a relative idea of them, without pretending to comprehend the related objects" (T1.2.6.9: 68; my emphasis). Later in Book 1 he argues that "we may suppose, but never can conceive a specific difference betwixt an object and impression" (T1.4.5.20: 241). This principle has profound implications for the interpretation of Hume's philosophy. Throughout Book 1 of the *Treatise* Hume details common sense *suppositions* we naturally make regarding the external objects,

to note that none of these theories denies that our sensory perceptions are correlated with changes in material objects. They all assume the existence of material objects corresponding to our perceptions and put forward different theories about the way the perceptions are caused.

suppositions which cannot be conceived through clear and distinct ideas. These inconceivable suppositions are based on what he calls an "irregular kind of reasoning from experience" through which we "discover a connexion or repugnance betwixt objects, which extends not to impressions."[46] They include the supposition of the existence of a necessary connection between cause and effect,[47] of an external world independent of our senses,[48] and of a simple and identical self which lasts throughout our lives.[49]

So far we have discussed Hume's account of the relation of perceptions, including those of the senses, to external objects. *But what exactly is a perception itself?* When he gives examples of perceptions in the quotation given in the first paragraph of this section he uses the infinitive form of the verbs: "To hate, to love, to think, to feel, to see; all this is nothing but to perceive" (T1.2.6.7: 67). The significance of this becomes clear at the beginning of Book 3, where he explicitly identifies perceptions as *actions*: "all the actions of seeing, hearing, judging, loving, hating and thinking, fall under ... the term of *perception*" (T3.1.1.2: 456). Perceptions are *actions* or even *events*. It would, perhaps, have been more accurate for him to write of 'perceivings,' rather than "perceptions." He writes toward the end of Book 1 that "perceptions ... succeed each other with an inconceivable rapidity, and are in a perpetual flux and movement" (T1.4.6.4: 252–3). They do not remain the same "for one moment."[50]

Luckily for us, certain of our perceptions – our sensory perceptions – are not taken in ordinary life to be what they really are.[51] When I look at the table in front of me I mistakenly think it is an external object. In everyday life we don't make a distinction between the act of seeing and the object seen (T1.4.2.31: 202). We take our sensory perceptions themselves to be independent lasting objects. However, this common sense supposition is mistaken, and we need

---

[46] See Chapter 4, pp. 143–5 for the immediate reference of this remarkable claim.
[47] Chapter 3, pp. 122–6.   [48] Chapter 4, pp. 143–50.
[49] Chapter 5, pp. 162–3.
[50] This account of what Annette Baier has called the "whirlwind" of our perceptions should make us thankful for the "the irregular kind of reasoning from experience" based on the association of ideas, which makes us believe that both we ourselves and external objects have some stability (Annette Baier, *Death and Character: Further Reflections on Hume* (Cambridge, Mass.: Harvard University Press, 2008), p. 158).
[51] See Chapter 4, pp. 137–40.

to do only a little bit of philosophy to recognize this. Philosophy discovers that "all our perceptions are dependent on our organs, and the disposition of our nerves and animal spirits" (T1.4.2.45: 211), and the sensory perceptions we take to be independent lasting external objects really are "interrupted, and perishing, and different at every return" (T1.4.2.46: 211). Perceptions really are neurologically dependent existences which last briefly, and are quickly replaced by others. Hume's perceptions have a double aspect, as short-lived neural events and fleeting acts of consciousness. This reading is, I think, confirmed when we consider what he has to say about the two kinds of perceptions, impressions and ideas.

6. IMPRESSIONS AND IDEAS

In the opening paragraph of Book 1, Section 1, Hume divides perceptions into two kinds which he calls "IMPRESSIONS and IDEAS" (T1.1.1.1: 1). He stresses that impressions and ideas are differentiated by "the degrees of force and liveliness, with which they strike upon the mind, and make their way into our thought or consciousness." Impressions are characterized as those perceptions "which enter with most force and violence." They include "passions and emotions," as well as "sensations" when "they make their first appearance in the soul." The perceptions you had when you saw and tasted a chocolate éclair yesterday were *impressions*. So are the feelings of desire and pleasure which now arise in your mind when you think about that chocolate éclair. On the other hand, the thought of the chocolate éclair which you might buy on your way home tonight is an *idea*. Hume writes that "by *ideas* I mean the faint images of these [impressions] in thinking and reasoning."

i) Impressions

In a footnote to the first paragraph Hume says that he is using the term "impression" in a new sense, "not ... to express the manner, in which our lively perceptions are produced in the soul, but merely the perceptions themselves." Before Hume, authors often limited the term *impression* to those motions which arise from external objects through the nerves. For example, in his article on "Imagination" in his 1728 *Cyclopædia* Ephraim Chambers contrasted "the first impression" made by external objects "on the external surface of the fibres of the nerves" with motions in the brain arising from the "Course of the animal Spirits, or in some other manner."[52] The first kind of motion causes us to perceive "an external object as present," while the latter causes us to imagine it and judge that it is absent. For Hume, on the other hand, *impressions* arise from inner as well as outer sources. As we have seen, for him passions and emotions as well as sensations are impressions.

John Laird argued that Hume "officially ... renounced all the physical implications of 'impressions' though sometimes it is hard to acquit him of an unconscious betrayal of pure phenomenalism."[53] I myself do not find any reason to believe that Hume renounced these implications of the term 'impression,' whether officially or unofficially. Hume's language in the first paragraph, where he writes of perceptions *striking* on the mind, suggests the opposite. In the fifth paragraph of the first section he writes of the impression of red "which strikes our eyes in sunshine" (T1.1.1.5: 3). Here he is considering the impression as a physical motion which exists before we can be conscious of it. It is certainly true that he generally takes impressions to have a conscious component; but this does not mean that he uses the term 'impression' only to refer to this component. In his first *Enquiry*, he characterizes *impressions* as "all our more lively perceptions, when we hear, or see, or feel, or love, or hate or desire, or will" – and then refers back to them all as "sensations or *movements*" (EHU 2.3; my emphasis). As perceptions, impressions appear to have a double aspect, both as movements of the body which make us conscious or aware, and as the consciousness content itself.

Hume's Scottish contemporary William Cullen understood him to include both a physical and conscious component in his notion of an impression.[54] In his 1771 lectures on the *Institutions of Medicine* at the University of Edinburgh, Cullen explained to his students that

---

[52] Chambers, *Cyclopædia*, Vol. II, p. 375.
[53] John Laird, *Hume's Philosophy of Human Nature* (London: Methuen, 1932), p. 27.
[54] Cullen, who held the post of Professor of Medicine at the University of Glasgow in 1751, was a major supporter of Hume's candidacy for the Moral Philosophy chair that year; see Hume to William Cullen, 21 January 1752, HL I, 163.

he followed Hume in distinguishing ideas from impressions, though he (Cullen) generally used the word 'sensation' where Hume used the word 'impression.' In contrast to Hume, Cullen used the latter term to refer to a sensation "only as so far as it arises from the body."[55] Cullen makes a distinction between impressions and sensations in order to argue that there are "certain impressions of the body .... [which] act on the nervous system without producing any sensation." In other words, he acknowledges that there are impressions which do not cause any consciousness. His terminological disagreement with Hume is based on the fact that Hume's 'impressions' must have a conscious as well as a physical component.

Hume characterizes the difference between impressions and ideas as a difference between "feeling and thinking" (T1.1.1.1: 1). The impression of sight which I have when I am looking at the computer in front of me is a *feeling* in the sense in which Hume is using the term here. It is contrasted with my thought or idea of the computer when I remember it, or imagine a new one. In using the term "feeling" to characterize the impressions of the senses Hume was following Malebranche who wrote that the perceptions of the mind when it "sees plains and rocks before its eyes ... are called *feelings* [*sentiments*] or *sensations* ..." (*Search*, 17). For Hume, like Malebranche, our impressions of sight are *feelings*, which like most feelings are forceful and lively.[56]

As we have seen, Hume divides impressions into two kinds, those of *sensation* and those of *reflection*. Impressions of sensation include those of the five senses, as well as the pains and pleasures which accompany them. They are also called *original* impressions because they arise in the soul "without any antecedent perception ... from the constitution of the body, from the animal spirits, or from the application of objects to the external organs" (T2.1.1.1: 275). He has little to say about their causes, which belong to "the sciences of anatomy and natural philosophy" (T2.1.1.2: 275–6). The second kinds of

---

[55] See my "Metaphysics and Physiology: Mind, Body and the Animal Economy in Eighteenth-Century Scotland," in M. A. Stewart, ed., *Studies in the Philosophy of the Scottish Enlightenment* (Oxford: Clarendon Press, 1990), pp. 251–301, p. 294.

[56] Malebranche distinguished different kinds of feelings: the "strong and lively sensations" which "forcefully rouse the mind" like heat and cold, and those that have less force and liveliness like the sensations of sight (*Search*, pp. 57–8).

impressions, those of *reflection*, are called "secondary," because they are derived from sensations. They include passions, as well as other internal feelings which arise from reflection on sensations, or on their ideas. It is the causes of these impressions which are of particular interest to him, both in his accounts of both the origin of ideas in Book 1 and the origin of passions in Book 2. These secondary impressions arise from the original impressions either directly or indirectly, via an association of ideas.[57]

ii) Ideas

In the opening paragraph of Book 1, Hume characterizes ideas as "the faint images" of impressions "in thinking and reasoning" (T1.1.1.1: 1). While, as we have seen, he began the paragraph by stating that the difference between impressions and ideas consists "in the degrees of force and liveliness, with which they strike the mind," it soon becomes clear that there is more to their difference than that. For he goes on to claim that under certain circumstances, namely "in sleep, in a fever, in madness ... our ideas may approach to our impressions," and that "it sometimes happens, that our impressions are so faint and low, that we cannot distinguish them from ideas." These claims, particularly the second, suggest that the *essential* difference between an impression and idea cannot be simply its force and vivacity.[58]

In his *Abstract* he characterizes an idea in terms of the *absence* of its object: "when we reflect on a passion or an object which is not present, this perception is an *idea*" (A5: 647). The reason that the perceptions we have in sleep, in a fever, or in madness are still ideas rather than impressions, in spite of their strong force and vivacity, is that the external objects which the ideas represent are *not present*. In Book 2 he applies this notion to the passions of other people: "these movements appear at first in *our* mind as mere ideas, and are conceiv'd to belong to another person, as we conceive any other matter of fact" which is not present to us (T2.1.11.8: 319). When the

---

[57] See especially Chapter 3 §6, pp. 114ff., and Chapter 6 §2, pp. 193ff.

[58] The claim that impressions can be indistinguishable from ideas is fundamental to his account of motivation and calm passion in Book 2, and his account of the development of

passions of others are represented by ideas, they are absent. It is only when they are transformed into impressions through the mechanisms of sympathy that they become present to us.[59]

In the footnote to the first paragraph of Book 1 Hume tells his reader that he is restoring "the word, idea, to its original sense, from which Mr. *Locke* had perverted it, in making it stand for all our perceptions" (T1.1.1.1n: 2). Unlike Locke, who wrote of "those *Ideas*, we have of *Yellow, White, Heat, Cold, Soft, Hard, Bitter, Sweet*" when we are affected by external objects (ECHU 2.1.3), Hume limits the term 'idea' to the perceptions we have when the object is absent from us – when we remember it, or imagine it, or reason about it.

In explaining Hume's use of the term 'impression' above, I suggested that impressions have a double aspect – physical as well as mental. This appears to be equally true of at least some *ideas*. We already saw that in Part 2 of Book 1 Hume writes of ideas as being placed in certain regions of the brain. In Book 2, he argues that even though our judgment of the size of an object is determined by its comparison with larger or smaller objects "the image and idea of the object are still the same, and are equally extended in the *retina*, and in the brain or organ of perception" (T2.2.8.3: 372). And in his discussion "Of the immateriality of the soul" he argues that our ideas of sight and touch are, like their corresponding impressions, "really extended" (T1.4.5.16: 240). He thinks that this fact supports the view of "the freethinker" who rejects the claim that the soul is immaterial. He also points out that other perceptions including tastes, smells, sounds – as well as passions – "exist no where," and he argues that this fact supports immaterialism (T1.4.5.10–14: 234–9). Nevertheless, as we have seen, he concludes the whole section with the claim that the fact that motions in the body cause thoughts in the mind supports materialism. It seems that, for Hume, ideas as well as impressions have a physical or material component.

Hume argues that ideas and impressions differ only "in degree, not in nature" (T1.1.1.5: 3). When he writes of a difference "in degree"

a common moral point of view in Book 3; see Chapter 7 §7, pp. 228ff., and Chapter 9 §6, pp. 278ff.

[59] We will see the importance of this claim in his account of *sympathy* in Chapter 6 §8, pp. 204ff.

he appears to mean a difference in force and vivacity.[60] But what does he mean when he affirms that ideas do not differ *in nature* from impressions? At the beginning of Part 3 of Book 1 of the *Treatise*, he berates mathematicians who "pretend, that those ideas, which are their objects, are of *so refin'd and spiritual a nature*, that they fall not under the conception of the fancy" – that is, the imagination (T1.3.1.7: 72; my emphasis). His target here seems to be the claim of philosophers such as Descartes and Malebranche that over and above the ideas of the imagination there are purely intellectual ideas. In his *Sixth Meditation* Descartes had appealed to the distinction "between imagination and pure understanding" to explain the difference between apprehending a thousand-sided figure ("a chiliagon") and a triangle (CSM II, 50). Unlike the triangle, the chiliagon cannot be apprehended by means of the imagination. It can only be understood. He suggested that when "the mind understands, it in some way turns towards itself," and that when it imagines "it turns towards the body and looks at something in the body which conforms to an idea understood by the mind" (CSM II, 51). Pure understanding for Descartes does not involve the body, only the mind. Malebranche also claimed that "images of spiritual things cannot be formed" in the brain (*Search*, 16–17). Through "*pure understanding*" the soul "perceives spiritual things, universals ... the ideas of perfection, and of an infinitely perfect being," as well as "extension with all its properties." In this latter category he includes "a perfect circle, a perfect square, a figure of a thousand sides ..."

In attacking the view that there are ideas which go beyond those of the imagination, Hume mentions in particular the claim that we "can form an idea of a triangle ... which shall neither be isosceles nor scalenum, nor be confin'd to any particular length and proportion of sides" (T1.3.1.7: 72). His example suggests that his target was Locke's view of abstraction as much as the ideas of "pure understanding" of the Cartesians. For Locke had claimed that we have an abstract "*general Idea* of a *Triangle*" which is "neither Oblique nor Rectangle, neither Equilateral, Equicrural, nor Scalenon; but all and none of these at once" (ECHU 4.7.9). In criticizing Locke on

---

[60] Before Hume, Malebranche had written that "the senses and the imagination differ only in degree" (*Search*, 88).

abstraction, Hume was following Berkeley who claimed that all "*abstract* or *general* ideas" are "*particular in the mind's conception of them*" (T1.1.7.1: 17). Of course, it is true that Berkeley rejected materialism, and the fact that Hume was following Berkeley in arguing that all ideas are particular, challenges my interpretation of Hume's ideas as having a dual nature as both physical and mental. But it is significant that nowhere in the *Treatise* does Hume adopt Berkeley's view that the being of any object is simply to be perceived.[61] In §8 below I shall discuss Hume's account of abstraction in connection with his *copy principle*.

7. SIMPLICITY AND COMPLEXITY

As well as dividing all perceptions into impressions and ideas in the opening pages of Book 1, he divides them into those which are simple and those which are complex. This is a division which includes both impressions and ideas. While his initial way of making this division seems straightforward, as he proceeds through Book 1 it becomes less so. He begins by claiming in Section 1 of Part 1 that "simple perceptions ... are such as admit of no distinction or separation. The complex are the contrary to these, and may be distinguished into parts" (T1.1.1.2: 2). He illustrates the distinction by means of the example of the perception of an apple, which may be divided into a "particular colour, taste, and smell" which "are at least distinguishable from each other." Of course, the parts he writes about here are not what we should normally consider to be parts of an apple itself. When I divide an apple into parts I divide it into quarters with a knife, which makes it easier to eat! The "parts" of the *perception* of the apple are themselves perceptions which constitute what we mean when we use the term 'apple'.

It is not difficult to see why he might consider the taste and the smell of the apple to be simple perceptions since, unlike the perception of the apple itself, they are not obviously divisible into further perceptions. The perception of the color is more problematic: for one thing, if I carefully attend to it, my perception of the bright red apple in front of me consists of different shades of red; for another

---

[61] Contrast Berkeley's *Principles*, I, 3: 42 *et passim*.

it is extended and divisible into spatial parts. In these two ways the color seems to "admit of" distinction and separation.

In fact, Hume's claims about what is and is not distinguishable and separable may surprise us. In his discussion of abstraction in Section 7 of Part 1, he claims that the shape and the color of an object such as the apple are "in effect the same and undistinguishable" (1.1.7.18: 25). In other words, both the particular shape and particular color of the apple constitute a simple perception. It is only through comparison with other perceptions – such as that of a red pear or a yellow apple – that we can 'distinguish' the shape from the color via what Hume calls a "*distinction of reason.*" But this is not a real distinction, and the perceptions of shape and color do not count as simple parts of the original apple perception. They are merely "different aspects" in which we view one and the same simple perception.

Moreover, in Part 2 of Book 1 of the *Treatise*, Hume argues that an extended perception is divisible into simple unextended parts which are themselves colored or solid. He holds that there are simple minimal parts of both our visual and tactual perceptions – perceptual atoms (T1.2.1–2). However, there is no indication when he refers to simplicity in the opening pages of Part 1, that he has this kind of simplicity in mind or, more importantly, that this is the notion of simplicity which enters into his *copy principle*.

8. IDEAS AS COPIES OF IMPRESSIONS: THE *COPY PRINCIPLE*

Hume formulates the principle concerning the relation of impressions and ideas in the seventh paragraph of Section 1: "*all our simple ideas in their first appearance are deriv'd from simple impressions, which are correspondent to them, and which they exactly represent*" (T1.1.1.7: 4). He argues that while complex ideas are commonly derived from complex impressions, there are many cases – he mentions the "*New Jerusalem*" – where there is no corresponding complex impression (T1.1.1.4: 3). In these cases, the complex idea must be put together from simple ideas, which are themselves derived from resembling simple impressions. While Hume says that "the full examination" of the causes of our ideas is "the subject of the present treatise" (T1.1.1.7: 4) – that is, of Book 1 of the *Treatise* – he sets out in these opening pages to defend it.

He begins by claiming that since there is a *constant conjunction* between our simple impressions and resembling simple ideas, there must be "a great connexion" between them "and that the existence of the one has a considerable influence on the other" (T1.1.1.8: 4–5). To determine which perception causes which, he asks us to consider which arises first in the mind. Hume appeals to human behavior to answer this question. He writes: "To give a child an idea of scarlet or orange, of sweet or bitter, I present the objects, or in other words, convey to him these impressions; but proceed not so absurdly, as to endeavour to produce the impressions by exciting the ideas." To give the child the idea, we show him the external objects and so "convey to him" the appropriate impressions. From this practice Hume concludes that it is the impressions which cause the ideas, not *vice versa*. Here we have a good example of Hume's use of the inductive method which he outlined in his Introduction. He is asking us to consider human behavior to find evidence that impressions cause ideas, rather than *vice versa*.

In the next paragraph he gives a further piece of objective evidence in order to show that the impressions cause the ideas: a person who "is born blind or deaf" not only fails to have the relevant sense impressions, "but also their correspondent ideas" (T1.1.1.9: 5). When "the faculties, which give rise to any impressions, are obstructed in their operation ... there never appear in the mind the least traces of either" the impressions or ideas. Once again in giving evidence, Hume does not appeal to introspection, or what passes in one's own mind.[62] It is true that he has not spelled out the evidence for the lack of ideas in the persons born blind or deaf; but there is no reason to think that he would appeal to anything but their behavior. Hume would have agreed with Locke when he wrote that "the Actions of Men [are] the best Interpreters of their thoughts" (ECHU 1.3.3).

Simple impressions, according to Hume, are the causes of their resembling simple ideas. But how do they cause them? Or, to put the question in a different way, what is the nature of the process by which an idea *copies* an impression? As we have just seen, in arguing that the impressions cause the ideas rather than the other way

---

[62] As I stressed in §2 above, he follows a Baconian method of induction which distinguishes the explanatory theory from the evidence in favor of it.

around, Hume appeals to evidence to show that the impressions are prior in time to the ideas. But, priority in time is not sufficient for Hume in establishing that one item is the cause of another: the effect must follow immediately on the cause.[63] Hume holds that it is an "establish'd maxim both in natural and moral philosophy, that an object, which exists for any time in its full perfection without produ- cing another, is not its sole cause" (T1.3.2.7: 76). This is Rule 8 of his "Rules by which to judge of causes and effects" in Section 15 of Part 3 of Book 1 (T1.3.15.10). Given this rule, as Galen Strawson reminds us, impressions are not normally the "sole cause" of their resembling ideas; for there is often a lapse in time before we have the idea which corresponds to the impression.[64] Suppose I am now thinking about the feeling of pleasure I had a half an hour ago when I read Rule 8 in Section 15 of Part 3 of Hume's *Treatise*. My thought right now is an idea of that feeling. But that feeling cannot be the *sole* cause of the idea: for if it were, I would have had the idea of the pleasure right after having the impression. Generally speaking, simple impressions are not by themselves the causes of later ideas which are derived from them. What more could be required?

Hume's principle that all ideas are derived from impressions is gen- erally referred to by commentators as *the copy principle*. He restates his principle in the second section of Part 1 where he distinguishes the two kinds of impressions:

An impression first strikes upon the senses, and makes us perceive heat or cold, thirst or hunger, pleasure or pain of some kind or other. *Of this impres- sion there is a copy taken by the mind, which remains after the impression ceases*; and this we call an idea. This idea of pleasure or pain, when it returns upon the soul, produces the new impressions of desire and aversion, hope and fear, which may properly be call'd impressions of reflection because deriv'd from it. These again are *copy'd* by the memory and imagination, and become ideas. (T1.1.2.1: 8; my emphasis)

---

[63] See Chapter 3 §2, p. 91.
[64] Galen Strawson, *The Evident Connexion: Mind, Self and David Hume*, (Oxford University Press, forthcoming), §2.5. Janet Broughton thinks that because Hume cannot appeal to "something non-mental … [such as] physical traces in the brain" this is "a serious problem for the general explanatory project Hume pursues in the *Treatise*" ("Impressions and Ideas," in *The Blackwell Guide to Hume's Treatise*, ed. Saul Traiger (Oxford: Blackwell, 2006), pp. 43–58, esp. pp. 48–9). It is not clear to me why Hume cannot appeal to something not directly perceived such as traces in the brain, since he so clearly appeals to indirectly per- ceived objects in his explanations throughout the *Treatise*.

What exactly could Hume mean when he says that the mind takes a *copy* of these impressions and that these copies are called ideas? And what is the status of these ideas, given that we are often not aware of them until some time "after the impression ceases?"

One suggestion that might occur to us is that Hume is referring to a universal, or idea type: after I have the impression of red, a copy is taken by the mind and redness exists as a universal type in my mind. But this suggestion is incompatible with Hume's denial of abstract general ideas in Section 7 of Part 1. As we have seen, he argues that there are only particular ideas in the mind. It is the resemblance of these particular ideas to other particular ideas and our use of a general term like 'red' which accounts for abstraction. There is, Hume argues, only a particular idea like that of my red pen which is actually present to the mind when I use the general term 'red'; the ideas of other red things like the red vase on the table upstairs are "not really and in fact present to the mind, but only in power" (T1.1.7.7: 20). That is, they can be recalled when we are "prompted by a present design or necessity." But in order for this to be possible they, or at least some representative of them, must *continue to exist* in some way in the mind or brain. Hume implicitly acknowledges this when he writes that "a particular idea becomes general by being annex'd to a general term; that is, to a term, which from a customary conjunction has a relation to *many other particular ideas*, and readily recals them in the imagination" (T1.1.7.10: 22; my italics). How could these other particular ideas be recalled unless they somehow exist before we become conscious of them?

It is hard to see how Hume can avoid the conclusion that *the copy* "which remains after the impression ceases" is a kind of trace or template in the brain which can later be brought to consciousness as an idea. As we have seen in §4, Hume writes that the animal spirits excite an idea when they run "into the proper traces, and rummage that cell which belongs to the idea" (T1.2.5.20: 61). However crude Hume's model, it suggests that impressions first cause some sort of change in the brain, before they can cause the ideas which later occur in the mind or soul. Of course, the existence of a brain trace is not itself *sufficient* to account for the fact that the idea "returns upon the soul" at some later time (T1.1.2.1: 8). For that we also require some new impression, perhaps one that resembles, is contiguous to, or is causally related to the original – that is, one which excites the idea via the principles of association.

Hume considers an exception to this first principle of the science of human nature which maintains that simple ideas are derived from their corresponding simple impressions, and much has been written about the fact that he would present an exception to a principle which he otherwise puts forward as being quite universal. The exception is one which may have been suggested to him by Rule 14 of Descartes' *Rules for the Direction of the Mind*: Descartes argued that while a person who is born blind can never obtain the ideas of any color, nevertheless "if someone at some time had seen the primary colours, though not the secondary or mixed colours, then by means of a deduction of sorts it is possible for him to form images even of those he has not seen, in virtue of their similarity to those that he has seen" (CSM I, 56–7). Hume's example is similar: we have seen a range of shades of a given color from lightest to darkest, but one shade has never been experienced. He asks "whether 'tis possible for him, from his own imagination, to supply this deficiency, and raise up to himself the idea of that particular shade" (T1.1.1.10: 6). His answer is that he can, but that "the instance is so particular and singular, that 'tis scarce worth our observing, and does not merit that for it alone we shou'd alter our general maxim." That Hume allows such an exception is not surprising considering the inductive method he pursues, and the fact that he makes no claim to discover ultimate principles of the mind. Moreover, if, as I have argued, Hume presupposed the standard model of the imagination presented by Malebranche, Chambers and indeed by Descartes himself,[65] which requires that ideas of imagination are formed by way of traces formed previously in the brain, why would he not accept that such a trace could be formed without an impression under very unusual circumstances?

Hume appeals to the *copy principle* to identify and clarify the ideas we actually have in our minds. He writes that "many of our ideas are so obscure, that 'tis almost impossible even for the mind, which forms them, to tell their exact nature and composition" (T1.2.3.1: 33; A7: 649). We need to identify the impressions from which they are

---

[65] See Descartes' *Treatise of Man*, in CSM, I, 99–108, esp. p. 106 where Descartes writes of ideas as "traced in the spirits on the surface" of the pineal gland.

derived in order "to tell exactly their nature and composition." These impressions "all are so clear and evident, that they admit no controversy." This passage may suggest that impressions themselves are completely transparent to us without attention and scientific analysis: but a consideration of specific cases reveals that this is not at all Hume's view. He argues that in everyday life we suppose our sensory impressions to be external and independent, when they are really internal and dependent – and even "appear" as such.[66] Moreover, while we naturally suppose causal power to be external and in the objects of our senses, the actual impression from which our idea of power arises is an internal impression of reflection which results from a change in our minds or brains.[67] It takes some degree of sophisticated philosophical or scientific analysis to identify the impressions from which our ideas are derived. It is only after such analysis that we can explain the "nature and composition" of our ideas.

Hume's *copy principle* is commonly regarded as a principle having to do with the meaning of words, as well as a principle concerning the origin of ideas. This is a claim which must be treated with some caution. [68] Hume does not have any systematic theory of meaning.[69] It is true that in his *Abstract*, he states that if he cannot find an impression corresponding to a philosophical term, he "concludes that the term is altogether insignificant" (A7: 649). And in his first *Enquiry*, he writes that when he suspects "that a philosophical term is employed without any meaning or idea . . . we need but enquire, *from what impression . . . that supposed idea* [*is*] *derived*" (EHU 2.9). These passages suggest that philosophical terms such as *vacuum, matter, substance*, and *soul* which Hume discusses in his *Treatise* are without meaning, for he argues that there are no impressions corresponding to them. At the same time, he gives accounts of why we naturally suppose that there *are* objects corresponding to these terms. As we shall see in Chapter 4, these suppositions are based on what he technically calls "illusions" or "fictions" of the imagination – that is, systematic

---

[66] T1.4.2.7: 190; see Chapter 4 §2, esp. p. 138.

[67] See Chapter 3, pp. 114–15 and pp. 122–6.

[68] See the excellent discussion of the copy principle and meaning in Peter Kail's *Projection and Realism in Hume's Philosophy* (Oxford University Press, 2007), pp. 31–6.

[69] For example, in his discussion of "power or efficacy" he writes of "meaning . . . unknown qualities" (T1.3.14.27: 168). We can *mean* or *signify* that of which we have no impression or coherent idea.

confusions of different impression-derived ideas.[70] He argues that controversies concerning their objects are not merely verbal.[71] We suppose the existence of such objects even though there are no coherent impressions corresponding to them. Moreover, Hume holds that it is not only philosophers, but ordinary non-philosophical thinkers who suppose the existence of these objects.

9. REASON: PHILOSOPHICAL RELATIONS AND SEPARATIONS

i) Reasoning and philosophical relations

Hume defines reasoning as "nothing but a *comparison*, and a discovery of . . . relations . . . which two or more objects bear to each other" (T1.3.2.2: 73). The distinction between reasoning and imagining is first suggested in Section 5 of Part 1 of Book 1 of the *Treatise* where he distinguishes "two senses considerably different" of the word *relation*. It is not only used for "that quality, by which two ideas are connected together in the imagination, and the one naturally introduces the other" through association, but also for "that particular circumstance, in which, *even upon the arbitrary union of two ideas in the fancy, we may think to compare them*" (T1.1.5.1: 13–14; my emphasis). As we saw in §3 above, the second relation is called a "philosophical relation" (T1.1.5.3: 14) and the first a "natural relation".[72] Unlike the natural relations produced by association, philosophical or scientific relations require a self-conscious *comparison* of objects or an act of reasoning. We can compare, as well as associate objects in terms of the relations of resemblance, contiguity, or causation. The mind operates in two different ways in relating objects in these ways.

What an act of reasoning does *not* do is transfer a feeling from one perception to another. It merely determines the relation of ideas and how their objects stand in reality. In so far as *belief* is determined by the vivacity of ideas, reason itself plays no role in generating it.[73]

---

[70] A 'fiction' in this sense is an idea which represents or is applied to something other than that from which it is derived (T1.2.3.11: 37); see esp. pp. 146ff. and pp. 156ff. of Chapter 4.

[71] For example, see T1.2.5.2: 54ff. and T1.4.6.7: 255.

[72] T1.3.6.16: 94; T.3.14.31: 170; see Chapter 3, pp. 106–7.

[73] Chapter 3 §5, pp. 108–9ff.

Hume distinguishes seven philosophical relations – resemblance, identity, relations in space and time, quantity or number, degrees of any quality, contrariety, and causation. As we shall see in Chapter 3, he further distinguishes these philosophical relations themselves into two kinds, depending on the way they are discovered and whether we have genuine insight into the nature of the relation or not.[74]

ii) *The separability principle: conceptual possibility*

Hume considers adding *"difference"* as an eighth philosophical relation to his list, but rejects this on the ground that difference is "a negation of relation" rather than "any thing real or positive" (T1.1.3.10: 15). *Difference* is a negation of either qualitative identity (resemblance) or quantitative (numerical) identity – the first two relations on his list of philosophical relations. The most important judgment of difference for Hume relates to the difference between ideas – what commentators have called his *separability principle*. He ascribes this principle to the power of imagination, though it would, perhaps, be more appropriately ascribed to reason. He writes that "wherever the imagination perceives a difference among ideas, it can easily produce a separation," that is, think them apart (T1.1.3.4: 10). He attributes this principle to the imagination because it is our ability to *imagine* one object existing without the other which convinces us that they can be conceived as numerically distinct. However, he generally writes of conceiving one object as different from another as a self-conscious operation of the mind, which presupposes comparison. It is an activity which we perform as philosophers. In this sense it is more like the operations of reason than it is like the association of ideas – the primary operation which Hume attributes to the imagination.

Hume's principles concerning separability and inseparability define *conceptual* possibility and impossibility for him. He writes in Part 2 of Book 1 that "Every thing, that is different, is distinguishable; and every thing that is distinguishable, may be separated ... If on the contrary, they be not different, they are not distinguishable; and if they be not distinguishable, they cannot be separated" (T1.2.3.10:

---

[74] See pp.83–4 and 87–8.

36).[75] Hume appeals to the second part of this principle, the "contrary" principle, to support the claim that *time* cannot be conceived apart from things ordered in time. "Five notes play'd on a flute give us the impression and idea of time; tho' time be not a sixth impression, which presents itself to the hearing or any other of the senses." The idea of time is not different nor distinguishable nor separable from the idea of things that appear in time. It arises merely "from the manner, in which impressions appear to the mind." Similarly, he argues that the idea of extension or space is merely the idea of colored or tangible points ordered in space (T1.2.3.4–5). "The ideas of space and time are … no separate or distinct ideas, but merely those of the manner or order, in which objects exist" (T1.2.4.2:39–40). As a result, it is "impossible to conceive either a vacuum and extension without matter, or a time, when there was no succession or change in any real existence." The Newtonian notions of absolute time and space are, on Hume's analysis, inconceivable through clear and distinct ideas.[76]

Similarly, the first part of the above principle, concerning the separability of what is different, is taken by Hume to show conceptual possibility. He appeals to the principle to establish that it is conceptually possible for something to begin to exist without a cause – though he denies that anything actually does so.[77] He argues that our ideas of causes and effects are different and separable, and hence it is *possible* for anything to cause anything.[78] This application of the principle to establish conceptual possibility, as we shall see in Chapter 3, is central to his radical account of causality.

iii) Separation of perceptions themselves and the solid principle

However, there is one instance where Hume uses the separability principle to establish *actual* separation, instead of merely possible separation – namely in the case of perceptions themselves. His main

[75] Cf. T1.1.7.3: 18; T1.4.5.5: 233
[76] See my *Sceptical Realism of David Hume* §10, pp. 100–7.
[77] See Chapter 3 §3, pp. 93–5.
[78] See Chapter 3 Introduction, pp. 79ff. and §4, p. 100. For the explicit use of the principle in the first *Enquiry* see my "Hume's Causal Realism: Recovering a Traditional Interpretation," in *The New Hume Debate*, eds. R. Read and K. Richman, revised edition (Routledge: London, 2007), pp. 92–3.

reason for doing so is based on what Annette Baier calls his "solid principle."[79] Hume writes that the following principle may "appear a mere sophism," but is actually "solid and satisfactory":

> Since we may suppose, but never can conceive a specific difference betwixt an object and impression; any conclusion we form concerning the connexion and repugnance of impressions, will not be known certainly to be applicable to objects; but … on the other hand, whatever conclusions of this kind we form concerning objects, will most certainly be applicable to impressions. (T1.4.5.20: 241)

Hume argues that since our ideas of objects are derived from impressions, the logical structure of those ideas – that is, their "connexion and repugnance" – must at least apply to the impressions. Thus, for example, from the fact that I think of the table in the corner of the room as distinct and separable from the fireplace, it must follow that their impressions themselves are distinct and separable (TApp.13: 634). Hume employs this *solid principle* to show not only that a distinct perception "*may be conceiv'd* as separately existent," but also that "every distinct perception … *is* a distinct existence."[80] It is this claim which leads Hume into the puzzles concerning the unity of the self which he confronts in the Appendix to the *Treatise*.[81]

10. CONCLUSION: IMAGINATION AND HUME'S SCIENCE OF HUMAN NATURE

In this chapter I have stressed the continuity of Hume's theory of the imagination with that of his contemporaries. I have argued that the Cartesian psychophysiological theory of the imagination is implicit in the first principles of the *Treatise*, including his *copy principle*. He profoundly developed this theory in applying it to explain a number of phenomena, including inductive inferences, indirect passions, sympathy – and the natural suppositions we make concerning space, causality, an external world and personal identity.

I have also argued that it is a mistake to think that by ridding himself of the pure intellect and resting our beliefs on the imagination

---

[79] Baier, *Death and Character*, pp. 159 and 189.
[80] TApp.12: 634 and T1.4.6.16: 259, my emphasis; for the latter claim cf. TApp.21: 636 and T1.4.5.5: 233. T1.4.6.16: 259; cf. T1.4.5.5: 233 and TApp.21: 636
[81] Chapter 4 §4 iv), pp. 163–6.

Hume is merely embracing a new Cartesian-like project of using clear and distinct ideas to construct reality. He does not, it seems to me, adopt what Don Garrett has called "reductive empiricism" – the reduction of our basic notions of space, time, causation, matter and person to what can be believed on the basis of clear and distinct impression-derived ideas.[82] In the next two chapters we shall see in detail that Hume's central goal is to show the *limits* of what we can legitimately believe on the basis of those ideas, and to postulate other processes of the imagination which explain how we construct the reality in which we naturally and inevitably believe.

---

[82] Don Garrett, *Cognition and Commitment in Hume's Philosophy* (Oxford University Press, 1997), pp. 36–8 *et passim*.

CHAPTER 3

Causation

In this Chapter, I consider what is undoubtedly the most original and influential part of the *Treatise*, namely Part 3 of Book 1, where Hume presents his theory of causation. It is easy to lose sight of his central discovery concerning causation as we go through the details of his theory. While Hume scholars disagree on some of these details, there is general agreement that this central discovery was epistemological and that it had profound results in our intellectual history. Hume expresses his central epistemological claim toward the end of Part 3 when he writes that

there are no objects which, by the mere survey, without consulting experience, we can determine to be the causes of any other; and no objects which we can certainly determine in the same manner not to be the causes. *Any thing may produce any thing.* Creation, annihilation, motion, reason, volition; all these may arise from one another, or from any other object we can imagine ... *The constant conjunction of objects determines their causation* ... (T1.3.15.1: 173; the first italics are mine)

Before Hume, major thinkers held that we have some knowledge independently of experience as to what kinds of things can and can't produce other kinds of things. Even Newton and Locke held that it is impossible for the order we discover in the universe to arise from anything but a thinking intelligent being.[1] However, Hume argued systematically that before we consult experience "*any thing may produce any thing*," and that only "*constant conjunction*" or unalterable experience can show us what actually does produce what. In Part 4

---

[1] Issac Newton, *Opticks* (New York: Dover, 1952), Query 31, esp. pp. 402–3. Cf. Locke, ECHU 1.4.9: "For the visible marks of extraordinary Wisdom and Power, appear so plainly in all the Works of the Creation, that a rational Creature, who will but seriously reflect on them, cannot miss the discovery of a *Deity*."

of Book 1 of his *Treatise*, he applies these claims to the question of whether changes in matter can cause changes in thought, and concludes that insofar as we have an idea of causality they can and actually do – a claim that went directly against the arguments of Locke as well as Malebranche.[2] In his *Dialogues Concerning Natural Religion* written over ten years later, he applies the principle that "any thing may produce any thing" to the question of the origin of order in the world – arguing systematically that experience did not support the generally accepted argument for an intelligent designer. But he did not have the facts to support any alternative theory. The development of a serious alternative based on experience had to await another great British philosophical genius who published 120 years after Hume's *Treatise*, namely Charles Darwin.

Hume's own central aim in Part 3 is to explain the mental processes which give rise to causal reasoning, and the idea of causal power or (what amounts to the same thing for him) the necessary connection between cause and effect. It is a project in what we would now call cognitive psychology. In explaining how our causal inferences and supposition of causal power are formed he appeals to a mental process which his predecessors had generally considered to be a source of false conclusions – namely the association of ideas as it arises from custom.[3] Hume argues that association provides the mechanism for our causal inferences when it is supplied with the input of nature herself. This input is nothing but the observation of the constant conjunction of objects discovered by experience. Hume regards his associational explanation of causal inference as giving strong support for his complementary claims that we have no insight into the power or force of nature, and that we must rely entirely on experience in identifying causal connections.

Thus far, there is general agreement on the interpretation of Hume's theory of causation. What Hume scholars mainly disagree about is his account of what causal power or causal connection really is – what

---

[2] See Chapter 2 §4, pp. 57ff.; cf. Locke, ECHU 4.10.10. Locke's view is somewhat complicated by the fact that he thought that God could "supperadd" thought to matter, and that our souls might possibly be material (ECHU 4.3.6): however, he held unequivocally that it was inconceivable that matter by itself could cause thought. God or the first being cannot be material.

[3] See p. 102 and §6, pp. 114ff.

we may call the *ontology* of causation. A common view is that objective causal power is no more than constant conjunction.[4] On this view, Hume is saying that there really is no power or force in nature, only a regular conjunction of objects found to be successive and contiguous in time and space. Hume writes in Book 3 of the *Treatise* that "all beings in the universe, consider'd in themselves, appear entirely loose and independent of each other" (T3.1.1.22: 466). According to the positivist[5] or reductionist interpretation, objects don't just *appear* loose and unconnected; they *really are* loose and unconnected. There is regularity in nature; but there is nothing which is the source of that regularity. The central basis for this interpretation is to be found in Section 14 of Part 3, "Of the idea of necessary connection." In that section, Hume traces the origin of our idea of power or necessary connection to a subjective impression in the mind of the observer. He argues that our idea of necessary connection can only legitimately represent this subjective impression. He goes on to give two definitions of cause, what we may call the 'regularity definition' and 'inference definition.' These definitions have, above all, led to the view that he denies that there are any necessary connections in objects (§6, pp. 118–20).

At the end of this chapter I argue that there are reasons to think that Hume's definitions and his account of the subjective origin of the *idea* of necessary connection are not his last word on the subject of the ontology of causation. In the Conclusion to Book 1 of the *Treatise* and the *Abstract* he appeals to his account of the subjective origin of our idea of power to support the claim that we are *ignorant* of objective causal power (§7). Moreover, he holds that in both ordinary life and scientific discourse we naturally suppose the existence of objective necessity, and he provides two explanations of this natural supposition (§8). These explanations provide support for two alternative interpretations of his view – quasi-realism and what I have called 'sceptical realism.'[6] I briefly discuss these interpretations

---

[4] See Helen Beebee, *Hume on Causation* (London: Routledge, 2006), esp. Ch. 5, "The Traditional Interpretation."

[5] This view can be traced to early-nineteenth-century interpreters of Hume's theory. See my "The Scientific Reception of Hume's Theory of Causation: Establishing the Positivist Interpretation …," in *The Reception of David Hume in Europe*, ed. Peter Jones (London: Continuum, 2005), pp. 327–47.

[6] In my *The Sceptical Realism of David Hume*, Chapter 4, and subsequent articles.

and give reasons for favoring the latter. I conclude the chapter in §9 with a discussion of the significance of Hume's claim in response to "the Cartesians" that we have "no adequate idea of power or efficacy in any object" (T1.3.14.8–10).

1. "OF KNOWLEDGE AND PROBABILITY"

Hume begins his discussion of causation and causal reasoning in Part 3 of Book 1 of the *Treatise* by drawing a twofold distinction between *knowledge* and *probability*, and placing causal reasoning firmly on the side of probability. Later on, in Section 11 of Part 3, he draws a three-fold distinction, putting causal reasoning in the category of *proofs*, and downgrading the term probability to mean something like what we mean by it today – namely, "evidence which is still attended with uncertainty" (T1.3.11.2: 124).[7] By placing our arguments from cause and effect under the category of "proofs" Hume wanted to stress that these arguments leave us without any doubt: "One would appear ridiculous who would say, that it is only probable the sun will rise to-morrow, or that all men must die; though it is plain we have no further assurance of these facts than what experience affords us." If it seemed silly in Hume's day to say that it was only probable that all men die or that the sun will rise tomorrow, it seems even sillier today. For we today commonly think of experience as giving us knowledge in the strongest sense of the word. Nevertheless, no matter how much Hume upgraded causal reasoning because it leads to conclusions "which are entirely free from doubt and uncertainty," he still maintained a strict division between proofs and probabilities on the one hand, and real knowledge on the other. To understand what Hume says about causal reasoning or reasoning from experience, it is important to understand his claim that it never results in genuine *knowledge*.

i) Knowledge and insight

What exactly did Hume and his predecessors mean by knowledge? Most fundamentally a knowledge claim is one which is intelligible.

---

[7] As we saw in Chapter 1 §6, he probably derived this threefold distinction from the Chevalier Ramsay.

It gives us *insight* or understanding of the relation of the objects conjoined. Think of a child learning the multiplication table after learning addition. One might first train the child to memorize the multiplication table, and then afterwards help her to understand, for example, that '3 × 7' = '7 + 7 + 7'. When the child understands the relation of equality between multiplication and repeated addition of the same quantity a certain number of times, then she has what Hume would have called knowledge of multiplication. It is useful to think of knowledge at the time we first attain it, at the point where we first attain insight. Then we have what some philosophers call an 'A-ha feeling.' When we get real knowledge we feel like saying: 'A-ha, I understand that now!'

At the beginning of his discussion of causal reasoning in Part 3 of Book 1 of the *Treatise* Hume places causal reasoning and its results *outside* of the realm of real knowledge in this sense. In fact, one should think of much of Part 3 as a sustained argument for the view that causal or experiential reasoning never gives us real knowledge. Causal relations are never intelligible. Hume's claim may seem counterintuitive. Think of a child discovering through experience that watering plants makes them grow and that they shrivel when not watered. "Surely", a critic might say, "the child gets an 'A-ha feeling' when she discovers the connection between the two events, just as she does when she understands a truth in mathematics. How can Hume deny that she *perceives* their connection?" But that is exactly what Hume does deny. He argues that experience never gives us any insight into the connection between the two distinct events; it merely accustoms us to them so that we associate the two in our minds. The distinction between an association of ideas and real knowledge of relations is fundamental for understanding Hume's theory of causation and causal reasoning. Causal reasoning or reasoning from experience never takes us beyond the assurance that arises from association of ideas. The most skillful physicist has no more insight into causal connections than our young child.

As we saw in Chapter 2, Hume distinguishes seven "philosophical relations" which are apprehended by reason.[8] At the beginning of Part 3 of Book 1, he identifies four which are objects of real

---

[8] §10, pp. 75ff.

knowledge: "*resemblance, contrariety, degrees in quality, and propor-tions in quantity or number*" (T1.3.1.2: 70). Hume claims that only the last set of relations – mathematical relations – form the basis for the kind of *reasoning* that results in knowledge, what he and his predecessors called *demonstration.*[9]

The first three sets of relations, according to Hume, are only *intu-ited*: that means that we immediately understand them when we perceive them. We immediately understand that one circle *resembles* another and "white differs less from gray than it does from black" (a relation of "degrees in quality").[10]

We also intuitively understand contrariety. Hume argues that nothing can be contrary except the idea of an object and its negation (T1.1.5.8: 15). In other words, there are no *a priori* impossibilities between distinct ideas. Locke, on the other hand, held that there is an *a priori* or intuitive impossibility that "bare incogitative mat-ter" can "produce a thinking intelligent being" and that "the order, harmony, and beauty which are to be found in nature" can arise either from matter or from a number of "finite cogitative beings" (ECHU 4.10.10). But, for Hume, there are no such *a priori* causal impossibilities.

Hume sharply narrows the number of truths which we appre-hend merely through intuition. It is the fundamental principles of mathematics, particularly those of arithmetic and algebra, which give Hume the paradigm for what counts as intuitive knowledge and genuine *insight* into the real nature of things.[11]

---

[9] Locke had extended demonstration to other realms besides mathematics such as morality (ECHU 3.11.16; 4.3.18; 4.4.10.), but as we shall see in Chapter 8, pp. 243ff. Hume opposed this extension.

[10] The example is taken from William James, *Pragmatism* (London: Longmans, 1925), p. 209. James gives this as an example of a relation "*among purely mental ideas*." He denies that such truths refer to anything but mental objects. As explained below, I do not think this is Hume's view.

[11] Hume held that geometry, unlike algebra and arithmetic, was not "a perfect and infallible science." He argued that "its first principles are ... drawn from the general appearance of the objects" (T1.3.1.4–5: 70–1). The problems with the first principles of geometry arise when it deals with "the prodigious minuteness of which nature is susceptible." Hume's account of geometry is notoriously difficult and I will not deal with it in this book; see Marina Frasca-Spada, *Space and the Self in Hume's Treatise* (Cambridge University Press, 1998), esp. Chapter 3, and Dale Jacquette, *David Hume's Critique of Infinity* (Leiden-Boston-Köln: Brill, 2001), Chapter 4, pp. 168ff.

At the beginning of his discussion of knowledge in Part 3, Hume gives a standard example of a relation known through *demonstration*: "'tis from the idea of a triangle, that we discover the relation of equality, which its three angles bear to two right ones; and this relation is invariable, as long as our idea remains the same" (T1.3.1.1: 69). In order to discover the truth of this proposition we need to do a bit of demonstrative reasoning. This involves finding intermediate links so that we can understand the relation of equality between the idea of the sum of the angles of the triangle and the idea of two right angles. Ultimately these intermediate links consist of relations which are known intuitively.[12]

To see this, let us take a simpler example than that given by Hume, again from arithmetic. Suppose we want to demonstrate that '3 + 1' = '2 + 2'. Then we would find intermediate links, namely the intuitive truths that '3 + 1 = 4' and that '2 + 2 = 4'. These are known directly, or by intuition. Having perceived these intermediate links we would then be able to perceive the demonstrative truth that '3 + 1' = '2 + 2'. For Hume, following Descartes and Locke, the most basic forms of knowledge are intuitive. Indeed, in going through the steps of a demonstrative argument repeatedly we come close to an intuitive understanding of the conclusion.[13]

While it is not obvious from the opening pages of Part 3 of Book 1 of the *Treatise*, Hume holds that real knowledge also involves a *necessity*, or a necessary connection between the ideas. Throughout his discussion of causality in the rest of Part 3, Hume refers to this feature of knowledge in order to show that it is lacking in the case of causal claims. If a claim is necessary, it is impossible to distinctly conceive of its contrary. In the case of an intuitive truth such as that '2 + 2 = 4' this is obvious: we cannot conceive or imagine that 2 + 2 is equal to any number besides 4. There is an absurdity in the claim that '2 + 2 = 5' or that '2 + 2 = 3'. But Hume thinks that this kind of necessity also applies to demonstrative truths such as '3 + 1' = '2 + 2', or 'the sum of the angles of a triangle equal two right angles.'

[12] For discussions of Hume and his predecessors on intuition and demonstration, see David Owen, *Hume's Reason* (Oxford University Press, 1999), and Beebee, *Hume on Causation*, Chapter 2.
[13] Descartes' views are found in his *Rules for the Direction of the Mind*, esp. Rules 3 & 7, CSM I, pp. 13–15 and 25. Compare Locke in ECHU 4.2.

Over and over again throughout Part 3, Hume stresses that any proposition which is the object of real knowledge – whether intuitive or demonstrative – is such that we cannot distinctly conceive of its contrary. On the other hand, if we *can* distinctly conceive or imagine the contrary, as is the case with causal claims, then they can never be demonstrated (or intuited) and cannot be the object of insight, or genuine knowledge.[14]

At the beginning of Part 3 of Book 1, Hume stresses that knowledge claims "depend entirely on the ideas, which we compare together" (T1.3.1.1: 69). He is often taken to be claiming that knowledge by its very nature is *only* about ideas, and not about objects in the real world – the view which he seems to adopt in the first *Enquiry*.[15] But this is not his view in the *Treatise*, where he makes the *adequate representation* of objects a condition of knowledge. In Part 2 of Book 1, in his discussion "Of the ideas of space and time," he writes that

> Wherever ideas are adequate representations of objects, the relations, contradictions, and agreements of the ideas are all applicable to the objects; and this we may, in general, observe to be *the foundation of all human knowledge*. But our ideas are adequate representations of the most minute parts of extension ... The plain consequence is, that whatever *appears* impossible and contradictory upon the comparison of these ideas, must be *really* impossible and contradictory, without any farther excuse or evasion.(T1.2.2.1:29; my emphasis)

It would take us too far afield to consider Hume's complex arguments showing the contradiction involved in the claim that bodies are infinitely divisible.[16] His point here is simply that since it is self-contradictory in idea, it must be self-contradictory in reality. It is important to realize that Hume was arguing *against* a philosopher, namely Pierre Bayle, who argued that "the objects of geometry ... are mere ideas in the mind; and not only never did, but never can exist in nature" (T1.2.4.10: 42).[17] It was in opposition to this claim

---

[14] See especially p. 121 & pp. 93–4.

[15] He writes that "though there never were a circle or triangle in nature, the truths, demonstrated by Euclid, would for ever retain their certainty and evidence" (EHU 4.1).

[16] For an interpretation of these arguments see my *Sceptical Realism of David Hume*, pp. 91–100.

[17] Bayle argued that the paradoxes of infinite divisibility show that space "can only exist in our minds" – that is, "they can only exist *ideally*." See his article "Zeno of Elea" in Pierre Bayle, *Historical and Critical Dictionary: Selections*, eds. Richard H. Popkin and Craig Brush

that Hume argued that "our ideas are adequate representations of the most minute parts of extension" (T1.2.2.1: 29).[18] Where our ideas are adequate representations of objects, "the relations, contradictions, and agreements of the ideas are all applicable to the objects." In the Conclusion to this chapter (§9), I shall consider the significance of this requirement for knowledge in relation to Hume's denial that we have genuine knowledge of causation.

ii) Probability

Hume describes probability in Section 2 of Part 3 much as Locke had in Book 4 of his *Essay Concerning Human Understanding*, by contrasting it with knowledge. Unlike knowledge relations which "have a constant, immutable, and visible connexion one with another" the relations of probability are "not constant, and immutable, or at least are not perceived to be so" (ECHU 4.15.1). Hume follows Locke in calling the probable relations "inconstant" (T1.3.2.2). Whereas relations of knowledge may be discovered simply from their ideas, we require something more to discover whether probable relations hold.[19] Hume identifies "*identity, situations in time and place, and causation*" as the probable relations (T1.3.2.1). One cannot tell the relative situations (i.e. positions) of two objects in space – your house and mine, say – merely from their ideas. Nor can one tell in this way that things we encounter at different times are identical: one cannot just compare our ideas of the Morning Star and the Evening Star in order to discover that they are the same object – namely Venus. Hume writes that "two objects, tho' perfectly resembling each other, and even appearing in the same place at different times, may be numerically different" (T1.3.1.2: 1). It is not inconceivable that the exact resembling computer I found on my desk this morning is a different one than I left there last night, though the probability of this is very low. It is not merely by comparison of ideas that I am convinced that

(Indianapolis: Bobbs-Merrill, 1965), p. 363. As we saw in Chapter 1 §6, p. 27, Hume advised his friend Michael Ramsay to read this article to help him understand the metaphysical parts of his reasoning in the *Treatise*.

[18] Locke's views on "the reality of knowledge" are discussed in ECHU 4.4. He too insists that knowledge requires the existence of objects corresponding to our ideas.

[19] Locke wrote that in the case of probable relations "that which makes me believe, is something extraneous to the thing I believe" (ECHU 4.15.3).

I am typing on the same computer, but rather because of my belief in cause and effect – in certain causal relations. Hume contrasts causal relations themselves with knowledge relations: "the power, by which one object produces another, is never discoverable merely from their ideas." That flame causes heat or that the movement and impact of an object on a second one causes the second one to move cannot be discovered simply by comparing their ideas. Nor, as we shall see, are the contrary claims inconceivable.

According to Hume, just as the relation of equality (or, more generally, any proportion in quantity or number) forms the basis of all our demonstrative reasonings, so the relation of causality forms the basis of all our reasonings concerning probabilities.[20] In order to reason about the relative positions of objects in space and time or their numerical identity, we must appeal to judgments about causality. When I reason about the unlikely possibility that the computer I am typing on this morning is different from the one I left on my desk last night, I consider the possibility of its being replaced in the night, of all the information being downloaded, of people breaking into my house without my knowledge, etc. These are all considerations based on causation. Hume writes that "of those three relations, which depend not upon the mere ideas, the only one, that can be trac'd beyond our senses, and informs us of existences and objects, which we do not see or feel, is *causation*" (T1.3.2.3: 74). The main aim of the rest of Part 3 of the *Treatise* is to explain the idea of causation and the reasoning about the existence of objects beyond our senses (and memory) which is based on it.

The tie between 'probability' and causal reasoning was much tighter and more explicit in Hume's philosophy than that of his predecessors. Locke had considered causal reasoning as the source of the "highest degree of Probability" (ECHU 4.16.8). However, unlike Hume later, he regarded testimony (the second highest degree) as an independent of ground of probability (ECHU 4.15.4 and 4.16.7). For Hume, on the other hand, our belief in testimony is itself based on causal considerations: "when we receive any matter

---

[20] To be more precise, this claim should be limited to what Hume calls "philosophical" or legitimate probabilities: it does not apply to what he calls "unphilosophical probabilities" in T1.3.13. Nevertheless, it is significant that Hume even claims that causation lies at the basis of reasoning concerning "the probability of chances" (T1.3.11.4–6: 125–6).

of fact upon human testimony, our faith arises from the very same origin as our inferences from causes to effects, and from effects to causes: nor is there any thing but our experience of the governing principles of human nature, which can give us any assurance of the veracity of men" (T1.3.9.12: 113). The study of human nature teaches us the principles which cause human beings to lie or tell the truth.

iii) *Hume's notion of reasoning in general*

Hume's full definition of reasoning is as follows: "all kinds of reasoning consist in nothing but a *comparison*, and a discovery of those relations, either constant or inconstant, which two or more objects bear to each other" (T1.3.2.2: 73). As we have just seen, the "inconstant" relation which allows us to draw inferences to objects beyond our senses and memory is causation. However, Hume goes on to argue that comparison is never *sufficient* for us to draw an inference from cause to effect, or from effect to cause. To draw such inferences we require an impression and an association of ideas. So paradoxically, causal *reasoning* in the sense of comparison is not able to make us draw an inference or *reason* from the existence of one object to another. For that, we need to join reason with further powers of mind, including sensation and imagination.

Hume's notion of reasoning, especially in so far as it concerns probability, is among the most difficult of the *Treatise* to sort out.[21] He writes later in Part 3 that "all probable reasoning is nothing but a species of sensation" (T1.3.8.12: 103). But nothing could be further from the notion of reason as comparison with which he begins Part 3 of the *Treatise*. Some commentators argue that Hume changes his notion of reason through the pages of the *Treatise*. But that view is not consistent with the fact that he denies in Books 2 and 3 that reason can motivate our actions, or form the fundamental basis of our moral judgments. We need to retain the notion of reason simply as comparison, unaffected by sensation or imagination, to account for his stress throughout the *Treatise* on its practical limitations.[22]

---

[21] See also Kail, *Projection and Realism in Hume's Philosophy*, Chapter 2.3.
[22] See §4 pp. 106ff., §5, pp. 113–14, and Chapter 7 §1, pp. 217–18.

It should be noted further that in Hume's philosophy there is no significant distinction between *reason as a faculty or power* on the one hand, and the *act of reasoning* on the other. Hume writes that "the distinction, which we often make between power and the exercise of it, is ... without foundation" (T1.3.14.34: 171). There is no such thing as unexercised power in Hume's philosophy. In Book 2, he allows that the distinction has a place in our everyday thinking, but stresses that it has no place in science or philosophy.[23]

2. PRELIMINARY EXAMINATION OF THE IMPRESSION OF CAUSATION

Hume begins his discussion of causation by noting that if we are to "reason justly" we need to understand "the idea concerning which we reason" (T 1.3.2.4: 74). In accordance with his *copy principle* he seeks the impression which is the source of the idea.[24] He begins by asking whether there are some "particular *qualities*" which we discover in all those objects which we call causes and effects, only to dismiss this suggestion as absurd (T. 1.3.5: 74). For any quality or property which belongs to one kind of cause or effect, there will be some other cause or effect which does not have it. Flame causes heat. The cue ball on the billiard table impacts the 8 ball, causing it to move. Our will causes the motions of our limbs. But there is no single property I can discover in these very different kinds of causes or effects which they have in common.

Hume then seeks common features of the *relation* of causation itself. What relations do we actually observe between the objects or events that we call cause and effect? He identifies two relations, namely *contiguity* and *succession*, which are found to hold between all causes and their effects.

Two events are *contiguous* if they are beside each other in time, *or* in space. They would *not* be contiguous if there were a ten-minute gap between the appearance of the first and the appearance of the second, *or* if the one were to occur across the room from the other. I shall return to temporal contiguity in the next paragraph. What

[23] See Chapter 5 §1, pp. 172–3.   [24] See Chapter 2 §8, pp. 68ff.

Hume says about *spatial* contiguity of causes and effects is somewhat cavalier – given that this was a major point of contention among physicists in his own day who disputed the question whether there was a mechanism causing gravitation between distant objects.[25] He claims without argument that when one object seems to produce a change at distance from it, one can generally find "a chain of causes" spatially linking "the distant objects" (T1.3.2.6).[26] He includes spatial contiguity in the first definition of cause which he gives toward the end of Part 3.[27] While he qualifies his commitment to spatial contiguity as a feature of all causal relations later in Book 1 of the *Treatise*, his qualification arises from observations in philosophy of mind, not natural philosophy.[28]

Hume considers temporal contiguity as more basic to causation than spatial contiguity. He discusses it in Section 2 along with the second relation he identifies, namely *succession*. Succession is simply "PRIORITY of time in the cause before the effect" (T1.3.2.7: 75). Hume notes that some people hold that causes can be simultaneous with their effects. However, he thinks that "experience in most instances seems to contradict this opinion" (T1.3.2.7: 76). In the course of arguing that cause and effect must be successive, he appeals to an "establish'd maxim in both natural and moral philosophy, that an object, which exists for any time in its full perfection without producing another, is not its sole cause." In other words, even though cause and effect are successive they are *temporally* contiguous: there is no gap in time between them. As we already saw in Chapter 2, he endorses this maxim in Rule 8 of his "Rules by which to judge of causes and effects" (T1.3.15.10: 174). Temporal contiguity is fundamental for him in the scientific identification of true causes.

While temporal contiguity and succession are necessary for causation, they are not sufficient. Hume writes that "an object may be

---

[25] See Lisa Downing, "Occasionalism and Strict Mechanism: Malebranche, Berkeley, Fontenelle," in *Early Modern Philosophy: Mind, Matter, and Metaphysics*, eds. C. Mercer and E. O'Neill (Oxford University Press, 2005), pp. 206–30.

[26] In his *Enquiry*, he favors the Newtonian hypothesis of an "ethereal active fluid," which presumably precluded action at a distance (EHU 7.25n16); see my *Sceptical Realism of David Hume*, pp. 144–7 and 161–4.

[27] See pp. 118–19. However, spatial contiguity drops out of his first definition of cause in EHU 7.29.

[28] T1.4.5.11: 236. He allows for causes of perceptions which have no location in space.

contiguous and prior to another without being consider'd as its cause." Just because one object temporally follows another object and is contiguous to it, it does not follow that the first is the cause of the second.[29] Night always and invariably follows day and is temporally contiguous to it, but no one would say that day *causes* night. What more is needed for causation?

Hume writes: "there is a NECESSARY CONNEXION to be taken into consideration; and that relation is of much greater importance than ... the other two ..." (T1.3.2.11). A cause is necessarily connected with its effect, so that if the cause occurs the effect *must* occur. Necessary connection is what we all naturally take as fundamental to causation, according to Hume.

Hume formulates his basic problem concerning causation as one of identifying the impression which is the source of our idea of necessary connection. Lest we miss the significance of his problem he later reminds us that he is dealing with "one of the most sublime questions in philosophy, viz. *that concerning the power ... of causes*" (T1.3.14.2: 156). Hume identifies the *power* or energy of the cause with the necessary connection between the cause and effect. He writes that "we can only define power by connexion" (T1.4.5.31: 248). Indeed, "the terms ... *efficacy, agency, power, force, energy, necessity, connexion,* and *productive quality*" are, he tells us, nearly synonymous (T1.3.14.4: 157). In asking for the origin of the idea of necessary connection, Hume is asking for the origin of our idea of power, energy, force, or whatever it is that makes one thing produce another.

After stressing the importance of the idea of necessary connection to our conception of causation, Hume denies that we ever observe this necessity in the objects themselves. We have no sense impression of necessary connection as we do of contiguity and succession. Has he then found "an idea, which is not preceded by any similar impression" (T1.3.2.12: 77)? Since he already has found sufficient evidence for the principle that all ideas are derived from similar impressions, he is not willing to reject it in this case without further investigation. However, Hume's further investigation into the impression which is the source of our idea of necessary connection takes a rather

---

[29] To assume that it does follow is an example of the fallacy which logicians have traditionally called "*Post hoc, ergo propter hoc.*"

roundabout route. He does not return directly to the question until Section 14 of Part 3,[30] hoping in the meantime to find what he is looking for by beating "about all the neighbouring fields" without any fixed plan (T1.3.2.13: 78).

3. THE CAUSAL MAXIM AND HUME'S REJECTION OF INDETERMINACY IN NATURE

The prey which flies out of the first field in which he starts to beat is the causal maxim. Hume writes that it is "a general maxim in philosophy, that *whatever begins to exist, must have a cause of existence*" (T1.3.3.3). This maxim is not only the basis of our experimental reasoning in science, but was also thought by his contemporaries to be a major support for the cosmological argument, which concludes that God must be the cause of the beginning of the universe.

In Section 3 Hume argues that the causal maxim is not based on intuition or demonstration – that is, our confidence in it is not based on either of the two forms of knowledge. He was accused by later critics of the *Treatise* of denying the *truth* of the maxim. He replied to one such critic that he was only discussing the source of our belief in it, not its truth. His claim is epistemological, not ontological. He states that he "never asserted so absurd a Proposition as *that any thing might arise without a Cause.*"[31]

Hume begins his account in Section 3 by giving a general argument to show that the causal maxim cannot be known in the strict sense of the word. All knowledge claims, he reminds us, are necessarily true and it is impossible to deny them without contradiction. But we can "conceive any object to be non-existent this moment, and existent the next, without conjoining to it the distinct idea of a cause or productive principle" (T1.3.3.3: 79). The idea of something *beginning to exist* and of something *being caused* are two *distinct* ideas, and we can think of the former without the latter. Since the

---

[30] See §6, p. 114.

[31] Hume to John Stewart, February 1754, HL I, 187. On Hume's exchange with John Stewart, who was Professor of Natural Philosophy at the University of Edinburgh, see my "The Scientific Reception of Hume's Theory of Causality: Establishing the Positivist Interpretation in Early Nineteenth-Century Scotland," in *The Reception of David Hume in Europe*, ed. Peter Jones (Bristol: Thoemmes-Continuum, 2005), pp. 327–47, esp. pp. 329–33.

ideas are separable "for the imagination ... the actual separation of [their] objects is so far possible, that it implies no contradiction or absurdity." Here we see Hume applying the *separability principle* to establish the conceptual or logical *possibility* that something can exist without a cause.

When Hume turns to the refutation of some specific attempts philosophers have made to prove the causal maxim, its significance for the cosmological argument becomes apparent. He cites what he takes to be an attempt to demonstrate the maxim by his predecessor John Locke. In his chapter on the existence of God in his *Essay Concerning Human Understanding*, Locke had argued for God's existence by way of the claim "that bare *nothing can no more produce any real Being, than it can be equal to two right Angles*" (ECHU 4.10.3; cf. T1.3.3.6). Hume takes Locke to be arguing that if *something* could begin to exist without a cause, then *nothing* would have to be its cause, and it is absurd to postulate *nothing* as the cause of something.[32] Hume claims that the first premise begs the question: unless one starts with the assumption that *whatever begins to exist has a cause*, then there is no reason to postulate *nothing* as its cause (T1.3.3.7).

Hume also considers arguments for the causal maxim put forward by Samuel Clarke and Thomas Hobbes (T1.3.3.4: 80). He claims that, like that of Locke, the arguments they put forward beg the question.

Hume concludes his discussion of the causal maxim by noting that since it does not arise "from knowledge" in the strict sense, it "must ... arise from observation and experience" (T1.3.3.9). His account of the experiential source of the maxim is given later in Part 3, where he describes the difference between unscientific and scientific reasoners. The unscientific reasoner attributes an apparent "uncertainty of events to ... an uncertainty in the causes" – that is, to chance. (T1.3.12.5: 132). The peasant, writes Hume, can give "no better reason for the stopping of any clock or watch, than to say, commonly it does not go right." In contrast, the scientific reasoner examines the clock or watch, and finds "a grain of dust, which puts a stop to the whole movement." He goes on to reflect that in almost "every part

---

[32] In fact, Locke took the claim quoted above to be known intuitively. It is not at all clear that he subscribes to the rather silly argument which Hume attributes to him.

of nature there is contain'd a vast variety of springs and principles, which are hid, by reason of their minuteness or remoteness," and that it is possible that any apparent irregularity arises from "the secret operation of contrary causes." Because of their subsequent success in finding the "contrary causes" of *many* of these apparent irregularities, scientific reasoners form "a maxim ... that the connexion betwixt *all* causes and effects is equally necessary" (my emphasis). Apparent irregularities in nature arise from the hidden operation of "contrary causes." This then is the way that "observation and experience" lead to the scientific thinker's adoption of the causal maxim.

Hume's philosophical commitment to the causal maxim should not be treated lightly. He writes in his discussion "Of the probability of chances" that "chance is nothing real in itself, and, properly speaking is, is merely the negation of a cause" (T1.3.11.4: 125). As we shall see in Chapter 5, his rejection of the view that there is any kind of chance in reality is even stronger in Book 2 of the *Treatise*.[33] In fact, throughout his metaphysical writings Hume rejects any kind of indeterminacy in the nature of things.[34]

Hume did not find his prey – the impression of necessary connection – in discussing the origin of the causal maxim. But when he beats about in the next field he visits, he is more successful. In addition, he discovers one of the greatest curiosities of modern philosophy, what later philosophers have called 'the problem of induction.'

4. THE INFERENCE FROM THE OBSERVED TO THE UNOBSERVED

When Hume writes "Of the inference from the impression to the idea" in the title to Section 6 of Part 3, what he has in mind is the fact that we draw inferences from what we observe, "the impression," to what we have not yet observed, "the idea." To take the example

[33] Chapter 5 §1, pp. 172ff.
[34] See EHU 8.23. In Section 8 of the *Dialogues Concerning Natural Religion* where Philo puts forward the Epicurean hypothesis that forms come into being through chance, he describes it as "justly ... esteem'd the most absurd system that has ever been proposed"(8.2), He only proposes to give it a "faint appearance of probability" (*Dialogues* 8.2). For a convincing account of the origins of the modern scientific acceptance of indeterminacy in the nineteenth century see Ian Hacking, *The Taming of Chance* (Cambridge University Press, 1990).

he uses in his *Abstract*, I draw an inference from my observation of the movement of one billiard ball impacting on another (the impression) to the movement of the second ball before observing it to move (the idea). This example involves a prediction about the (immediate) future. But that is not the case in all inferences from what is observed to the unobserved. We also draw inferences from observed objects to unobserved objects in the past. For example, I infer that the e-mail I received yesterday was written the day before by my friend in Scotland. We draw inferences from what we observe to unobserved objects in the past and present, as well as making predictions about the future.

As I said, it is in this section that Hume is generally thought to have discovered what philosophers have come to call 'the problem of induction.' *Induction*, which is the name philosophers now give to these inferences, was not a word used by Hume in this sense.[35] More importantly, the problem as generally conceived by later philosophers is usually considered solely a problem of whether the inference is *justified*. However, Hume's central problem concerns the *cause* or *explanation* of induction. He argues negatively that the inference is not caused by reason, and positively that it is caused by the association of ideas. For Hume, the question whether the inference is justified is *at best* a secondary concern.[36]

Hume begins his discussion of the cause of the inference from the impression to the idea by denying that it is based on demonstration or intuition. He uses the language of 'essence' to discuss this possibility:

The inference we draw from cause to effect, is not derived merely from a survey of these particular objects, and from such a penetration into their essences as may discover the dependence of the one upon the other. There is no object which implies the existence of any other, if we consider these objects in themselves, and never look beyond the ideas which we form of them. Such an inference would amount to knowledge, and would imply the absolute contradiction and impossibility of conceiving any thing different. (T1.3.6.1: 86)

---

[35] Hume uses the term only once in the *Treatise* (T1.2.2.2) and once in the Appendix (T1.3.7.7: App. 628): in the first case he clearly uses the word in a context where we would talk of deduction.

[36] In his first *Enquiry* he writes that he allows "that the one proposition may *justly* be inferred from the other" (EHU 4.16, my emphasis).

If we could penetrate into the essence of the cause and discover the dependence of the effect on it, then we could infer the effect from it in a new case without experience. His model here is mathematics: just as we can infer the properties of a triangle from insight into the essence or nature of a triangle, so if we had intuitive or demonstrative knowledge of causation then we would be able to infer the existence of the effect by way of insight into the essence or nature of the cause.

He dismisses this possibility by appealing to an argument of the form with which we became familiar in §3. If the inference were based on knowledge then its denial would be self contradictory. It would be impossible to deny that motion of the second billiard ball follows on the motion and impact of the first. However, there is no contradiction in imagining that the cue ball rolls along the table, hits the 8 ball, and the 8 ball turns into a butterfly which flits around the room and lands on a player's nose. None of us expects such a result, but the point is that it is perfectly conceivable or imaginable. If the inference were based on intuition or demonstration, then any result other than that which actually occurs would be unimaginable. It would be impossible to conceive the idea of the effect separately from that of the cause, and think that something else occurs.

i) 'Experience' and the nature of Hume's problem of induction

Hume writes that it is "by EXPERIENCE only, that we can infer the existence of one object from that of another." He explains what we generally mean by experience in the following way:

> We remember to have had frequent instances of the existence of one species of objects; and also remember, that the individuals of another species of objects have always attended them, and have existed in a regular order of contiguity and succession with regard to them. Thus we remember to have seen that species of object we call flame, and to have felt that species of sensation we call heat. We likewise call to mind their constant conjunction in all past instances. Without any further ceremony, we call the one cause, and the other effect, and infer the existence of the one from that of the other.

What Hume calls "constant conjunction" is key to his conception of experience. We remember one kind of object as being always joined with another kind of object in the past. This constant conjoining includes the succession and contiguity which Hume already identified in Section 2. When we remember an object of one kind as always succeeding and contiguous to an object of another kind, we draw an inference from the appearance of a new individual of the first kind to the existence of an individual of the second kind. His example here is flame and heat: I remember flames like the one which is now present to my senses as being constantly conjoined with heat, and so infer the existence of heat in this new instance.

Hume stresses that we would never draw the inference if we had not observed constant conjunction of resembling objects in the past. He makes this point vividly in his *Abstract* when he asks us to consider a newly created adult human suddenly arriving at a game of billiards:

> Were a man, such as *Adam*, created in the full vigour of understanding, without experience, he would never be able to infer motion in the second ball from the motion and impulse of the first ... It would have been necessary, therefore, for *Adam* (if he was not inspired) to have had *experience* of the effect, which followed upon the impulse of these two balls. He must have seen, in several instances, that when the one ball struck upon the other, the second always acquired motion ... [Then] his understanding would anticipate his sight, and form a conclusion suitable to his past experience. (A11–12)

Of course, people being brought up in this world, as all of us are, and having seen balls and other objects strike each other, might well be able to make the inference without specific experience of billiard balls. Hume's point is that our minds anticipate our senses in making the inference only when we have observed similar objects conjoined in the past.

The importance of experience in leading us to draw an inference to unobserved objects was well recognized in Hume's day. In his *Essay Concerning Human Understanding*, Locke identified "constant and never-failing Experience in like cases" as the source of our belief in cause and effect, and of our reasoning to what he called "*particular matter of fact*" (ECHU 4.16.6). Hume's problem was *why* we draw this inference, a problem to which he may have been alerted by his reading of the Introduction to Joseph Butler's *Analogy of Religion*.[37]

---

[37] Butler writes that his own purpose in his book is not to inquire "whence it proceeds that *likeness* should beget that presumption, opinion and full conviction, which the human

Why should constant experience of objects related by contiguity and succession make us draw an inference in a new case? Each instance is completely separate from every other one, and does not affect it. Hume emphasizes that we don't *discover* any new connection in the objects when we reflect on those similar instances in the past, or even when we reflect on their repetition: "From the mere repetition of any past impression, even to infinity, there never will arise any new original idea, such as that of a necessary connexion; and the number of impressions has in this case no more effect than if we confin'd ourselves to one only" (T1.3.6.3: 88). Hume's problem can be seen as one of *relevance*: why is it relevant to the case now under investigation that all objects similar to the present impression always appeared in the past along with the same type of object? For in none of the subsequent cases did we find any relation which was not present in the first case.

As we have seen, the power of the mind by which we make discoveries about the world beyond what we immediately sense is *reason*. What has been called Hume's problem of induction is based on his claim that reason is not the source of our inference from the observed to the unobserved. He argues that if it was reason that made us draw the inference, "it would proceed upon that principle, *that instances, of which we have had no experience, must resemble those, of which we have had experience*" (T1.3.6.4.: 89). In other words, if the inference were based on reason it would be based on the discovery that "*the course of nature ... continues uniformly the same.*" This principle has come to be called the *principle of the uniformity of nature*.[38] One of its corollaries is the principle "*that the future will resemble the past*" (T1.3.12.9: 134). Hume proceeds to argue that the truth of the principle and its corollary are not discovered by reason.

mind is formed to receive from it" but that this problem constitutes a part of the subject of logic which "has not yet been thoroughly investigated" (Joseph Butler, *Analogy of Religion*, in *The Works of Joseph Butler*, ed. W. E. Gladstone, 3 vols. (Oxford: Clarendon Press, 1896), Vol. I, p. 7; cf. p. v of the second edition of 1736). Butler's *Analogy* was published three years before the first two books of Hume's *Treatise*. On the likelihood that Hume read Butler's *Analogy*, see Chapter 1 §7, esp., pp. 28–9.

[38] In fact, Hume uses the expression "uniformity of nature" only once, in his first *Enquiry* (EHU 9.5n).

ii) The inference from the observed to the
unobserved is not based on reason

In the first place, he argues that the principle of the uniformity of nature is not an object of knowledge; that is, it is not discovered merely by intuition or demonstration. Once again we find Hume appealing to his familiar form of argument. If the principle were demonstrable then it would be impossible to conceive or imagine its not holding. However, "we can at least conceive of a change in the course of nature; which sufficiently proves, that such a change is not absolutely impossible" (T1.3.6.5). Hence the principle is not known through demonstration. The same argument proves that it cannot be known by intuition.

What is it to "conceive of a change in the course of nature"? At the very least, Hume is telling us that we can conceive or imagine that past regularities might fail to hold in new instances – that flames not be followed by heat, bodies impacting on other bodies not be followed by the motion of those other bodies, and so on. On a minimalist reading of his suggestion, he is arguing that we can conceive that these regularities might be replaced by new ones. However, he might be making an even more radical claim: for we can conceive a world without any regularity at all, a world very much like that of our dreams. Not only would it be the case that all previously identified laws of nature would cease to hold, but there would be no regularity on the basis of which we could postulate any new laws of nature at all.

In the second place, Hume argues that we cannot discover the truth of the principle of uniformity of nature by reasoning from past experience – that is, through probable reasoning. What we discovered through past experience is that one kind of object was always followed by another kind of object. But, all inferences from this past experience to any claim about what is not yet experienced *presuppose* that instances of which we have not yet had experience will resemble those of which we have had experience. In other words, such inferences *presuppose* the principle of uniformity of nature. Hence the principle itself cannot be proved by past experience. To put the same point in another way, all we can discover through past experience is that the principle of uniformity of nature has held in the past – that past futures have resembled their pasts. As Hume puts the point in his first *Enquiry*, to attempt to prove the principle that "the future will be conformable to the past ... by probable arguments ... must be evidently going in a circle, and taking that for granted, which is the very point in question" (EHU 4.19). In the *Treatise* he puts the same point more obscurely when he writes that "the same principle cannot be both the cause and effect of another" (T1.3.6.7: 90).

Hume considers and dismisses another argument for the claim that we discover the basis for our inference when we consider past experience. The argument is put in terms of 'power' and 'production' – terms which, as we have seen, Hume considers to be roughly synonymous with 'cause.' The argument is that the past experience of regularity shows us that unless an object were "endow'd with a power of production," it would not be found always to be conjoined with another object (T1.3.6.8: 90). In other words, it is only because there is power of production that we find regularity in the past. From this knowledge we have gained of production in past instances we can infer that the same kind of object will produce the same kind of effect in a new case. To take Hume's example from his first *Enquiry*, from the fact that bread has always nourished us in the past, we can infer it must have a power to produce nourishment. Then we can infer that we will be nourished by the next piece of bread that we encounter (cf. EHU 4.16.).

Hume's response to this argument is revealing: he replies that objects which *appear* to be exactly similar to us could have completely different causal powers. Even if it were true that in the past certain sensible qualities were always followed by certain effects, that would not establish that "a like power is always conjoin'd with like sensible qualities" (T1.3.6.10: 91). Note Hume's use of term "sensible qualities." He implies that the same "sensible qualities" may be accompanied by different powers of production in future cases. The sensible qualities of bread do not reveal the underlying causal powers of bread, and therefore there is no guarantee that the next bread-like object we encounter will nourish us.[39]

---

[39] Compare Peter Kail's analysis of what he calls "the switching argument" in §4.3.5 of *Projection and Realism in Hume's Philosophy*; see the confirmation of this reading of Hume's argument from the passages from the first *Enquiry* which Kail cites on pp. 97–8.

It may be thought that Hume is claiming that it is *in principle* impossible to discover sensible qualities which would reveal the secret powers. But, it seems to me, this is a mistake. That would make his claim an *a priori* truth. But his claim is derived *from experience*: we never discover the power of the cause by observing the sensible qualities of objects. If we ever did, we would apprehend the necessary connection between cause and effect. With respect to other relations, sensible qualities *do* reveal necessity. This is the case in mathematics. After all, we never doubt that the sum of the angles of the next Euclidean triangle that we encounter will be equal to two right angles. Hume presupposes that if we had genuine knowledge of production or power in the way that we have genuine knowledge of relations in mathematics, then we would be able to draw an inference to unobserved instances without experience.

iii) Custom and association are the cause of the inference: Hume's critique of Locke

What then is the role of repetition of like instances in the past in making us draw the inference from the observed to the unobserved? Hume argues that the repetition brings about an association of ideas. He writes: "When ev'ry individual of any species of objects is found by experience to be constantly united with an individual of another species, the appearance of any new individual of either species naturally conveys the thought to its usual attendant" (T1.3.6.14: 93). The role of constant conjunction and experience in making us infer an effect from a cause (as well as a cause from an effect) is now made clear. Hume now calls the principle which causes the inference "a true principle of association of ideas," and to be "the very same" as the associative principle which he originally labeled cause and effect (T1.3.6.15: 93).

In Section 8, Hume identifies the principle of human nature which causes us to associate the two ideas and infer one from the other as *custom* or habit. He does not define this principle in the *Treatise*, except to say that "we call every thing CUSTOM, which proceeds from a past repetition, without any new reasoning" (T1.3.8.10: 102). In his first *Enquiry* he states that by using that word he is not identifying the ultimate cause of the propensity to draw an inference from one object to another (EHU 5.5). Nevertheless, he identifies it as "an instinct or mechanical tendency" (EHU 5.22). As we shall see in §5 (pp. 109–12), in the *Treatise* itself he drew on standard contemporary accounts of the mechanisms of the imagination to explain how we come to draw the inference.

The radical nature of Hume's claim that custom and the association of ideas are the source of the inference from the observed to the unobserved becomes clear when his views are compared with those of Locke. As we have seen, Locke had already identified "constant Experience" as the source of our belief in cause and effect, and of what he called "particular matter of fact" (ECHU 4.16.6). He identified causal reasoning as the source of the "*highest degree of Probability*."[40] He even recognized that "Probability on such grounds carries so much evidence with it, that it naturally *determines* the Judgment, and leaves us as little liberty to believe, or disbelieve, as a Demonstration does" (ECHU 4.16.9; my emphasis). But Locke never inquired into the *cause* of this determined judgment.

As we also saw in Chapter 2, Locke considered association of ideas to be a kind of *pathological* thinking.[41] He contrasted ideas which "have a natural Correspondence and Connexion one with another ... [and which] it is the Office ... of our Reason to trace ... and hold ... together" with those which are connected through "Chance or Custom" (ECHU 2.33.5). What Locke called a "natural" connection is a reasoned connection discovered through probability or demonstration.[42] On the other hand, the artificial associational connections with which he *contrasts* these probable and demonstrative connections are the source of prejudice and a kind of irrationality to which all human beings are prone. Locke points to early childhood education (i.e. indoctrination) as the major source of these associational connections, and argues that they "prevent men from seeing and examining" – that is, discovering the reasoned connections between ideas (2.33.18).

---

[40] ECHU 4.16.6.   [41] §3, pp. 48–9.
[42] See ECHU 4.17. Locke's "natural ... Connexion" is what Hume calls a "philosophical relation." *Hume's* "natural relations" are the associational connections which Locke sees as the source of prejudice and misguided thinking.

What is striking is that Locke never saw any relation between his discussions of probable reasoning and of the association of ideas.[43] Hume clearly did. Echoing Locke, he wrote that "all those opinions and notions of things, to which we have been accustom'd from our infancy, take such deep root, that 'tis impossible for us, by all the powers of reason and experience, to eradicate them" (T1.3.9.17: 116). But Hume recognized that the same principle of human nature which is the basis of childhood indoctrination is also the source of our probable beliefs. He wrote that indoctrination is "built almost on the same foundation of custom and repetition as our reasonings from cause and effect" (T1.3.9.19: 117).[44] The difference is what we would now call the *input*: in the case of our reasonings from cause and effect the input is *nature herself*, not artificial connections established by human beings. The input of nature is the regular succession of resembling objects in our experience. Hume's remarkable discovery is that *nature herself teaches us through the same principle of association which is also the source of our prejudice and pathological thinking.*

Hume notes that since the connections which arise from indoctrination are "frequently contrary to reason, and even to themselves in different times and places," they are considered unwarranted by philosophers (T1.3.9.19: 117; cf. T1.4.4.1: 225). Unlike the beliefs which arise from nature herself, they "may easily be subverted by a due contrast and opposition" (T1.4.4.1: 225). In spite of the fact that custom is the source of both sorts of connections of ideas, only those which arise from our observation of natural regularity are the source of a consistent set of beliefs which stand up under reflection. This idea is developed by Louis Loeb in his book *Stability and Justification in Hume's Treatise*. Loeb argues that induction is justified for Hume because it results in stable beliefs which stand up under reflection, unlike the beliefs arising from indoctrination.[45]

---

[43] Part of the reason may be that Locke's discussion of the association of ideas only appeared in the 4th edition of the *Essay*. Locke also never suggested that association is the source of complex ideas or of abstraction as Hume did (p. 48 above).

[44] Of course, as a matter of historical development it was clearly the other way round: Hume was arguing that our reasonings from cause and effect were built on almost the same foundation as indoctrination.

[45] Louis Loeb, *Stability and Justification in Hume's Treatise* (Oxford: Clarendon Press, 2002), esp. pp. 81, 159, 238.

Hume goes on to argue that we don't need memory and reflection on past experience to draw the inference from cause to effect in the case of "the most establish'd and uniform conjunctions of causes and effects, such as those of gravity, [motion by] impulse, solidity, & c." (T1.3.8.13–14: 104). Our past experience operates unconsciously – "in such an insensible manner as never to be taken notice of, and may even in some measure be unknown to us." This, according to Hume, is at least part of the reason we don't realize that custom and habit is the principle operating in forming our inferences in these common cases.[46]

It is worth noting that in the case of these established and uniform conjunctions of cause and effect such as motion by impulse, Locke thought that we have some *insight* into the connection of cause and effect. We don't entirely rely on experience. He wrote "that the size, figure, and motion of one Body should cause a change in the size, figure, and motion of another Body, is not beyond our Conception ... and the change from rest to motion, upon impulse; these, and the like, seem to us to have some *connexion* one with another" (ECHU 4.3.13).[47] For Hume, on the other hand, the mistaken belief that one has insight into the connection of physical causes arises entirely from the association of ideas. One becomes so accustomed to such familiar cases that one mistakes the customary association with a genuine knowledge of a real connection.[48] *Moreover*, he argues that there is an even stronger association of ideas in the case of motion by impulse (e.g. our billiard balls) than in other familiar cases like flame and heat. This is because of the resemblance of the cause and the effect to each other: motion causes other motion. Hume writes that "the reason, why we imagine the communication of motion to be more consistent and natural ... than any other natural effect, is founded on the relation of *resemblance* betwixt the cause and effect" which is combined with the effects of experience "and binds the objects in the closest and most intimate manner to each other, so as to make us imagine them to be absolutely inseparable" (T1.3.9.10:

---

[46] Compare what Hume says regarding the effects of custom and habit in his moral philosophy, Chapter 9 §4, pp. 272–3.
[47] Locke also wrote that motion by impulse "is the only way which we can conceive Bodies to operate in" (ECHU 2.8.10). Compare what he says at ECHU 4.10.19.
[48] Compare pp. 124–6 below.

111–12). We shall reconsider the significance of this remarkable claim in §8 ii).

iv) *Reasoning about causes*

In other cases, after custom habituates us to believe in the uniformity of nature, we don't even need to have repetition of particular objects in order to draw inferences from the observed to the unobserved. Hume writes that we "may attain the knowledge of a particular cause merely by one experiment, provided it be made with judgment, and after a careful removal of all foreign and superfluous circumstances" (T1.3.8.14: 104).[49] This is the kind of reasoning which we do in science when we find the "contrary causes" which are the source of irregularity in our observations.[50] Hume argues that such reasoning still arises from custom and habit, "but in an *oblique* and *artificial* manner" (cf. T1.3.12.7: 133). In science we form a general rule that when we have found the causes or effects by a "clear experiment" we ought to "immediately extend our observation to every phenomenon of the same kind" (T1.4.15.6: 173).[51] Hume stresses that while scientific reasoning goes beyond everyday reasoning in the way he has described, it is still founded on a general habit rooted in experience, which makes us suppose "*that the future resembles the past*" (T1.3.12.9: 134).

At the end of Section 6 of Part 3, Hume remarks that "tho' causation be a *philosophical* relation, as implying contiguity, succession, and constant conjunction, yet 'tis only so far as it is a *natural* relation, and produces an union among our ideas, that we are able to reason upon it, or draw any inference from it" (T1.3.6.16: 94). When we *reason* philosophically (i.e. scientifically) we *compare* the objects according to the relations of contiguity, succession, and (wherever possible) constant conjunction. But this comparison is not sufficient to make us draw any inference from the one object to another. We only draw an inference from such a comparison because of a further operation of the mind, namely an association which forms "a

---

[49] He is, of course, not using the term 'know' here in the strong and official sense he introduced at the beginning of Part 3.

[50] See §3, pp. 94–5 above and Chapter 5, pp. 180–1.

[51] This is the sixth of Hume's "Rules by which to judge causes and effects" and the one which "is the source of most of our philosophical reasonings."

natural relation." Our comparisons of ideas through reason do not by themselves make us draw an inference from the observed to the unobserved. Reason alone is never the source of our inferences. What we require for the inference is an association of the ideas formed by custom and habit.[52]

As I pointed out earlier,[53] Hume uses the term reason and its cognates in two very different senses. When he denies that our inferences from the observed to the unobserved are based on reason or reasoning, he is using the term for the comparison of ideas which results in the discovery of philosophical relations. All that we can discover through comparison of ideas is succession, contiguity, and constant conjunction. In this sense, "reason can never satisfy us that the existence of any one object does ever imply that of another" (T1.3.7.6: 97). But on the same page, in a note, Hume writes that we reason or "infer a cause immediately from its effect; and this inference is not only *a true species of reasoning*, but the strongest of all others" (T1.3.7.5n: 97; my emphasis). Of course, this "true species of reasoning" is infected by custom and association of ideas. While some have held that this ambiguity in Hume's conception of the term reason and its cognates is dropped at the end of Book 1 or even after Part 3 of Book 1,[54] I believe it is to be found throughout the *Treatise*. When Hume denies in Book 2 that reason alone can ever motivate action he is using the term in the more limited sense which involves a mere comparison of ideas – that is, reason uninfected by our senses or the imagination.

5. BELIEF

When we draw an inference from what is observed to what is unobserved, we don't merely form an idea of what is unobserved: we *believe*

---

[52] For an important recent discussion of Hume's distinction between causality as a philosophical relation and as a natural relation see Beebee, *Causation in Hume*, pp. 99–106, esp. p. 105.

[53] §1, p. 89.

[54] If I understand her correctly, this is something like the view which Annette Baier put forward in her *A Progress of Sentiments: Reflections on Hume's Treatise* (Cambridge, Mass.: Harvard University Press, 1991). She argued that Hume's skepticism was directed at overinflated claims concerning "pure intellect," and that he progressively replaced a purely intellectualist conception of reason with "animal reason."

that it exists. Reflecting on this fact leads Hume to a discussion of the nature, causes and effects of belief.

i) The nature of belief

Before presenting his own theory of the nature of belief Hume considers and rejects an alternative theory. According to this theory when we believe that something exists, we add a distinct idea of existence to the idea of the thing itself. Thus, for example, the belief in the existence of God consists in an idea of God which the unbeliever can share, plus the general idea of existence. Or the belief that Julius Caesar died in the Senate House in Rome on the Ides of March 45 BC consists of a complex idea plus the distinct idea that this event really took place, or existed.

What is right about this theory is that we all form the same ideas in these cases whether we believe the object to be real or not. *What is wrong, according to Hume, is the claim that existence is a distinct idea, which the believer adds to the idea of whatever is proposed.* Hume argues that if this view were correct then we could just believe in whatever we pleased. For we can voluntarily put distinct ideas together in any way we choose. For example, we can put together the ideas of a horse or a man together with the distinct idea of wings to form the idea of a winged horse or an angel. But, according to Hume, *belief is not a voluntary act.* There are fixed principles of the mind determining our beliefs. So belief in real existence cannot be a distinct or separate idea which we can simply add to any other idea we have in our minds.[55]

Hume also rejects the suggestion that belief consists in any special order of ideas, or in thinking about only one side of a question. You and I may dispute about whether Caesar really died in the Senate House or not – and still form exactly the same complex idea of the proposition in the same order in our minds. We still need to answer the question as to what constitutes my belief that it really happened and your disbelief in the same proposition.

According to Hume's theory, belief in real existence consists in "the *manner* of our conceiving" the ideas (T1.3.7.4: 96). He describes

[55] T1.3.7.4: 95–6; TApp 2: 623–4 [Norton & Norton, p. 396]; A19: 653. The same point is made, though somewhat more obscurely in the Section "*Of the idea of existence, and of external existence*" at T1.2.6: 66–8.

this manner of conception as a superior "force and vivacity" to that of the idea of an object or proposition which we merely entertain (T1.3.7.5: 96). He is, of course, using the same terms as he used in the first section of the *Treatise* to distinguish impressions from ideas. Belief in an unobserved object is a "*peculiar feeling, different from the simple conception*" which makes the ideas "approach nearer to the impressions, which are immediately present to us" (TApp 3: 624–5). He ends up with an array of different terms to describe how belief goes beyond the mere entertaining of an idea of something: it involves "a superior *force*, or *vivacity*, or *solidity*, or *firmness*, or *steadiness*" (T1.3.7.7App: 629). These last three terms are particularly favored in his Appendix.[56] In the *Abstract* he states it is "impossible by words to describe this feeling, which every one must be conscious of in his own breast" (A22: 654). In the final analysis, he is clearly more interested in the causes and effects of belief than in describing the phenomenon of belief itself (TApp 6–9: 626–7). Indeed the original definition he offers "Of the nature of the idea or belief" in Section 7 of Part 3 anticipates the account of its causes which he gives in the following section: "belief, may be most accurately defined, [as] A LIVELY IDEA RELATED TO OR ASSOCIATED WITH A PRESENT IMPRESSION" (T1.3.7.5: 96).

ii) The causes of belief: mental mechanisms

In giving "*the causes of belief*" in Section 8 Hume explains the mechanism by which an idea becomes lively and vivacious and more firmly fixed in our minds. He writes that he seeks to establish "a general maxim in the science of human nature, *that when any impression becomes present to us, it not only transports the mind to such ideas as are related to it, but likewise communicates to them a share of its force and vivacity*" (T1.3.8.2: 98–9). There are two factors which are key to this account of the causes of the belief in real existence – first, the impression of an object which is either sensed or remembered, and second, its association with a related idea. The impression supplies

---

[56] Annette Baier argues that Hume changes his view of belief in the Appendix, allowing "different dimensions of mental 'feel' to a conception" (*Death and Character*, p. 197). In contrast, my own view is that he further stresses the *causes* and *effects* of belief in the Appendix, rather than its phenomenal "nature."

the psychic energy or elevation of the animal spirits, which is then transferred to the related idea via the associational pathway. Hume writes that "according as the spirits are more or less elevated, and the attention more or less fix'd, the action will always have more or less vigour and vivacity." The object presented to the senses or memory "elevates and enlivens" the animal spirits or nervous fluids, and there is a "natural transition of the disposition" from the "present impression" to the related idea. This transition *fixes* the attention and results in "a more lively idea of the related objects."

Hume employs the standard eighteenth-century model of the imagination here. We saw in Chapter 2 that Locke writes in the *Essay* of how custom causes the animal spirits to form a "smooth path" in the brain so that their motion "becomes easy and as it were Natural" (ECHU 1.33.6). In the *Treatise*, Hume describes his "present hypothesis" as the claim that "from custom" there is formed "an easy transition to the idea of that object, which usually attends" the present impression (T1.3.9.16: 115–16). By constant repetition the pathway linking their corresponding brain traces gets deeper, facilitating the motion of the animal spirits and making us conceive the "idea in a stronger and more lively manner." As the pathway grows deeper the belief grows stronger.

While the transfer of force and vivacity occurs to some extent by way of any of the three principles of association – resemblance, contiguity, and causality – the effect of the first two is much weaker than that of the third, and they alone are not able to raise the vivacity of the associated ideas to the level of belief in the existence of their objects (T1.3.9.6: 109). Hume gives examples of how one's feelings for family and friends grow stronger when we return from a trip and are a few miles away from home (*contiguity*), and how a picture revives our feelings for an absent friend through *resemblance* (T1.3.8.5: 100; T1.3.8.3: 99). But in neither of these cases, he argues, do these associations operate independently of causation in creating a belief in real existence.

The reason for the superior strength of the relation of causation is that when we have invariably experienced one type of object followed by another on a number of occasions, the impression of the first "draws along with it a precise idea, which takes its place in the imagination, as something solid and real, certain and invariable" (T1.3.9.7:

110). Hume states that as a result of such an experience "the thought is always *determin'd* to pass from the impression to the idea, and from that particular impression to that particular idea, without any choice or hesitation" (my emphasis). In the case of resemblance and contiguity, on the other hand the associations are more diffuse and the mind does not fix itself for any time on a particular related object.

The use of the word "determin'd" in connection with Hume's account of causal inference and belief in the existence of the unobserved object is significant. When Hume originally raised the question of the nature of belief he drew a contrast between the kind of belief we form in propositions which are demonstrated and the belief we form in the conclusions of arguments from causation. In the former case, we are "*necessarily determin'd* to conceive [the ideas] in [a] particular manner … Nor is it possible for the imagination to conceive any thing contrary to a demonstration" (T1.3.7.3: 95; my emphasis). In apparent contrast, "in reasonings from causation, and concerning matters of fact, this absolute necessity cannot take place, and the imagination is free to conceive both sides of the question." Nevertheless, as we have now seen, there is still *determination and necessity* in the latter case, though it is not the sort which makes the denial of the proposition inconceivable and absurd. The observation of a constant conjunction of causes and effects produces "such a habit of surveying them in that relation, that we cannot without a sensible violence survey them in any other" (T1.3.11.3: 125). Indeed, as we have seen, in cases like the transference of motion by impact he goes so far as to say that the association binds the ideas so closely together that we "imagine them to be absolutely inseparable" (T1.3.9.10: 112). As we shall see, Hume thinks that we systematically mistake the one kind of necessity for the other, and this is key to one explanation he gives of why we naturally suppose that there is genuine necessity in nature.[57]

Hume considers this "determination" of the mind to transfer the force or vivacity of the impression to the related idea to develop gradually, at least in young children before they have gained much experience. He writes that the association arrives "at its full perfection by degrees, and must acquire new force from each instance, that falls under our observation … 'tis by these slow steps, that our judgment arrives at a full assurance" (T1.3.12.2: 130). Below this full assurance

---

[57] §8 ii), pp. 124–6.

there are lesser degrees of probability, including what Locke called " ... Conjecture, Guess, Doubt, Wavering ... " (ECHU 4.16.9). Our belief in the reality of the related unobserved object increases by degrees as the associational link is made stronger by custom or habit. As we shall see, Hume draws a parallel between his account of degrees of belief in reality and his later account of sympathy, where our empathy with another person varies with the strength of our natural relation to that person.[58]

The strengthening of the customary connection between cause and effect results in what Hume calls "a new system ... of *realities*" which extends beyond those which we have directly sensed (T1.3.9.3: 107–8). The system of unobserved objects which we judge to be real is formed "by custom, or, if you will, by the relation of cause or effect." He writes that this system of *judgment* "peoples the world," and acquaints us "with such existences, as by their removal in time and place, lie beyond the reach of the senses and memory" (T1.3.9.4: 108).

iii) The effects of belief

Hume begins his discussion of the effects of belief by reminding us that the perception of pain and pleasure is "the chief spring and moving principle" of all our actions (T1.3.10.2: 118). Pain and pleasure cause actions through sense impressions, as when we get too close to a hot stove, or experience the delectable smells of baked goods being taken out of the oven. But, they also cause actions when we have enlivened ideas of them through the imagination. My vivid anticipation of the pain that I will feel if I fail my philosophy exam tomorrow leads me to study today. My vivid idea of the pleasure I will experience from a good dinner at my favorite restaurant tonight leads me to make reservations this morning. These imagined pains and pleasures are lively and vivacious ideas of a kind which have been associated with past impressions of their causes. Hume stresses that ideas of this kind affect my passions and actions just as much as the impressions of pleasure and pain of my senses.

He reflects on the purpose of nature in making enlivened ideas affect us, as well as impressions. If impressions alone affected the will, "we should every moment of our lives be subject to the greatest

[58] Chapter 6 §8, pp. 206–7ff.

calamities" (T1.3.10.2: 119). We would not protect ourselves from these calamities "tho' we foresaw their approach."[59] On the other hand, we "would never enjoy a moment's peace and tranquility" if every imagined idea were to affect us as much as every other. It is only those lively and vivacious ideas which are the foundation of our beliefs in reality which affect us and cause us to take actions to avoid pain and seek out pleasure. According to Hume, "the effect … of belief is to raise up a simple idea to an equality with our impressions, and bestow on it a like influence on the passions" (T1.3.10.3: 119). It is in this way that we learn in "what manner our reasonings from causation are able to operate on the will and passions" (T1.3.10.3: 120).

This latter claim raises an important question concerning the consistency of his conception of reasoning.[60] For as I indicated earlier, he goes on to argue in Book 2 that "reason alone can never be a motive to any action of the will" (T2.3.3.1: 413). But if, as he argues here in Book 1, our "reasonings from causation" cause belief, and belief affects our passions and actions, then it would follow that causal reasonings affect our passions and move us to act. It seems that causal reasoning both is, and is not, the motive of action.

The only escape from this paradox, it seems to me, is to recognize that Hume uses the term 'reasoning' and its cognates in both a narrower and a wider sense. The narrower sense is the sense in which reasoning merely involves a comparison of ideas. In this sense, it operates independently of impressions and the association of ideas. In this narrower sense of the term, *reason* cannot cause belief, any more than it can cause a passion or action. It operates in this narrow sense when it discovers that objects are successive, contiguous and constantly conjoined – that is, when it compares and simply determines the relations between objects. This is the sense of the word which he employs in Section 6 of Part 3 of Book 1 when he denies that our inferences from the observed to the unobserved are caused by reason. On the other hand, when Hume argues that "reasonings

---

[59] Hume's account implies that the belief-forming mechanisms which he describes play a fundamental role in human adaptation and survival, though this point is made far more explicit in the corresponding discussion in the first *Enquiry* (EHU 5.22) than it is in the *Treatise*.

[60] See also Kail, *Projection and Realism in Hume's Philosophy*, Chapter 8.3, and Rachel Cohon and David Owen, "Representation, Reason and Motivation," *Manuscrito* 20 (1997), pp. 47–76.

from causation ... operate on the will and passions" in Section 10 he
is writing about reason in the wider sense – where we are affected by
an impression of either the senses or memory, and the association
which transfers its force and vivacity to the related idea.

6. THE SUBJECTIVE ORIGIN OF THE IDEA OF NECESSARY CONNECTION

In Section 14, "*Of the idea of necessary connexion,*" Hume finally
returns to the question of the origin of the idea of causation which he
left off in Section 2 of Part 3 (see §2 above). There he had stated that
when we attribute causation to objects we ascribe a necessary connection to them. We think that the cause must make the effect occur;
it must necessitate or produce it. However, he pointed out that when
we examine the sense impressions of the objects we call cause and
effect, we discover that the only relations we observe in the object
are contiguity and succession. There is no information discovered
through our senses which corresponds to the 'mustness' or necessity
which, we all naturally believe, makes the second billiard ball move
when struck by the first. What then is the source of the idea of necessity which we ascribe to the object we call the cause?

In Section 6 of Part 3 Hume showed how after experience, or
repeated observations of one kind of object succeeded by another
kind of object we draw an *inference* from an observation of an instance
of the first kind to the (as yet unobserved) existence of an object of
the second kind. He stressed that the repeated observations do not
reveal anything new about the connection between the two objects:
"what we learn not from one object, we can never learn from a hundred, which are all of the same kind, and are perfectly resembling
in every circumstance" (T1.3.6.3: 88). Hume attributes the inference
to custom rather than reason. In discussing the inference in the following sections of Part 3 he argued that the effect of custom was to
"determine" the mind to pass from an unobserved object to an object
like those which are constantly conjoined with it, and to conceive it
with greater vivacity.

It is this discovery which, he now tells his reader, has given him
the clue to the origin of the idea of the necessary connection. After
observing the resembling instances "the mind is *determin'd* by custom

to consider its usual attendant" and it is "this impression, then, or *determination* which affords me the idea of necessity" (T1.3.14.1: 156). Custom produces a new pathway in the brain linking the brain traces of the perceptions, and this change in the brain is the natural connection from which the impression of necessity arises.[61] Repetition not only causes the mind to associate the perceptions of cause and effect and infer the one from the other, but also produces a change in the structure of the mind from which the idea of the necessary connection of objects is derived.

i) The impression of necessity

In the *Treatise*, Hume stresses that this impression is nothing but "an internal impression, or impression of reflection" (T1.3.14.22: 165). It arises from the "propensity, which custom produces to pass from an object to its usual attendant." Since, as we have discovered, we never perceive any necessity in objects, we must "draw the idea of it from what we feel internally in contemplating them" (T1.3.14.28: 169). "Power and necessity ... are qualities of perceptions, not of objects, and are internally felt by the soul, and not perceiv'd externally in bodies" (T1.3.14.24: 166).

Hume sometimes writes as though it is necessity itself which is found in the mind of the observer. He writes that the new "propensity, which custom produces, to pass from an object to the idea of its usual attendant ... is the essence of necessity" and that "upon the whole, necessity is something, that exists in the mind, not in objects" (T1.3.14.22: 165; cf. T1.3.14. 23: 166). He argues that when we change our "point of view, from the objects to the perceptions" and consider the impression of the observed cause as itself a cause, and the idea of the (as yet) unobserved effect as its effect, then their "necessary connexion is that new determination, which we feel to pass from the idea of the one to that of the other" (T1.3.14.29: 169). After experience, the impression of the first billiard ball striking the second *determines* the mind to form the idea of the second one moving, and it is this *determination* of the mind itself which is the source of the idea of necessity. Our idea of necessity is not derived from any

---

[61] §5 ii), p. 110 above.

necessity in the billiard balls themselves which, if it exists, is unobserved by us. We apprehend necessity, not in the objects perceived, but in the mind of the perceiver.

Consider the following two propositions:

1. Object A *determines*[1] (or causes) object B.
2. The impression of object A *determines*[2] (or causes) the idea of object B.

Hume's claim is that it is *determines*[2], not *determines*[1], which is the source of our idea of necessary connection. In fact, Hume insists, we have no idea of *determines*[1] since we never observe it. *Determines*[2] is founded on the associational pathway formed by experience – that is, the repeated observation of objects of type A followed by objects of type B. It is the "new determination" of the mind which is formed through experience.

Hume argues further that our idea of necessity can *represent* nothing more than this determination or necessity of the mind itself, for an idea can only legitimately represent the impression from which it is derived. He writes that "the ideas of necessity, of power, and of efficacy … represent not any thing, that does or can belong to the objects, which are constantly conjoin'd" (T1.3.14.19: 164). Nor can we legitimately *mean* anything more than the subjective determination of the mind when we use the terms power or necessity.

Hume considers the response of a critic of his view who insists that the necessity must really be in the objects we call cause and effect, not in the mind:

What! the efficacy of causes lie in the determination of the mind! As if causes did not operate entirely independent of the mind, and wou'd not continue their operation, even tho' there was no mind existent to contemplate them, or reason concerning them. Thought may well depend on causes for its operation, but not causes on thought. This is to reverse the order of nature … (T1.3.14.26: 167)

Hume replies that the critic doesn't understand her own "meaning" when she ascribes necessary connection or efficacy to objects independent of the mind of the observer (T1.3.14.27: 168). She is like a blind person who insists that the color scarlet must be like the sound of a trumpet. Like the blind person, the critic has no idea of what she is talking about. Indeed, when the critic applies the actual idea of necessary connection she has to the external objects, then she is applying something "incompatible" with them. Hume does allow that "there may be qualities ... with which we are utterly unacquainted" and even writes of "*meaning* these unknown qualities" (my emphasis). But to transfer the subjective idea we have of necessity "to external objects, and suppose any real intelligible connexion betwixt them" is the source of a "false philosophy." Hume writes that this "real intelligible connection" can only belong to the mind of the perceiver, not to external objects. (But see §7 below!)

Thus, when we attribute causality to objects we either "contradict ourselves or talk without meaning" (T1.4.7.5: 267). We talk without meaning when we ascribe a power to the objects of which we have no idea. We contradict ourselves when we ascribe what does have meaning – namely our internal impression of determination – to external objects, where it cannot exist.

How then does Hume answer his imagined critic's claim that "the operations of nature are independent of our thought and reasoning" (T1.3.14.28: 168)? He says that he is willing to acknowledge that they are independent in so far as "objects bear toward each other the relations of contiguity and succession," *and* that before the mind operates, "like objects may be observ'd in several instances to have like relations." He allows the objective relations of succession and contiguity, and that we regularly observe pairs of objects related in these ways.

But it is clear that Hume deflects the critic's objection here. *Her* concern was that what is independent of the mind is causation itself – one event making another occur. It is not sufficient to tell her that we observe regularity in nature – though, as I mentioned in the introduction to this chapter, many have taken regular succession and contiguity to be Hume's definitive answer as to what causation in the objects really is. However, his critic knows exactly what she is looking for, and Hume does too. Otherwise he would not be so sure that we have no objective idea of it.[62] She is looking for the intelligible

---

[62] Compare Kail, *Projection and Realism in Hume's Philosophy*, p. 35: "He knows full well what it would be to be acquainted with power and exploits that knowledge to argue that we cannot be so acquainted."

connection between cause and effect which would make it impossible to think the first without the second. I will return to this point.

ii) *Hume's two definitions of cause: defining causation in terms of regularity of objects or the determination of the mind*

Hume proceeds to tell his reader that he is now in a position to give "a precise definition of cause and effect" (T1.3.14.30: 169). The interpretation of Hume as holding that there is no more to causation in nature but regular succession and contiguity receives its strongest support on the basis of the two definitions of causation which he goes on to give. He first defines cause as "an object precedent and contiguous to another ... where all the objects resembling the former are plac'd in like relations of precedency and contiguity to those objects, that resemble the latter" (T1.3.14.31: 170). Causation, to put the matter more simply, is defined as universal regularity. *A* is the cause of *B*, just in case *A-like* objects are always succeeded by *B-like* objects. Hume says that in defining a cause in this manner he is defining it as a "philosophical relation" – that is, in terms of features we can discover through the comparison of the objects. Or at least this is true in so far as the "objects" to which he is referring in the definition are those which have existed in the past.

What is striking about this first definition is that it defines a cause without any reference to that feature which Hume considers to be essential to it – namely necessary connection. The notion of necessity appears neither in the *explanans* nor in the *explanandum*. It is small wonder that many readers have gone on to claim that he reduces causation to regularity.

But Hume goes on to remark that some may find this definition defective because it is "drawn from objects foreign to the cause" (T1.3.14.31: 170). It is important to understand the relevance of this objection. He has defined a cause, not in terms of its relation to its effect, but only in terms of its relation to other resembling sequences of objects. He defines 'A causes B' as 'All A-like things are constantly conjoined with B-like things.' But if the critic is right this means that we can only define causation indirectly – through the observations which are the source of our belief in it. This critic's concern is reinforced by Hume's reformulation of this definition in his first *Enquiry* where, instead of putting the objection in the mouth of a critic, he himself states categorically that both his definitions are "drawn from something extraneous and foreign" to the cause (EHU 7.29).

What exactly *would* it be to define causation directly? Hume makes this clear at the beginning of Section 14, in a passage which is seldom noticed. In opposition to Cartesian philosophers, principally Malebranche, he argues that the power or necessity of a cause cannot be anything general like what is called a law of nature.[63] General or even universal regularities don't have the power to make anything occur. Hume writes that

we must be able to place this power in some particular being, and conceive that being as endow'd with a real force and energy, by which such a particular effect necessarily results from its operation. We must distinctly and particularly conceive the connexion betwixt the cause and effect, and be able to pronounce, from a simple view of the one, that it must be follow'd or preceded by the other. (T1.3.14.13: 161)

This is the "true manner of conceiving a particular power in a particular body," and if we were able to conceive the relation of cause and effect in this way our definition would not be foreign to what we are defining.[64] However, he points out that we cannot give such a definition because "the human mind cannot form such an idea of two objects, as to conceive any [necessary] connexion betwixt them."

What are we to say of Hume's second definition of cause, which apparently *does* define it in terms of a necessary relation between two particular entities? He writes that "a CAUSE is an object precedent and contiguous to another, and so united with it, that the idea of the one determines the mind to form the idea of the other, and the impression of the one to form a more lively idea of the other" (T1.3.14.31: 170). Note Hume's use of the word "determines" in this definition. It surely means the same as "necessitates." It seems that Hume is defining cause *directly* by identifying it as a necessary relation between the perceptions in the mind of the observer. It is defined in terms of the necessary relation between the impression

---

[63] Malebranche had written that "because ... laws are efficacious, they act, whereas bodies cannot act (*Search*, 449).

[64] Compare his claim in the first *Enquiry* where he writes that "a more perfect definition" would "point out that circumstance in the cause, which gives it a connexion with its effect" (EHU 7.29).

and the idea. Has he not found the source of a genuine idea of necessary connection where we would least expect it, namely in the mind
of the perceiver, rather than in the objects perceived?

But Hume considers that this definition too will "be rejected for
the same reason" as the other, namely its being foreign to the cause
(T1.3.14.31: 170; cf. EHU 7.29). This definition can only be foreign to
the cause in so far as it defines causation by what goes on in the mind
rather than objects. But didn't Hume just tell us that that was where
the necessity really was located? How can he allow that *this* definition
is foreign to causation itself?

7. SKEPTICISM CONCERNING CAUSATION

It is a striking fact that Hume does not identify his view of causation as *skeptical* anywhere in Part 3 of Book 1 of the *Treatise*.[65] He
only does so in the famous skeptical Conclusion to Book 1. There
he states that "our aim in all our studies" is to discover the "energy
in the cause, by which it operates on its effect; that tie, which connects them together ..." (T1.4.7.5: 266–7). He goes on to say how
disappointed we must be when we find "that this connexion, tie, or
energy lies merely in ourselves." *But then there is an important shift
in his thinking.* He remarks that the problem arises from "*deficiency
in our ideas,*" and that we are "*ignorant* of the ... principle, which
binds*" the cause and effect together in the most usual as well as the
most extraordinary cases (my emphasis). Can one be ignorant of
what does not exist? And why attribute our ignorance to a *deficiency*
in our ideas unless those ideas fail to represent what actually exists in
external reality? In the *Abstract*, after summing up his account of the
origin of the idea of necessary connection, he notes that his account
is "very sceptical" and that it shows "the imperfections and narrow
limits of human understanding" (A27: 657).

A closer look at Hume's account of the origin of the idea of necessary connection in the *Treatise* indicates that he overstates his case in
those statements where he asserts that we apprehend power or necessity in the mind itself, and especially when he suggests in Section 14 of

---

[65] See Janet Broughton, "Hume's Skepticism about Causal Inferences," *Pacific Philosophical
Quarterly* 64 (1983), 3–18.

Part 3 that there is a "real intelligible connexion" which is to be found in the mind of the observer (T1.3.14.27: 168). In the same paragraph where he seems to say that we apprehend the necessity in the operations of the mind itself, he goes on to stress that "the uniting principle among our internal perceptions is as *unintelligible* as that among external objects," and that even experience of our own minds "never gives us any *insight* into the operating principle . . ." (T1.3.14.29: 169; my emphasis). Experience "only accustoms the mind to pass" from one perception to another. In other words, we should not be misled into thinking that we have found genuine necessity when we identify the impression of the mind which is the source of our idea of necessary connection. Finding a genuine necessity connecting the cause and effect would require *knowledge* and *insight*, and that we never have – even when we consider the operations of the mind itself.

Indeed, Hume explicitly denies that we have any genuine idea of power or necessity from the mind itself. In a paragraph which he added to Section 14 in the Appendix to Book 3 of the *Treatise*, Hume writes that "no internal impression has an apparent energy, more than external objects have" (T1.3.14.12App: 633). Hume is considering the view that the idea of power or necessary connection arises from the mind itself when we reflect on the operation of our wills in bringing about the motions of our own bodies. He refutes it by pointing out that an act of will can be distinctly conceived apart from the effects it brings about, and that we only learn its connection with these effects through custom and habit – just like the relation between physical causes and their effects. In his *Abstract*, he concludes from these considerations "our own minds afford us no more notion of energy than matter does" (A26: 656).[66]

From the very beginning of his discussion of causal reasoning in the first *Enquiry*, Hume identifies his account as *skeptical*.[67] He prefaces the paragraph in which he gives the two definitions of cause by

---

[66] This argument concerning power and the will is discussed at length in Section 7, "Of the idea of necessary connexion," of the first *Enquiry* (EHU 7.9–20).

[67] His negative account of the inference from the observed to the unobserved is called "Sceptical doubts concerning human understanding" (EHU 4) and his positive account "Sceptical solution to these doubts" (EHU 5). It must be admitted that Hume's overstatement of his view on the subjectivity of necessity does not entirely disappear from the first *Enquiry*: in a footnote to his discussion "Of Liberty and Necessity" he writes that "the necessity of any action . . . is not, properly speaking, a quality in the agent, but in any thinking or

stating that his account of the idea of necessary connection shows "the surprizing ignorance and weakness of the understanding" (EHU 7.29). He writes that "so imperfect are the ideas we form concerning ... [the relation of cause and effect], that it is impossible to give any just definition of *cause*, except what is drawn from something extraneous and foreign to it." As we have seen, both definitions are clearly identified as describing causation by what is foreign to the causal relation itself. In his second definition Hume replaces the term "determines" with the term "conveys," thus making it clearer that we have no more insight into the necessity of the operations of our own minds than those of external objects.[68]

8. THE NATURAL SUPPOSITION OF OBJECTIVE NECESSITY

i) *Projection*

In spite of his own philosophical analysis of the origin of the idea of necessary connection, Hume clearly recognizes that both in our everyday lives and in natural science we cannot help ascribing the necessary connection to the external objects themselves. In order to explain this fact, in Section 14 of Part 3 of Book 1 of the *Treatise* he appeals to a further associational principle beyond that which forms our inference from the impression to the idea: we may call this the principle of projection.[69] According to this principle, "the mind has a great propensity to spread itself on external objects, and to conjoin with them any internal impressions, which they occasion, and which always make their appearance at the same time that these objects discover themselves to the senses" (T1.3.14.25: 167). This principle

intelligent being, who may consider the action; and it consists chiefly in the determination of his thoughts ..." (EHU 8.22n.). However, he does qualify the view here with the adverb "chiefly."

[68] A cause is defined as "*an object followed by another, whose appearance always conveys the thought to that other.*" Annette Baier argues for the importance of Hume's replacement of the term "impression" used in the second definition in the *Treatise* with the term "appearance" used here; see her *Death and Character*, Chapter 10, esp. pp. 217–18.

[69] For an extended discussion of this principle, its source and the uses that have been made of it in the interpretation of Hume, see Kail, *Projection and Realism in Hume's Philosophy*, esp. 110ff.

explains "why we suppose necessity and power to lie in the objects we consider, not in our mind, that considers them." It is the same principle which Hume uses later in Book 1 to explain why we suppose that non-spatial perceptions such as smells and tastes are located in visible spatially extended objects, and, arguably, in Book 3 of the *Treatise* to explain why we think of moral value as located outside of us in the characters and actions which we evaluate.[70] In the former case, Hume argues that non-spatial impressions such as the smell and taste of an orange become so closely associated with the visual (and tactual) perceptions of the orange that we come to think of them as actually located outside of us in the orange itself (T1.4.5.11–14: 236–9). The same principle also explains why we think of the *internal* impression of necessity as located in the constantly conjoined objects which we observe in the world outside of us which give rise to it. Hume writes that our natural supposition that necessity exists in external objects is "so riveted in the mind" that it will lead his readers to treat his own theory of the subjective origin of the idea "as extravagant and ridiculous" (T1.3.14.26: 167).

Hume's talk of the mind spreading itself on to external objects has led to an interesting interpretation of his view which has been championed by Simon Blackburn,[71] and more recently developed by Helen Beebee and Angela Coventry. This is the view called *projectivism* or quasi-realism. According to this interpretation, our talk of necessary connections in objects is *expressive* rather than *descriptive*. We express our "inferential habits in propositional form," adopt "the 'objective mode of speech'" and so bring "the resources for thinking of those habits as susceptible to critical scrutiny."[72] Once the operations of our imagination come into play we no longer perceive the events of the world as loose and unconnected; we perceive them as necessarily connected. When we do so we project our inferential habits on to the world and experience it as consisting of objects which necessarily produce one another. But what we are actually doing on this interpretation is projecting "an attitude, habit or other commitment

---

[70] See Chapter 8 §7, pp. 248ff.
[71] See Simon Blackburn, "Hume and Thick Connexions," in *The New Hume Debate*, eds. R. Read and K. Richman, revised edition (Routledge: London, 2007), pp. 100–12.
[72] Beebee, *Hume on Causation*, p. 145.

which is not descriptive onto the world."[73] For example, we treat the relation between events as law-like, and as supporting contrary to fact conditionals: "*if the first object had not been, the second never had existed*" (EHU 7.29). The projectivist interpretation, unlike the traditional regularity theory, legitimizes our talk of necessary connections in objects. But like the regularity theorist, the projectivist rejects the claim that there are genuine mind-independent necessary connections in objects.

It goes beyond the scope of this book to consider how far this account represents Hume's true intentions.[74] What I want to stress here is that Hume himself did not give any such account of language as expressive rather than descriptive. His explanation of why we suppose that there is power or necessity in matter is based entirely on his associational psychology – not on any thoughts about language having more than a descriptive function.

ii) *The natural supposition of inseparability*

Moreover, it is important to note that Hume also has another entirely independent associational explanation of our supposition of causal necessity – the natural supposition of inseparability. According to this account we come to suppose that there is a necessary connection *between* the objects that we perceive. We do not conceive of the impression of necessity as a separate impression apart from the felt connection between the perceptions of the cause and the effect. This explanation dispenses entirely with the metaphor of the mind spreading itself on external objects. Custom alone leads us to think of the objects we call cause and effect in such a way "that we cannot without a sensible violence survey them in any other" (T1.3.11.4: 125).We "imagine them to be absolutely inseparable" (T1.3.9.10: 112). Indeed, "because custom has render'd it difficult to separate the ideas" of the objects which we find constantly united in experience, we naturally imagine "such a separation to be in itself impossible and absurd" (T1.4.3.9: 223). In other words, custom and association make us suppose that cause and effect are conceptually inseparable, just

---

[73] Simon Blackburn, *Spreading the Word* (Oxford University Press, 1984), p. 171.
[74] But see Kail, *Projection and Realism in Hume's Philosophy*, pp. 116ff.

as they would be if we had *insight* into their real natures. As Hume puts it in his first *Enquiry*, after experiencing a constant conjunction between two successive events we "suppose, that there is some connexion between them; some power in the one, by which it infallibly produces the other, and operates with the ... strongest necessity" (EHU 7.27).

This interpretation of Hume's account of our natural supposition of necessary connection in objects as inseparable has a distinguished pedigree. In his *Prolegomena to any Future Metaphysics*, Immanuel Kant argued that Hume's own British contemporaries misunderstood him when they thought he denied that causes necessitate their effects.[75] Hume showed only that our supposition of the necessity of causes does not arise "*a priori* and from concepts" (*Prolegomena*, p. 7). We cannot discover it through conceptual analysis, through what Kant called an analytic judgment. Rather, according to Hume, our idea of causation is "nothing but a bastard of imagination, which ... having brought certain representations under the law of association, passes off the resulting subjective necessity (i.e. habit) for an objective necessity (from insight)." On Kant's interpretation, Hume argues that we naturally mistake the "subjective necessity" arising from association of ideas for a genuine "objective necessity" discovered though *insight* and the use of reason. Reason mistakes the necessary connection of causes and effects "for her own child." Hume's claims, on Kant's reading, were purely epistemological and genetic: he claimed to discover the origin of our idea of causal necessity, not to challenge the view that there is genuine necessity in objects.

This interpretation was further developed by Norman Kemp Smith, who argued that, according to Hume, we apprehend the objective necessity between objects through *feeling* rather than reason.[76] This is the natural way to read Hume's claims about the feeling which is the origin of the idea of necessity in "Of liberty and necessity" in Book 2

[75] Immanuel Kant, *Prolegomena to any Future Metaphysics That Will Be Able to Come Forward as Science*, ed. and trans. Gary Hatfield, revised edition (Cambridge University Press, 2004) pp. 8–9.
[76] See Norman Kemp Smith, "The Naturalism of Hume (I)," *Mind*, n.s.14 (1905), 149–73, esp. 150–3 and *The Philosophy of David Hume: A Critical Study of its Origins and Central Doctrines* (London: Macmillan, 1941), Chapter 17.

of the *Treatise*: there he writes that while it is "impossible for the mind to penetrate" into the relation of the objects, after experiencing their constant conjunction, the mind *"feels* the necessity"(T2.3.1.16: 406).[77] Even more clearly, in his first *Enquiry* he writes that a person *"feels ...* events to be *connected* in his imagination" after experiencing their constant conjunction (EHU 7.28). Here, clearly, we feel a necessary connection between *events*, not merely between subjective *perceptions*.

The text of the first *Enquiry*, where Hume also frequently refers to the unknown powers of nature, provides a stronger support for what I have called the skeptical realist interpretation of his theory of causation than does the *Treatise*.[78] Nevertheless, I believe that there is good evidence in the *Treatise* itself, particularly in considering his remarks concerning the inadequacy of our ideas of cause and effect, to ground this interpretation.

9. CONCLUSION: HUME'S REJECTION OF OCCASIONALISM, AND THE INADEQUACY OF OUR IDEAS

Toward the beginning of his discussion of the idea of necessary connection in Section 14 of Part 3 of Book 1 of the *Treatise*, Hume considers the view of the occasionalists (principally Malebranche) that there is no energy, force, power or necessary connection in matter, and that God is the only repository of power. Hume writes that *"the Cartesians ...* having establish'd it as a principle, that we are perfectly acquainted with the essence of matter, have very naturally inferr'd, that it is endow'd with no efficacy" (T1.3.14.8: 159). Hume's own arguments that we have no idea of a necessary connection between *physical causes and their effects* follow closely those of Malebranche and other Cartesians.[79] Indeed, Charles McCracken has claimed

---

[77] See Chapter 5, §7, pp. 182ff.
[78] See my *Sceptical Realism of David Hume*, esp. Chapter 4; Stephen Buckle, *Hume's Enlightenment Tract: The Unity and Purpose of An Enquiry Concerning Human Understanding* (Oxford: Clarendon Press, 2001), esp. pp. 193ff.; Beebee, *Hume on Causation*, pp. 221–5. For discussions of the relevant passages of the first *Enquiry* see articles by myself, Galen Strawson, Edward Craig and Peter Kail in *The New Hume Debate*, eds. R. Read and K. Richman, revised edition (Routledge: London, 2007); see also John Yolton, *Realism and Appearances* (Cambridge University Press, 2000), Chapter 6.
[79] By "the Cartesians," Hume is referring to those followers of Descartes who adopted the theory called "occasionalism." It is very questionable whether Descartes himself held this view; see my *Sceptical Realism of David Hume*, pp. 136–45.

that Malebranche anticipated Hume's view that we "mistake a *habit-ual association* of ideas for a *necessary connection* between them."[80] Nevertheless, there is good reason to think Hume is opposed to the conclusion which he says the Cartesians naturally draw from their "establish'd ... principle" – namely that matter "is endow'd with no efficacy."

To see this one needs to consider his *reductio ad absurdum* of the Cartesian view. He notes that after denying that there is any power or necessary connection in matter or in finite minds, the Cartesians went on to conclude that God's will is the only source of power in the universe. The only necessary connection in the universe, accord-ing to them, is between the will of an all-powerful being and the effects of that will.[81] Hume argues that, given the falsity of the the-ory of innate ideas, any idea of power in the Deity would have to be derived from that of particular objects, a possibility the Cartesians have already excluded. Given their principle that the ideas we have are adequate representations of reality, they are left with the absurd conclusion that there is no power anywhere in the universe. Hume goes on to argue that in order to *avoid* this absurdity they should conclude "from the very first, that they have *no adequate idea* of power or efficacy in any object ... [,] neither in body nor spirit, nei-ther in superior nor inferior natures" (T1.3.14.10: 160; my emphasis). They need to recognize the *inadequacy* of all the ideas we have of causes – that is, that they do not adequately represent reality. These inadequate ideas include not only causes in body or matter, but also those in mind or spirit.[82]

We have seen (§6, pp. 115–18) that, at certain points in his own discussion of power, Hume seemed to be arguing that the necessary connection we ascribe to causes and effects really only exists in the minds of observers. We have also noted that his more carefully con-sidered view is that we have no more idea of necessary connection

---

[80] McCracken, *Malebranche and British Philosophy*, p. 38. He cites *Search*, p. 224.

[81] Malebranche wrote that "it is impossible to conceive that He wills a body to be moved and this body not be moved" (*Search*, 448). In other words, if God wills a body to move, it must necessarily move.

[82] For another interpretation of Hume's critique of Malebranche, in criticism of my own, see Martin Bell, "Sceptical Doubts Concerning Hume's Causal Realism," in *The New Hume Debate*, eds. R. Read and K. Richman, revised edition (Routledge: London, 2007), pp. 122–37, esp. §§3–4.

or power in our own minds than we do in external objects (§7). However, this leaves him in the same absurd position which he ascribes to the Cartesians, with no place for power anywhere in the universe – neither in mind nor matter. *Does not the answer which he gave to them apply to his own philosophy as well?* To avoid the absurd conclusion that there is no power in the universe, he must acknowledge that our impression-derived ideas of cause and effect are *inadequate representations* of reality. He must reject the "establish'd ... principle" of the Cartesians who claim that we are acquainted with the essence of things through our ideas. Indeed, we have seen, this is the view which Hume adopts in the Conclusion to Book 1 of the *Treatise* where he writes of the *deficiency* of our ideas of cause and effect, and in the *Abstract* and first *Enquiry* where he writes of their *imperfections*.

What exactly is the significance of the claim that our ideas of cause and effect are *inadequate representations* of reality? We saw at the beginning of this chapter that Hume makes the adequacy of our ideas a necessary condition for *knowledge* (pp. 86–7). In denying that our ideas of cause and effect are adequate, he is denying that we have knowledge of cause and effect. He is denying that "the relations, contradictions, and agreements of the ideas" need be "applicable to the objects." Now, what we actually discover through examination of our ideas of cause and effect is that they are distinct and separate. By calling these ideas inadequate, Hume opens up the possibility that the objects they represent may, in a way we do not understand, be necessarily connected.

But why, beyond escape from what common sense considers to be an absurd conclusion, should a philosopher believe that there are necessary causes in the world? The most straightforward answer within Hume's own philosophy is that this belief, like the belief in external existence which I consider in the next chapter, is one which we naturally believe, and that it is absolutely necessary for human survival.

CHAPTER 4

Skepticism

There could not be a greater contrast than that between the optimism which pervades Hume's announcement of his ambitious project of founding all the sciences on that of human nature in the Introduction to the *Treatise* and the pessimism with which he describes his *total skepticism* in the Conclusion to Book 1. Here, after running through the "manifold contradictions and imperfections in human reason" he announces that he is "ready to reject all belief and reasoning, and can look upon no opinion even as more probable or likely than another" (T1.4.7.8: 268–9). In this state of total skepticism or doubt, he is stuck in inaction – "utterly deprived of the use of every member and faculty." He is overwhelmed by "philosophical melancholy and delirium" (T1.4.7.9: 269). His only means of escape is to leave his study and "dine, ... play a game of back-gammon, ... converse, and ... [be] merry with ... [his] friends" – where he is forced to believe in the "general maxims of the world" (T1.4.7.10: 269). But he calls his belief in this state an "indolent" or lazy belief, and when he once again remembers his former state he is ready to renounce philosophy entirely and "throw all [his] books and papers into the fire." For philosophy can provide no remedy either for his "spleen and indolence" (T1.4.7.11: 270). It is small wonder that many readers have inferred that his philosophical project of discovering the causes of mental phenomena has collapsed by the end of Book 1 even before he turns to the study of the passions and morals in Books 2 and 3, and that his 'naturalism' has run aground on the shoals of his skepticism.

However, this would be a mistake. Hume's dramatic portrayal of his own psychological state in the Conclusion to Book 1 is intended to illustrate his own theory of human nature, as well as draw epistemological lessons from it. Unlike the total skepticism of Descartes, who artificially induces it at the end of his first *Meditation* with his hypothesis of an evil demon, Hume's total skepticism is embedded in his experience-based science of human nature – particularly his study of reason and the senses in Part 4 of Book 1, "*Of the sceptical and other systems of philosophy.*" His goal is to show that reason itself can never find its own way out of this skepticism, as Descartes had claimed in his *Meditations*. In the Conclusion Hume writes that since "philosophy has nothing to oppose" total skepticism, she must rely on "the returns of a serious good-humour'd disposition" (T1.4.7.11: 270). It is through certain favorable passions that Hume thinks we can and ought to escape from total skepticism. In §5 (pp. 166ff.) we shall see that Hume's dramatic Conclusion to Book 1 provides a literary and philosophical transition to the study of the passions in Book 2.

The skeptical doubt which leads to the "philosophical melancholy" of the Conclusion to Book 1 is based on his own philosophical project of identifying the principles of the imagination which form the basis for scientific or philosophical reasoning. Earlier in Part 4 he wrote that according to his philosophy the imagination is "the ultimate judge of all systems of philosophy" (T1.4.4.1: 225–6). He went on to make a distinction between the principles of the imagination which are "permanent, irresistible, and universal" and those "which are changeable, weak, and irregular." The former, such as "the customary transition from causes to effects, and from effects to causes" are necessary for human survival: "upon their removal human nature must immediately perish and go to ruin." As an example of the second kind of principle of the imagination he mentions that which leads to superstitious beliefs, such as "spectres in the dark." Hume argues that such weak principles "may easily be subverted by a due contrast and opposition" with those principles which are necessary for our survival. When systemized and corrected, these necessary principles form the basis for our scientific reasoning. It is "the general and more establish'd properties of the imagination" which form the basis of "the understanding" (T1.4.7.7: 267).

It is the difficulty of maintaining this distinction between these two kinds of principles of the imagination, as well as inconsistencies in the operation of the necessary principles themselves which lead Hume to reflect on the "manifold contradictions and imperfections in human reason" in the Conclusion (T1.4.7.8: 268). In the first place, he argues that there is an opposition between two of the necessary principles of the imagination – the one which makes us believe in cause and effect, and the other which makes us believe in the independent existence of the objects of our senses. He argues that the first undermines belief in the second.[1] In the second place, he argues that in order to do science we need to embrace a trivial quality of the imagination, namely that which prevents us from following a certain abstract argument to its skeptical conclusion. At the same time, science requires abstract reasoning: "Very refin'd reflections have little or no influence upon us; and yet we do not, and cannot establish it for a rule, that they ought not to have any influence; which implies a manifest contradiction."[2]

The third source of total skepticism which Hume reflects on in the Conclusion to Book 1 focuses on the "deficiency" of our idea of causal power, and the "illusion of the imagination" which prevents us from recognizing our ignorance of the necessary connection between cause and effect (T1.4.7.6: 267). As we saw in Chapter 3, that illusion arises from our mistaking the strong association of ideas which results from custom and habit for a genuine insight into the necessary connection between cause and effect.[3] In the Conclusion Hume raises the question of "how far we ought to yield to these illusions" and says "that this reduces us to a very dangerous dilemma, which-ever way we answer it." He goes on to argue that while we must reject the trivial suggestions of the imagination which have led to "the flights of the imagination" of philosophers, we must in other cases rely on them. Indeed, earlier in Part 4, in Section 2, he admitted that the belief in the external world, which he clearly considers as necessary for human survival, is based on "trivial qualities of the fancy" (T1.4.2.56: 217).

It is Hume's exploration of some of these "trivial" qualities of the imagination which leads to his deepest form of epistemological skepticism.[4] This is based on the illusions or fictions of the imagination

---

[1] T1.4.7.4: 265–6.; see §2, pp. 153–5 below.
[2] T1.4.7.4: 267–8; see §1, pp. 133–6 below.   [3] See pp. 124–6.
[4] Contrast the view of Don Garrett who writes that Hume's "epistemological scepticism does not concern the intelligibility of a domain of propositions" ("A Small Tincture of Pyrrhonism: Skepticism and Naturalism in Hume's Science of Man," in *Pyrrhonian Skepticism*, ed. W. Sinnott-Armstrong (Oxford University Press, 2004), pp. 68–98, esp. 71).

which form the content of our beliefs in the continued and independent existence of bodies (§2), in material substances (§3), and in a substantial soul (§4).[5] While Hume explicitly argues that the two latter beliefs cannot be based on the *copy principle*,[6] the same is clearly true of the first. The belief in external existence of bodies is based on "a gross illusion" which makes us "suppose ... that our resembling perceptions are numerically the same" (T1.4.2.56: 217). It is based on the *identity substitution* principle, a principle which generates belief by way of "a propensity to confound ... ideas" and in particular to "confound identity with relation" (T1.4.6.6: 254–5). It is an instance of the more general principle which Hume identified in Part 2 of Book 1 where he wrote of our tendency to systematically "confound ... ideas" and substitute one for the other as a result of their resemblance (T1.2.5.21: 61).

There is a basic lack of intelligibility which underlies the beliefs which Hume seeks to explain in the *Treatise*, including the beliefs in an external world and in objective causes. This lack of intelligibility links up historically with the "*mitigated* scepticism, or ACADEMICAL philosophy" which he later adopted in his first *Enquiry* (EHU 12.24). While he does not explicitly follow this ancient school of Academic philosophy in the *Treatise*, he does adopt one of its major tenets. In contrast to Pyrrhonian skeptics who simply suspended judgment, the Academics accepted probabilities, while denying that they can be "comprehended and perceived."[7] Cicero wrote that the proponent of the Academic philosophy accepts as probable what is "not grasped [non comprehensa] nor perceived nor assented to."[8] If such propositions were not accepted "all life would be done away with." They

---

[5] Compare Louis Loeb's discussion of what he calls "quasi content" or defective meaning in *Stability and Justification in Hume's Treatise* (Oxford University Press, 2002), 162–72, esp. 167.

[6] T1.1.6.1: 15–16; T1.4.5.3: 232–3; T1.4.6.2: 251–2.

[7] Cicero, *Academica*, in *Cicero*, 28 vols. Trans. H. Rackham (Cambridge, Mass.: Harvard University Press, 1933) Vol. xix, II, §xxxviii, p. 620–1. This passage is quoted in Bayle's article on Carnaedes, in Pierre Bayle, *The Dictionary Historical and Critical of Mr. Peter Bayle*, 5 vols., ed. and trans. P. des Maizeau, 2nd edn. (London, 1735), Vol. I, p. 326. Compare also Sextus Empiricus who claimed that "the adherents of the New Academy ... affirm that all things are non-apprehensible" (Sextus Empiricus, *Outlines of Pyrrhonism*, Book I, in Sextus Empiricus, 4 vols., trans. R. G. Bury (Cambridge, Mass.: Harvard University Press, 1961), Vol. I, p. 139.

[8] "Etenim is quoque qui a vobis sapiens inducitur multa sequitur probabilia, non comprehensa neque percepta neque adsensa sed similia veri" (Cicero, *Academica*, pp. 594–5).

provide the Academic philosopher "with a canon of judgment both in the conduct of life and in philosophical investigation" (pp. 508–9). Like Cicero, Hume held that our probable judgments are not clearly comprehended. They are based on *illusions* or *fictions* of the imagination, which like the probabilities of the ancient Academic skeptics are mere objects of belief. Echoing Cicero, Hume writes that his aim is to explain "probabilities and those other measures of evidence on which life and action intirely depend, and which are our guides even in most of our philosophical speculations" (A4: 646–7).

In spite of its basis in a systematic confusion of ideas, Hume endorses the belief in an external world beyond our senses. It is necessary for our survival. He tells his reader that it is useless to ask whether or not there *is* an external world. That must be taken "for granted in all our reasonings," including his own subsequent reasoning explaining the origin of the belief (T1.4.2.1: 187). Before turning to that explanation in §2, I will consider his puzzling argument that reason undermines itself, and that we are only saved from total skepticism by a trivial quality of the imagination.

I. "OF SCEPTICISM WITH REGARD TO REASON"

At the beginning of Section 1 of Part 4, Hume writes that "our reason must be consider'd as a kind of cause, of which truth is the natural effect; but such-a-one as by the irruption of other causes, and by the inconstancy of our mental powers" may fail to achieve truth (T1.4.1.1: 180). He goes on to point out that while the rules of any demonstrative reasoning in science are certain, we make mistakes in applying them, particularly when the calculations are very intricate and complex. On Hume's view these mistakes arise from other principles than reason itself – for example, our biased desire to reach a presupposed result. He notes that reflection on our past errors should weaken the trust we put in our ability to carry out any piece of demonstrative reasoning successfully. In this way "all knowledge degenerates into probability."

He then turns to probable reasoning, and argues that repeated reflection on the trustworthiness of our reasoning abilities leads *in principle* to "a total extinction of belief and evidence" (T1.4.1.7: 183). When we reason on the basis of probabilities we compare the number of positive results with the negative ones, and arrive at a measure of the probability that an event will occur. Suppose that we are studying the probability that a mortgage lender will make a risky loan under the condition that he can sell it at a profit to another lender. We might find from past experience that this event occurs in nine cases out of ten. Thus we arrive at a .9 probability that such an event will occur in the future. However, Hume says that "we ought always to correct the first judgment, deriv'd from the nature of the object, by another judgment, deriv'd from the nature of the understanding" (T1.4.1.5: 181–2). He recognizes that a person who has extensive experience of the subject matter – in our example, people's self-interested economic behavior – will have more reason to trust her results than a novice. However, she will also be conscious of having made mistakes in the past, and through this "reflex act of the mind" she should correct her original probability based on this experience. He thinks that such a reflection should cause our researcher to lower her original estimate of probability of the event occurring – in this case of a person making a risky loan. A further reflection on *that* judgment should, he thinks, lower her original estimate still further, and so on with every new reflex judgment until all confidence in our original probability is completely eliminated.

There is, however, a problem with the argument which Hume presents. It occurs at the first reflective step where he claims that the probability of our original judgment – for example, of someone making a risky loan – should *decrease* because of one's lack of confidence in one's own faculty of judgment. For that lack of confidence could result in one's being either too high or too low in one's estimate of the original probability. There is no reason why one's reflection on one's fallibility in making judgments of this kind should *lower* one's estimate of the original probability.

But perhaps Hume's argument can still be saved. Suppose that one's original margin of error is .01 and that one's estimate of probability should be between .89 and .91. Then reflection on one's own past errors and fallibility might increase the margin of error by another .01. Then the probability of one's original judgment becomes anywhere from .88 to .92. On each subsequent reflection on the fallibility of one's judgment the margin of error grows greater, so that eventually the probability of one's original result is anywhere from 0 to 1. In the end we have no clearer sense of the truth than when we started. This, then, is at least a plausible route to what Hume calls "*total* scepticism" (T1.4.1.7: 183).

Hume's aim in presenting this argument is to show that abstract theoretical reasoning has no effect on our beliefs. Our original estimates of probability remain the same, in spite of our reflective doubts about our abilities to make accurate assessments of probability. He asks rhetorically whether he is "really one of those sceptics, who hold that all is uncertain, and that our judgment is not in *any* thing possest of *any* measures of truth and falshood" and replies no one can be "sincerely and constantly of that opinion" – or rather lack of opinion (T1.4.1.7: 183). Indeed, the aim of this whole exercise is to show that such doubt is *in practice* impossible: "Nature, by an absolute and uncontroulable necessity has determin'd us to judge as well as to breathe and feel; nor can we any more forebear viewing certain objects in a stronger and fuller light, upon account to their customary connexion with a present impression." He appeals to the theory of belief which he developed in Part 3.[9] It is the *force and vivacity* of an idea which determines belief, and as we continually reflect on the probability of error because of our own past failures the argument becomes too abstract to weaken our belief. Belief is not merely a function of our reasoning faculty, but is determined by the natural judgments of the imagination.

Hume goes on to give a psychophysiological explanation of our inability to reach a state of total doubt. He notes that "the mind, as well as the body, seems to be endow'd with a certain precise degree of force and activity, which it never employs in one action, but at the expence of all the rest" (T1.4.1.11: 186). The mind only has a limited amount of mental energy. Hume appears to be applying the principle of mental economy which he learned from the illness of his youth.[10] He argues here that in abstract reflections "the posture of the mind is uneasy; and the [animal] spirits being diverted from their natural course" do not have the same force "as when they flow in their usual channel" (T1.4.1.10: 185). The result is that we cannot lose the force and vivacity of our original belief in probability.

---

[9] T1.4.1.8: 183–4; see Chapter 3 §5, pp. 107ff. [10] See Chapter 1 §2, pp. 8–9ff.

It is worth noting that Hume's account of the impossibility of total skepticism differs significantly from traditional accounts of its impossibility. Traditionally it was argued that it is *logically* impossible to be a total skeptic because the very statement that "all is uncertain" is self-defeating. Hume may well have read the following passage in the article on 'Pyrrhonians' in Chambers' *Cyclopedia*: "The very Principle of the *Pyrrhonians* destroys itself: for if there is nothing ... more probable or likelier to Truth than another, why shall [this] Principle of the Pyrrhonians be believed preferably to the opposite one."[11] According to Chambers, the statement that nothing is more probable than another reflectively undermines itself. In contrast, Hume's own explanation of the impossibility of total skepticism is based on what he takes to be experimentally discovered principles of our mental economy and the nature of belief.

2. "OF SCEPTICISM WITH REGARD TO THE SENSES"

Just as Hume argued in Section 1 that while reason cannot undermine our natural belief in probability, so he begins Section 2 by asserting that reason cannot undermine our natural belief in the senses. The skeptic "must assent to the principle concerning the existence of body, tho' he cannot pretend by any arguments of philosophy to maintain its veracity. Nature has not left this to his choice, and has doubtless esteem'd it an affair of too great importance to be trusted to our uncertain reasonings and speculations" (T1.4.2.1: 187). Hume considers the belief in an external world to be absolutely necessary for our survival. It is on this basis that he sets out to explain "*What causes induce us to believe in the existence of body?*" and to show us why it can, in practice, never be doubted.[12]

Hume defines a "body" as an object which has a "CONTINU'D existence" while unperceived, and which is "DISTINCT from the mind and perception" (T1.4.2.2: 188). Under the heading of distinctness, he includes both the "*external* position" of objects outside of our own body, and "the *independence* of their existence and operation." In explaining the belief in body, he concentrates on the question of

---

[11] Ephraim Chambers, *Cyclopædia: or, an Universal Dictionary of Arts and Sciences* (London, 1728), Vol. II, p. 921.
[12] But for a qualification see pp. 155–6.

why we believe in the *continued existence* of objects, and holds that their *independent existence* follows as a consequence (T1.4.2.44: 210).[13] His chief skeptical argument runs the other way round: he argues that sensory perceptions have *no independent existence*, and their lack of *continued existence* is taken to be a consequence (T1.4.2.46: 211). I begin by discussing his skeptical argument.

i) The roots of skepticism with regard to the senses: "a few ... experiments"

Hume's skepticism with regard to the senses arises from some simple "experiments" which he only cites toward the end of Section 2 of Part 4 (T1.4.2.45: 210–11). These experiments show that our sensory perceptions are not independent objects – as we unreflectively think they are in ordinary life. Hume first describes an experiment in which one presses one's eyeball with one's finger, and discovers that there are two images where there was one before. This experiment is supposed to prove that the immediate objects of sight "are dependent on our organs, and the disposition of our nerves and animal spirits." By performing it, we discover that what we naturally suppose to be an external and independent object really is an entity which is dependent on ourselves, on our sense organs and our nervous systems. This experiment is "confirm'd by the seeming encrease and diminution of objects, according to their distance"; by their changes of shape as they are viewed from different angles; by the changes of their qualities when we are ill; "and by an infinite number of other experiments of the same kind." In sum, these experiments are supposed to show that our sensory perceptions are not distinct from us: they are neither spatially external to us, nor do they operate independently of us.

The skepticism concerning the senses which results from these "experiments" illustrates what in his first *Enquiry* Hume called a "scepticism ... *consequent* to science and enquiry" (EHU 12.5). According to Hume, prior to science and reflection we all believe that the very objects we perceive, our sensory perceptions, can exist

---

[13] Hume is not concerned with explaining why we believe bodies to be *spatially external* to ourselves. Berkeley had already done that at length in his "An Essay towards a New Theory of Vision" (1710) in *The Works of George Berkeley, Bishop of Cloyne*, Vol. II, eds. A. A. Luce and T. E. Jessop (London: Nelson, 1949).

independently of us. We make no distinction between the mind and its contents, and external objects. The perception of the computer I am typing on, that of the table in front of me, and of the houses I see outside the window are, according to the natural common sense view of the world, independent objects which go on existing whether I perceive them or not. What the "experiments" show us is that they are not independent: they are dependent for their existence on our sense organs, and ultimately our brains. From the conclusion that they are dependent we can draw the further conclusion that they will not go on existing when we cease to perceive them: "The natural consequence of this reasoning shou'd be, that our perceptions have no more a continu'd than an independent existence" (T1.4.2.46: 211). The common sense view of our sense perceptions is *false*.[14]

The results of Hume's "experiments" are assumed throughout the earlier paragraphs of Section 2 where he argues that the belief in body cannot arise from *the senses*.[15] For example, he begins his discussion of whether our senses "suggest any idea of distinct existences" by noting that if they did it would have to be "by a kind of fallacy and illusion" (T1.4.2.5: 189). This, he reminds us two paragraphs later, is because all the strong and lively perceptions of our minds – sensations as well as pains, emotions, etc. – are really "originally on the same footing" (T1.4.2.7: 190). From the context it is clear that he means that they are all really internal and mind-dependent. He goes on to argue that it is impossible that the senses themselves can generate the illusion that their objects are external and independent because then we would have to admit that "even where we are most intimately conscious, we might be mistaken." Since these strong and lively impressions "must necessarily appear in every particular what they are," and since "every thing that enters the mind" is "in *reality* a perception," it follows that it is impossible that "any thing shou'd to *feeling* appear different." In this remarkable argument Hume is presenting us with a conclusion about the way things *appear* to our senses on the basis of a claim about the actual nature of sense impressions: they cannot appear as external and independent because they actually are internal and dependent. Fallacy and illusion are not possible in this case.

---

[14] T1.4.2.43: 209; T1.4.2.48: 213; T1.4.2.56: 217.   [15] Paragraphs 3–15.

Hume also makes a distinction between what we can determine from the "object of the senses" itself, and what can be determined about it through "experience and observation":

The *independency* of our [sensory] perceptions on ourselves ... can never be *an object of the senses*; but any opinion we form concerning it, must be deriv'd from *experience and observation*: And we shall see afterwards, that our conclusions from experience are far from being favourable to the doctrine of the independency of our perceptions. (T1.4.2.10: 191; my emphasis)

In claiming that "independency" can never be an "object of the senses," he makes clear that the characteristics of sense impressions cannot be discovered simply through an inspection of the phenomena. Rather, we must use "experience and observation," as he does in the experiments which he anticipates in this passage. There is clearly more to our sense impressions, than what we can ever determine by simple inspection of them. Hume is not what philosophers call a 'phenomenalist.'

Hume also presents "three ... considerations" to show that something more than the impressions of the senses is needed "to convince us of the external existence of body" (T1.4.2.9: 190–1). First, he asserts that what I actually "perceive," when I "regard" my legs and arms is not my legs and arms "but certain impressions, which enter by the senses."[16] In other words, I don't perceive the parts of my body as they actually exist in space, but as they exist my mind. Secondly, he appeals to the fact that "sounds, and tastes, and smells, tho' commonly regarded by the mind as continu'd independent qualities, appear not to have any existence in extension, and consequently cannot appear to the senses as situated externally to the body." His point is that sensory impressions such as sounds, while we consider them to exist externally and at a distance from us, are not presented to our senses that way. In themselves they have no spatial qualities and it is only by associating them with sight and touch that we ascribe spatial location to them.[17] Thirdly, Hume appeals to writers on the theory of vision who argue that "even our sight informs us not of distance and

---

[16] Cf. Malebranche, *Search after Truth*, pp. 572–3.

[17] Cf. Locke, ECHU 2.13.24. Locke is arguing against the Cartesians who think that "they cannot imagine any sensible Quality of any Body, without extension." Hume's explanation of why we consider them external is given at T1.4.5.11–14.

outness (so to speak) immediately and without a certain reasoning and experience." Hume's words "distance and outness" echo those of Malebranche[18] and Berkeley. In his *Principles of Human Knowledge* Berkeley stated that "*distance* or outness" is not "immediately of it self perceived by sight," a point he had defended at length in his *Essay Towards a New Theory of Vision*.[19]

ii) We have no legitimate idea of body

The implications of Hume's denial that the senses are the source of our belief in independent existence are profound. They establish that any subsequent judgment of the independent and continued existence of objects must contain a certain internal incoherence. According to his *copy principle*, every idea is derived from a corresponding impression and can only represent that impression from which it is derived (T1.1.1.7: 4). But the upshot of Hume's argument that the senses cannot be the source of the belief in independent existence is that all our sensory *impressions*, including those of sight and touch, are internal and dependent. How then can we ever form an *idea* of what is external and independent? Given Hume's theory of ideas and the results of his "experiments," it follows that any legitimate idea can only represent what is internal and dependent. It is impossible ever to have a fully coherent idea of external and independent existence.

Hume faces a problem here which he did not have in the case of the origin of our belief in objective necessity in Part 3. For while he argued there that we have no idea of objective necessary connection, he clearly characterized what it would be like to have such an idea. He described what he was looking for, and explained what our knowledge would be like if we had it.[20] However, here, in the case of the independent existence of body, we have no separate way of specifying what it would be like to have such an idea. We can only have an incoherent grasp of the meaning of independent existence through the processes of the imagination which Hume goes on to describe. We need always to recognize that, no matter how successful his explanation, it can never succeed in giving us a clear and distinct

---

[18] *Search after Truth*, p. 572.   [19] *Principles*, I, 43.
[20] See pp. 124–5 above; cf. Kail, *Projection and Realism in Hume's Philosophy*, esp. pp. 34–5.

understanding of what it is to judge that an object exists independently of us.

It may be thought that since Hume goes on to explain how the imagination generates the belief in the *continued* unperceived existence of body, this notion has a greater legitimacy than that of *independent* existence. But a little reflection will convince us that that is incorrect. There can be no impression of continued unperceived existence, and therefore no legitimate idea of it. Hume writes in the third paragraph of Section 2 that our senses "are incapable of giving rise to the notion of the *continu'd* existence of their objects, after they no longer appear to the senses. For that is a contradiction in terms, and supposes that the senses continue to operate, even after they have ceas'd all manner of operation" (T1.4.2.3: 188). There is no other plausible source of such an impression and Hume never suggests one. The belief in continued existence must be formed by some kind of confusion of ideas.

Perhaps such an idea can arise through *reason*? Apart from Hume's general view that no original ideas can arise from reason, he presents specific arguments why this idea of distinct existence cannot arise from that source. First, even if philosophers produced good arguments "to establish the belief of objects independent of the mind," they would not be known to ordinary people who falsely "attribute a distinct continu'd existence to the very things they feel or see" (T1.4.2.14: 193). Secondly, the only way that reason could establish the belief in an independent external object would be to *prove* that such an object is the *cause* of our sensory perceptions. But as Hume showed in Part 3, a relation of cause and effect can only be established through the past experience of a constant conjunction between the two. In this case such an experience is impossible because we never observe the independent object – only the dependent sensory perception. Hence we can never draw a legitimate inference from the existence of latter to the existence of the former (T1.4.2.47: 212).

It is worth noting that Hume rejects a plausible account of the origin of the idea of the independent operation of bodies which Descartes presented in the course of his proof of the existence of bodies in his sixth *Meditation*. In that proof Descartes concluded from the fact that his sensory ideas "are produced without [his] ... cooperation and often against [his] ... will" that there must be "an active faculty ... in another substance distinct from [him]" (CSM II, 55). In other words, the idea of the independence of an object acting on us comes from the recognition that our will lacks control over our sensory ideas. However, Hume argues that "our pains and pleasures, our passions and affections, which we never suppose to have any existence beyond our perception ... are equally involuntary, as the impressions of figure and extension ..." – those to which Descartes ascribed an external and independent existence (T1.4.2.16: 194). Thus, it cannot be "the involuntariness of certain impressions, as is commonly suppos'd, nor ... their superior force and violence" which makes us ascribe to them an independent existence.[21]

iii) Constancy and coherence

For all Hume's assertions that the belief in body does not arise from the senses, he thinks the way objects appear to the senses is still key to understanding the workings of the imagination which do generate that belief. He identifies two characteristics of sensory impressions – or rather sequences of such impressions[22] – which, when reflected on by the imagination generate the belief in body – *constancy* and *coherence*. These characteristics, he claims, are not exhibited by 'internal' impressions such as pains, pleasures, and passions.

He calls sensory impressions *constant* when they repeat themselves in similar patterns after an interruption in observation. He looks at the "mountains, and houses, and trees" outside his window, looks away, and then looks back again: they "return upon [him] without the least alteration" (T1.4.2.18: 194). Or rather, to be more precise, *another* sensory impression appears to him which exactly resembles the earlier one. For, as the "experiments" such as pressing the eyeball have taught us, our sensory impressions are "interrupted, and perishing, and different at every return" (T1.4.2.46: 211). The first

---

[21] This is not the place to defend the Cartesian account of the origin of our idea of an independent existence. I will only suggest that for Descartes our pains and passions no less than our sensory perceptions give us the idea of a substance independent of our own minds which is acting on us.

[22] Cf. Donald Baxter, "Identity, Continued Existence, and the External World," in *The Blackwell Guide to Hume's Treatise*, ed. Saul Traiger (Oxford: Blackwell, 2006), pp. 114–32, p. 119.

impression of the scene outside his window ceases to exist as soon as he looks away, and then when he looks back a new one appears.

There is a further characteristic of "constant" impressions which becomes important as his exposition proceeds: during continuous observation they do not change. Hume can observe those mountains, houses, and trees for some time without interruption, and the impression itself will remain unchanging and uninterrupted. This is clear from the first stage of Hume's explanation of the origin of the belief in body which we will consider on page 147 below.

Hume calls impressions *coherent* when they change in regular ways indicating a dependence of one object on another:

This constancy, however, is not so perfect as not to admit of very considerable exceptions. Bodies often change their position and qualities, and after a little absence or interruption may become hardly knowable. But ... in these changes they preserve a *coherence*, and have a regular dependence on each other ... (T1.4.2.19: 195)

He gives as an example the impressions he has of the fire burning down in his fireplace which appear in a similar order whether he is continuously present in the room observing them, or goes out and comes back again. He interprets this as a "regular dependence" of the sequential parts of the fire on each other.

iv) Imagination as the source of belief in body: coherence and the mental inertia principle

The belief in the continued and distinct existence of body arises from the imagination – that is, the association of ideas. The imagination leads us to believe that our sensory perceptions themselves are external objects. It is the source of the natural direct realism that we adopt in our everyday lives. According to Hume, we naturally believe that our sense perceptions themselves are external and independent objects which continue to exist when we cease to perceive them. He writes that "tho' this opinion be false, 'tis the most natural of any" (T1.4.2.48: 213).

He postulates two principles of the imagination which make us believe in the existence of unperceived objects – or what are really unperceived perceptions. The first principle which he postulates is a principle of *mental inertia*[23] which extends the regularity of our sense impressions beyond their appearance. He states the principle as follows: "the imagination, when set into any train of thinking, is apt to continue, even when its object fails it, and like a galley put in motion by the oars, carries on its course without any new impulse" (T1.4.2.22: 198). This principle causes us to ascribe a greater regularity to our *coherent* sense impressions than we actually observe through our senses. When Hume hears the hinges of the door to his room squeak without observing the opening of the door, he naturally supposes the existence of the unobserved door; and when, a moment later, he sees the porter coming toward him with a letter he naturally supposes the unobserved existence of the stairs which allowed the porter to rise to the second floor of the house. These suppositions avoid a "contradiction to all past experience" (T1.4.2.20: 196). By supposing the existence of these unperceived objects which have been regularly associated with the objects when he directly observes them, he constructs a richer world than that given to him by his past sense impressions. He refers to the reasoning caused by the principle of mental inertia as an "irregular kind of reasoning from experience" through which we "discover a connexion ... betwixt objects, which extends not to impressions" (T1.4.5.20: 242).

However, he does not regard the principle of mental inertia as sufficient by itself to generate the belief in the external existence of body. He writes that it is "too weak to support alone so vast an edifice, as is that of the continu'd existence of all external bodies" (T1.4.2.23: 198–9). He is not explicit about why he considers the principle to be weak, but the answer may be implicit in his whole account. He considers the principle of inertia to be directly contrary to the principle of custom and habit, the most powerful principle of the human mind. He writes that "to consider these phaenomena of the porter and the letter in a certain light, they are contradictions to common experience, and may be regarded as objections to those maxims, which we form concerning the connexions of causes and effects" (T1.4.2.20: 196). The principle of mental inertia works in opposition to the rules of cause and effect in making us believe in

[23] The principle was given this name by H. H. Price, in *Hume's Theory of the External World* (Oxford: Clarendon Press, 1940), pp. 54–5. The principle is called "custom and galley" by Louis Loeb in *Stability and Justification in Hume's Treatise* (Oxford University Press, 2002).

a greater regularity than we actually observe. In the case of direct observation, whenever we hear a squeak without its being preceded by the impression of a door opening, we weaken our belief that the opening of the door is the cause of the squeak. However, the principle of mental inertia works in the opposite manner, increasing our belief in the unperceived existence of the object (the door opening) just when it fails to accompany the object which we observe (the squeak).[24]

Hume does not appear to place much faith in the principle of *mental inertia* and in fact his appeal to it appears rather *ad hoc*. He does refer back to a discussion in Part 2 of Book 1 where he employed the principle to explain why, in mathematics, "after considering several loose standards of equality, and correcting them by each other, we proceed to imagine ... [an] exact standard."[25] But the principle does not play any role in other major topics of the *Treatise*.

But even if we were to admit that the *mental inertia* principle is not *ad hoc*, and it really does supplement custom and habit in making us judge that there is a regular conjunction of objects which goes beyond what can be observed, the question still arises whether it can generate the kind of belief in independent existence which Hume is looking for. There is as much reason to say it generates the kind of hypothetical view of external existence proposed by Berkeley. Berkeley held that when we speak of things existing unperceived this really means that *if* we were present to them *then* we would perceive them: "If I were out of my study I should say ... [the table I write on] existed, meaning thereby that if I was in my study I might perceive it, or that some other spirit actually does perceive it" (*Principles* I,3: 42). Unperceived existence is really hypothetical perception (or God's perception). This is hardly the robust judgment of continued unperceived independent existence which Hume sought. Perhaps this is the reason why he considered the principle of mental inertia to be "too weak to support alone so vast an edifice, as is that of the continu'd existence of all external bodies."

---

[24] For a very different view of Hume's analysis of the role of the relations of custom and the inertial principle; see Loeb, *Stability and Justification in Hume's Treatise*, esp. Chapters V and VI. Rather than seeing custom and mental inertia in conflict Loeb argues that they co-operate with each other in producing the belief in the unperceived object.

[25] T1.4.2.22: 198. Hume's reference is back to T1.2.4: the relevant paragraph is T1.2.4.25: 49.

v) Imagination as the source of belief in body: constancy and the identity substitution principle

The basic principle of the imagination which Hume postulates to account for our belief in the continued and independent existence of body is based on the *constancy* of the sense perceptions – the fact that they appear in resembling patterns after a break in observation, and that during continuous observation they do not change. The principle involves an association of ideas whereby the mind systematically mistakes *resemblance* for *identity*: "resemblance is the cause of the confusion and mistake, and makes us *substitute* the notion of identity, instead of that of related objects" (T1.4.6.6: 254; my emphasis). This is what I call the *identity substitution* principle. Because of its wide range of application in producing the belief in material substances (§3) and personal identity (§4), and the fact that it is an instance of a more general principle which causes us to mistake any relation for any other, it does not suffer from the fault of being *ad hoc* which infects the principle of *mental inertia*. Hume writes that it is "constancy … [which] has the most considerable effect" in making us believe in the unperceived and continued existence of the objects of our senses (T1.4.2.56: 217).

Hume divides his account of the effects of constancy in making us believe in an unperceived object into four parts (T1.4.2.25: 199–200). In the first place, he explains how we come to think of any sense perception as identical under conditions of continuous observation. He gives an account of what he later calls "perfect identity." Secondly, he explains how the *identity substitution* principle leads us through conflicting beliefs to ascribe an identity to interrupted resembling perceptions. Thirdly, he explains that we postulate the *fiction* of an unperceived perception and how we think of it as disappearing from and reappearing to the mind without undergoing any essential change. Fourthly, he explains the source of the vivacity which makes us believe in this *fiction*.

Before running through all the steps of his account, Hume reminds his reader that the view he seeks to explain is that of "the vulgar," that is, of common sense which makes no distinction between perceptions and external objects (T1.4.2.31: 202). He says that in giving his explanation he supposes with common sense "that there is only a single existence, which I shall call indifferently *object* or *perception* … understanding by both of them what any common man means by a hat, or shoe, or stone, or any other impression, convey'd to him by his senses." This switching between the terms *object* and *perception* engenders a certain kind of ambiguity in the next fourteen paragraphs, but it is a systematic ambiguity which Hume thinks necessary to explain the reasoning processes of common sense. We need to keep in mind that his main point is that in our ordinary lives we never think about the real nature of our sensory perceptions: we never treat them as mind-dependent existences and make no distinction between what is perceived and the act of perceiving itself.

In the *first stage* of his account Hume identifies our most basic apprehension of identity as involving a confused idea or "fiction of the imagination" (T1.4.2.29: 200–1). He considers the case where one simply contemplates an unchanging object, such as the mountain outside of his window. He notes that the perception of the mountain by itself won't give us the idea of identity because it itself gives us no idea of time or multiplicity. To get the idea of time we must think of changing perceptions, for example the background of our changing inner thoughts as we stare at the mountain. Suppose that while he is contemplating the mountain out of his window Hume thinks of writing his friend Michael, then of going out to buy a new pen, then of the pastry shop beside the stationery store, and then of a rich chocolate éclair. This change of ideas accompanies his contemplation of the unchanging mountain and allows him to suppose it "to participate of the changes of the co-existent objects, and in particular that of [his] perceptions." This thought is technically called a "fiction" because he is using ideas (the succession of his thoughts) to represent an impression (the unchanging mountain) other than that "from which they are deriv'd" (T1.2.3.11: 37).[26] However, in later discussions he disregards this incoherence at the heart of what he calls "perfect identity" (T1.4.2.33: 203), and even allows that "we have a distinct idea of an object, that remains invariable and uninterrupted thro' a suppos'd variation of time" (T1.4.6.6: 253).

---

[26] "Ideas always represent the objects or impressions, from which they are deriv'd, and can never without a fiction represent or be apply'd to any other."

In the *second stage* he employs the *identity substitution* principle in order to explain "the source of the error and deception with regard to identity" in those cases where sense perceptions are interrupted (T1.4.2.32: 202). He judges that he is looking at the numerically identical mountain every time he looks out of his window, even though there is a long gap in his observation of these resembling perceptions. "This resemblance is observ'd in a thousand instances, and naturally connects together our ideas of these interrupted perceptions by the strongest relation, and conveys the mind with an easy transition from one to another" (T1.4.2.35: 204). He argues that the act of the mind when he thinks of the discontinuous but resembling perceptions of the mountain is so like the action of the mind when he thinks of a continuous unchanging perception of the mountain that he substitutes the idea of the second for the first. "The passage betwixt related ideas is … so smooth and easy, that it … seems like the continuation of the same action" of the mind (T1.4.2.34: 204). Since we have the same kind of feeling when we contemplate the two kinds of perception, we think of the resembling but interrupted perceptions of the mountain as one and the same continuous perception of the mountain.

Hume refers back to his psychophysiological account of the association of ideas which he gave in Part 2 in order to explain this tendency of the mind to mistake resembling ideas for identical ones (T1.4.2.32n: 202). When we reflect on the resemblance, the "animal spirits" get misdirected into contiguous brain traces and "present other related ideas in lieu of that which the mind desir'd at first to survey" (T1.2.5.20: 60–1). This happens unconsciously and the mind makes "use of the related idea, which is presented to us" instead of the idea it originally sought. In the case at hand, the resembling sequence of sense impressions gets mistaken for an identical uninterrupted one.

We are then involved in a "contradiction" between the way the objects appear to us and the way they are conceived by way of the *identity substitution* principle (T1.4.2.36: 205). At the *third stage* the resulting "uneasiness" (T1.4.2.37: 206) is resolved by "the fiction of a continu'd existence" (T1.4.2.36: 205 and T1.4.2.43: 209). We embrace the notion that the resembling perceptions are identical by postulating a continuing being which links them, and which exists while they are unperceived. He writes that "we disguise, as much as possible, the interruption, or rather remove it entirely, by supposing that these interrupted perceptions are connected by a real existence, of which we are insensible" (T1.4.2.24: 199).

In order to explain how we can think of perceptions as existing while unperceived Hume appeals to the conception of the mind as "a heap or collection of different perceptions, united together by certain relations, and suppos'd, tho' falsely, to be endow'd with a perfect simplicity and identity" (T1.4.2.39: 207). Since this is what the mind is, he can naturally think of the mountain outside his window as both a *perception* and an *object*. As a *perception* it is considered as part of the heap of related perceptions which constitute his mind. It is a 'seeing of a mountain,' which may cause him in the next few moments a feeling of awe, a memory of mountains at home in Scotland, and a feeling of homesickness. But at the same time it is regarded as an *object*, a mountain, which may leave the collection of his perceptions which constitutes his mind when he turns his head. And when it does so, it will go on existing without being part of his mind until he looks back out of the window. Hume writes that "if the name of *perception* renders not this separation from a mind absurd and contradictory, the name of *object*, standing for the very same thing, can never render their conjunction [with a mind] impossible" (T1.4.2.40: 207). The mountain can come back and join the collection of his perceptions without itself undergoing any change in its intrinsic nature.

Hume is here anticipating the account of the mind which he develops in Section 6 of Part 4, "Of personal identity."[27] He is using that account to explain the common sense view of the external world. Unlike the philosopher, common sense does not regard sense perceptions as dependent on the brain, or on an immaterial mind. Since the mind just is a collection of distinct perceptions, any one of which can exist separately from the others, so there is no contradiction in thinking of some perceptions – mountains, houses, trees, doors, and human bodies – as existing unperceived. This does not mean that common sense adopts Hume's 'bundle theory' of the mind; merely that that theory accounts for the fact that these perceptions can be thought to exist independently of what common sense unreflectively takes a mind to be.

---

[27] §4 ii), pp. 160ff. below.

In the *fourth and final stage* of his account, Hume explains how we come not just to form the fiction of the unperceived perception, but actually *believe* in its existence. Since the "propensity to feign the continu'd existence of all sensible objects ... arises from some lively impressions of the memory, it bestows a vivacity on ... [the] fiction" of the continued existence of the unperceived object (T1.4.2.42: 209). The force and vivacity of Hume's memories of the interrupted but resembling perceptions of the mountain outside his window are transferred to the fiction he forms of its unperceived existence, and this is what makes him actually believe it.

Finally, at the end of this account Hume reminds us that while he has explained how the imagination directly generates the belief in the *continued existence* of body, the belief in its "*distinct* or *independent* existence ... follows ... as a necessary consequence*" (T1.4.2.44: 210). Body or matter is not thought of as the distinct unperceived cause of our sense perceptions (as on the indirect realist theory); rather the sense perceptions (which constitute matter) are thought to exist independently of the mind or soul when they cease to be perceived.

vi) *The primacy of common sense belief: it is not a "natural belief" as defined by Kemp Smith*

This primary or original belief in continued and independent existence generated by the imagination has, along with the belief in necessary connection of Part 3, been called a "natural belief" by Norman Kemp Smith in his influential book *The Philosophy of David Hume*[28] – and this label is still commonly used by Hume scholars. However, it is not always understood that Kemp Smith meant something very special when he used the term 'belief' in this context. He wrote that belief here is "more than, and other than, any mere enlivening. It is a quite distinctive *attitude* of mind. It carries the mind beyond its immediately experienced perishing states – in sense-perception to independently existing bodies" (p. 444). Kemp Smith placed great

---

[28] "Natural belief takes two forms, as belief in continuing and therefore independent existence, and as belief in causal dependence," (Norman Kemp Smith, *The Philosophy of David Hume*, p. 455); see my "Kemp Smith and the two kinds of Naturalism in Hume's Philosophy," in *New Essays on David Hume*, eds. Emanuele Ronchetti and Emilio Mazza, (Milan: FrancoAngeli, 2007), pp. 17–36.

weight on the claim that the common sense belief is primary and original, and claimed that for this reason it was beyond skeptical doubt. He tied up this special status of the common sense belief in body with a claim that it is "a kind of instinct" – a concept Hume only uses once in his *Treatise* account of the common sense belief in body (T1.4.2.51: 214), but went on to form the basis of the corresponding account in his first *Enquiry* (EHU 12.10, 14 and 16).

It is important to realize that Hume gives no such special cognitive status to his account of vulgar or common sense belief in body, at least in the *Treatise*. It is *primary* only in the sense that it is the origin of our belief in body, and that any further belief in body – such as that of philosophers – must rely on it, while correcting it. Throughout his account of the genesis of the belief based on constancy Hume stresses its falsity. It is not merely shown to be false by the "experiments" which he goes on to present after explaining the origin of the belief (T1.4.2.45: 210), but it contains an internal inconsistency as well. Constancy has "the most considerable effect" in generating the belief in continued and independent existence, and it "is attended with the greatest difficulties" (T1.4.2.56: 217). The difficulty which he goes on to describe is that connected with the *identity substitution* principle: "'tis a gross illusion to suppose, that our resembling perceptions are numerically the same; and 'tis this illusion, which leads us into the opinion, that these perceptions are uninterrupted, and are still existent, even when they are not present to the senses." It is through the illusion of *identity substitution* that we superimpose the idea of an identical object which lasts without change on to a series of interrupted resembling objects, and generate the belief in a continued and independent existence. As we saw in §2 (pp. 140–2), Hume has clearly rejected the possibility of generating a belief in body through a genuine impression-derived idea.

vii) The "double existence" view of philosophers, or indirect realism

The "experiments" which we considered on pp. 137–40 above are performed by philosophers who discover the mind or brain dependence of our sensory experiments. Hume says that "the natural consequence of this reasoning" is that philosophers reject the independent existence of the sensory perceptions and "distinguish, (as we shall do in the future) betwixt perceptions and objects" (T1.4.2.46: 211). Like other philosophers, Hume distinguishes between dependent sensory perceptions and independent external objects. When Hume turns away from the window and no longer sees the mountain, 'the seeing of the mountain' no longer exists: it is a "perishing" thing; and every time he looks out of his window subsequently there is a new 'seeing of the mountain' which is "different at every return." He conceives of the continually existing mountain, of which the two perishing instances of 'the seeing of the mountain' are representations, as numerically different from his sensory perceptions of it. This is the theory of "double existence of perceptions and objects" adopted by philosophers, including Hume himself.

Hume then proceeds with his skeptical critique of this philosophical system, *not*, it must be stressed, on grounds of its falsity (it corrects the mistake of common sense regarding the independence of sensory perceptions), but rather on grounds that it cannot be independently verified by reason, and it relies on imagination to generate the basic belief in continued and independent existence. He writes that it has no "*primary recommendation, either to reason or the imagination*" (T1.4.2.47: 212). For firstly, as we have already seen on page 141, he argues there is no way to independently prove the existence of the external object (the mountain) by inferring that it is the cause of the sensory perceptions which represent it. Secondly, the fundamental belief that there exists a continually existing object (the mountain) which exists between the different sightings of it is borrowed from the misleading mechanisms of the imagination, and in that sense it inherits the difficulties of the system of common sense. Thirdly, on the philosophical view which Hume examines in Section 2, the philosopher thinks of the distinct external object (the mountain) as *resembling* his perceptions. (But see pp. 153–5 below.) Philosophers "arbitrarily invent a new set of perceptions" to which they ascribe the qualities of continued and independent existence (T1.4.2.56: 218). While numerically distinct, the mountain is generally thought to have the same shape and color as one's sense perceptions of it. Hume offers two further principles of the imagination to account for this fact that philosophers ordinarily think of the independent object as resembling their sensory perceptions (T1.4.2.54–5: 216–17).

This theory of double existence generally adopted by philosophers is characterized by Hume as "the monstrous offspring of two principles," namely, reason and imagination (T1.4.2.52: 215). Reason shows us that our sensory perceptions are mind-dependent. But it is only because of our original imagination-generated belief in their continued existence that we now postulate an independent object which causes them. And it is only because of a further principle of the imagination that we consider the independent objects which cause our sensory perceptions to resemble them.

In spite of this skeptical critique, Hume clearly accepts the truth of what philosophers today call indirect realism. In Section 2 of Part 4 he notes that he himself adopts the double existence view throughout the *Treatise, except for* the fifteen paragraphs in which he explains the origin of the direct realist view of common sense (see T1.4.2.31: 202 and T1.4.2.46: 211). As we saw in Chapter 2,[29] in the section entitled "Of existence and external existence" at the end of Part 2 of Book 1, he clearly distinguishes between perceptions and external objects. Even more succinctly, in Section 5 of Part 4 he writes that "the most vulgar philosophy informs us, that no external object can make itself known to the mind immediately, and without the interposition of an image or perception" (T1.4.5.15: 239).

viii) Skepticism concerning the modern philosophy

When Hume considers the "double existence" view of philosophers in Section 2, he assumes that philosophers think of the independent objects as entirely *resembling* the perceptions which represent them. But that is *not* the theoretical view adopted by modern science, beginning with Galileo and further developed by thinkers such as Descartes, Boyle and Locke. Hume discusses this view in Section 4 of Part 4 under the title "Of the modern philosophy." "The fundamental principle of that philosophy" is that "colours, sounds, tastes, smells, heat and cold" are "nothing but impressions in the mind, deriv'd from the operation of external objects, and without any resemblance to the qualities of the objects" (T1.4.4.3: 226). It is only the impressions of primary qualities such as motion, extension,

---

[29] Chapter 2, pp. 58–60.

shape and solidity which resemble the causes in the objects used in physical explanations. Hume argues that the modern philosophy gives rise to an even deeper skepticism concerning the senses than that which he considered in Section 2. Indeed it is the discussion in this Section which gives rise to the first of the manifest contradictions which Hume cites in the Conclusion to Book 1.

Hume thinks that the fundamental principle of modern philosophy is based on an argument from cause and effect.[30] He writes that "when different impressions of the same sense arise from any object, every one of these impressions has not a resembling quality existent in the object" (T1.4.4.4: 227). He cites phenomena like the different tastes of food when we are sick and in good health, different colors reflected from objects resulting from varying distance and perspective, etc. When the same object causes us to have these contrary impressions then the causes of these impressions cannot resemble them. Hume concludes more generally that all impressions of taste, color, sound, etc. – impressions of what Locke called secondary qualities – must "arise from causes, which noways resemble them" (T1.4.4.4: 227). From this argument it is a short step to conclude that these causes must consist only of the "primary qualities" of "extension and solidity, with their different mixtures and modifications" (T1.4.4.5: 227).

Hume then follows Berkeley (*Principles* I, 9–10: 44–5) in arguing that these so-called primary qualities cannot be conceived without the secondary ones. One cannot think of something extended which does not consist of colored or felt parts; "solidity or impenetrability" cannot be conceived "without having recourse to the secondary and sensible qualities" (T1.4.4.11: 229–30). But when we exclude these latter qualities "there remains nothing in the universe" with "a continu'd and independent existence" (T1.2.4.15: 231).

In Berkeley's philosophy that is the end of *matter*, that is of objects which exist independently of the perceiver. But Hume's point is very different. In the present section he says that this argument leads to "the most extravagant scepticism" (T1.4.4.6: 228). In the first *Enquiry*,

---

[30] This is historically inaccurate. Galileo and Locke's arguments are clearly based on what they consider to be questions of conceivability; see Galileo's *Assayer*, in *The Discoveries and Opinions of Galileo*, ed. & trans. Stillman Drake (New York: Anchor Books, 1957), p. 274 and Locke, ECHU 2.8, esp. §§ 9–10, 15 & 21.

after attributing the argument to Berkeley, he calls it "merely skeptical" and says it "produce[s] no conviction" (EHU 12.15n32). In Book 3 of the *Treatise* (published after Books 1 and 2) he writes of the view that colors, etc. "are not qualities in objects . . . as a considerable advancement of the speculative sciences; tho' it has little or no influence on practice" (T3.1.1.26: 469).[31] He acknowledges the theoretical value in physics of thinking of causes in terms of primary qualities.

But how can the notion of matter of modern philosophy have any place in physics if we have no genuine idea of it? If one holds that all beliefs for Hume are limited to genuine impression-derived ideas, then the problem is intractable. However, we have seen that the same problem arises both in the case of belief in causality (Chapter 3, pp. 120ff.) and in the case of belief in independent existence (pp. 140–2 above). We must be able to "suppose in general" the existence of what we cannot distinctly conceive (T1.4.2.56: 218; cf. T1.4.5.20: 241–2 and T1.2.6.9: 68). We must be able to think in general terms of external objects as having a nature different from that of our perceptions (Chapter 2, pp. 58–60 and 73–4).

Hume takes a purely skeptical lesson from Berkeley's argument. It shows that it is impossible "for us to reason justly and regularly from causes and effects, and at the same time believe in the continu'd existence of matter" (T1.4.7.4: 266). It is this conflict of two necessary principles of the imagination which, as we have seen, Hume uses to generate the total skepticism which he appeals to in the Conclusion to Book 1.

ix) *Skepticism and the inevitability of belief in the senses*

It is still another question whether, after all these skeptical arguments Hume can actually doubt the existence of external objects like the mountains, houses, and trees outside his window. In fact, he writes that this doubt "has been peculiar to a few extravagant sceptics; who after all maintain'd that opinion in words only, and were never able to bring themselves sincerely to believe it" (T1.4.2.50: 214). As we have just seen, after presenting Berkeley's critique of the modern philosophy in his first *Enquiry*, he identifies him as a skeptic of just this kind.

---

[31] See Chapter 8, §7, pp. 248ff.

And yet in the final paragraphs of Section 2, Hume himself admits, however briefly, to such a doubt with regard to his senses. He writes that while he began by "premising ... that we ought to have an implicit faith in our senses," he feels "*at present* of a quite contrary sentiment" and is "inclin'd to repose no faith at all in [his] senses" (T1.4.2.56: 217). It seems that even though he cannot doubt the belief in his senses for any extended time, he still can doubt it while he is in his study, thinking about it. And this doubt is not simply based on the fact that he cannot find "any arguments of philosophy to maintain its veracity." Rather it is based on his discovery that the belief arises from "trivial qualities of the fancy, conducted by ... false suppositions." Hume's temporary doubt arises from the discovery that the imagination makes us suppose falsely that our distinct perceptions are really numerically identical.

But that doubt must leave him, and us, as soon as we leave the study. In the final paragraph of Section 2, Hume expresses confidence that however much his reader may presently be puzzled, "an hour hence he will be persuaded there is both an external and internal world." (T1.4.2.57: 218). Doubt cannot be cured by further explanation: "Carelessness and in-attention alone can afford us any remedy."

3. MATERIAL SUBSTANCE AND ARISTOTELIAN PHILOSOPHY

Hume argues that the *identity substitution* principle plays the fundamental role in our belief in external existence. He appeals to this principle again in his explanation of the belief in material substance in Section 3 of Part 4. But in this case, unlike the belief in the existence of body, there is no question of explaining a belief which is required for human survival. His aim is to study "the fictions of the antient philosophy" in order to uncover the principles of the operation of the imagination (T1.4.3.1: 219). And yet, as we shall see, by the end of this section it becomes clear that Hume holds that in our everyday common sense way of thinking we are susceptible to the same core illusion as the ancient philosophers.

Hume considers the appeal to a *substance* which underlies the different properties of a plant or animal to be unnecessary in science.

On his view, what we call a Monarch Butterfly, for example, is just a collection of qualities existing in sequence – an egg laid on a milkweed plant, a caterpillar with certain markings and feeding patterns, a chrysalis of a certain shape and color, a butterfly with very distinctive markings, etc. "We have," he writes, "no idea of substance, distinct from that of a collection of particular qualities" (T1.1.6.1: 16; cf. T1.4.3.2: 219). It is true that these qualities are closely related by "relations of contiguity and causality," and when we discover a new quality related to it in these ways – like that of the genome structure of the Monarch (to take an up-to-date scientific example) – we "immediately comprehend it among" the rest of the qualities, "even tho' it did not enter into ... [its] first conception" (T1.1.6.2: 16).

The ancient Aristotelian philosophy went beyond this legitimate idea of a particular natural kind of thing, and considered the collection of qualities to be "ONE [simple] thing" which continues "the SAME under very considerable alterations" (T1.4.6.2: 219). Hume's psychological explanation of the source of this fiction is as follows. We survey the series of qualities from two very different points of view. First, when we survey the continuous successive stages of an animal's history "the smooth and uninterrupted progress of the thought" is so like that of our conception of an unchanging object that we take it as one simple continuously existing thing (T1.4.3.3: 220). In this case we ascribe identity, not on the basis of interrupted resembling qualities as in the case of the belief in body, but on the basis of their very gradual continuous changes. But, just like the case of body, we mistake another relation for that of identity because of their similar influence on the mind. We overlook the gradual changes and regard the whole as one unchanging uninterrupted thing.

But we can also survey the series at two distinct periods of its existence, such as the butterfly stage and the caterpillar stage, and this seems "entirely to destroy the identity" (T1.4.3.4: 220). The result is a "contrariety in our method of thinking, from the different points of view, in which we survey the object." In order to reconcile the contrary views "the imagination is apt to feign something unknown and invisible, which it supposes to continue the same under all these variations" and it is to this "unintelligible something" that it gives the name "*substance*."

The Aristotelian philosophy also ascribes to each species of objects "a distinct *substantial form*, which it supposes to be the source of all those different qualities they possess, and to be a new foundation of simplicity and identity to each particular species" (T1.4.3.6: 221). This substantial form is an invisible essence which is supposed to be the source of the observed qualities of the species. Hume argues that through "custom" we associate the qualities with this fiction of a substantial form and believe that the one must always accompany the other (T1.4.5.7: 222). This leads to the further fictions of the Aristotelian philosophy, which involve no genuine understanding.

Hume goes on to distinguish this system of Aristotelian philosophers from that of both common sense (i.e. "the vulgar"), and what he calls the "true philosophy" (T1.4.5.9: 222). The true philosopher is the Humean who is satisfied with giving the natural history of the object and explaining the causal connections. But what is puzzling about this discussion is that Hume now appears to assume that common sense is as much inclined to ascribe the notion of substance as ancient philosophers. He writes that "'tis natural for men, in their common and careless way of thinking, to imagine they perceive a connexion betwixt such objects as they have constantly found united together; and because custom has render'd it difficult to separate the ideas, they are apt to fancy such a separation to be in itself impossible" (T1.4.5.9: 223). The objects which the vulgar imagine they perceive to be connected are the changing qualities of a plant or animal and the underlying simple and unchanging material substance. Hume writes of the "vulgar error, that there is a natural and perceivable connexion betwixt the several sensible qualities and actions of matter."

4. PERSONAL IDENTITY

i) *Understanding Hume's Problem*

When Hume comes to his discussion of personal identity in Section 6 of Part 4, it is clear that he believes that common sense is as susceptible to the *identity substitution* principle as ancient philosophers. It is not merely the latter who adopt the belief in a simple and identical self or soul; this is part of the natural thinking of every one of us. It is true that he begins his discussion by ascribing the belief to "some philosophers" who think we are "intimately conscious" of an underlying "SELF" which is endowed with "perfect identity and simplicity" (T1.4.6.1: 251). But as his account proceeds it becomes clear that the application of the *identity substitution* principle to form the notion of a simple identical self is universal. We all have the tendency to believe in a substantial self or soul which lasts throughout our lives. He insists that this tendency is not a mere artifact of language: "when we attribute identity . . . our mistake is not confin'd to the expression" (T1.4.6.7: 255). It is not, for example, just because we have the first person personal pronoun 'I' that we attribute all our perceptions to a simple identical substance; this and similar facts about our language are based on deep psychological principles.

Hume's central aim in his account of personal identity in Section 6 of Part 4, is to defend the thesis that the identity and simplicity which we naturally attribute to ourselves is really a "fiction" of the imagination (T1.4.6.6: 253–4).[32] He holds that there really is no substantial thing which constitutes "a *soul*, and *self*, and *substance*," or at least none with which we are acquainted. The identity which we ascribe to the self is like that which we ascribe to plants, animals, ships or republics whose parts are constantly being replaced by new ones, and are not single unchanging substantial things. It is the relation of the temporal parts and stages to one another which leads us, mistakenly, to ascribe a "perfect identity" to these items. Hume's goal is to explain the psychological process which makes us ascribe such a perfect identity to separate distinct perceptions which are actually constantly changing and are even interrupted by sleep.

It is important that we don't misunderstand the problem of personal identity which Hume is dealing with in this section. He is not *here* raising the question whether there is some continuity of character which manifests itself throughout our lives. Hume's other writings, including his Letter to a Physician and his later autobiography which we discussed in Chapter 1, show that he was quite convinced that there is such continuity of character. But continuity of character, even if it involved exact resemblance of character traits at different times of one's life, would not be "personal identity" in the sense he is using the term here. Theoretically two different persons, say identical

---

[32] Cf. T1.4.6.7: 254 and T1.4.6.21: 262.

twins brought up together, could share many or most character traits. But no matter how similar, they would still be numerically different persons. Hume's concern is with the belief that each of us is *numerically* identical, not *qualitatively* identical, throughout our lives. This is what he means when he says that his "present subject" in this section is with identity with regard to the imagination, rather than the passions (T1.4.6.5: 253). It is true that he argues that the latter kind of 'identity' *contributes* to the belief that we are a single self throughout our lives (T1.4.6.19: 261), but his concern in Book 1 is with the former kind of identity.

When we ascribe personal identity to a simple identical soul we attribute "invariableness" as well as "uninterruptedness" to it. (T1.4.6.7: 255). This single invariable soul can in principle vary its character – become 'reborn' as it were, and so turn from a vicious mean person who causes others untold harm to a kind loving person who improves the lives of her fellow beings.[33] That is to say that the "invariableness" which we ascribe to a simple identical soul underlying our perceptions need not manifest itself in outward characteristics. This is also true of the "uninterruptedness" which is ascribed to such a soul. We recognize that we go to sleep and have periods of unconsciousness. However, the soul or self we believe in involves an "uninterrupted existence" whether it is manifest or not (T1.4.6.5: 253).

ii) The Bundle Theory

In denying that there really is any such soul or substantial self, Hume makes the remarkable claim that each of us really is "nothing but a bundle or collection of different perceptions, which succeed each other with an inconceivable rapidity, and are in a perpetual flux and movement" (T1.4.6.4: 252–3). He draws an analogy between our minds and a theater, where perceptions are like actors who "successively make their appearance; pass, re-pass, glide away, and mingle in an infinite variety of postures and situations." He denies that there is anything simple and identical which combines the perceptions at any one time, or at successive times. He carefully notes the limits of

---

[33] *In fact*, Hume thinks that as adults it is almost impossible to vary our characters; see T3.3.4.3: 608 and Chapter 9, p. 274.

the analogy with a theater: "they are the successive perceptions only, that constitute the mind," and denies that we "have ... the most distant notion of the place, where these scenes are represented, or of the materials, of which [the mind] is compos'd."

There are two objections to what Hume says here which may immediately occur to us. First, it is true that when we go to a theater and see a play or a movie we are focused on the scene in front of us. But there must also be a single identical perceiver of all these scenes, namely oneself. One can compare the different scenes at intermission and think about their relevance to one another. *Doesn't one have to be really one and the same simple identical self to do that?* Secondly, after the play is over and the lights come on, one can see the walls and seats, examine the stage and props, and note the materials out of which they are constructed. *Isn't that like discovering that one's mind consists of a brain and that it contains neurons which when stimulated in a certain way will cause one to have certain perceptions?* What has happened to those animal spirits and organs of perception which Hume writes about in other parts of the *Treatise?* Do not these too constitute the mind?

To answer the first objection, let us consider the action of the self or mind when one reflects back at intermission and compares the different scenes of the play. There is no reason to think that this action consists of anything but a *new* complex perception which includes the act of comparison and memory perceptions of what one experienced earlier. What Hume calls a perception is simply an act of perceiving. "The mind can never exert itself in any action, which we may not comprehend under the term of *perception*" (T3.1.1.2: 456). He includes under the term perception, not only "the actions of seeing, hearing ... loving, [and] hating" but also of "judging" and "thinking." The act of judgment whereby we compare our memories of the different scenes of the play is nothing but *a new perception.*

Secondly, when Hume says that mind is constituted by perceptions this does not mean that the perceptions themselves are taken for what they really are. It is clear, as we saw on page 137, that Hume holds that in everyday life we take our sensory perceptions to be independent external objects when they are really dependent on our nerves and animal spirits. There is nothing in Hume's philosophy which commits him to the view that our perceptions are entirely perspicuous – though many have interpreted him this way. We have seen that he writes of ideas as being located in cells in the brain.[34] Also, he thinks that there is strong evidence that all perceptions are caused by matter in motion.[35] In saying that the mind is constituted by its perceptions, he is not saying that we are immediately aware of everything that a perception is.

This second answer, I think, goes only part way in meeting the objection.[36] Even with the clarifications of the last paragraph, it seems that Hume himself often attributes more to the mind than perceptions. For example, he writes of "the organs of the human mind" as having a "certain disposition fitted to produce a peculiar impression or emotion" (T2.1.5.6: 287) and that the mind "has certain organs naturally fitted to produce a passion" (T2.2.11.6: 396). If the mind has organs, doesn't it have to consist of more than perceptions? And how exactly are we to understand Hume's talk of "a faculty, which nature has ... implanted in the mind" (T1.4.1.7: 183) which makes us believe in spite of his skeptical arguments? Also, if we include Hume's references to the 'self' and to 'soul' as well as 'mind' we will find many other passages in which it is difficult to read these items as *mere* collections of different perceptions.

iii) Explanation of the belief in personal identity

But however we read these passages we must recognize that Hume's goal is to explain our belief that we consist in a single simple unchanging substance when we are really a multiplicity of changing parts. He holds that there are two relations which cause us to ascribe an identity to ourselves when we reflect over our past perceptions. The first is the *resemblance* which results from the repetition of our past experiences in memory. He writes that one "always preserves the memory of a considerable part of past perceptions" and that it is this "frequent placing of these resembling perceptions in the chain of thought" which conveys "the imagination more easily from one

---

[34] Chapter 2 §4, p. 52.   [35] *Ibid.*, p. 57.
[36] See Robert F. Anderson, *Hume's First Principles* (Lincoln: University of Nebraska Press, 1966), esp. Part I.

link to another, and make[s] the whole seem like the continuance of one object" (T1.4.6.18: 260). As in the case of the belief in body, it is the easy transition of the imagination caused by the relation of resemblance which makes us think of ourselves as one invariable and uninterrupted being.

The second relation, which Hume thinks of as having an even greater influence than resemblance, is *causation*. He states that "the true idea of the human mind, is to consider it as a system of different perceptions ... which are link'd together by the relation of cause and effect, and mutually produce, destroy, influence, and modify each other" (T1.4.6.19: 261). It is such causal links between our perceptions which Hume began describing from the opening pages of Book 1 where he put forward the *copy principle*. He is arguing now that when we reflect back over these past causal links in memory we associate the perceptions so closely that we mistake the causal connections for an invariable and uninterrupted sequence. One perception brings about the existence of the next, and that of another. Using the analogy of a republic in which members, laws and constitutions give rise to new members, laws and constitutions, he argues that perceptions, character traits and dispositions give rise to new perceptions, character traits and dispositions. It is when we remember these causal connections of our past impressions that the smooth passage of the imagination from one mental state to the next leads us to mistake the causal sequence for an unchanging uninterrupted one, and to postulate the existence of the fiction of an unchanging uninterrupted soul. Once again, the *identity substitution* principle plays a decisive role.

iv) Second thoughts: the Appendix

It is this *explanation* of the belief in such an unchanging mental substance which came to dissatisfy Hume when he reconsidered his account of personal identity in the Appendix which he added to Book 3 of the *Treatise*. He writes that "having ... loosen'd all our particular perceptions, when I proceed to explain the principle of connexion, which binds them together, and makes us attribute to them a real simplicity and identity; I am sensible, that my account is very defective" (TApp 20: 635). Unfortunately, Hume never spells out clearly just what it is about his explanation which now dissatisfies him, and this has led to a variety of speculations among Hume scholars.[37]

It seems to be the *second* application of the *identity substitution* principle in producing the belief in personal identity which particularly troubles Hume – the substitution of identity when he reflects on the causal connections of his past perceptions. The problem appears to arise from his principle that "every distinct perception ... is a distinct existence" (T1.4.6.16: 259).[38] In his Appendix he states that if the mind did "perceive some real connexion among ... [perceptions], there wou'd be no difficulty in the case" (TApp 21: 636). He also writes that there would be no difficulty if our perceptions would "inhere in something simple and individual," but that solution seems a non-starter because it overturns everything he originally wrote against the idea of the mind as a simple unchanging substance. As we have seen, he does refer to the "true idea of the human mind" as involving causal links between its different perceptions (T1.4.6.19: 261), so the first suggestion seems the more plausible one. His central problem is that he has never perceived anything but a regular succession and contiguity between internal perceptions, and that does not provide a sufficient basis when we reflect on it to account for the substitution of identity for causality.

In the case of physical objects we ascribe causal connection to *objects* only on the basis of observation of the regular succession and contiguity of our distinct sensory *perceptions*. The perceptions themselves appear distinct, but as a result of the association of ideas and smooth transition from the impression of the one to the idea of the other we ascribe the necessary connection to the external objects which they represent.[39] But Hume's concern is now with the ascription of necessary connection to the perceptions themselves: it is difficult to explain how we could ever ascribe a connection to them since their apparent distinctness, he holds, indicates their actual distinctness, and precludes their being causally connected. The problem is one of explaining how we ascribe causal connection, and subsequently perfect identity, to our distinct internal perceptions.

[37] See Corliss Swain, "Personal Identity," in *The Blackwell Guide to Hume's Treatise*, ed. Saul Traiger (Oxford: Blackwell, 2006), pp. 132–50, esp. 141–7.
[38] See Chapter 2, §9 iii), pp. 76–7.
[39] Chapter 3 §8, pp. 122ff.

Hume states that there are two principles which are inconsistent and which he cannot reconcile, namely *"that all our distinct perceptions are distinct existences,* and *that the mind never perceives any real connexion among distinct existences"* (TApp 21: 636). These principles are not in themselves inconsistent, so he must mean that they are jointly inconsistent with a third, namely *the supposition* that there is a real connection between the perceptions themselves. He seems to think that the distinctness of perceptions should be so obvious that it should preclude the natural supposition of a causal connection between them. And yet he has assumed that causal connection in order to explain the further supposition that we have an uninterrupted and unchanging mind, self or soul.

In his original account in Section 6 of Part 4 of Book 1, Hume argued that the source of our natural supposition that we consist of an unchanging and uninterrupted mind or soul was the causal connection of our perceptions. In the Appendix he rehearses the steps of his argument which led him to the conclusion that our perceptions are distinct existences and are perceived as such, a conclusion which, he thinks, invalidates that explanation.

Like other commentators, I find it tempting to suggest a solution to Hume's problem, a solution which he himself did not propose. My own candidate is to drop the first of his principles, namely the principle that *"all our distinct perceptions are distinct existences"* (TApp 21: 636). Why not argue that internal perceptions give us no more insight into the separation of their (mental) objects than external perceptions? The fact that our internal perceptions appear to be distinct should give us no more insight into the distinctness of their objects than the same fact about external objects. The nature of the mind is unknown, just like the nature of external objects.[40]

Hume wrote at the beginning of Section 5 of Part 4 that "the intellectual world, tho' involv'd in infinite obscurities, is not perplex'd with any such contradictions, as those we have discover'd in the natural" (T1.4.5.1: 232). He retracts this claim at the beginning of his reconsideration of his account of personal identity in the Appendix, where he admits that he is "involv'd in such a labyrinth" that he admits that

---

[40] I first put forward this suggestion in "Hume, Descartes and the Materiality of the Soul," in *The Philosophical Canon in the 17th and 18th Centuries,* ed. G. A. J. Rogers, and Sylvana Tomaselli (Rochester: University of Rochester Press, 1996), pp. 175–90.

he neither knows "how to correct [his] former opinions, nor how to render them consistent" (TApp 10: 633). If the analysis given above is correct, he expects to find real causal connections among his perceptions themselves, and yet this is precluded by the two principles *"that all our perceptions are distinct existences, and that the mind never perceives any real connexion among distinct existences"* (TApp 21: 636).

In the Appendix, Hume writes that the difficulties he has run into in explaining the belief in personal identity have given him a "good *general* reason for scepticism" and "sufficient one ... for ... a diffidence and modesty" in all his decisions (TApp 10: 633). The problem he has encountered has, it seems, gone to the core of the theory of mind which he presents in Sections 5 and 6 of Part 4. It is significant then that in subsequent writings, including his first *Enquiry*, he makes no further attempt to explain personal identity; he also drops the principle that all our distinct perceptions are distinct existences. Indeed, the *identity substitution* principle, which plays such a central role in his explanations of our suppositions of external existence, material substrata, and immaterial souls, also makes no appearance in his later philosophy.

5. CONCLUSION: HUME'S ESCAPE FROM TOTAL SKEPTICISM

Nothing better characterizes Hume's escape from total skepticism in the Conclusion to Book 1 than his famous dictum that "reason is, and ought only to be the slave of the passions, and can never pretend to any other office than to serve and obey them" (T2.3.3.4: 415).[41] In the Conclusion, Hume writes that reason or philosophy "ought only to be assented to" where it is "lively, and mixes itself with some propensity" (T1.4.7.11: 270). From the context it is clear that by a "propensity" here he means a passion. He writes that where reason does not mix itself with some passion "it never can have any title to operate upon us."[42]

---

[41] See also Chapter 9, p. 268.

[42] Don Garrett has called this the "Title Principle" and argued that it provides Hume with an epistemic, and not merely a practical, "ought" to carry on with his philosophical studies ("Hume's Conclusions," in "Conclusions in 'Conclusion of this Book'," in *The Blackwell Guide to Hume's Treatise*, edited by Saul Traiger. Oxford: Blackwell, 2006, 151–76, esp. pp. 169–70).

He goes on to identify two passions which give him the right to carry on with his reasoned study of human nature – "curiosity and ambition" (T1.4.7.13: 271). *Curiosity*, or "the love of truth" is motivated by doubt, which he characterizes in Book 2 as the *uneasy* state wherein the mind moves restlessly from one idea to another, without settling on any one (T2.3.10.12: 453). In the Conclusion, Hume describes the state of doubt which leads him forward in his study of human nature as an *uneasiness* he has when he thinks about the problems he has not yet solved: "I am *uneasy* to think that I approve of one object, and disapprove of another; call one thing beautiful, and another deform'd; decide concerning truth and falshood, reason and folly, without knowing upon what principles I proceed" (T1.4.7.12: 271; my emphasis). This uneasiness will only be satisfied by discovering the causes of these moral, aesthetic and scientific judgments – or, at the very least, developing some fixed idea or belief concerning them.

Hume's *ambition* is to contribute to "the instruction of mankind" and to acquire "a name by my inventions and discoveries." He writes that if he were to give up his philosophical project he would "be a loser in point of pleasure" and he frankly admits that "this is the origin of [his] philosophy" (T1.4.7.12: 271). It is important to realize that Hume is only using himself as a kind of case study in identifying *curiosity* and *ambition* as justifying any scientific activity. While he puts his point in purely personal terms, he is clearly formulating the justifications of any scientific inquirer. Curiosity and ambition are, according to Hume, both necessary and sufficient conditions of any scientific inquiry.

It is sometimes said that Hume thinks our only escape from Pyrrhonian or excessive skepticism is to simply follow the natural judgments of common life – those which make us believe, for example, "that fire warms, or water refreshes" (T1.4.7.11: 270). While he stresses that our scientific worldview is parasitic on such natural judgments, he clearly thinks that most people cannot help *but go beyond them*. In the Conclusion to Book 1, he notes that human beings are naturally led into "speculations without [i.e. outside of] the sphere of common life," for it is "almost impossible for the mind of man to rest, like those of beasts, in that narrow circle of objects, which are the subject of daily conversation and action" (T1.4.7.13:

271–2). For many this need is filled by religion or by "superstition of every kind or denomination." But, Hume writes, superstition generally disturbs "the conduct of our lives and actions." Religion is an unstable source of belief and as such is associated with unpleasant passions.[43] Given that we have this tendency to go beyond the sphere of common life, it is much safer and more pleasant to pursue science, which "contents itself with assigning new causes and principles to the phænomena, which appear in the visible world," than religion, which arbitrarily creates a whole new world of spiritual objects.

At the same time, having faced the contradictions and imperfections of our reasoning, we ought to pursue our scientific tasks in a new way. We ought to recognize that "hypotheses embrac'd merely for being specious and agreeable" are not likely to provide any stability, being too far from "common practice and experience" (T1.4.7.14: 272–3). He thinks that by avoiding such hypotheses he might be able to "establish a system or set of opinions, which if not true ... might at least be satisfactory to the human mind, and might stand the test of the most critical examination." Even if the particular principles he has discovered do not outlast the scrutiny of later generations of philosophers, Hume thinks that, at the very least, his studies in human nature will point out the kind of investigations in which some "assurance and conviction" can be expected. He resolves to continue his philosophical investigations in a "careless [i.e. carefree] manner" by following his natural inclinations and avoiding being overwhelmed by those earlier "doubts and scruples" which led to his philosophical melancholy and delirium. As a "true sceptic" he will distrust his "philosophical doubts, as well as ... his philosophical conviction."

---

[43] See Chapter 6, p. 192.

CHAPTER 5

Determinism

Hume opposes a doctrine – freedom of the will – which was supported in his day not only by philosophers, but by preachers. He alludes to this fact at the end of the two sections of Part 3 of Book 2 devoted to this topic (T2.3.1 & T2.3.2). He states that the question of free will should not be decided "by declamations before the people," but by fair arguments before philosophers (T2.3.2.8: 412). We should remember that shortly before Hume left Scotland in 1734, his neighbor William Dudgeon had been prosecuted by the local church presbytery for writing a book in which he denied the freedom of the will. He was accused of thereby making God the source of human evil.[1] In the sections on liberty and necessity in the *Treatise* Hume does not consider this theological problem which arises from denying that human beings have free will, though he did so when he recast this discussion in his *Enquiry Concerning Human Understanding*.[2] He points out that even if the denial of the freedom of the will had the negative consequences for religion and morals that many clergy claimed, this would be irrelevant to the question of its truth and falsity. He writes that "there is no method of reasoning more common, and yet none more blamable, than in philosophical debates to endeavour to refute any hypothesis by a pretext of its dangerous consequences to religion and morality" (T2.3.2.3: 409). This kind of attack commits the *ad hominem* fallacy: it is an attempt "to

---

[1] See Chapter 1, §1, p. 3.

[2] EHU 7.32ff. Of course, this could have been removed from the original draft of these sections of the *Treatise* when he castrated his text before publication (see Chapter 1, pp. 28ff & 34). In the Section "Of the immateriality of the soul" Hume does refer to the general problem of considering God to be the direct source "of all our volitions and perceptions," as "*Malebranche* and other *Cartesians*" believed – but he does not go on to elaborate on the problem of evil which results from doing so (T1.4.5.31: 248–9).

make the person of an antagonist odious" or hateful in the minds of one's audience, and does nothing to further the pursuit of truth.

I. LIBERTY AND NECESSITY

Hume argues in "Of liberty and necessity" that the will is determined or necessitated. His argument is based on the claim that the same kind of experimental reasoning that we employ about physical objects is also employed in reasoning about human actions. In so arguing he gives a clear illustration of what he meant in the Introduction to the *Treatise* when he wrote that his aim was to apply to the science of man the same method of "experience and observation" which had already proved so successful in the natural sciences (TI 7: xvi).

How we interpret the conclusion of "Of liberty and necessity" depends a great deal on how we interpret Hume's account of scientific method and its ontological implications. For in this discussion he applies the account of inductive inference and causality which he develops in Part 3 of Book 1. A central question which arises here, as it did there, is whether Hume reduces the meaning of causal necessity to uniformity and predictability – or whether he regards the latter as a sign of a genuine but unintelligible necessity. I shall argue that the latter assumption runs throughout his reasoning about liberty and necessity.

In Hume's discussion of liberty and necessity in the *Treatise*, he argues that human liberty and necessity are *incompatible*. He does, however, briefly mention another sense of the word liberty which is compatible with necessity – what he calls the "liberty of *spontaneity*" (T2.3.2.1: 407). According to this notion, we are free whenever our actions are produced by our wills – when we are not forced to do what we do by external forces outside of us. This use of the term 'liberty' figures prominently in the recasting of his discussion of liberty and necessity in his first *Enquiry*, where he argues for the view which has come to be called *compatibilism* – the view that 'liberty' and necessity are compatible.[3] But, as I said, in the discussion in the *Treatise*

---

[3] He argues in the first *Enquiry* that "by liberty … we can only mean *a power of acting or not acting, according to the determinations of the will*" (EHU 8.23). This is what he means by "liberty of spontaneity" in the *Treatise*.

Hume only mentions this "liberty of *spontaneity*" in passing, and it does not play any role in his argument. In this respect, his argument in the *Treatise* is more straightforward than in the first *Enquiry*: his question concerns *the causes of the will* and *not what the will causes*. We call those actions that the will causes voluntary actions. But in the *Treatise* Hume holds that "it is not a just consequence, that what is voluntary is free" (T3.3.4.3: 609). In other words, just because we have liberty of spontaneity it does not follow that we have liberty of indifference.

In both the *Treatise* and the later first *Enquiry* Hume argues against freedom of the will, that is, against the "liberty of *indifference*" (T2.3.1: 407). *Liberty of indifference* just implies that the will itself is free of necessitating causes; there is no combination of motives, character traits, circumstances, or any other factors which cause our will or act of choice. Earlier in Book 2 he had referred to the theory that we have liberty of indifference as "the scholastic doctrine of *free-will*" (T2.1.10.5: 312). Hume is opposed to this theory. According to it, "motives deprive us not of free-will, nor take away our power of performing or forbearing any action." If the theory were true, no matter how strong my fear of punishment if I break the law and murder my enemy, I am still free to do so. Fear of consequences never takes away my power to perform an action. Hume's own view is that in most circumstances "the fear of the civil magistrate is as strong a restraint as ... iron" and takes away my power of performing the prohibited action as much as chains and iron bars. More generally, he thinks that motives together with character and circumstances prevent as well as determine actions.

Nevertheless, it is clear that, from a subjective point of view, we all think that we have the power to choose differently than we actually do. Hume writes of a person who has been a miser all his life, who never spends his money on his own pleasure, but who, nevertheless, thinks that it is still within his power to do so. He attributes this belief to a "false sensation of liberty, which makes us imagine we can perform any thing" (T2.1.10.9: 314). Even though he has never done so, the miser thinks he can always change his behavior and choose to go on a spending spree; but this, according to Hume, is really "an *illusion of the fancy*." Hume goes on in the second section "Of liberty and necessity" (T2.3.2.2) to explain this illusion – that is, why we think we could always have chosen to do something different than we did do. But more of this in a moment.

It is sometimes said that Hume's view of necessity allows that there can be uncaused events, as well as irregularities in men's actions. Don Garrett, for example, writes that "Hume's doctrine of necessity is ... distinct from both strict determinism and universal causation. It ... permits irregularities and even occasional uncaused events."[4] But this is not the doctrine of necessity which Hume presents in his discussion "Of liberty and necessity" in the *Treatise*. He argues that the will is determined, that necessity and liberty are incompatible, and that there are no uncaused actions. Hume writes that "according to [his] definitions, necessity makes an essential part of causation; and consequently liberty, by removing necessity, removes also causes, and is the very same thing with chance" (T2.3.1.18: 407). In Book 1, he writes that "chance is nothing real in itself, and, properly speaking, is merely the negation of a cause" (T1.3.11.4: 125). Here, in Book 2, he writes that chance "is commonly thought to imply a contradiction," and that, at the very least, it is "directly contrary to experience" (T2.3.1.18: 407). When he reflects back on this discussion in Book 3, he claims he has shown that free will "has no place with regard to the actions, no more than the qualities of men" (T3.3.4.3: 609). Certainly, he is prepared to argue that we perform actions which are *voluntary*, that is that follow from our wills. However, as we have seen, he denies that it is a consequence of the claim that an action is voluntary that it is free. In §5 below we shall see that Hume explicitly argues against those who maintain that there are genuine irregularities in human actions.

Moreover, in Book 2, he makes it clear that the notion of a cause which is merely potential and does not necessarily bring about its effects is not a philosophical or scientific conception. In a "just and *philosophical* way of thinking" there is no distinction between "*power* and the *exercise* of it" (T2.1.10.4: 311). Nevertheless, Hume argues that this is "not *the philosophy* of our passions." The miser is not alone in thinking his own actions are free and always subject to exceptions.

---

[4] Garrett's view is based on his reconstruction of what he thinks is required by what he calls "Hume's argument." He does go on to admit that Hume "does nevertheless *endorse* both strict determinism and universal causation" (Don Garrett, *Cognition and Commitment in Hume's Philosophy* (New York: Oxford University Press, 1997), p. 128.

We all do, as *subjects* of our own actions. But this puts us, as philosophers, in the typical position of the skeptic: our science conflicts with our common sense. Hume rejects the philosophical view that liberty or chance has any objective existence. He does acknowledge that we can be uncertain about what people are going to do. But he argues that there is no more indeterminacy in human actions themselves than in physical events, and that our uncertainty in these cases lies in the knower, not the known.[5] When there is epistemic uncertainty because a person behaves in different ways in apparently similar situations, a scientifically minded person postulates "contrary and conceal'd causes" (T2.3.1.12: 404; cf. T1.3.12.5: 132). In so doing she is recognizing that "the chance or indifference lies only in our judgment on account of our imperfect knowledge, not in the things themselves, which are in every case equally necessary." The belief in necessity is a fundamental assumption of the scientific method, one which is made in physics, and needs also to be made in the case of the science of human nature.

2. THE AGENT AND THE SPECTATOR POINTS OF VIEW

Most of those who defend the freedom of the will do so from the subjective or agent-centered point of view. They claim that it is from their own case that they have evidence that they are free. Just as you can be completely certain of your own existence in a way that you cannot be certain of anyone else's existence (remember Descartes' famous '*cogito*' argument), so you can be certain of your freedom of choice from your special position as agent of your own actions.[6] It may look to *me* like your actions are necessitated, because of their regularity and predictability; but *you yourself* have evidence that you could have chosen to do otherwise. After all, so goes the argument, who is in a better position than you to know whether your will is free – that is, whether you really could have chosen to do something else than you actually did do?

---

[5] A consideration of the person's motive in such cases will leave "the imagination [of the knower] perfectly indifferent" (T1.3.11.4: 125).

[6] Descartes argued that "*the freedom of the will is self evident*" and that it is "experienced within us." (René Descartes, *Principles of Philosophy* I, 39, in CSM I, pp. 205–6).

Hume rejects this argument from subjectivity. It is not that he does not recognize the difference between the subjective view that we take on our own actions, and the objective view that we take on the actions of others. In fact, he acknowledges that there is "a certain looseness" which we often experience in our own case (T2.3.2.2: 408). When we consider the connection between our own motives and actions we do not feel that determination of the mind which we often feel in considering the motives and actions of other people. But, for him, that "looseness" between motives and actions is the source of the "false *sensation or experience* ... of the liberty of indifference."

Hume reports an experiment which, he seems to think, forms the basis for the libertarian's view. After one performs an action one can often imagine that one could have willed the opposite. As Hume puts it, one feels that one's will "moves easily every way, and produces an image of itself even on that side, on which it did not settle" (T2.3.2.2: 408). For example, suppose you made a nasty remark to someone because something the person said irritated you. Now, when you reflect back on the action, you can imagine yourself willing the opposite – not saying anything nasty, or even responding to the person with a nice remark. The libertarian thinks that, in this way, you show that you could have acted otherwise than you did act. But, says Hume, a new motive has entered on this second round that wasn't present the first time, namely "the desire of showing [your] liberty." Or, it could simply have been your regret in seeing the other person's reaction to what you said which has made you do this 'double-take' on your own action. In either case, Hume's point is that the circumstances existing before you exerted your will have changed, and that the experiment does *not* prove that you could have willed differently in the first place. The experiment of reflecting back on your actions in order to prove that you could have acted otherwise simply does not work.

We appear to have here an application of the concern that Hume raises about introspection in the Introduction to the *Treatise*. As we have seen, he writes there that "reflection and premeditation ... so disturb the operation of my natural principles, as must render it impossible to form any just conclusion from the phænomenon" (TI

10: xix).[7] For this reason, he argues, we must determine the principles of human nature by way of observation of people's behavior. One's own self-observation interferes with the phenomenon of one's own mind which one is trying to study. If Hume is right, far from being in the best position to decide whether your own actions are caused or necessitated by your motives, you are in the worst.

It may be objected that while Hume's argument is successful in ruling out the relevance of reflective experiments which we do *after* the action is performed, it does not rule out the validity of the subjective point of view altogether. What of that *looseness* which he himself acknowledged that we all experience when we actually perform intentional actions? We do not feel any determination when we ourselves make a decision to act. When you feel angry at the person who makes a nasty remark to you and want to retaliate, you are not forced to do so. Between your desire and your action lies your will. You choose whether or not to act on your desire. A Humean philosopher would answer that if you do not act on your anger, it is because another stronger motive has slipped in – perhaps your desire to avoid uncomfortable confrontations, or even your sense of the wrongness of retaliating. *You* might reply that while you do have these different motives, none are determining; you don't have to act on the one that is 'strongest.' You can choose the motive which seems to you to have the most value, and so act on it. Perhaps you decide that it would be morally wrong to lash out at the other person, and so you disregard his insult. Have you not freely chosen which of the possible motives to act upon? And do you not know this from reflecting on what exactly has gone on in your own mind?

One answer to this objection – a Humean answer – is that it assumes that we are always conscious of which motive influenced us. In the following sections of the *Treatise*, Hume argues that we are often motivated by desires and tendencies of which we are barely, if at all, aware. This will become clear in our discussion of Hume's theory of "calm desires and tendencies" in Chapter 7.[8] Briefly, Hume argues that when a motive becomes part of our character through

---

[7] See p. 45 above. In this case, we have what may more accurately be described as *postmeditation*, rather than premeditation.

[8] §7, pp. 228ff.

custom and habit, it manifests itself without any emotional intensity. Thus introspection, even if it does not interfere with what originally went on in our own minds, may well fail to identify the desire which actually motivated us.

Let us apply this analysis to the example above where you argue that you freely chose not to strike back at the person who insulted you. Perhaps you claim that the reason you did not retaliate was because of moral considerations: you believe that one ought to turn the other cheek when another person insults you. But there was another possible reason for your not retaliating – namely that you tend to dislike direct confrontation with others. It may well be that a spectator who knows your character from observing you in other situations would determine that what really influenced you was this desire to avoid confrontation. She notes that, in other situations where there is no direct confrontation, you have no qualms about retaliating in kind against people who insult you. This shows that it was not moral considerations – your supposed belief in turning the other cheek – which influenced you after all.

Hume argues that it is the spectator's point of view that we must adopt in settling the question of freedom of the will. He writes that

We may imagine we feel a liberty within ourselves; but a spectator can commonly infer our actions from our motives and character; and even where he cannot, he concludes in general, that he might, were he perfectly acquainted with every circumstance of our situation and temper, and the most secret springs of our complexion and disposition. (T2.3.2.2: 408–9)

The person who is in the best position to determine the motives of my action is a spectator who can infer my actions from my "motives and character." Of course, her belief in my motives and character would have to be derived by observing my behavior in a number of different situations. But that is exactly what Hume thinks a spectator may be able to do in a more accurate way than the person himself. Moreover, even if she were unable to infer my actions from my motives and character in a specific situation, she would conclude that she could do so if she knew "the most secret springs of [my] complexion and disposition." Hume concludes that this belief forms "the very essence of necessity, according to the foregoing doctrine."

3. NECESSITY IN PHYSICAL OBJECTS

In Section 1 of Book 2 Part 3, before turning to his reasons for thinking that the spectator's point of view implies that human actions are necessitated, Hume discusses necessity as it is ascribed to material objects. Given his overall aim in the *Treatise* of applying to the study of man the same methods of reasoning which have already been successfully applied in the physical sciences, this is a natural place for him to begin. His argument here is that we have exactly the same grounds to ascribe necessity to human actions as we have to ascribe it to material objects; since we ascribe it to material objects, we must also ascribe it to human actions.

Hume begins his discussion by considering the necessity which we ascribe in the case of the physical world:

> 'tis universally acknowledg'd, that the operations of external bodies are necessary, and that in the communication of their motion, in their attraction, and mutual cohesion, there are not the least traces of indifference or liberty. Every object is determin'd by an absolute fate to a certain degree and direction of its motion, and can no more depart from that precise line, in which it moves, than it can convert itself into an angel, or spirit, or any superior substance. The actions, therefore, of matter are to be regarded as instances of necessary actions ... (T2.3.1.3: 399–400)

There are two things to note about this passage. First, Hume unambiguously ascribes necessity to external objects themselves. There is no suggestion that necessity is merely in the mind of the spectator. Secondly, Hume describes this necessity as absolute and as excluding the possibility of anything occurring besides what actually occurs in the given circumstances. When he rewrote this passage in his first *Enquiry*, he was even more unequivocal: the effect is so precisely determined by its cause "that no other effect, in such particular circumstances, could possibly have resulted from it" (EHU 8.4). We appear to have necessity ascribed to objects in the strongest sense of the word.

Some commentators have claimed that Hume is not writing in his own voice in this passage, and is only reporting what is "universally acknowledg'd" by other philosophers.[9] However, Peter Millican has

---

[9] See James Harris, "Hume's Reconciling Project," *British Journal for the History of Philosophy* 11 (3), 2003, 451–71, esp. 464.

correctly pointed out that Hume uses this and similar expressions in cases where he is without question reporting his own views.[10] In any case, Hume unequivocally expresses his own view when he states a few paragraphs later that "we must certainly allow, that the cohesion of the parts of matter arises from natural and necessary principles, whatever difficulty we may find in explaining them" (T2.3.1.8: 401). Hume is clearly expressing a view which he himself endorses when he writes of the necessity of the operations of "external bodies."

Having adopted the view that the actions of physical or material objects are instances of necessary actions, Hume turns to the question of the basis for this belief. He argues, as he does in Book 1, that it is not based on any penetration "into the essence and construction of bodies" which would allow us "to perceive the principle, on which their mutual influence depends" (T2.3.1.4: 400). Rather the belief in the necessity of the operations of physical objects arises from the observation of their "constant union." When we have observed two objects constantly conjoined on a number of occasions, the one following the other without exception, there results "a determination of the mind to pass from one object to its usual attendant," and it is this "determination" which is the source of the idea that the existence of the second object is necessitated by the first. The belief in this necessity is drawn from our psychological propensity to infer the one from the other after we have observed the constant union, not from any "insight" into nature itself. Hume stresses that "the absence of this insight" will not in any case lessen our belief in the necessity, so long as "the union and inference remain."

Similarly, he argues that in the case of human actions, all we have to do is "prove a constant union ... in order to establish the inference, along with the necessity of these actions" (T2.3.1.4: 400–1). Hume sets out in the rest of this section to "prove from experience, that our actions have a constant union with our motives, tempers,

[10] Millican points out that Hume uses this expression in one of the most quoted passages in the *Treatise* where he writes that "'tis universally allow'd by philosophers, and is besides pretty obvious of itself, that nothing is ever really present with the mind but its perceptions or impressions and ideas ..." (T1.2.6.7: 67). The phrase is repeated in his account "Of liberty and necessity" in the first Enquiry (EHU 8.4). Other unequivocal uses of the expression are at T1.2.1.2: 26 and EHU 8.22–3. Millican cites these passages in his "Hume's Determinism," read to the 32nd meeting of the Hume Society in Toronto in August, 2005, which is in preparation for publication.

and circumstances," and that we infer that future actions follow necessarily from this regularity.

4. UNIFORMITY IN HUMAN BEHAVIOR

Hume thinks that it is sufficient to take a "general view of the common course of human affairs" in order to convince us of the uniform connection between these three factors and behavior (T2.3.1.5: 401). He presents a number of examples to show that people's behavior is correlated with their sex (T2.3.1.6: 401), their age (T2.3.1.7: 401), their rank or social status (T2.3.1.9: 402), and their national characteristics (T2.3.1.10: 402–3). These factors, which cause differences in behavior, are both biological and social. In fact, Hume does not clearly distinguish between the two in this discussion. He mentions the differences between the physical condition of "a day-laborer" and "a man of quality" which correlate with differences in their "sentiments actions, and manners" (T2.3.1.9: 402); but then he goes on to discuss the development of social and political conditions which cause such differences in the "ranks of men."

Some of the factors he discusses relate to behavior of human beings in general, and some to behavior of specific human groups. He argues, for example, that anyone with a knowledge of human nature in general would be disinclined to believe that there were anywhere people similar to those described in Plato's *Republic* or Thomas Hobbes' *Leviathan* (T2.3.3.10: 402) – that is, people wholly altruistic (like Plato's guardians), or wholly selfish (like those in Hobbes' state of nature). But, as I have said, he also mentions that we find different behaviors correlated with different national characteristics. Earlier in Book 2 he argues that these latter differences are caused by sympathy with one's fellow countrymen, not with soil and climate, as is commonly believed (T2.1.11.2: 316–17). This anticipates his famous argument against Montesquieu in his essay "Of national characters."[11]

While many of the factors he mentions only give us the ability to predict general tendencies in human behavior, others show correlations which are so strong that they allow us to predict the behavior

[11] *Essays*, pp. 197–215.

of individuals. Hume asks whether it is "more certain, that two flat pieces of marble will unite together, than that two young savages of different sexes will copulate? Do the children arise from this copulation more uniformly, than does the parents' care for their safety and preservation?" (T2.3.1.8: 402). Presumably, in these cases the correlation between behavior on the one hand, and circumstance, character, and motive on the other, is so universal that it allows us to predict the behavior of these "young savages" with near certainty.

5. HUME'S ANSWER TO THE OBJECTION THAT THERE IS IRREGULARITY IN HUMAN ACTION

Hume considers an objection to his view that intentional actions "have a constant union and connexion with the situation and temper of the agent" (T2.3.1.11: 403): "For what is more capricious than human actions? What more inconstant than the desires of man? And what creature departs more widely, not only from right reason, but from his own character and disposition?" In short, according to Hume's imagined critic, human nature really is very "irregular and uncertain."

Hume's answer, which we already considered briefly above, is that we need to use the same methods in explaining apparent irregularities in human behavior that we use to explain apparent irregularities in the physical world. When there are exceptions to an observed regularity in nature, scientists do not remove "the notion of causes and necessity" (T2.3.1.12: 403–4). They reason that the irregularity in appearances has resulted from "the operation of contrary and conceal'd causes" and that "the chance or indifference lies only in our judgment on account of our imperfect knowledge." Chance does not exist "in the things themselves, which are in every case equally necessary." As we saw in Chapter 3, on Hume's view it is the scientist or philosopher's belief that every event has a determining cause – her adoption of the "maxim, that the connexion betwixt all causes and effects is equally necessary" – that leads her to search out the hidden "contrary causes" (T1.3.12.5: 132).[12] Hume concludes that we need to

---

[12] §3, pp. 94–5ff. Compare here EHU 8.13 where this discussion of scientific method is incorporated into his discussion "Of liberty and necessity."

follow a similar line of reasoning in connection with human actions in those cases where they appear not to correlate regularly with motives and character. We need to assume that there is a necessity in the nature of things and look for the hidden causes that account for the apparent irregularity. As we saw earlier, this is the essence of the scientific method as Hume conceives of it.

Hume accuses his opponent of inconsistency when he appeals to the irregularity of human behavior in order to prove human freedom. He points out that it is madmen who behave erratically, and that it is universally recognized that they have no liberty (T2.3.1.13: 404).[13] But according to the assumptions of his critic, madmen should be considered to have more liberty than men who behave in a regular and uniform manner. Hume states that such inconsistencies are the result of people arguing about this matter using "confus'd ideas and undefin'd terms."

In fact, according to Hume's own definitions where "necessity makes an essential part of causation ..." (T2.3.1.18: 407), the actions of both the madman and the wise man are equally necessitated. The difference lies in the first appearances. In the case of the wise man, the factors indicating necessity are apparent from the regular way in which his actions follow upon his motives, character, and situation; in the case of the madman the causal factors are commonly hidden. If we follow the same reasoning we use in natural science, we will accept the "maxim, that the connexion betwixt all causes and effects is equally necessary" (T1.3.12.5: 132) even when this is not always directly apparent from experience.

6. THE INFERENCE OF THE MIND AND THE NECESSITY OF VOLUNTARY ACTIONS

Hume stresses the difference between the *theory* of those who claim to believe in free will and their *actual practice* in drawing inferences. Despite their commitment to the "fantastical system of liberty" in theory, they draw inferences from "*moral evidence*" based on people's "motives, temper and situation" in practice (T2.3.1.15: 404–5). Like everyone else, the defenders of free will draw conclusions about

---

[13] Cf. Locke, ECHU 2.21.50, where he makes a related remark about madmen.

actions of others based on their beliefs about human nature. In believing historical accounts of the murder of Julius Caesar, "the success of *Augustus,* the cruelty of *Nero*" they assume that people tell the truth unless they have particular motives of "interest" to do otherwise. Everyone recognizes that if these historians had reported what was false they would have exposed themselves to "the derision of all their contemporaries, when these facts were asserted to be recent and universally known." Similar inferences concerning the necessary causes of human actions are made when a general counts on "a certain degree of courage" in the actions of the soldiers under his command, when a merchant gives orders to those he has hired to look after his business or goods, when "a man, who gives orders for his dinner, doubts not the obedience of his servants." Hume claims that so long as his opponents reason in these ways about human actions, they "believe the actions of the will to arise from necessity" and fail to understand what they are saying when they deny it.

Hume's point is that when any of us considers the voluntary actions of people in practice, we think of them as following with as much necessity as the actions of physical objects. His final example, which is meant to show the way "*natural* and *moral* evidence cement together," is particularly striking. He writes of "a prisoner, who has neither money nor interest," and who "discovers the impossibility of his escape, as well from the obstinacy of the gaoler, as from the walls and bars with which he is surrounded" (T2.3.1.17: 406). He treats the actions of the jailer as no less determined than the physical properties of the walls of his prison. "The same prisoner, when conducted to the scaffold, foresees his death as certainly from the constancy and fidelity of his guards as from the operation of the ax or wheel." In fact, in his reasoning to his inevitable doom the prisoner goes through a "connected chain of natural causes and voluntary actions" and "feels no difference betwixt them."

7. THE THEORETICAL MISTAKE OF THOSE WHO BELIEVE IN FREE WILL

The mistaken belief in free will, as Hume sees it, arises from two different sources. First, there is the natural mistake we make when we focus on the first person point of view. Second, there is a theoretical mistake which some philosophers make when they assume that there is a fundamental difference between physical causation and mental causation. This mistake arises because these philosophers think we have insight or comprehension of necessity in the case of physical causes, and what we there comprehend is lacking in the case of mental causes.[14] Hume argues that in *neither* case is the "*necessary connexion ...* discover'd by a conclusion of the understanding" (T2.3.1.16: 405–6). It "is merely a perception of the mind." This perception is a *feeling* which is derived from custom and habit. Hume writes:

> Motion in one body in all past instances, that have fallen under our observation, is follow'd upon impulse by motion in another. 'tis impossible for the mind to penetrate farther. From this constant union it *forms* the idea of cause and effect, and by its influence *feels* the necessity. As there is the same constancy, and the same influence, in what we call moral evidence, I ask no more.

In both cases our belief in the necessity is derived from feeling. Those who refuse to speak of necessity in the case of mental causes are only involved in "a dispute of words." For, "'tis impossible for the mind to penetrate farther" into the necessity either in the case of physical or mental causation. Hume's point here is that in neither case can we *understand* the underlying necessity, and in both cases we apprehend it through *feeling*. As we saw in Chapter 3, this is the account of our belief in necessity which Hume goes on to present in his discussion "Of the idea of necessary connexion" in his first *Enquiry*.[15] His account is clearly skeptical, rather than reductionist.

However, in returning to this point in the second of the two sections of the *Treatise* devoted to the discussion "Of liberty and necessity" Hume appeals to the two definitions of cause which he gives in Book 1. As I noted in Chapter 3, these definitions tend to support the view that Hume reduces objective causation to mere regularity, and necessity itself to a subjective determination of the mind of the observer.[16] Here in Book 2, Hume writes:

> I define necessity two ways, conformable to the two definitions of *cause*, of which it makes an essential part. I place it either in the constant union and conjunction of like objects, or in the inference of the mind from the

---

[14] This is the view Locke adopts at ECHU 4.10.19 where he contrasts the intelligibility of motion by impulse with voluntary action, where we only learn of our own ability to cause motion by "constant Experience."
[15] §8 ii), p. 126. [16] §6 ii), pp. 118–20.

one to the other. Now necessity, in both these senses, has universally, tho' tacitely, in the schools, in the pulpit, and in common life, been allow'd to belong to the will of man, and no one has ever pretended to deny, that we can draw inferences concerning human actions, and that those inferences are founded on the experienc'd union of like actions with like motives and circumstances. (T2.3.2.4: 409)

Here, Hume is explicitly defining "necessity" itself, and not just "cause" as he did in Book 1. Both definitions are said to be definitions of necessity. We get no qualifications about the definitions being "foreign to the cause." His aim here is clearly to disarm his opponents' arguments by getting them to admit that they accept necessity in the two senses he allows in his definitions.

Hume recognizes that his opponents may "refuse to call" what is allowed by his official definitions "necessity," and may claim that when we ascribe necessity to matter we mean something stronger (T2.3.2.4: 409–10). His answer is that even if there *is* such an unknown necessity in matter, it is not what he is ascribing when he claims that people's actions are necessary. He is not claiming that our wills are moved by anything like the force which makes a billiard ball move when another one strikes it. In stressing that we have no understanding of the force or necessity of physical objects, he says he has changed "nothing in the receiv'd systems, with regard to the will, but only with regard to material objects." He is arguing, in effect, that he has taken the sting out of the tail of physical or material necessity, and applied this new domesticated breed of necessity to human actions. In accord with his two definitions, he writes, "I place it in the constant union and conjunction of like objects, or in the inference of the mind from one to the other." It is only in these two senses that he is ascribing necessity to both physical events and to human actions.

It is difficult to believe that Hume is being entirely ingenuous here, given his unequivocal statements in the first section of "Of liberty and necessity" that in the physical world "every object is determin'd ... to a certain degree and direction of its motion" (T2.3.1.3: 400), and that there is no indifference or chance in the nature of things. Did he not begin his whole discussion by ascribing necessity to physical objects in a stronger sense than that authorized by his two definitions? Moreover, there is reason to question whether he really does believe that the force which moves our wills is of an entirely different kind than that which moves physical objects. As we have seen, at the end of Section 5 of Part 4 of Book 1, "Of the immateriality of the soul," he argues that experience shows us that "matter and motion may often be regarded as the causes of thought, as far as we have any notion of that relation" (T1.4.5.32–33: 250) and that this evidence gives support "to the materialists." In other words, he suggests that mental causation is probably ultimately based on physical causation.

The key philosophical question is whether Hume can legitimately claim that he is *only* ascribing necessity to objects in the two senses given by his two definitions. Does he not clearly deny any "liberty of indifference" to both the physical and the mental world independent of the observer? And is it not this liberty which is demanded by his opponent, the libertarian? Indeed, the libertarian can even allow that there is a complete regularity or constancy observed in human actions, and that they can be predicted with complete accuracy. She only insists on the *possibility* that she can do otherwise in given circumstances, a possibility for which she claims to have evidence from her own subjective, agent-centered point of view. Constant conjunction and predictability of one's actions do not in themselves preclude liberty of indifference.[17] But Hume's theory does.

To see this, one just needs to take into account Hume's own language in describing those cases where he claims that a spectator infers as much necessity in the moral as in the physical world. Consider again what Hume says about the unfortunate prisoner. He "discovers the *impossibility* of his escape, as well from the obstinacy of the gaoler, as from the walls and bars with which he is surrounded" (T2.3.1.17: 406; my emphasis). He infers his unhappy future from the "*inflexible nature*" of his guards, no less than from the physical properties of the stone and iron out of which his cell is constructed. Hume clearly uses the word "impossibility" and the expression "inflexible nature" here to refer to features of the objective world of agents and material bodies, and not mere features of the mind of the prisoner who observes them. The prisoner who has a realistic assessment of human behavior judges that, given their motivations, characters and circumstances,

---

[17] I take this to be Garrett's point in the passage I cited in footnote 4 above; see also James Harris's article which I cited in footnote 9.

the guards cannot act otherwise than they do. He does not simply believe in the constant conjunction of loyal jailors who have not been bribed on the one hand and unreleased prisoners on the other; nor does he simply predict his own death from past observation of similar cases. But rather, based on the evidence, he naturally supposes that the actions of his jailors as well as the properties of stone and iron bars are necessarily determined. As the late John Yolton has argued, one cannot reduce the objective language of causality and necessity which Hume uses in his philosophical discussions of these topics to the language of regular successions of events.[18] Our supposition of necessity outdistances the evidence that we have for it, not only because we naturally make predictions about the future, but because we naturally judge that there is a necessary connection between the objects that we have observed to have been constantly conjoined.

8. NECESSITY AND MORAL RESPONSIBILITY

In the last three paragraphs of his discussion "Of liberty and necessity" Hume considers the objection that his view, because it denies free will, subverts religion and morality. His response is to turn the charge against his libertarian opponents – first by claiming that their view fails to explain the effectiveness of both human and divine laws, and then by arguing that the belief in free will actually undermines moral responsibility.

Let us begin with Hume's second response, which presupposes his later account of moral praise and blame. He argues that we would never hold a person responsible for an uncaused act of will such as that which the libertarian requires for human freedom. If the act of will "proceeded from nothing in him, that is durable or constant, and leaves nothing of that nature behind it, 'tis impossible he can, upon its account, become the object of punishment or vengeance" (T2.3.2.6: 411). It is only just to blame a person for an action if it derives from something lasting in his character and personality. "Actions," he writes, "are by their very nature temporary

---

[18] See John Yolton, *Realism and Appearances: An Essay in Ontology* (Cambridge University Press, 2000), Chapter 7, "Hume's Ontology," esp. pp. 124–32.

and perishing; and where they proceed not from some cause in the characters and disposition of the person, who perform'd them, they infix not themselves upon him, and can neither redound to his honour, if good, nor infamy, if evil." It is only if intentional actions are determined by something fixed and durable in a person's character that they are the proper subject of praise and blame, and of moral responsibility.[19] According to the libertarian view, on the other hand, "a man is as pure and untainted, after having committed the most horrid crimes, as at the first moment of his birth, nor is his character any way concern'd in his actions."

Indeed, Hume claims that, in spite of the popularity of the libertarian view of moral responsibility, it is disregarded in practice. The law excuses people or at least assigns diminished responsibility for actions which are done "hastily and unpremeditately" – for example, so-called *crimes of passion* (T2.3.2.7: 412). This is because they do not derive from the person's established character. On the other hand, the law *does* hold a person fully responsible for actions done with "thought and deliberation" because they give evidence that the actions are caused by lasting dispositions of the entire person. A person who is fully repentant and undergoes a genuine character change is, according to Hume, excused for his past crimes.[20] But if the libertarian doctrine were true, the change in her character would be irrelevant to whether we still hold her responsible for these crimes.

Moreover, he charges, the libertarian can never account for the effectiveness of human laws. These are based on promises of rewards and threats of punishment – particularly the latter. Unless the threat of punishment has "an influence on the mind" in producing good and preventing evil actions, laws would be useless (T2.3.2.5: 410). He says that this "influence" implies that the motive is "*usually* conjoin'd with the action" and therefore should be considered "an instance of that necessity, which I wou'd establish" (my emphasis).

It has been argued that this passage shows that Hume allows for a sense of necessity which does not require a constant conjunction between the cause and the effect, but only a "usual" one. But we need to remember that Hume does not claim that motives *by*

---

[19] Compare Chapter 6 §5, pp. 199ff. and Chapter 9 §4, pp. 271–5.
[20] The possibility of this actually occurring seems pretty slim on Hume's view; see. T3.3.4.3: 608 & p. 274 below.

themselves necessitate actions, but motives together with character and circumstance – that is, what he calls "temper and situation" (T2.3.1.15: 404; cf. T2.3.1.4: 401). He holds that the usual, but not constant conjunction of specific motives with specific actions *indicates* a necessity. But whether or not I am actually motivated by the threat of the law's punishment also depends on my character and the specific situation which I find myself in. There are no irregularities in the nature of things, according to Hume, and a scientifically minded person supposes necessity, even in the case of a less than constant experience.[21]

9. CONCLUSION

Hume argues that the correct point of view from which to decide the philosophical problem of liberty and necessity is that of the spectator or observer, not the agent. This is, of course, the point of view we inevitably take when we contemplate external physical objects, whose absolute necessity is never doubted. Nevertheless, Hume points out, we have no insight into the necessity in the physical world. We don't understand *why* when the first event occurs, the other always follows. The belief in necessity is based on a feeling of the mind which we have when we have experienced two objects as invariably conjoined – and infer the one from the other. While uneducated people only ascribe necessity when they actually experience a constant exceptionless conjunction, a scientifically minded person believes that there is such necessity in the objects, even when there is apparent irregularity. She forms a maxim that all causes are equally necessary in reality, and this belief forms the basis for the discoveries she makes about the hidden causes underlying the apparent irregularities.

Hume argues that we have exactly the same basis to suppose necessity in the causes of the human will as we have to suppose necessity in the physical world. First, he claims that we observe as much regularity in human actions as physical events. We commonly experience a constant conjunction between motives, characters and circumstances on the one hand, and actions on the other – and we form the same

---

[21] See Chapter 3 §3, pp. 93ff.

belief that the actions are necessitated. Second, when we discover an apparent irregularity in human actions, we have as much reason to postulate a necessity as in physical ones. The scientist of human nature believes that there is an underlying necessity even when there is an apparent irregularity, and so will look for the underlying hidden causes.

The question which Hume scholars dispute is the question concerning the meaning of this necessity which is ascribed to human agents as well as material objects. Those who consider Hume to be a reductive empiricist hold that he thinks that necessity means no more than constant conjunction and the ability to make inferences about what will occur in the future. They deny that he holds that we really lack knowledge of objective necessity – that he is a skeptic with regard to causal necessity. In opposition to this view, I have stressed first, that Hume opens his discussion in "Of liberty and necessity" by unequivocally ascribing physical necessity to external bodies in the strongest sense: he argues that such a body is "determin'd by an absolute fate to a certain degree and direction of its motion" and could not possibly act otherwise. It is this notion of necessity which he then applies to the human will. Secondly, as a scientist of human nature he rejects any kind of chance or liberty of indifference in the objective world, whether natural or social, ascribing all uncertainty to the ignorance of the spectator. He writes of the absurdity or falsity of the liberty of indifference. Thirdly, Hume argues that our judgment of objective necessity is rooted in a *feeling* rather than any kind of insight into the nature of causation. We feel the necessity rather than understanding it. Finally, Hume's own claims concerning the necessity which we suppose to exist in physical objects and agents simply do not make sense when we try to translate them into his imperfect definitions of it. The function of these definitions is to identify the epistemological basis of our ascription of causal necessity, not to tell us what we intend to convey when we make such ascriptions.

CHAPTER 6

Passions, sympathy, and other minds

At the beginning of Book 2, Hume characterizes passions as secondary impressions which arise from reflection on primary impressions or sensations – or on ideas derived from them (T2.1.1.1: 275; cf. T1.1.2.1: 7–8). Sensations, as Hume analyzes them in Book 1, are of three kinds – impressions of primary qualities, impressions of secondary qualities, and finally "the pains and pleasures, that arise from the application of objects to our bodies" (T1.4.2.12: 192). It is this third kind of sensation, pleasure and pain, which plays a particularly important role in Hume's account of the arousal of the passions. Hume writes that passions "are founded on pain and pleasure, and that in order to produce an affection of any kind, 'tis only requisite to present some good or evil" – that is, some object which causes pleasure or pain (T2.3.9.1: 438). Reflection on such an object is fundamental to Hume's account of the origin of the passions.[1]

Hume divides the passions into those which arise simply from reflection on the pleasure or pain caused by some object, and those which *also* involve a relation of the object either to oneself or another person. "By direct passions I understand such as arise immediately from good or evil, from pain or pleasure. By indirect such as proceed from the same principles, but by the conjunction of other qualities" (T2.1.1.4: 276). Hume only briefly discusses the first – the "direct passions." Over two-thirds of Book 2 involves his extensive and original discussion of what he calls "indirect passions." Here we will reverse the order of Hume's own exposition in the *Treatise*, and begin

---

[1] However, in Chapter 7 §7, pp. 228ff. we shall see that Hume allows that there are also some purely instinctive passions which arise independently of perceptions of pleasure or pain.

with his brief account of the direct passions, before turning to his account of the origin of the indirect passions.[2]

I. THE DIRECT PASSIONS: DESIRE, AVERSION, JOY, GRIEF, HOPE, AND FEAR

Hume's list of direct passions includes desire and aversion, joy and grief, and hope and fear. These different passions arise according to the possibility, certainty or probability of their objects – what we might call their modalities.

Desire and aversion are those passions which arise from considering pleasure and pain as possibilities. Desire arises from reflecting on the pleasure which some object may bring – say a new electronic gadget which a friend has told me about, or a cake which I see in the window of the pastry store. Aversion arises when I reflect on pain, such as the uneasiness I would feel should a very irritating relative decide to visit me. Both desire and aversion have a direct connection with "volition," or an act of the will (T2.3.9.2 & 7: 438–9).

In his discussion of the direct passions Hume treats desire as a distinct passion arising directly from thoughts of pleasure and pain. However, elsewhere Hume recognizes that many other passions incorporate desire.[3] I not only have desires for new electronic gadgets or for different kinds of pastry, but when I am angry I desire the punishment of my enemy, and when I feel benevolent I desire the good of my friend. A person who feels cowardice desires to run away, whereas a courageous person wants to stand and fight. Passions such as anger, benevolence, cowardice, and courage have a strong motivational aspect and Hume regards them as closely linked with the will.

Joy and grief arise when the pleasure or pain one reflects on is *certain* or *highly probable*. I feel joy in reflecting on the pleasure I received from the new car I bought last week, and I felt grief in the irretrievable loss of my closest friend.

Hope and fear arise when the pleasure and pain are *merely probable* and are accompanied by uncertainty. My hope arises when I think of

---

[2] Hume himself followed this order when he recast Book 2 in his *Dissertation on the Passions*.
[3] See Chapter 7 §6, pp. 226ff.

the pleasure I would feel if I were to get a top grade in the philosophy course I am taking, and my fear in reflecting on the uneasiness I would feel if I were to fail.

Most of Hume's discussion of the direct passions is focused on hope and fear. His interest in these two passions relates to their mixture, which he argues is inevitable – considering the uncertainty involved in their generation. He writes that "all kinds of uncertainty have a strong connexion with fear ..." (T2.3.9.27: 446–7). This is because "uncertainty alone is uneasy, and has a relation of impressions to the uneasy passions." When I feel hope, it is inevitably combined with fear, and other melancholy passions. Hope is inherently unstable, and the more we waver between hope and fear, the more fear tends to predominate.

It is likely that when he wrote this discussion Hume had in mind the hopes and fears of an afterlife which lie at the basis of Christianity; in any case, this discussion in the *Treatise* has direct relevance to his later reflections on this subject in his *Dialogues Concerning Natural Religion*. In Dialogue 12, Philo (whose views are generally thought to represent Hume's own) argues that both "fear and hope enter into religion" and that each "forms a species of divinity, suitable to itself."[4] When a religious person is "melancholy and dejected," he has "nothing to do but brood upon the terrors of the invisible world, and to plunge himself still deeper in affliction." After such religious opinions become engraved "deep into his thought and imagination" there may come "a change of health or circumstances, which may restore his good humour" and lead him to feel hope in the prospects of a future life, and "run into the other extreme of joy and triumph." But such episodes are short lived, and since "terror is the primary principle of religion, it is the passion which always predominates in it." Philo states that human happiness depends on a "calm and equitable" state of mind. However, "this state it is impossible to support, where a man thinks, that he lies, in such a profound darkness and uncertainty, between an eternity of happiness and an eternity of misery" and it will always be "gloom and melancholy" which predominates "in all devout people."

---

[4] *Dialogues*, 12: 29, p. 100.

Hume's study of the passions forms a major part of his project of applying the experimental method to the study of human nature. In summarizing his purpose in his *Dissertation on the Passions*, he wrote that it would be sufficient if he had "made it appear, that, in the production and conduct of the passions, there is a certain regular mechanism, which is susceptible of as accurate a disquisition, as the laws of motion, optics, hydrostatics, or any part of natural philosophy."[5] Hume's account of the predominance of fear which results from reflections on the uncertainty of future pleasure and pain is only one example of such a regular mechanism – one which he thought had a particular application in explaining a general feature of the religious life.

2. INDIRECT PASSIONS: PRIDE, HUMILITY, LOVE, AND HATRED

Two-thirds of Book 2 of the *Treatise* consists of an account of the origin of what he calls the indirect passions – pride, humility, love, and hatred, as well as related passions such as benevolence, anger, pity, malice, and envy. To a modern-day reader this discussion may seem tedious and drawn out. But its purpose for Hume is to base his account of the natural mechanisms which give rise to these passions on careful observations of human life and especially to show that our moral feelings about them arise from purely natural causes. The indirect passions arise from what Hume calls the double relations of ideas and impressions – that is the associational relations which are so central to Hume's science of human nature.

Hume begins his discussion of pride and humility by separating what he calls their *object* from their *cause* (T2.1.2.4: 278). In the cause itself he distinguishes between what he calls the *subject* and the *quality* (property) of that subject (T2.1.2.6: 279). We need to be clear about his distinctions here because what in ordinary language we often call the *object* of pride (e.g. my beautiful house) is what Hume calls the *subject* of pride.

---

[5] *Dissertation on the Passions*, in *A Dissertation on the Passions and The Natural History of Religion*, ed. Tom L. Beauchamp. Oxford: Clarendon Press, 2007), §6.19, p. 29.

Hume notes that if we carefully reflect on these passions them-selves we will discover that the *object* of both of them is always the *self*. He puts forward the hypothesis that the self is the natural or ori-ginal object of both these passions. Many philosophers would con-sider this to be simply a conceptual matter: a necessary condition for a passion to count as pride or shame is that it concerns ourselves.[6] But that was not Hume's view. The passion of pride and the self are two distinct perceptions.[7] Just as we can discover that the object of hun-ger is always food or of thirst is drink, so we discover that whenever we feel the passions of pride or humility arise in us then we think of ourselves. It is true that Hume argues that these passions have the self as their object "not only by a natural but also by an original property" (T2.1.2.2: 277). By the word 'original', Hume means something like 'innate.' He means that the connection between these passions and the self is built into our thinking processes. But it is not a conceptual or necessary connection, according to his *separability principle*.

What is this *self* to which the mind turns in the case of pride and humility? The view Hume develops here at the beginning of Book 2 is consistent with the analysis of the self or person which he gives in the section "Of personal identity" at the end of Book 1. That is to say it is a self without any true identity or simplicity. Hume writes of the self to which the mind turns in the case of pride and humility as "that succession of related ideas and impressions, of which we have an intimate memory and consciousness" (T2.1.2.2). When we feel pride or humility our idea of self "is more or less advantageous." This suggests that there is a different succession in the case of the two pas-sions which he is here explaining. Consider the different memories which flood into your mind when you are proud and when you are ashamed. We might even think of two different selves as appearing to us, one constituting the proud memories and one constituting the memories of things of which we are ashamed. Each is constituted by a different set of successive impressions and ideas.

---

[6] See Pall S. Ardal, *Passion and Value in Hume's Treatise* (Edinburgh University Press, 1966), p. 34.

[7] Terry Penelhum writes that for Hume "every passion is a unique, simple secondary impres-sion ... Questions about how it arises and how it leads to other experiences or to actions, are construed by Hume as causal questions to be dealt with within his Newtonian mental science" *Themes in Hume: the Self, the Will, Religion* (New York: Oxford University Press, 2000), p. 135.

3. THE SUBJECT OF PRIDE AND HUMILITY

In contrast to the self which is the *object* of the passion, the *subject* which *causes* these passions is not originally or innately connected with the passions (T2.1.3.6: 281–2). Hume notes that a person might invent a new kind of machine tomorrow which will be a source of pride, and it would be absurd to think that it was innately built into her that she should be proud of it. At the same time, he argues that the causes of pride and humility must have certain general features in common, features that we can discover by induction from experience.

To discover those features Hume reflects on the subjects in which people take pride – including "qualities of the mind; wit, good-sense, learning, courage, integrity: … those of the body; beauty, strength, agility, good mein [or demeanor], address in dancing, riding, fencing: … external advantages; country, family, children, relations, riches, houses, gardens, horses, dogs, cloaths" (A30: 659–60). The list is endless. It includes moral attributes, various mental abilities, physical attributes, possessions, family relations. These same general categories can be subjects of humility or shame. As we have seen, the list of things in which we take pride – or of which we are ashamed – may include kinds of things which do not even exist yet. Hume himself couldn't have envisioned the pride or shame we take in our cars or electronic gadgets. He asks of the vast numbers of things we take pride in – or are ashamed of – what they have in common. His answer is that they all include "either parts of ourselves, or something nearly related to us" (T2.1.5.2: 285). They are related to us by way of resemblance, contiguity and, above all, causal relations. Hume thinks ownership, parenting, creativity, etc. all fall under the category of causal relations. I am proud of my new car, my sons, the picture I painted, the paper I wrote.

Hume notes that each of these three relations produces an association of ideas in our minds. When I think of my fellow philosophers (resemblance), my neighbors (spatial proximity), and the essay I wrote (causality), each of those thoughts is connected with the thought of myself.

But the relation to the self is still *not sufficient* by itself to produce pride or humility. We need to take into account what Hume calls the *quality* of the subjects which produce these passions – that is to say their tendency to produce pleasure or uneasiness in any observer (T2.1.5.3: 285–6). He thinks that if we consider all those things we are proud of we find that they are the sorts of things which would produce pleasure in anyone whether he is related to them or not. All those things of which we are ashamed are such that they tend to make people feel uneasy. In order to produce pride or humility, the subjects must *independently* produce pleasure or uneasiness in *any* observer or spectator of them. The ability to produce pleasure or uneasiness is another necessary condition for the production of pride and humility.

Putting these factors together, we discover that anything which is in itself pleasurable and which is related to ourselves, produces pride. Anything which is inherently unpleasant and which is related to us produces humility or shame. Having established this, Hume concludes that these passions originate in a "double relation of ideas and impressions" (T2.1.5.5: 286). To see what this means, let us return to the example of the house. Suppose it is a beautiful house, one which would produce pleasure in any spectator. Then if the house happens to be mine, the pleasure is transferred from the thought of the house to the thought of myself. Moreover, since pleasure is a feeling related to the emotion of pride – the feelings resemble each other in respect of their pleasantness – then the passion which is produced when my thoughts turn to myself is pride. On the other hand, if the house is broken down and dilapidated it would cause pain or uneasiness, and therefore shame through the same mechanism. Pleasure and uneasiness cause these different passions by being transfused along the relation of ideas. The house that I own makes me think of myself, and the pleasure or uneasiness that it produces is transformed into the appropriate passion related to self – whether it be pride or shame.

4. THE MECHANISM OF THE INDIRECT PASSIONS

There are then three key factors in the generation of pride and humility. The first is the fact that each of these passions has the self as its object. The second is that there is a subject which is related to the self. The third is that the subject which is related to the self, quite independently of that relation, produces pleasure or pain in any spectator. Hume thinks that once these factors are present to the mind the passions are produced with little thought or reflection, in a purely mechanical way. Hume describes this mechanism in the following way:

When an idea produces an impression, related to an impression, which is connected with an idea, related to the first idea, these two impressions must be in a manner inseparable, nor will the one in any case be unattended with the other. 'tis after this manner, that the particular causes of pride and humility are determin'd. (T2.1.5.10: 289)

The "first idea" is that of the subject, for example, the house. The impression it produces is pleasure or pain. This pleasure or pain is related to the passion, the first to pride and the second to humility. Finally, pride and humility produce the idea of self, which is related to the "first idea," the idea of the house. The relations of the ideas (the self and the house) make the relations of the impressions (pleasure and pride; pain and humility) "in a manner inseparable."

In summing up the "hypothesis" which he has put forward to explain the generation of pride and humility, Hume argues that the same basic principles are operating here as in his account of belief in Book 1 (T2.1.5.11: 289–90). I will not dwell on the parallels here, since they are much clearer in his subsequent account of sympathy. What we need to note is the fundamental role in Hume's explanation of the phenomena of the human mind of the principles of the association of ideas, *and* of their role in the transfer and (in this case) generation of feeling.

The same principles of association operate in producing the other two indirect passions – love and hatred. The *object* of these passions is another person. The *subject* is something related to that person which, quite independently of its relation to her, produces pleasure or uneasiness. By 'love' Hume often means what we would call 'admiration' or 'esteem.' By 'hatred' he means 'contempt.' Let us return to the example of the beautiful house which would produce pleasure in any spectator. If it now turns out to be related to you, then, when I think of the house, my mind will move to thoughts of you, and the pleasure which the house causes will be transformed into the related passion connected with another person, namely love or admiration for you. If the house is ugly, it will cause an uneasiness in me, and contempt for you, its owner.

Hume does not seem to feel any need to explain how another person can be the object of the passions of love and hate, as he had felt the need in Book 1 to explain how an external object can be the object of our senses. I shall offer some reflection on this asymmetry in the conclusion to this chapter. For now, I just want to stress Hume's overall scheme of the indirect passions.

The same beautiful house that produces pride in me will produce love or esteem in you for me, and the same ugly house that produces shame in me will produce your hatred or contempt for me. Love and hatred have other persons as their objects. Pride and love have in common the fact that they are produced by intrinsically pleasant subjects, and humility and hatred (i.e. shame and contempt) have in common the fact that they are produced by intrinsically painful subjects. Pride and humility have in common the fact that they are produced by subjects related to the self, and love and hatred have in common the fact that they are produced by subjects related to another person.

Here is Hume's schema of the indirect passions:

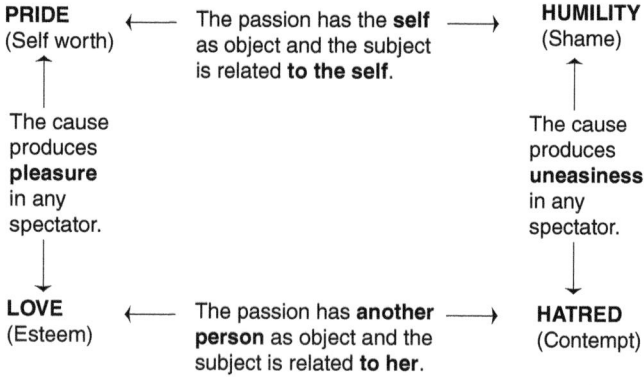

5. QUALIFICATIONS

After presenting the basic principles of the double relations of impressions and ideas which generate the passions of pride and humility Hume presents five "limitations" to his original schema. These qualifications are important since they are central to Hume's subsequent discussion of the variations of these basic indirect passions.

The first qualification is that the subject in which we take pride be strongly related to us (T2.1.6.2–3: 290–1). Hume notes that if the subject is pleasurable to us, but has no strong relation it merely produces joy. He gives the example of a fine feast where only the host feels the indirect passion of pride, and the guests feel only the direct passion of joy.

Hume's second qualification is that the subject must be "peculiar to ourselves" (T2.1.6.4: 291). We don't take pride in things which everyone else also possesses, no matter how pleasant and closely related to ourselves. For example, I don't take pride in my computer even though it gives me much pleasure; but I do in my rare book collection. In explaining the reason for this, Hume introduces two principles which are important in his account of human nature. First, any subject to which we become overly accustomed loses value in our eyes. Second, and more importantly in this case, we "judge of objects more from comparison than from their real and intrinsic merit." The uniqueness of the subject in which I take pleasure (e.g. my rare book), and my comparison with other people who lack it, increases my pleasure and thus my pride.

Hume's third qualification is that pride depends on whether the subject which causes pride "be very discernible and obvious" (T2.1.6.6: 292) This is because our own pleasure in any subject depends very much on the feelings of others, which are transferred to us through *sympathy*. As we shall see, Hume thinks that we cannot sustain pride without its being reinforced by the feelings of others. Similarly, a subject which is "discernible and obvious" is required to sustain the feeling of shame. If my unpleasant subject can be hidden from others, my shame will considerably decrease.

The fourth qualification is that the subject in which I take pride, or of which I feel ashamed, must be something which lasts. "What is casual and inconstant gives but little joy, and less pride" (T2.1.6.7: 293). This principle is also central in Hume's moral theory. We judge the moral worth of ourselves and others only by character traits which are *durable*, not by transient actions which have little to do with our established characters.[8]

---

[8] Compare Chapter 5 §8, pp. 186ff., and Chapter 9 §4, pp. 270ff.

Finally, Hume stresses the influence of *"general rules"* on the pride or shame we feel in different subjects (T2.1.6.8: 293). He writes of a human being "full-grown, and of the same nature as ourselves" who is "suddenly transported into our world" and who would be at a loss to know how much pride or shame, love or hate to feel as a result of her relation to any subject. The reason is that "custom and practice ... have settled the just value of everything ... and guide us, by means of general establish'd maxims, in the proportions we ought to observe in preferring one object to another." Hume is stressing the importance of what we would call *culture* in determining what things are worth. If anything, he underestimates the diversity of these customs or general rules in determining those things which are subjects of pride and humility. Could I really take pride in my rare books unless there were an established practice of doing so among other scholars?

6. VIRTUE AND VICE AS SOURCES OF PRIDE AND SHAME

Hume first introduces *virtue* and *vice* in the *Treatise* as subjects of pride and humility. Virtue and vice are stable features of one's character which produce pleasure or uneasiness, when one reflects on them. One's virtuous characteristics produce pleasure and pride, and one's vices cause uneasiness and shame.

Initially we might consider such a view implausible. In fact, in many people's minds, *it is quite the opposite.* Many people think that vices cause a great deal of pleasure for the person who possesses them. They associate vice with, for example, unrestrained sexual pleasure, and virtue with its restraint. Virtue itself is not naturally pleasurable. Similarly, they think that we naturally take pleasure in selfish behavior, and that generous behavior, which involves restraining our natural selfishness, is originally unpleasant to the person who practices it. We only need to think of how young children cry when other children take their toys away from them. To teach them the virtue of generosity we must teach them to share and so limit their natural unrestrained pleasure in keeping things for themselves.

In fact, Hume alludes to a moral theory which begins with the view that selfish passions are inherently pleasurable and altruistic ones inherently painful. This is a theory which, in the language of

Hume's day, considered virtue and vice to be *artificial*. According to this view, put forward in Hume's day by the philosopher Bernard Mandeville, our own virtue is connected with pleasure, and our vice with shame, only through artifice and education. Mandeville does hold that we receive pain from the vice of others, and pleasure from their virtue and the restraint of their natural selfish passions. But we need to be taught to make these connections in our own case and this, he holds, comes about through praise and blame by other people. At the beginning of society, according to Mandeville, clever politicians realized that the overall good of society required that people restrain their selfishness and, in general, their natural passions. They taught men to value generosity and the restraint of their passions through praise and flattery. Mandeville wrote that "Moral Virtues are the Political Offspring which Flattery begot upon Pride."[9] The process by which people originally learned to recognize their own generosity as virtuous and their own selfishness as vicious was similar to that in which we inculcate virtue in a young child. In general, through praise and blame, adults come to make children feel pleasure in the restraint of natural passions and feel uneasiness and shame when they are indulged in. The restraint is called virtue and the indulgence vice. Through education we artificially reverse the pains and pleasures we naturally associate with our own passions.

Hume's own consideration of this theory in Book 2 stresses its end result, namely that when we reflect on our own virtue (as well as that of other people) we feel pleasure and when we reflect on our own vices we feel pain or uneasiness. "If all morality be founded on pain or pleasure … that may result from our own characters, or from those of others, all the effects of morality must be deriv'd from the same pain or pleasure, and among the rest, the passions of pride or humility" (T2.1.7.4: 295–9). We feel pride when our own characters produce pleasure in ourselves and others, and shame when they produce uneasiness.

Hume also considers another theory of morals put forward in his day which held that we *originally* take pleasure in what is virtuous and are *originally* pained by what it vicious. This was the view put forward by Lord Shaftesbury and Francis Hutcheson. According to

---

[9] Bernard Mandeville, *The Fable of the Bees*, ed. F. B. Kaye (Oxford: Clarendon Press, 1924), 2 vols., Vol. I, p. 51.

them, we naturally feel pleasure in our own virtue and pain in our own vice. We naturally take pleasure in helping other people, though (and this was particularly important in the theory of Hutcheson) we do not approve of generous behavior *because* it is pleasurable. The pleasure constitutes our approval of generous behavior and pain constitutes our disapproval of selfish behavior. For Hutcheson, there are pleasures of different kinds and the specifically moral pleasure is the one we take in generous behavior – whether our own or that of other people.

Hume tells us in this section of Book 2 of the *Treatise* that he will not here directly address "the controversy, which of late years has so much excited the curiosity of the publick, *whether these moral distinctions be founded on natural and original principles, or arise from interest and education*" (T2.1.7.2). What is curious is that in this first discussion of moral theory in the *Treatise* he only presents the views of his predecessors. The fact that he does not present his own moral theory in Book 2 of the *Treatise* may indicate that he had not finally formulated it at this time. We need to remember that Hume published Book 3 of the *Treatise* in 1740, nearly 21 months after Book 2, rewriting it extensively in the light of the criticisms of Hutcheson. We shall see in Chapter 9 that when he finally presents his own theory in Book 3, it is an interesting synthesis of the two views he outlines here, those of Mandeville and Hutcheson.

In treating virtue and vice as sources of pride and humility Hume brings morality down to earth and makes it a regular part of our general psychological makeup. He recognizes that in connecting virtue with pride, and vice with humility, he is going against traditional Christian moral doctrine which makes pride a sin and humility a virtue. For this reason he expects many of his readers to be "surpriz'd to hear [him] talk of virtue as exciting pride, which they look upon as a vice" (T2.1.7.8: 297; cf. T3.3.2.13: 600). What many Christian writers of his day called conscience became for Hume nothing more than shame. There is no need to postulate some special faculty by which we apprehend morals. For Hume, shame, rather than guilt, is the natural feeling which results from reflection on our own vice.[10]

---

[10] For a discussion of some of the issues related to this distinction see Bernard Williams, *Shame and Necessity* (Berkeley: University of California Press, 1993).

7. SYMPATHY, AND THE MIND AS MIRROR OF OTHER MINDS

Each of the five factors which Hume alludes to as "limitations" of his system of pride and humility is central in his account of the indirect passions. They provide ways in which Hume's basic associational model for the indirect passions accounts for the variations discovered through experience. We shall consider in detail the factor behind his third limitation, namely that the subjects of pride and humility must be discernable to others. This factor is sympathy. From this factor, above all, we see how Hume's psychology takes us into the social realm. Sympathy makes it clear that we are social creatures through and through. Sympathy plays a major role not only in his discussion of all four indirect passions but, as we shall see, is also core to his whole theory of moral judgment.

In §6, I mentioned Mandeville's view that we are taught to value certain character traits through praise, and condemn others through blame. In this way, according to him, we come to take pleasure in performing actions like generosity to others, to which we are not naturally inclined. But Hume criticizes Mandeville's account because it does not explain why we care about praise and blame in the first place. How do the opinions of others ever get a hold over us? Why do we care about them? Hume's answer is, in a word, *sympathy*.

Sympathy is first introduced in the *Treatise* as a *secondary* cause of pride and humility. Hume argues that the praise and blame of others can only affect us if we are being praised or blamed for qualities which would themselves directly produce these passions. Praise is only given for such things as "power, or riches, or family, or virtue" which would "if real, produce, of itself, a pride in the person possest of it" (T2.1.11.9: 320). In other words, praise and blame get a hold on us because they are given for qualities which in themselves cause pleasure and uneasiness to ourselves.

But while Hume argues that sympathy is a secondary cause of pride and shame, he argues that these passions cannot be sustained unless they are "seconded by the opinions and sentiments of others" through sympathy (T2.1.11.1: 316). We need to feel the admiration and disapproval of others in order to maintain our feelings of pride and humility. The importance of this influence of other people on our sense of self worth cannot be underestimated. "The minds of men are mirrors to one another, not only because they reflect each others emotions, but also ... [their] sentiments and opinions ..." (T2.2.5.21: 365).

What exactly is sympathy? In the first place, it is important to understand that sympathy is not itself a sentiment or feeling. It is rather the *mechanism* by which we come to enter into the feelings of other people including their admiration and disapproval of ourselves. Sympathy allows us to feel what others feel.

8. THE MECHANISM OF SYMPATHY

Hume begins his discussion of sympathy with an explanation of how sympathy operates. Sympathy begins with what Hume calls "the idea, or rather impression of ourselves [which] is always intimately present with us" (T2.1.11.4: 317). Secondly, we have an idea of the other person's feelings, derived from the "external signs in [their] countenance and conversation." Thirdly, there is a relation between ourselves and the person with whom we sympathize. Finally, through this relation the idea of the person's passion becomes enlivened and it is transformed into the passion itself. We feel what the other person feels.

Our first surprise in reading Hume's account of the mechanism of sympathy comes in what he says about the role of the self in this process. Hume writes:

the idea, or rather impression of ourselves is always intimately present with us, and that our consciousness gives us so lively a conception of our own person, that 'tis not possible to imagine, that any thing can in this particular go beyond it. (T2.1.11.4: 317)

What can Hume mean by this lively idea or impression of self (he seems unsure which to call it) which is "always intimately present with us"? At the beginning of the section "Of personal identity" in Book 1 he rejects the view of those who hold that "we are every moment intimately conscious of what we call our SELF" (T1.4.6.1: 251) and he argues that there is no "constant and invariable impression of self," and therefore no such idea. I suggested earlier in this chapter that the account of self which Hume gives in his explanation of the object of pride, that is, as "that succession of related ideas and impressions, of which we have an intimate memory and consciousness" (T2.1.2.2: 277), appears to be compatible with his Book 1 account. But here Hume's account of self is, if not in downright contradiction with it, very hard to reconcile with it. It is difficult to see how he could be referring to anything but that impression of self which he rejected in Book 1. The impression of self which forms the basis of Hume's account of sympathy is present to our consciousness at every moment of our lives and must somehow be distinguished from and related to other selves with whom we sympathize. It is not clear how it can have those qualities without the constancy and invariability which Hume denied to the self in Book 1. It is true that Hume leaves us a path to reconcile what appear to be two very different accounts of the self. In "Of personal identity" he tells us that we "must distinguish betwixt personal identity, as it regards our thought or imagination, and as it regards our passions or the concern we take in ourselves" (T1.4.6.5: 253). Here, in his account of sympathy that distinction appears to become crucial. But Hume does not explain how the passions are able to generate an impression of self which is identical at every moment of our lives.[11]

No less remarkable is the second element of Hume's account of sympathy, the idea of the other person's feelings – an idea which arises from their words and physical expressions. He writes that "when we sympathize with the passions and sentiments of others, these movements appear at first in *our* mind as mere ideas, and are conceiv'd to belong to another person, as we conceive any other matter of fact" (T2.1.11.8: 319).[12] Ideas, as Hume makes explicit here, are representative. We think of them as representing something beyond themselves – in this case the other person's passions. We shall return to this aspect of sympathy in the conclusion to this chapter.

Thirdly, for sympathy to operate, there must be a relation between the person with whom I sympathize and myself. This is central to Hume's account, for the relation results in an association of ideas,

---

[11]   At T1.4.6.19: 261, where Hume writes of the mind as a causal system, he argues that his account shows how "our identity with regard to the passions serves to corroborate that with regard to the imagination." For reasons I have explained on p. 212, I do not think the idea of self generated in this way can serve the dynamic role required by the "impression of self" to which Hume appeals in the case of sympathy.

[12]   See also Chapter 2 §6, pp. 64ff.

which allows a transfer of feelings. Hume stresses that the relation may only be one of *resemblance*. He notes that there is "a great resemblance among all human creatures" (T2.1.11.5: 318) and that this allows us to sympathize with any human being. At the same time, he stresses that sympathy is greater with those who more closely resemble me – those who speak the same language as I do, who have the same manners, or have the same kind of character. Moreover, the relations of *contiguity* and *causation* increase the degree to which I sympathize with others. Under this latter relation, as we have seen, Hume includes family relationships: I sympathize more with my parents and siblings, and less with my distant cousins. The relation between ourselves and the other person is crucial in Hume's explanation of sympathy because it controls the transfer of psychic energy or vivacity from the idea of myself to that of the other person, and to the idea I have of her feelings: "The stronger the relation is betwixt ourselves and any object, the more easily does the imagination make the transition, and convey to the related idea the vivacity of conception, with which we always form the idea of our own person."

Finally, the result of the transition of psychic energy from the impression or idea of myself to "the ideas of the affections of others" is that they "are converted into the very impressions they represent, and that the passions arise in conformity to the images we form of them." The representation or idea of the other person's feelings is converted into the feelings themselves. Hume glides over a fundamental problem his account does not solve, namely that in the conversion of the idea into the passion the perception would lose its representative quality and cease to be conceived as the passion of the other person. He does say that "we are convinc'd of the reality of the passion, with which we sympathize" through "the relation of cause and effect" as well as the relations of contiguity and resemblance. But while these relations contribute to the enlivening of the idea of the passion, it is difficult to see how they help us to recognize the enlivened feeling as that of the other person, rather than as our own. I shall return to this problem.

Hume stresses the parallel between his explanation of sympathy in Book 2 and the explanation of belief he gave in Book 1: the theory of sympathy, he writes, gives "strong confirmation ... to the foregoing system concerning the understanding" (T2.1.11.8: 319). The parallel he draws is between the enlivening of an idea which makes us believe in matters of fact beyond our senses and memory, and the conversion of an idea of another person's feelings or passions into the very feelings or passions themselves. In the latter case, the case of sympathy, the vivacity of the impression of self is transferred to the idea we have of the other person's feelings, and that idea is then converted to the impression or feeling itself. But Hume is not merely concerned to point out that the vivacity of an impression is transferred to the related idea in both cases, but he argues that the degree of vivacity transferred is regulated by the particular relations involved, be they resemblance, contiguity or cause and effect. And here again, we have a direct parallel to the account of belief in Book 1.

Hume notes that sympathy is a principle which operates in herding animals as well as humans, though he stresses that mankind is "the creature of the universe, who has the most ardent desire for society, and is fitted for it by the most advantages" (T2.2.5.15: 363). He argues that our own feelings become unbearable when they are not shared with another person: "Every pleasure languishes when enjoy'd a-part from company, and every pain becomes more cruel and intolerable." Hume gives a vivid portrayal of a man who can control all nature and yet is completely miserable because he has no one to share it with:

Let the sun rise and set at his command: the sea and rivers roll as he pleases, and the earth furnish spontaneously whatever may be useful or agreeable to him. He will still be miserable, till you give him some one person at least, with whom he may share his happiness, and whose esteem and friendship he may enjoy.

We have the deepest need for another consciousness to reflect back our own feelings if those feelings are to have any meaning or importance for us. For this whole account to work we must recognize the feelings we receive by sympathy as belonging to the other person.

9. THE NATURE OF SYMPATHY

Hume originally introduces the phenomenon of sympathy in Book 2 to explain the effect of the feelings and opinions of other people on our own feelings of pride and humility. Sympathy explains why we are concerned about how others perceive us. Our concern for the opinions of others is not merely an abstract matter of what others think of us. We actually come to share their feelings and opinions[13] about us through sympathy, even when they are at odds with those we ourselves originally held. Hume gives a variety of examples to make this clear. For example, he asks why someone who is madly in love cares if you happen to have a low opinion of his beloved (T2.1.11.19: 324). What effect can your opinion have on his proud feelings? And yet he *will* care a great deal and try to change your opinion of her beauty, wit, or intelligence. Your feelings are transmitted to him through sympathy, and come thereby to make a great deal of difference to his own feeling of pride in his lover.

But we don't care about what just anyone feels about us. We care particularly about the opinions and feelings of those who are closely related to us and those for whom we have some respect. This is evidence, according to Hume, that our "love of fame" is not based in any "original instinct" (T2.1.11.11: 321). It is regulated by sympathy and therefore, as we have seen, by the association of ideas. Hume's theory of relations explains variations in the degree to which we care about the feelings of others, just as his theory of understanding can explain the various degrees of belief in what is real.[14]

Hume describes sympathy as the ability to feel with others while still recognizing that the feelings are those of the other person – as we should now say, to *empathize* with them. He says at different points that we actually "*enter into* the sentiments of others."[15] It is true that he sometimes writes of sympathy as though it merely involved a kind of infection of feelings received from other people: "A cheerful countenance infuses a sensible complacency and serenity into my mind; as an angry or sorrowful one throws a sudden damp upon me."[16] But his considered view is that in sympathy one recognizes the feelings

---

[13] Which are, of course, themselves feelings, according to Hume's analysis of belief in Book 1. In this discussion Hume stresses that opinions "have a peculiar influence, when we judge of our own worth and character" (T2.1.11.9: 321).

[14] Chapter 3 §5ii), p. 112 above

[15] T2.1.11.5: 318; the emphasis is mine. Cf. T2.2.5.7: 360 and T2.2.5.14: 362.

[16] T2.1.11.2: 317. Similarly, in Book 3, in applying the principle of sympathy to his explanation of moral judgment he uses a purely physical analogy which gives little hint that we recognize the feeling received as belonging to another center of consciousness: "As in strings equally wound up, the motion of one communicates itself to the rest, so all the affections readily

as those of the other, and that one never loses sight of the difference between one's own feelings and that of the other person. Hume writes that "in sympathy our own person is not the object of a passion, nor is there any thing, that fixes our attention on ourselves" (T2.2.2.17: 340). When I feel what the other feels, her feelings are still recognized as hers and not my own. If I sympathize with someone who is angry I do not just feel a generalized anger, but I recognize the direction of that anger, even if it is toward myself.

That this is Hume's view becomes clear from a discussion in Part 2 of Book 2, in a section entitled "Of our esteem for the rich and powerful." He stresses that we are not only able to "enter into the sentiments of the rich and poor, and partake of their pleasure and uneasiness" through sympathy, but also partake of their very *interests* (T2.2.5.14: 362). He describes a situation in which a wealthy man takes us on a tour of his house, pointing out the convenience of the rooms and the utility of his possessions. Hume stresses that "our own interest is not in the least concern'd" in the matter (T2.2.5.16: 364). "We enter into his interest by the force of imagination, and feel the same satisfaction, that the objects naturally occasion in him."

Similarly, he explains how, through sympathy, we come to feel the "affliction and sorrow" of those in misery, and so come to pity them (T2.2.7.2: 369). "Their persons, and therefore their interests, their passions, their pains and pleasures must strike upon us in a lively manner, and produce an emotion similar to the original one." He defines pity as a "desire of happiness of another, and aversion to his misery" (T2.2.9.3: 382). He opposes the view of philosophers like Hobbes and Mandeville who claim that when we pity the poverty or wretchedness of others we do so from "subtile reflections on the instability of fortune" and reason that we are "liable to the same miseries we behold" (T2.2.7.4: 370).[17] Hume argues that the automatic nature of sympathy precludes such a rationalistic and

---

pass from one person to another, and beget correspondent movements in every human creature" (T3.3.1.7: 576).

[17] Mandeville argues that "there is no Merit in saving an innocent Babe ready to drop into the Fire" because in saving her "we only gratified ourselves." According to Mandeville, we reason that if we were to see the baby fall, "and not strove to hinder it," that "would have caused a Pain, which Self-preservation compell'd us to prevent" (B. Mandeville, "An Enquiry into the Origin of Moral Virtue," in *The Fable of the Bees*, Vol. I, p. 56); see Chapter 9 §4, pp. 273ff. for the importance of Hume's criticism of Mandeville for his theory of moral judgment.

self-interested account of pity.[18] Pity is based on the imagination and not reason.

In his account of pity, Hume's analysis of sympathy as involving us in the interests and intentions of the other person becomes crucial. If our passions arose merely from the double relations of impressions and ideas we would simply feel contempt for the person in misery, a familiar enough experience when we casually pass a beggar in the street. "Nothing," Hume writes, "has a greater tendency to give us... contempt [for a person], than his poverty and meanness" (T2.2.5.1: 357). For the casual sight of poverty causes nothing but uneasiness in us, and that is the source of hatred or contempt. "A weak impression, that is painful," he writes, "is related to anger and hatred by the resemblance of sensations" (T2.2.9.15: 387). However, through what Hume calls the *"extensive sympathy"* which operates in pity I don't merely feel the other person's misery; I "concern myself in his good fortune as well as his bad" (T2.2.9.12: 386; my emphasis). Hume attributes this ability to empathize with another to the strength of one's original idea of the other person's misery: "When the present misery of another has any strong influence upon me, the vivacity of the conception is not confin'd merely to its immediate object, but diffuses its influence over all the related ideas, and gives me a lively notion of all the circumstances of that person, whether past, present or future; possible, probable or certain." The person's *interests* are felt by me, not merely his present pain and suffering.

Hume stresses that the pity and the related benevolence I feel toward the other person from extensive sympathy "arises from a great degree of misery, or any degree strongly sympathiz'd with" (T2.2.9.15: 387). He uses an analogy from hydraulics to explain the principle he is appealing to here: "If I diminish the vivacity of the first conception, I diminish that of the related ideas; as pipes can convey no more water than what arises at the fountain" (T2.2.9.14: 386). Unless there is sufficient pressure at the source, I will not carry my feelings beyond the person's present misery to a concern for his future interest and welfare.

---

[18] In support of his view, Hume claims that women and children are more liable to pity than men. He is appealing to a standard view of his day that women have much livelier imaginations than men. As evidence he appeals to the 'fact' that they will "faint at the sight of a naked sword, tho' in the hands of their best friend"!

This vivacious idea of the other person's suffering does not need to arise from any direct observation. Indeed, Hume argues that through imagination and the influence of "general rules" we may develop a lively idea of the person's suffering which goes well beyond what the person actually feels. He argues that pity can arise in situations where the person being sympathized with actually feels little or no pain: "The communicated passion of pity sometimes acquires strength from the weakness of its original, and even arises by a transition from affections, which have no existence" (T2.2.7.5: 370). Hume's example is "a person of great merit" who "falls into what is vulgarly esteem'd a great misfortune," but who patiently bears it without the usual suffering. He rises above it through "greatness of mind," and yet for all that we still feel sorry for him through sympathy. A "*general rule*" is applied from our experience of what people normally feel in like situations, and we ascribe to him a pain which he does not actually feel (T2.2.7.5–6: 371). Perhaps even more to the point is Hume's historical example of our pity for the "infant prince, who is captive in the hands of his enemies" and has no consciousness "of his miserable condition" before he is murdered. We generalize from what an adult who is fully conscious would feel in such a situation. We feel the infant prince's sorrow all the more, according to Hume, because of his own insensibility. We are concerned for him for pains he cannot himself feel, and our sense of his suffering becomes greater when we compare his insensibility with the suffering we would feel in the situation. Such is the power of imagination in transferring feeling.[19]

Thus, a vivid idea of another's pleasure or pain may arise merely from our observation of its usual causes. In order to sympathize with others, we do not require the presence of those external signs in the person's "countenance and conversation" which Hume describes in his initial account (T2.1.11.3: 317). We only need to observe the cause from which such pleasure and suffering generally result in order to concern ourselves in a person's future welfare. This is sufficient to communicate "the pains and pleasures of others which ... we only anticipate by the force of imagination" (T2.2.9.13: 385). Hume gives

[19] One may wonder if the extensive sympathy which Hume describes here may be at work in current debates regarding the use of discarded embryos for stem cell research. Is it possible that opponents may have concern for the non-existent future welfare of these embryos through the power of imagination which Hume describes in this discussion!?

the example of seeing a stranger sleeping in a field who is "in danger of being trod under foot by horses." We anticipate and concern ourselves in the person's future welfare merely from our awareness of the causes in the present situation which will bring it about. The causal antecedents of his pain and suffering are sufficient for us to sympathetically concern ourselves in his future interests.

It seems questionable whether the principles to which Hume appeals here are sufficient to account for extensive sympathy and the pity and compassion, and benevolence which follow it. Unfortunately, he never returns to a key element of his original mechanism of sympathy, namely that the whole process begins with the force and vivacity of the idea of ourselves being transferred to those of the other person. As Jennifer Herdt has pointed out, our ability to partake of the interests of others depends fundamentally on our own self esteem and the strength of our own egos.[20] It is only because we have a healthy and strong sense of self that we can have a full sense of the other person, and of her interests as well as her present pleasures and pains. It seems clear that the strength of our sense of self varies, and that that variation plays an essential role in our ability to empathize with others. Hume's basic scheme of the generation of sympathetic feeling provides for such an account, but he seems not to have taken full advantage of it in explaining how we develop an extensive sympathy for others.

10. CONCLUSION: SYMPATHY, THE PASSIONS AND THE PROBLEM OF OTHER MINDS

Before leaving this topic I want to consider more broadly the implications of Hume's claim that in sympathy we have access to the feelings and interests of other minds. This claim is quite remarkable, for it seems clear that through sympathy, and the passions generally, we have the ability to get outside of ourselves, which ability Hume seems to deny us in Book 1 of the *Treatise*. There he writes that if we "chace our imagination to the heavens, or to the utmost limits of

---

[20] "What is required for the sort of sympathy which enables compassion is not self-forgetfulness but a stable self-esteem which is capable of appreciating fully the reality of others." (Jennifer Herdt, *Religion and Faction in Hume's Moral Philosophy* (Cambridge University Press, 1997), p. 46.

the universe; *we never really advance a step beyond ourselves*, nor can conceive any kind of existence, but those perceptions, which have appear'd in that narrow compass" (T1.2.6.8: 67–8; my emphasis). As we have seen in Chapter 4, one of the major problems of Book 1 is to explain how we can think of a physical object as independent of ourselves, since all perceptions are merely mind-dependent entities. The best Hume can do to solve this problem is to claim that the mind plays a kind of trick on us through a "fiction" of the imagination, which makes us believe that our perceptions exist while unperceived.[21] But in Book 2, where he is constantly writing about our access to the feelings of others, Hume seems to think there is no problem to be solved. He never refers to other persons or their feelings as *fictions*. Not only does sympathy allow us to "enter into" the feelings and interests of other people, but the passions of love and hatred have for their object a "thinking, conscious being" (T2.2.5.13: 262) quite independent of ourselves. In Book 3 of the *Treatise* he writes that the principle of sympathy "*takes us so far out of ourselves*, as to give us the same pleasure or uneasiness in the characters of others … as if they had a tendency to our own advantage or loss" (T3.3.1.11: 579; my italics). How can Hume deny in Book 1 that we can ever legitimately think of an external object as independent of us, and in Books 2 and 3 allow that we are genuinely aware of other people as independent? Especially when at the beginning of the latter book he insists that the same principles operate as in Book 1, and repeats his earlier claim from Book 1 that "nothing is ever present to the mind but its perceptions" (3.1.1.2: 456)?

This remarkable feature of Hume's *Treatise* has been stressed by various commentators. Terence Penelhum writes of "the cultural shock that one experiences when passing from Book I to Book II," when one finds Hume simply taking for granted "the self-other distinction."[22] Norman Kemp Smith thought that the fact that Hume simply assumes that the passions are outwardly directed indicates that he has just accepted this theory from his predecessor Hutcheson.[23] This historical claim seems wrong: Hume himself

---

[21] Chapter 4, pp. 146–50.   [22] Penelhum, *Themes in Hume*, p. 123.
[23] Norman Kemp Smith, *The Philosophy of David Hume: A Study of its Origins and its Central Doctrines* (London: Macmillan, 1941), pp. 550–1.

ascribes the claim that "even the passions commonly esteem'd self-ish, carry the Mind beyond Self, directly to the Object" to Joseph Butler, not Hutcheson.[24] Moreover, Hume clearly contrasts his own account of moral judgment, which bases our fellow-feeling on sympathy, with Hutcheson's idea of an instinctive moral sense.[25] At the same time, Kemp Smith seems to have been right that Hume never succeeds in explaining our belief in other minds. While Hume's associational account of the conversion of an idea of another person's passion into the passion itself plays a fundamental role in explaining the hold which other people's feelings and opinions have on us, it still does not fully explain our belief in the independence of those feelings from our own. Hume himself seems to acknowledge this when he writes that the phenomenon which sympathy is supposed to explain is "an object of the plainest experience, and depends not on any hypothesis of philosophy" (T2.1.11.8: 319–20). The phenomenon of sympathy which Hume seeks to explain through his mechanistic principle of association outdistances the explanation which he provides for it.

While it is important to note that Hume takes for granted our access to other minds, it is also important to note that he seeks to explain the variations in our fellow feeling through association of ideas, and other principles of the imagination. As we have seen in this chapter, Hume stresses the role of association of ideas in generating our concern for the feelings of others through sympathy. In his *Abstract* he writes that the three principles of association are "so far as regards the mind ... the only links that ... connect us with any person or object exterior to ourselves. For it is by means of thought only that any thing operates on our passions" (A35: 662). It is the natural relations of association which regulate the transference of psychic

---

[24] Hume's remark is from a note to the first two editions of his *Enquiry Concerning Human Understanding*, where he gives examples of two philosophers – Hutcheson and Butler – who have contributed to the distinctions of "the parts of the mind" (EHU 1.14). In criticising Hobbes' selfish account of pity or compassion in Sermon 5, Butler asked rhetorically: "For does not every body by compassion mean an affection, the object of which is another in distress?" ("Sermons V, Upon Compassion," in *The Works of Joseph Butler*, ed. W. E. Gladstone, Vol. II (Oxford: Clarendon Press, 1896), p. 93. For the distinction which Hume ascribes to Hutcheson see Chapter 8, p. 236.

[25] See Chapter 9, pp. 284–8.

energy from the idea or impression of self to our idea of other selves in sympathy. Such transference is strong in the case of those closely related to ourselves but, as we have seen, the factors determining its strength where strangers are concerned are complex. And yet, as we shall see in Chapter 9, they are crucial in Hume's account of moral judgment.

CHAPTER 7

Motivation: reason and calm passions

Hume begins his discussion "Of the influencing motives of the will" (T2.3.3) by noting that most moral philosophy, both ancient and modern, is founded on the idea that there is a "combat of passion and reason," and that a person is virtuous only in so far as reason is the victor in this combat (T2.3.3.1: 413). On this view, we "ought to oppose" our passions by way of reason. In criticizing this view Hume argues that "reason alone" is impotent, and that therefore it can never act in opposition to our passions. Also, that *calm passions* are mistaken for reason. To the extent that there is anything like a combat which characterizes our moral life it is really a conflict between "calm passions" and violent ones. But, as we shall see, Hume's own moral theory tends to downplay any such combat. Moral feelings are a subset of calm passions which can, at least in principle, overcome our violent passions "without... opposition" (T2.3.4.1: 419).[1]

The theory that Hume attacks in this section is clearly Platonic. In Book 4 of the *Republic* Plato wrote of a "civil war of the soul" and argued that it is "appropriate for the rational element to rule" over the spirited and desiring parts of the soul.[2] More directly, Hume is concerned with modern theories such as those of the Newtonian philosopher Samuel Clarke, who wrote that virtue is founded in

the Domination of Reason, and *Religion* over all the irregularities of *Desires* and *Passions*. Every *Vice*, and every instance of *Wickedness*, of *whatever* kind it be; has its Foundation in *some unreasonable Appetite* or *ungoverned Passion, warring against the Law of the Mind.*[3]

---

[1] Chapter 9 §4, pp. 270ff.
[2] See Plato, *Republic*, trans. Tom Griffith, (Cambridge University Press, 2000), 440ᶜ–441ᶜ.
[3] Samuel Clarke, "The Difference Between Living after the Flesh and Spirit," *Sermons on Several Subjects*, 7ᵗʰ edn., 11 vols. (London, 1749), Vol. VIII, p. 19.

We find here the image of a war or combat between an unreasonable desire or "ungoverned Passion" on the one hand and "the Law of the Mind" or reason on the other. Clarke says that virtue lies in the "Dominion of Reason" over the "*Desires and Passions.*" As we shall see in Chapter 8, Clarke was also a major proponent of the rationalist theory of moral judgment which Hume criticizes at the beginning of Book 3.[4]

While Hume's *section* "Of the influencing motions of the will" is perhaps the one most commented on and discussed of the *Treatise*, there is widespread disagreement on its interpretation. A great deal hangs on the question of what Hume means by "reason" and what he means by the "calm passions" or "calm desires" which have been mistaken for it (T2.3.3.8–9).

I. ONCE AGAIN, WHAT HUME MEANS BY 'REASON'[5]

Hume gives a consistent account of what he means by *reason* in the section "Of the influencing motives of the will" (T2.3.3) and the closely allied section of Book 3 where he criticizes the rationalist theory of moral judgment (T3.1.1). This account reflects the representative notion of ideas which he assumes throughout the *Treatise*. In the section on motivation in Book 2 he writes of reason as a faculty in our minds "which judges of truth and falshood" (T2.3.3.8: 417) and tells his reader that the contradiction "to truth and reason ... consists in the disagreement of ideas, consider'd as copies, with those objects, which they represent" (T2.3.3.5: 415). Again, in Book 3 he writes that "reason is the discovery of truth or falshood ... [and] truth or falshood consists in an agreement or disagreement either to the *real* relations of ideas, or to *real* existence and matter of fact" (T3.1.1.9: 458). The type of reasoning which determines whether or not our ideas correspond to "the *real* relations of ideas" is demonstration, and to "*real* existence and matter of fact" is probability.

What seems to me important for our present topic in these passages is Hume's claim that the faculty of reason is concerned with discovering what is *real* – that is, what is represented by our ideas. Even in the

⁴ Chapter 8, pp. 243–4ff.
⁵ Cf. Chapter 2, pp. 74ff. and Chapter 3, pp. 89–90 and pp. 106–7.

case of demonstration, which for Hume is limited to mathematical reasoning, our aim is to discover real or objective relations. This view accords with his discussion of mathematics in Part 2 of Book 1 where, as we have seen, he defends a form of mathematical realism.[6] While we might find this general account of reason puzzling, we need to recognize that this was not a passing conception for Hume. In his *Enquiry Concerning the Principles of Morals*, first published in 1752, well over a decade after the *Treatise*, he writes that reason is the faculty by which "one discovers objects, as they really stand in nature" (EPM, App.1.21). Its standard, he claims, is "founded on the nature of things," a nature which is not only independent of our will, but is "eternal and inflexible, even by the will of the Supreme Being."

Reason, then, is the power in our minds by which we make discoveries about what is real. As we shall see in Chapter 8, the contrast between moral judgment and scientific judgment is fundamental for Hume.[7] At the same time, the reasoning which we do in both spheres is the same. Hume argues that this reasoning can never give us the primary impulse to act, or to make moral judgments. The primary basis for human action must come from a different power of the mind than that which is concerned with the discovery of truth and falsehood.

2. REASON ALONE DOES NOT PROVIDE ANY MOTIVATION TO THE WILL

Hume bases his argument that reason alone does not motivate the will on an account of the actual role which reason plays in our everyday actions. He begins by discussing the role of demonstrative reason. It may seem superfluous to us to show that demonstrative reasoning does not determine the ends or goals of our actions. But, in fact, this is the role which was given to demonstrative reason by philosophers like Clarke who argued that morality is based in reason. Hume himself limits demonstrative reasoning to mathematics, but he still needs to contend with philosophers such as Clarke and Locke[8] who think that demonstrative reasoning is the source of moral distinctions.

---

[6] Chapter 3, pp. 86–7.   [7] Chapter 8, §9, pp. 253ff.
[8] ECHU, 3.11.16; 4.3.18; and 4.4.10.

Hume does not turn to a direct consideration of these theories until Part 1 of Book 3 of the *Treatise*. In his discussion of the motives of the will in Book 2 he contents himself with arguing that the most obvious form of demonstrative reasoning – namely that which we employ in mathematics – does not determine the ends of human actions, but merely the means by which those ends can be fulfilled. A merchant uses arithmetic to calculate how much he owes his debtors. But that is only to determine the means by which he may achieve his goals of "paying his debt, and going to market" to buy new goods to sell (T2.3.3.2: 414). Similarly, mathematical calculation is necessary to build machines like those we use to pump water or spread seeds. But it does not cause us to build the machines in the first place or have the desires for which we need such machines.

What about probable reasoning, or reasoning about matters of fact? Hume provides the following account of the way such reasoning enters into human action. Desire or aversion arises from the consideration of "the prospect of pain or pleasure from any object" (T2.3.3.3: 414). For example, I might see a beautiful house which arouses in me the desire to own it. I anticipate the great pleasure I will have in living in this house. Hume states that probable reasoning then takes place in order to discover "whatever objects are connected its original one by the relation of cause and effect." Those causes and effects are "pointed out to us by reason and experience." They would be used to learn whether the house is well constructed, whether it is made of materials which are likely to last, whether I am likely to find neighbors who are congenial, whether there are schools close by for my children as they grow up, whether this is an area which is flooded during heavy rains, etc. In other words, I use probable reasoning to learn whether buying this house is likely to cause the pleasure which I originally anticipated from owning it.

While it may be true that the primary desire to achieve the pleasure of home owning is not a result of reasoning, reasoning does result in the creation of a number of secondary desires. In casting around for the means of achieving my primary goal I will develop desires such as the desire to borrow money at a low rate of interest, to hire an expert to inspect the house for any serious building flaws, etc. Hume stresses that I would not have such secondary desires unless I had the primary one: "Where the objects themselves do not affect us, their connexion [which we discover through probable reasoning] can never give them any influence" (T2.3.3.3). The primary impulse to action must come from some direct feeling ultimately based in our senses and memory.

Consider the following objection, based on our example, to Hume's claim that the original impulse to act cannot come from reason. The desire to own a house, it may be argued, may come simply from observing the pleasure of others who own houses. Perhaps I have a number of friends who own houses and note the great pleasure they take in house owning. May I not generalize from their experiences and so reason that I too would gain pleasure from owning a house – without in any way actually feeling such pleasure? Couldn't my desire to own a house, and even this particular house arise purely from reason in this way?

Hume's answer would, I think, be something like the following. One could certainly discover through reason that others take pleasure in owning their houses. But unless I somehow feel that pleasure myself, I will have no desire to act. Perhaps I felt my friends' pleasure through sympathy, and it is that which leads to my having the desire to own a house myself. Or after generalizing from my friends' experiences I started thinking about what it would be like to own a house myself, and comparing it with the pleasure of other experiences of ownership I have had. As a result, a desire arises in me to own a house. But, and this is Hume's point, reason by itself cannot be the source of this desire. It can only discover what is true or false about reality.

The objection and reply should remind us of the exact nature of Hume's claim. Hume is arguing that *reason alone*, the faculty by which we compare objects and determine what is true and false, does not by itself give us any desire or impulse to act.

3. THERE IS NO OPPOSITION BETWEEN REASON AND PASSION

Having argued that reason alone is not the primary source of any action, Hume proceeds to argue that there can be no opposition between reason and the passions, as philosophers like Plato and

Clarke had believed. He thinks that this simply follows from the conclusion he has already reached. Since reason by itself is not an original source of any motivation, because in itself it is impotent, it cannot "oppose or retard the impulse of passion" by providing a contrary impulse (T2.3.3.4: 415).

Again it is important to focus on the precise nature of Hume's claim. He does not deny that through reason we can make a discovery which will make us give up a passion – or what for him in this context is the same thing, a *desire*. For example, our homebuyer might reason from certain signs in the basement that the house has serious drainage problems, and as a result cease to have any desire to buy the house. But Hume correctly points out that this does not imply that there is any combat between reason and our original desire: he writes that "our passions" in such a case "yield to our reason without any opposition" (T2.3.3.7: 416). The original desire disappears because I discover that the pleasure which I anticipated from owning the house would be outweighed by the pains of having to solve such major problems. It is not as a result of a conflict between reason and desire.

One might object that there certainly are examples of unreasonable desires or passions which are in conflict with a person's reason. What about a person who is seriously ill with diabetes, and who desires and eats rich desserts? The person may well know the serious possibility of diabetic shock and even death which may result from the satisfaction of her craving, and therefore try to overcome it. Is this not an example of a conflict of a passion and reason – which each of us experiences in a lesser way every day of our lives? I am sitting here writing about Hume, but I feel a desire to go to the kitchen and find a snack. I know that doing so would distract me from thinking through and writing about his theory of motivation. I reason that I may also overeat and so lose my ability to concentrate on the idea I am writing about. Reasoning about these consequences, I overcome my desire and decide to keep working. Or perhaps my desire to have a snack is so strong that I get up and go to the kitchen. Surely, in such cases there is a combat between a passion on the one hand, and reason on the other. They are pulling me in opposite directions.

4. ARE THERE UNREASONABLE DESIRES?

Is the craving of our diabetic for rich desserts really an unreasonable desire? Hume recognizes that we do *call* such cravings unreasonable; however, he insists that it is "not the passion, properly speaking, which is unreasonable," but the accompanying false "judgment or opinion" (T2.3.3.6: 416). If the diabetic judges falsely that she can eat sweets without any danger to her life, then she has a misconception about the world; and her craving for sweets is only called unreasonable in relation to this false judgment.

Our secondary desires may also be called unreasonable in the sense that they may be based on false judgments about cause and effect. Suppose I desire to buy the house because I think that it will make my life easier and more satisfying, when the exact opposite is the case. Perhaps, having failed to have the house inspected properly, I find myself with innumerable repairs to make and have no relish for such tasks. Then my failure of reason has given me what may, by extension, be called an unreasonable desire. But it is because of a false supposition about means to ends that the desire is called unreasonable. Strictly speaking, the original desire itself is not unreasonable, only the false opinion about the world which led me to have it.

Hume allows that there are two kinds of false suppositions which may make our passions or desires, *in a sense*, unreasonable: "A passion can never, in any sense, be call'd unreasonable, but when founded on a false supposition, or when it chuses means insufficient for the design'd end" (T2.3.3.7: 416–17). When one realizes the falsity of the suppositions connected with one's desire, the desire ceases. Hume's example of the first case is of someone who desires some "fruit as of an excellent relish" and who becomes convinced that it is not. What she has desired – say a sweet lemon – does not exist, and when she becomes convinced of the falsity of this supposition the desire disappears. The desire of our home buyer who falsely supposes that buying the house will bring him great pleasure is unreasonable in the second sense: it involves a false supposition about the means to a desired end. Once he learns that buying the house will not result in "the design'd end" he gives up the original desire. Also, the desire of our diabetic who supposes that eating sweets would bring her no harm is unreasonable in this second sense. Once she understands the falsity of her supposition, her desire should cease.

But suppose the diabetic is under no illusions, and fully recognizes that the satisfaction of her craving for sweets endangers her life. Nevertheless, she continues to want sweets and acts on her desire. Then Hume would argue that her desire is not unreasonable in any sense. He writes: "'tis as little contrary to reason to prefer even my own acknowleg'd lesser good to my greater, and have a more ardent affection for the former than the latter" (T2.3.3.6). Of course, he would recognize that we can criticize her desire in other ways: it may well be immoral to have such wanton disregard for one's own life and to care more for the satisfaction of a purely sensual desire. Like other eighteenth-century philosophers Hume holds we have duties to ourselves as well as other people. But our disregard for our duties to ourselves is not a failure of reason: "'tis not contrary to reason for me to chuse my total ruin, to prevent the least uneasiness of an Indian or person wholly unknown to me." The moral fault of the person who does not care properly for herself lies in her affections or feelings, not in her faculty of reason.

5. THE NON-REPRESENTATIVE NATURE OF PASSIONS AND DESIRES

We certainly are tempted to use the term 'unreasonable' for the desire of someone who wantonly chooses short-term pleasure at the expense of her own greater happiness. However, Hume argues that to be opposed to reason the desire itself would somehow have to fail to correspond to the facts. According to him, a desire for pleasure just is what it is: it does not represent anything beyond itself. Unlike an idea, a desire or passion is not the sort of mental content which does or does not correspond with the facts: "A passion is an original existence ... and contains not any representative quality, which renders it a copy of any other existence" (T2.3.3.5: 415). He uses the example of anger: "When I am angry, I am actually possest with the passion, and in that emotion have no more a reference to any other object, than when I am thirsty, or sick, or more than five foot high."

Annette Baier once argued that in this passage Hume disregards what he had written of the passions earlier in Book 2. She stated that what Hume writes in this "very silly paragraph … has perversely dominated the interpretation of his moral psychology."[9] Specifically, she claimed that he disregards what he had previously written about anger – which makes it clear that this passion has an object (another person), a cause (the belief that the other person has caused some harm or displeased one in some way),[10] and a goal (that the other person be miserable).[11]

Baier went on to suggest that Hume's claim about the non-representative nature of passions is "a temporary aberration, an atypical and counter-productive blind swipe at his rationalist opponents."[12] However, at least from a historical point of view, this seems wrong. The view that Hume expresses here is essentially that expressed in Descartes' third Meditation where he noted that acts of will and passions cannot be false. Descartes wrote that "as for the will and the emotions … one need not worry about falsity; for even if the things which I may desire are wicked or even non-existent, that does not make it any less true that I desire them" (CSM II, 26). Cartesian passions, unlike ideas, do not have what he called "objective reality" (p. 27); they do not have any representative content. Like Hume later, Descartes held that passions themselves, unlike the judgments and ideas connected with them, do not represent anything beyond themselves.

To understand Hume's point let us return to his example of anger and focus on what he considers to be its usual *cause*, namely the opinion that the person one is angry at has caused some harm, or at least displeased one in some way.[13] Hume would allow that there is *an extended sense* in which anger can be said to be unreasonable, namely if this *opinion* is false. But now, consider someone who is angry at

---

[9]   Annette Baier, *A Progress of Sentiments: Reflections on Hume's Treatise* (Cambridge, Mass.: Harvard University Press, 1991), p. 160.

[10] "Whoever harms or displeases us never fails to excite our anger or hatred" (T2.2.3.2: 348; cf. 2.2.1.2: 329).

[11] While Hume insists that anger and hatred are distinct passions he holds that the latter as well as the former result in a desire for the "misery of the person" who is the object of the passion (T2.2.6.6: 368).

[12] Baier, *Progress of Sentiments*, p. 163.

[13] Strictly speaking, anger is the corresponding desire for the misery of another person which is caused by our hatred for them. Hume stresses that it is an independent passion which is naturally conjoined with hatred (T2.2.6). I am here treating the hatred/anger complex as one, as Hume generally does, considering the cause of hatred as also the cause of anger.

another *without its usual cause* – that is, as we commonly say, without any reason. Suppose we convince Sally, who is angry at Tom, that Tom has caused her no harm, and that the harm she thought he had caused was actually caused by another person – and yet she remains angry at Tom. When pressed, she denies that Tom has displeased her in any way. Wouldn't *we* now want to say that Sally's anger is unreasonable? However, what *Hume* would insist on is that Sally's anger does not fail to correspond to the facts. For there is no longer any misapprehension of the facts on Sally's part. He would allow that Sally's passion, her continuing anger at Tom, is *inappropriate* – just like the continued craving of our diabetic for sweets when she knows that eating them will endanger her life. But the passion and desire themselves do not misrepresent anything in the world. Since they are not the kind of perception which purports to represent anything at all, they cannot be considered as *unreasonable* in the strict and philosophical sense of the word.

To criticize a person who feels a passion or desire in inappropriate circumstances is not to criticize her for making a false judgment about reality. There is no failure of reason in this case. Rather, the person is lacking an appropriate or preferred affective response. Hume captures this general point earlier in Book 2 when he stresses the difference between what he calls the "*the philosophy* of our passions" and the philosophy of the understanding (T2.1.10.4: 311). Our passions have, as it were, a completely different logic than our reason or understanding. When passions *go wrong*, as in the case of the person who remains angry after the appropriate causes are removed, or in the case of the person who continues to have a craving which she knows will endanger her life, there is no failure to understand reality.

Hume's claim that "a passion is an original existence" which does not contain "any representative quality" is, it seems to me, fundamental to his theory of the passions (T2.3.3.5: 415). From the beginning of Book 2 Hume stresses that the causes and objects of the passions are entirely distinct from the passions themselves. As we have seen in Chapter 6, for Hume it is a contingent matter that pride has the self for its object and is caused by a subject related to the self which is an independent source of pleasure. These are relations that must be discovered by experience. Hume's *separability principle* applies to all perceptions and passions, as well as ideas. Just because passions have opinions or beliefs as their causes, beliefs that can be true or false, this does not mean that the passions themselves can be true or false. Fundamentally, they are not the kind of mental content which represents – or misrepresents – anything in the world.

6. CALM VS. VIOLENT PASSIONS

Let us return to the claim that there is an opposition between passion and reason in cases like those of our diabetic who fights her craving for sweets with the full knowledge that she is endangering her life. In this case, Hume would argue that, properly speaking, what is contending with her craving for sweets is a certain instinct "originally implanted in our natures," namely "the love of life" (T2.3.3.8: 417). This is an example of what he calls a calm desire or passion which, because it produces "little emotion in the mind," is mistaken for reason. Like reason, such a calm desire "exerts itself without producing any sensible emotion," that is any feeling of pleasure or pain. Nevertheless, the love of life *is* a passion, and one which constantly operates within each of us, leading us to avoid those things which will lead us into danger. Similarly, what is contending with my desire to go to the kitchen for a snack is my strong desire to complete my writing, based on ambition and similar passions. For reasons which I will explain in a moment, Hume argues that such ambition does not manifest itself in an overt feeling. His point is that in each of these cases, the impulse which is contrary to my conscious passion or desire is itself a passion – even though it manifests itself without any emotional intensity, and we may not even be conscious of its operation. But it does not arise from reason – from the faculty which discovers what is true and false.

Hume's own example of such a calm passion is long-range self-interest. Consider an industrious business person whose life is dominated by the desire to increase his wealth, and who is constantly finding opportunities to do so. Such a calm love of gain would be part of what Hume calls the person's "*general* character," and there would be no indication of any violent feelings of emotion as he daily pursues his business. Hume notes that such persons would "often counter-act a violent passion in prosecution of their interests and designs" (T2.3.3.10: 418). Nevertheless, even a person dominated by such a calm passion may on occasion be overcome by a violent passion. Hume notes that when we are angry we often desire the harm of a person who has injured us without thinking of our own self-interest: we "desire his evil and punishment, independent of all considerations of pleasure and advantage to myself" (T2.3.3.9–10: 418). Thus, "men often act knowingly against their interest." On the whole, however, a strong character such as that of our business person who has a "calm desire of riches and a fortune"[14] would normally be able to resist such immediate "sollicitations of passion and desire" and overcome the anger he feels at the harm which another has done to him (T2.3.3.10: 418). Hume notes that "what we call strength of mind, implies the prevalence of the calm passions above the violent."

Thus the so-called war between reason and the passions is really a conflict between calm and violent passions. Hume writes that both calm and violent passions "operate on the will; and where they are contrary ... either of them prevails, according to the *general* character or *present* disposition of the person" (T2.3.3.10: 418). He holds that violent passions will generally win out over calm ones, though "the calm ones, when corroborated by reflection, and seconded by resolution, are able to controul them in their most furious movements" (T2.3.8.13: 437–8). A calm passion *can* be stronger than a violent passion and so be able to control it.

There are also factors which can, he says, change the calm passions back into violent ones, especially what he calls the "circumstances and situation of the object" (T2.3.8.13: 438). When an object is brought close to us it produces "a turbulent and sensible emotion."[15] Think here about our industrious business person, when he is about to lose a deal by making the wrong decision. In such a situation, he may lose all sense of his long-range self-interest, through his greed in the present moment. Hume notes that "contiguous objects ... have an influence much superior to the distant and remote."[16]

---

[14] *Dissertation on the Passions*, in *A Dissertation on the Passions and The Natural History of Religion*, ed. Tom L. Beauchamp (Oxford: Clarendon Press, 2007), §5.2, p. 24.

[15] *Dissertation on the Passions*, 5.3, p. 24.

[16] T2.3.7.3: 428. This principle plays a fundamental role in his explanation of the need for government and punishments for violations of the laws of justice.

7. STRONG CALM PASSIONS AND THE DEVELOPMENT OF CHARACTER

How do strong calm passions arise? Hume holds that some, like the "love of life" which contends with our diabetic's craving for sweets, are *instinctively* built into us. Other instinctive calm passions which he mentions, besides the love of life, are "benevolence and resentment ... and kindness to children" (T2.3.3.8: 417). The inclusion of *benevolence* and *resentment* in this list is puzzling, but what he seems to mean is that we have an instinctive calm desire to do good to those we love, and harm to those we hate.[17] The idea that every human being has an instinctive calm desire to be kind to children is more plausible. Hume stresses that "besides these calm passions, which often determine the will, there are certain violent emotions of the same kind" (T2.3.3.9: 417). *Circumstances* will determine whether they are calm or violent. For example, while I naturally and instinctively feel kindness to the young children of strangers who I meet, my feelings of kindness for my own children are full of emotional intensity. The same instinctive passion operates in both cases, but it is only *calm* when considering children who are not closely related to me.

However, Hume recognizes that there are other passions which are originally violent and only become calm through *custom and habit*. What he says about this is particularly important for understanding his account of the development of *character* – a concept which, as we shall see, is central to his moral theory. A passion which is originally violent can become calm, and come to predominate in our actions:

> When a passion has once become a settled principle of action, and is the predominant inclination of the soul, it commonly produces no longer any sensible agitation. As *repeated custom* and its own force have made every thing yield to it, it directs the actions and conduct without that opposition and emotion, which so naturally attend every momentary gust of passion. We must, therefore, distinguish betwixt a calm and a weak passion; betwixt a violent and a strong one. (T2.3.4.1: 418–19; my emphasis)

---

[17] Hume says that "the desire of the happiness or misery of others, according to the love or hatred we bear them ... [is] an arbitrary and original instinct implanted in our nature" (T2.2.7.1: 368). Benevolence is the desire for the happiness of others. He is arguing that there is no necessary connection between love and benevolence, because love could conceivably have resulted in any other desire, such as the desire to harm the beloved.

It is through custom that a passion, say the desire for continually increasing wealth in our industrious business person, can become a settled principle of action and lose its original emotional intensity. Through habit, a passion gains *strength* at the same time as it becomes *calm*. It comes to "direct our action without ... opposition and emotion."[18] A similar process would account for the development of predominant calm passions such as love of power, love of pleasure or, as Hume said of himself, "Love of literary Fame."[19]

In a section called "Of the effects of custom," Hume argues that custom gives us both "a *facility* in the performance of any action ... and afterwards a *tendency or inclination* towards it" (T2.3.5.1: 422). He argues that the "facility" in performing an action results from the "orderly motion" of the animal spirits which can "sometimes be so powerful as even to convert pain into pleasure, and give us a relish in time for what at first was most harsh and disagreeable" (T2.3.5.3: 423). In support of this claim he appeals to the view of Joseph Butler who had argued that "custom encreases all *active* habits, but diminishes *passive*" (T2.3.5.5: 424). Any habit results from repetition. "Active habits" are those which relate to changes in our practices and actions; "passive habits" relate to changes in perception.[20]

The discussion to which Hume refers had appeared in Butler's *Analogy of Religion, Natural and Revealed* ... which was first published in 1736, three years before the first two books of Hume's *Treatise*. As we have seen, Hume was particularly concerned to get Butler's opinion of the first two books of the *Treatise*.[21] Butler had argued in Chapter 5 of the *Analogy* that the fact that we can morally improve ourselves in this life provides a basis for the belief that we are preparing ourselves for a life to come. While Hume was not

---

[18] Annette Baier has written that "a typically calm passion counteracts a typically violent one ... during the time of opposition" (*A Progress of Sentiments*, p. 168). This seems to me wrong. It would be more accurate to say that a calm passion overcomes the violent passion at the time of opposition by becoming firmly infixed in our character through custom and habit.

[19] "My Own Life," HL I, 7.

[20] Joseph Butler, *Analogy of Religion, Natural and Revealed, to the Constitution and Course of Nature*, 2nd edn. (London, 1736), p. 119–21. Hume's reference at T2.3.3.5: 424 is to "a late eminent philosopher." Butler was alive at the time Hume was writing, but this is compatible with the eighteenth-century usage of the adjective 'late' to mean 'recent.' See my article "Butler and Hume on Habit and Moral Character," in *Hume and Hume's Connexions*, eds. M. A. Stewart and John P. Wright (Edinburgh University Press, 1994), pp. 105–18.

[21] See Chapter 1, §7, pp. 28–9.

sympathetic with this theological conclusion,[22] he did accept its chief premise – that in our present existence "we are capable of … getting a new Facility in any Kind of Action, and of settled Alterations in our Temper and Character."[23] Butler wrote, that "by accustoming ourselves to any course of Action, we get an Aptness to go on, a Facility, Readiness, and often Pleasure in it. The Inclinations which rendered us averse to it, grow weaker; the Difficulties in it, not only the imaginary but the real ones, lessen …"[24] Butler anticipated Hume in arguing that through custom we can overcome sensations which make the relevant action unpleasant and difficult for us.

Butler anticipated Hume's claim that passions become calm at the same time as they gain strength and come to predominate in our actions. He wrote that:

Active Habits may be gradually forming and strengthening, by a Course of acting upon such and such Motives and Excitements, whilst these Motives and Excitements themselves, by proportional Degrees, growing less sensible, *i.e.* are continually less and less sensible felt while the active Habits strengthen. (Butler, *Analogy*, pp. 122–3)

His concern here is with the development of moral character, and he gives the examples of courage and benevolence. The apprehension of danger originally causes the passive impression of fear and the action of defending ourselves. But as a person constantly confronts such situations in practice and becomes habituated to defending himself, his feeling of fear becomes less and less. In this manner he becomes a courageous person. Similarly, when we see others in distress, we feel pity and are inclined to relieve their distress:

But let a man set himself to attend to, inquire out, and relieve distressed Persons, and he cannot but grow less and less sensibly affected with the various Miseries of Life, with which he must become acquainted; when yet, at the same time, Benevolence, considered not as a Passion, but as a practical Principle of Actions will strengthen; and whilst he passively compassionates the distressed less, he will acquire a greater Aptitude actively to assist and befriend them. (Butler, *Analogy*, pp. 123–4)

---

[22] See Paul Russell, "Butler's 'Future State' and Hume's 'Guide to Life'," *Journal of the History of Philosophy* 17 (2004), 425–48.

[23] Butler, *Analogy of Religion*, Chapter V, pp. 119–20.

[24] *Ibid.* p. 121. In this discussion Butler may well have been developing ideas he found in John Locke's *Essay Concerning Human Understanding*, 2.9.9–10 and 2.21.69.

Such is the character of a benevolent person. Butler says that through habit "active Principles" are "wrought ... thoroughly into the Temper and Character" of such a person so that they "become more effectual in influencing ... Practice" at the same time as they become "less lively in Perception."

Of course, the development of moral character through habit or custom has a long history going back to Aristotle,[25] and it is not surprising that it is stressed by both Hume and Butler. But what is apparently original, the idea which Hume got from Butler, is that as motives become part of a person's character through habit, they are reduced in emotional intensity. The more they affect our actions, the more they become calm and we become less conscious of their operation. This is at the core of Hume's notion of 'calm passions.'

The idea of a development in human character is central in Hume's moral philosophy – both in his theory of justice and in his account of moral sentiments. Hume describes a process very similar to that outlined by Butler in his account of the origin of the artificial virtue of justice. In this account Hume describes the civilizing process that allows us to live peacefully with one another in spite of our original natural greed. According to him, a civilized person "adheres to justice ... from a calm regard to a character with himself and others."[26] Moreover, Hume's account in Book 3, Part 3 of the development of the general sentiment of moral praise and blame is directly related back to his discussion of calm passions in Book 2. Through a process like the one that he describes here, we develop "calm judgments concerning the characters of men" (T3.3.3.1: 603). I argue in Chapter 9 that Hume holds that the development of our ability to make moral judgments is itself part of the development of our own moral character.[27]

8. CONCLUSION: HUME'S CONCEPT OF A CALM PASSION AND HUTCHESON'S "CALM DESIRES"

Hume's notion of the 'calm passions' seems paradoxical because the very concept of a passion seems to imply high emotional intensity,

---

[25] Aristotle stated in Book 2 of the *Nicomachean Ethics* that "moral and ethical virtue is the product of habit (ethos)" and that "our moral dispositions are formed as a result of the corresponding activities" (trans. H. Rackham (London: W. Heinemann, 1968), pp. 71, 75.

[26] *Dissertation on the Passions*, 5.1. p. 24.   [27] Chapter 9 §4, pp. 270ff.

as well as a receptive or passive state of mind. He himself appears to acknowledge the problem when he writes that "what we commonly understand by *passion* is a violent and sensible emotion of mind, when any good or evil is presented, or any object, which, by the original formation of our faculties, is fitted to excite an appetite" (T 2.3.8.13: 437). At the same time, once we appreciate the close connection between Hume's notion of calm passion and *character*, his terminology makes sense. We certainly do speak and write of an ambitious person, a resentful person, a revengeful person, as well as a courageous and kind person – without in any way implying that the person is overtly feeling the related passions. Persons who have developed the strong character traits associated with such passions are able to overcome violent passions through what Hume calls "strength of mind" (T2.3.3.10: 418). Consider, for example, an ambitious person who is rarely overwhelmed by violent sexual passions, or is able to use them to further his prevailing ambition.[28]

The idea that there is a continuity between calm passions and violent ones is important for Hume's philosophy. We have already seen how, in the *Treatise*, he insists that there are "certain violent passions of the same kind" as what he calls "calm desires" or "calm passions" (T2.3.3.8–9: 417). In a letter written to Francis Hutcheson three years after the publication of Book 2 of the *Treatise*, Hume criticizes him for drawing an absolute distinction between the "calm desire of happiness" and violent passions such as "lust, ambition, anger, hatred, envy, love, pity, or fear."[29] Hume pointed out that any of these latter passions can also be calm: "There is a calm Ambition, a calm Anger or Hatred, which tho' calm, may likewise be very strong, & have the absolute Command over the Mind."[30] Thus it is clear that Hume thought he was making an important point about human psychology in claiming that any passion may be calm and at the same time become the predominant inclination which influences a person's will.

---

[28] Two films of the last few years bring out this universal theme – Woody Allen's *Match Point*, and the portrayal of Julius Caesar in the BBC/HBO series *Rome*.

[29] Francis Hutcheson, *Philosophiae Moralis Institutio Compendiaria, with A Short Introduction to Moral Philosophy*, edited with an Introduction by Luigi Turco (Indianapolis: Liberty Fund, 2008), p. 29. Hutcheson had sent Hume the manuscript of this book before publication.

[30] Hume to Hutcheson , 10 January 1743, HL I, pp. 45–8, esp. p. 46.

In his *Essay on the Nature and Conduct of the Passions and Affections* Hutcheson distinguishes what he called "the *calm Desire* of Good ... either selfish or publick as it appears to our *Reason* or *Reflection*" from "*particular Passions* towards Objects immediately presented to some Sense" (I, II, p. 30). He distinguishes both the calm general desire for long-range self-interest from "selfish Passions, such as *Ambition, Covetousness, Hunger, Lust, Revenge, Anger*," as well as the "*general calm Desire of the Happiness of others*" from "*the particular ... Passions of Love ... Compassion, natural Affection.*" Moreover, following Malebranche, Hutcheson differentiates these general desires for our own good or that of others from passions themselves: unlike the former, the passions themselves contain "*a confused Sensation* either of Pleasure or Pain, occasioned or attended by some violent bodily Motions ...*" which often keeps our attention focused on "the present Affair," and keeps us from "*deliberate Reasoning* about our Conduct" (pp. 30–1). The term 'passion', according to Hutcheson, was to be used specifically for this physical component of our feelings which prevents us from reasoning about what serves our overall good, or the good of others. Thus, even Hutcheson seems to describe some form of conflict between reason and passion.

At the same time, as we shall see in the next chapter, in denying that reason can be the foundation of morals, Hume follows Hutcheson who forcefully argues that virtue should not be "called *reasonable antecedently to all Affection.*" It was Hutcheson who first argues that it is the opposition between calm desire and passions, which led philosophers to set reason "in opposition to what flows from *Instinct, Affection, or Passion*" (*Essay on the Passions*, p. 175). Like Hume later, Hutcheson denies that it is ever strictly speaking correct to "set rational Actions in Opposition to those from *Instinct, Desire or Affection.*" Hutcheson comes very close to anticipating Hume's claim that reason itself can never be opposed to our passions, though he still makes the sharp distinction between calm rational desires and passions which Hume himself rejects.[31]

In distinguishing the calm rational desire for good and aversion to evil from particular passions, and ascribing the first to our minds and

---

[31] In fact, elsewhere, Hutcheson himself comes close to saying that reason can oppose our violent passions when he writes that we should "prevent the *Violence* of ... *confused Sensations*, and stop [our] *Propensities* from breaking out into Action" by reflecting on their harmful

the second to our bodies, Hutcheson identifies a natural and original hierarchy in our affections and passions. In criticizing that distinction, and allowing that any passion can become calm and dominant, Hume removes the hierarchy. He does think it is important to both personal and social well-being that certain passions come to "Command the Mind," but for him, unlike Hutcheson, there is no natural hierarchy of principles in the mind. The greatest villain, whose personality is dominated by a calm greed and vengeance, can exhibit "strength of mind" (T2.3.3.10: 418) equal to that of the greatest benefactor to mankind.

effects (*Essay on the Passions*, II.VI, p. 110). Even if we reject this interpretation, this very Lockean passage (see ECHU 2.21.47) illustrates the difference between Hutcheson's normative approach to these questions, and Hume's objective science of human nature.

CHAPTER 8

Moral sense, reason, and moral skepticism

In the title to the second section of Book 3 Hume announces that "Moral distinctions [are] deriv'd from a moral sense" (T3.1.2). The phrase "moral sense" is taken from the philosophies of Francis Hutcheson and Lord Shaftesbury, whose writings Hume had clearly studied very carefully as he was writing Book 3 of the *Treatise*. However, apart from the title to this section, Hume uses the phrase "moral sense" only one other time in the *Treatise*, in Book 3, Part 3, where he claims to give his own "explication of the moral sense" (T3.3.1.25: 588). It is never used in his later recasting of his moral theory in the *Enquiry Concerning the Principles of Morals*. It is true that later in Book 3 of the *Treatise* he does sometimes use the phrase "sense of morals." But in the Conclusion to Book 3 of the *Treatise* he *contrasts* his own account of the "sense of morals" with the account of "those who resolve the sense of morals into original instincts of the human mind" – an apparent reference to the theory of moral sense of Hutcheson (T3.3.6.3: 619). His own view, he tells us, accounts "for that sense by an extensive sympathy with mankind."[1]

As we have seen in Chapter 1, Hume's personal relations with Hutcheson, which began as he was revising Book 3 for publication, were complex.[2] Hume sought Hutcheson out as an authority who would recommend his philosophy to others. At the same time, it must have become clear to him as they corresponded, if it had not been clear beforehand, that their views differed in fundamental respects. As James Moore and Luigi Turco have argued, the final

---

[1] See the conclusion to Chapter 9, pp. 286ff.   [2] Chapter 1, pp. 32ff.

structure of Book 3 of the *Treatise* reflects the complexity of the relationship between the two philosophers.[3]

In Part 1 of Book 3, entitled "Of virtue and vice in general," Hume defends the common features of his own and Hutcheson's theory against the latter's rationalist critics. It is only toward the end of Section 2 that he hints at his break with Hutcheson. The nature of that break becomes clear in Part 2 of Book 3, "Of justice and injustice," where he develops his theory of the "artificial virtues." Finally, in Part 3, published under the innocuous title "Of the other virtues and vices," the fundamental differences between Hume's and Hutcheson's accounts of moral evaluation are made clear. I will carefully explore those differences in presenting Hume's own theory of the foundations of morals in Chapter 9.

In this chapter, I stress those points of Hume's moral theory which coincide with that of Hutcheson. Hume agreed with Hutcheson that morality is based on feelings rather than reason. He wrote that Hutcheson "has taught us, by the most convincing Arguments, that Morality is nothing in the abstract Nature of Things, but is entirely relative to the Sentiment or mental Taste of each particular Being."[4] Of course the "particular Being" that interested both Hutcheson and Hume was a human being. However, in the conclusion of this chapter we will consider a matter of disagreement which came up in the exchanges of letters between them – the question of the existence of a sense of morals in a Divine being.

I. MORAL SENSE IN HUTCHESON'S PHILOSOPHY

To understand Hutcheson's philosophy we need to gain some grasp of what he means by the "moral sense." By a sense in general he meant a passive faculty of the mind. It is any *"Determination of our Minds to receive Ideas independently [of] our Will, and to have Perceptions*

---

[3] See Luigi Turco, "Moral Sense and the Foundations of Morals," in *The Cambridge Companion to the Scottish Enlightenment*, ed. Alexander Broadie (Cambridge University Press, 2003), 136–56, esp. 136–46; James Moore, "Hume and Hutcheson," in *Hume and Hume's Connexions*, eds. M. A. Stewart and J. P. Wright (Edinburgh University Press, 1994), pp. 23–57.

[4] This passage appeared in a footnote included in the first two editions of his *Enquiry Concerning Human Understanding* (then entitled *Philosophical Essays Concerning Human Understanding*); see the critical edition edited by Tom Beauchamp (Oxford: Clarendon Press, 2000), pp. 232–3.

of Pleasure and Pain."[5] In his *Inquiry into Beauty and Virtue* (1725), in addition to our five external senses, he identified two internal senses – a sense of beauty and harmony, and a moral sense. Unlike the pleasures of the five external senses, the pleasures of our internal senses arise from the perception of complex ideas.[6] In the first part of the book Hutcheson gives an account of the sense of aesthetic beauty which arises from the observation of "Uniformity amidst Variety" in nature and art (II.II.III, p. 28). He argues that there is a particular pleasure that is felt in the mind which makes us admire these works – quite independently of our understanding of their objective features. In the second part, he argues, there is a pleasure of *moral* beauty which closely parallels this pleasure of aesthetic beauty when we contemplate "those Affections, Actions, or Characters of rational Agents, which we call virtuous" (Preface, p. 9). In his later *Essay on the Nature and Conduct of the Passions and Affections, with Illustrations on the Moral Sense* (1728), Hutcheson identified two other internal senses, including the "*Publick Sense*" and the "*Sense of Honour*" (I.I.I, p. 17).

Hutcheson conceives of the sensations of the moral sense as arising immediately from the observation of a person's character, actions or passions. Just as I judge that some things just taste good and are healthy for me without my knowing anything about their chemical composition, so writes Hutcheson, "it is as easy to conceive, how a Character, a Temper, as soon as they are observ'd, may be constituted by Nature the necessary occasion of Pleasure, or an Object of Approbation, as a Taste or a Sound" (*Inquiry into Beauty and Virtue*, Preface, p.10). We immediately feel a sense of moral approval in contemplating the character of a virtuous person, and a sense of moral outrage in contemplating the character of a vicious person without understanding in any detail the good or harm that each of them does in society. "Human Nature," he writes, "was not left quite indifferent in the affair of Virtue, to form to it self Observations concerning the Advantage, or Disadvantage of Actions, and accordingly to regulate its Conduct" (p. 9). The moral sense gives us an immediate judgment of virtue or vice without any reasoning on the utility of actions,

---

[5] *Essay on the Passions*, I.I.I, p. 17.
[6] Francis Hutcheson, *An Inquiry into the Original of Our Ideas of Beauty and Virtue*, ed. Wolfgang Leidhold (Indianapolis: Liberty Fund, 2004), I.I.VIII, p. 22.

though it can later be corrected by reason – just like the perceptions of our external senses.[7]

Hutcheson stresses the unselfish or disinterested nature of the moral sense, as well as of the actions of which it approves. He writes that "There is in human Nature a disinterested ultimate Desire of the Happiness of others; and ... our moral Sense determines us to approve only such Actions as virtuous, which are apprehended to proceed partly at least from such Desire."[8] What the moral sense approves of is a person who desires the good of others, from a generous motive, not from her own self-interest. Hutcheson asks us to consider a situation where two persons act towards another in a way which is equally advantageous: however, one acts out of self-interest and the other "from Delight in our Happiness, and Love toward us" (*Inquiry into Beauty and Virtue*, p. 90). Think of two sisters, Sally and Annie, who are equally helpful to their aging mother: both come to visit her, bring her presents, call her every day, and generally try to make her life more comfortable. However, Annie does these actions because she is trying to get her mother to change her will in her favor, and Sally because she genuinely cares for her mother and her welfare. On Hutcheson's view, the moral sense condemns Annie and commends Sally. This illustrates that moral judgments involve something more than just considering the advantage or utility which results from such behavior. We naturally and immediately feel moral disapproval of the one sister and moral approval of the other.

According to Hutcheson, there is really only one moral virtue – namely benevolence – and all others are reducible to it. The traditional four cardinal virtues – temperance, courage, prudence and justice – are only considered virtues in so far as they are practiced with the motive of benefiting others (*Inquiry into Beauty and Virtue*, II.II.I, pp. 101–2). A person who abstains from excess in his appetites is only virtuous if his temperance is intended to benefit others – his children for example. For that he requires a form of benevolence, and it is this motive alone which is approved of by the moral sense.

---

[7] "Illustrations on the Moral Sense," in *Essay on the Passions*, pp. 150–1.
[8] Francis Hutcheson, *An Inquiry into the Original of Our Ideas of Beauty and Virtue*, 3rd edn., corrected (London, 1729), 151; cf. *Inquiry into Beauty and Virtue*, ed. Leidhold, p. 225.

Hutcheson's first publication, his *Inquiry into Beauty and Virtue*, was directed against philosophers like Thomas Hobbes and Bernard Mandeville, who argued that moral principles are based on rational self-interest.[9] In opposition to these thinkers Hutcheson argued that we act out of genuine regard for others, and that we have a moral sense which approves of such altruistic behavior. But shortly after it was published, Hutcheson's own theory was criticized by Gilbert Burnet who argued that while we feel pleasure in moral actions, we do so because of their rationality. Rational understanding of the rightness or wrongness of actions is prior to the feeling of pleasure and moral approval.[10]

In the public exchange of letters between Burnet and Hutcheson, Burnet maintained that it is "reasonable and fit, that the *Advantage of the Whole* should be regarded more than a *Private Advantage, or the Advantage of a Part . . .*" (*Letters*, p. 15). Thus, for Burnet, we know simply through reason that the happiness of the greatest number is preferable to the happiness of some lesser number of persons who constitute that number (p. 19). Hutcheson responded that without a moral sense there is no reason to accept such a proposition any more than "a Man, who has no Desire of Heaps" has reason to prefer twenty stones to one (p. 52). Preferences, including those embodied in moral judgments, require more than facts or relations known simply by reason. In his *Illustrations upon the Moral Sense* Hutcheson went on to consider the rationalist theories of earlier writers such as Samuel Clarke who claimed to base moral judgments on "eternal and unalterable Relations in the Natures of Things themselves."[11] He concluded that the relations between agents on which these thinkers attempt to base morality are only approved of because they give rise to "a grateful Perception" in the mind of an observer which "moves the Observer to love the Agent" (p. 160).

---

[9] In the subtitle to the first edition, Hutcheson wrote that he was defending "the principles of the late Earl of Shaftesbury . . . against the Author of the *Fable of the Bees*," that is, Mandeville (*Inquiry into Beauty and Virtue*, p. 199). On Hutcheson's defense, see Chapter 9 §1, pp. 260ff.

[10] See *Letters between the Late Mr. Gilbert Burnet, and Mr. Hutchinson, Concerning the True Foundation of Virtue or Moral Goodness* (London, 1735), p. 12. The exchange between Burnet and Hutcheson was originally published in the *London Journal* in 1725, together with Hutcheson's *Illustrations on the Moral Sense*.

[11] Section II, in *Essay on the Passions*, p. 155ff.

2. MORAL JUDGMENTS ARE NOT BASED ON REASON

The first section of Book 3 of Hume's *Treatise* is entitled "Moral distinctions not deriv'd from reason" (T3.1.1: 458). In this section it is often difficult to decide where the voice of Hutcheson ends and the voice of Hume begins – so well has Hume integrated Hutcheson's criticisms of the rationalist theory of moral evaluation.[12]

We already saw in Chapter 7 that in this section Hume defines reason as "the discovery of truth or falshood" (T3.1.1.9: 458).[13] In so doing he was following Hutcheson's *Illustrations* where Hutcheson defined reason as the "Power of finding out true Propositions," and "Reasonableness" as "Conformity to true Propositions, or to Truth."[14] Hutcheson went on to argue that their being reasonable or unreasonable cannot constitute the difference between "a *generous kind Action*" and "a *selfish cruel Action*" since both "are equally *conformable to* their several Truths." Hume uses the same conception of reason to argue that since "our passions, volitions, and actions, are ... original facts and realities, compleat in themselves ... implying no reference" to anything independent of them, their reasonableness or unreasonableness cannot be the factor which determines their morality or immorality (T3.1.1.9: 458). Since reason is conformity to truth, and passions, volitions and actions don't conform or fail to conform to anything independent of themselves, their rightness or wrongness is not determined by reason.

Hume had already argued in Book 2 that passions do not represent anything beyond themselves (T2.3.2).[15] He draws two more arguments from his earlier discussion of reason and motivation in Book 2 to show that reason cannot be the basis for our moral judgments.

The first is based on his earlier claim that reason alone is impotent. He now points out that moral judgments affect our actions. "Common experience" shows us that "men are often govern'd by their duties, and are deter'd from some actions by the opinion of injustice, and impell'd to others by that of obligation" (T3.1.1.5: 457). They are discouraged from stealing by the moral judgment that stealing is wrong, and encouraged to give to charity by the moral judgment that we have duties to those in need. But if reason were the sole

[12] See Turco, "Moral Sense and the Foundations of Morals." [13] §1, pp. 217ff.

[14] "Illustrations on the Moral Sense," in *Essay on the Passions*, Section I, p. 137.

[15] Chapter 7 §5, pp. 223–6.

source of these moral judgments we would not be affected by them. Hume sums up his argument as follows: "Reason is wholly inactive, and can never be the source of so active a principle as conscience, or a sense of morals" (T3.1.1.10: 458). More formally,

1. Reason does not cause any actions;
2. Moral judgments cause people to act in certain ways; Therefore,
3. Moral judgments are not based on reason.

It is worth reflecting a bit on this Humean argument. It rests on a distinction, which is central to Hume, between our faculties of reason and volition. It is a fact discoverable through reason that if people generally stole commerce would break down. But one can conceive of someone being able to rationally understand this truth, and its not affecting her actions at all: 'Why should I care about what would happen if everyone stole' the person might ask, 'so long as I can get what I want right now without paying for it?'

3. MISTAKES IN ACCOMPANYING BELIEFS DO NOT MAKE ACTIONS MORAL OR IMMORAL

Hume derives yet another argument against the rationalist theory of moral evaluation from his discussion of reason and motivation in Book 2. He thinks that having recognized that "no will or action can be immediately contradictory to reason" the rationalist may then argue that there is something contrary to reason in the accompanying "causes or effects" which makes it immoral (T3.1.1.11: 459; cf. T2.3.3.7: 416–17). Hume then shows that the falsity of the accompanying causally related beliefs does not make the action immoral.

In the first place, consider a situation in which my action is caused by a false belief in what Hume (somewhat awkwardly) calls *existence*. I pick up a coat from the stack at a party and take it home, believing that it is my own – while in fact it is yours. Here my action was caused by the false belief that I was taking home my own coat. It is caused by my belief in the *existence* of this coat as mine. However, this mistaken belief is not the cause of any immorality in the action. Indeed, because of my false belief, you wouldn't even call my action stealing. This mistake in reason, far from being the source of the immorality of the action, shows that the action is not really morally wrong.

Now consider another case, this time where my action is caused by a false belief that something is the means of attaining something else I desire. Suppose I give money to an organization which I believe is dedicated to helping the victims of a devastating earthquake in northern Pakistan. However, as I find out later, money given to this organization is being siphoned off to go to the training of terrorists who are threatening my own country. I wanted my action to help earthquake victims, while in fact it resulted in the support of terrorism. My failure of reason in this case was a failure to know the means to a certain end – that of giving charity to help earthquake victims. But once again, my failure of reason does not cause my action to be immoral. (It may be argued that I am morally culpable for not taking sufficient care to investigate the credentials of the charitable organization I was giving money to. But, now 'not taking sufficient care to investigate ...' is the action being morally judged – not the action of giving money to a charity. Hume's first argument, that showing that the moral fault of the action itself is not its failure to correspond to the facts (T3.1.1.9: 458), can now be applied to *this* action. Carelessness is not a fault because it fails to correspond to the facts.)

Hume then considers a case where a false belief is the *effect*, rather than the cause of the action (T3.1.1.15: 461). He asks whether it is this false and unreasonable belief which makes the action immoral.[16] Suppose, writes Hume, that I am committing adultery with my neighbor's wife and someone looks in the window and, seeing us together, falsely believes that she is my own wife. His mistaken belief is the effect of my immoral action. However, Hume points out, the immorality of adultery does not lie in its tendency to cause the mistaken belief. For this belief was not intended by me, who was only seeking to indulge my wrongful passion for my neighbor's wife. The immorality lies in that passion and its accompanying action, not in the accidental fact that it caused a false belief in an observer.

---

[16] Hume is responding to a claim made by William Wollaston in his *Religion of Nature Delineated* (London, 1724); see T3.1.1.15 n.68: 461–2.

4. AGAINST THE RATIONALISTS: MORALITY IS NOT THE DISCOVERY OF IMMUTABLE RELATIONS

The main target of both Hume's and Hutcheson's attack on rationalism is on the view that moral judgments consist in "eternal immutable fitnesses and unfitnesses of things" (T3.1.1.17: 463). In Section 2 of his *Illustrations*, Hutcheson identified the main defender of this theory as Samuel Clarke. Clarke wrote that moral obligation is discovered by reason which shows that "some things are in their own nature Good and Reasonable and Fit to be done; such as *keeping Faith, performing equitable Compacts,* and the like" and others "are in their own nature *absolutely Evil*; such as *breaking Faith, refusing to perform equitable Compacts, cruelly destroying those who have neither directly nor indirectly given any occasion for such treatment, and the like.*"[17] By tying the language of good and evil to that of reasonableness and fitness, Clarke meant to indicate that moral judgments have the same kind of certainty as the propositions of mathematics. He argued that the denial of these basic moral truths was like claiming "that the *Whole* is not *equal to all its parts,* or that a *Square* is *not double to a Triangle* of equal base and height" (p. 39). According to Clarke, moral judgments, like those of mathematics, show relations or proportions. Just as we know through reason that the whole is greater than the parts, so we recognize that it is *more fit* to help other beings like ourselves than to harm them.

Both Hume and Hutcheson complain that Clarke and other moral rationalists never explain this relation of *fitness* which is supposed to constitute the morality of actions. Hume reminds us that he has shown earlier that there are only four relations which "are susceptible of certainty and demonstration," namely "*resemblance, contrariety, degrees in quality,* and *proportions in quantity and number*" (T3.1.1.19–20: 463–5). But these relations apply to material objects. If one of them constituted the morality of actions, we would have to say that material objects were themselves good and evil. But that is absurd.

Hume goes on to argue that if there were any immutable relations of moral fitness and unfitness which determined the rightness and

---

[17] Samuel Clarke, *A Discourse Concerning the Unchangeable Obligations of Natural Religion, and the Truth and Certainty of the Christian Revelation,* 3rd edn. (London, 1711), pp. 43–4.

wrongness of actions, they would have to relate the internal actions in the mind of the agent to external objects (T 3.1.1.21: 464–5). For if relations were between the internal actions of mind alone, agents would be morally praiseworthy or blameworthy merely for their own thoughts, independent of anything else in the universe. If the relations just held among external objects then inanimate beings and non-human animals would be morally praiseworthy or blameworthy.

5. MATRICIDAL TREES AND INCESTUOUS ANIMALS

Hume proceeds to take examples of actions which he thinks all his readers will morally condemn – matricide (or patricide) and incest – and argues that there is nothing in the objective relations involved which constitutes their immorality. He argues that the same relations exist in non-humans, and that since we do not morally condemn the latter, these relations are not sufficient to account for moral condemnation.

His first example is that of the murder of one's own parent. He compares a man murdering his parent[18] with that of a sapling oak or elm which grows up and destroys its parent tree by depriving it of sunlight and water. He argues that the same relations hold in both cases: the parent causes the existence of the child and the child destroys the parent. To the objection there is a different kind of cause – namely choice and will which makes us condemn the human act and not that of the sapling – he argues that the difference in cause is irrelevant to the relations between the killer and victim: "a will does not give rise to any *different* relations, but is only the cause from which the action is deriv'd" (T3.1.1.24: 467).

Hume's second example of incest in animals is presented as one which is "still more resembling" to the same action in human beings – since animals have "sense, and appetite, and will" (T3.1.1.25: 467–8). In the case of animals there is "not the smallest moral turpitude and deformity" in incestuous relations. Thus it cannot simply be these relations which make the act of incest immoral in humans. To the objection that incest is immoral in humans and not in animals because

---

[18] From Hume's use of the same example in his *Enquiry Concerning the Principles of Morals* it is clear that he had in mind the Roman emperor Nero's murder of his mother Agrippina (EPM, App. 1.12).

the animals do not have sufficient reason to discover its immorality, Hume replies that the wrongness of the action must exist before it is discovered by reason. The lack of reason in an animal may prevent it "from perceiving the duties and obligations of morality, but can never hinder these duties from existing; since they must antecedently exist, in order to their being perceiv'd." So it can't be their lack of reason which makes incest morally innocent in animals.

Hume's discussion of the example of incest clearly brings out the nature of his claim that moral distinctions are not derived from reason. If moral distinctions were to be derived from reason, then they must exist in reality prior to the act of reason which discovers them. In denying that the morality of actions is based in reason, Hume is denying that their rightness or wrongness exists in the nature of things. Reason is a faculty that discovers "the *real* relations of ideas" or "*real* existence and matter of fact." (T3.1.1.9: 458). According to Hume, vice and virtue do not exist in either.

6. MORAL VALUE IS NOT DISCOVERED *A POSTERIORI* IN OBJECTIVE MATTERS OF FACT

As we have seen, Hume uses these examples of the killing of a parent and incest to directly attack those who hold that morality is discovered in the same way as the propositions of mathematics – simply through a discovery *a priori* of relations between ideas. However, he goes on to argue that the same reasoning "will prove with equal certainty" that vice and virtue do not consist "in any *matter of fact*, which can be discover'd by the understanding" (T3.1.1.26: 468). When he refers to *the same reasoning* he can only mean his argument that if immorality were discovered by reason, it must already exist in the nature of things before it could be discovered. He now claims that in the case of "wilful murder" all that reason can discover *a posteriori* is facts about the person's "passions, motives, volitions, and thoughts" (T3.1.1.26: 468). There is no fact of immorality itself "as long as you consider the object" – that is the agent and the action themselves. Hume is not denying that these matters of fact are *relevant* to our judgment that the action is immoral. But, he denies that they in themselves constitute the wrongness of the action.

What follows is one of the most commented-on passages of Book 3, if not of the whole of the *Treatise*:

The vice entirely escapes you, as long as you consider the object. You never can find it, till you turn your reflexion into your own breast, and find a sentiment of disapprobation, which arises in you, towards this action. Here is a matter of fact; but 'tis the object of feeling, not of reason. It lies in yourself, not in the object. So that when you pronounce any action or character to be vicious, you mean nothing, but that from the constitution of your nature you have a feeling or sentiment of blame from the contemplation of it. Vice and virtue, therefore, may be compar'd to sounds, colours, heat, and cold, which, according to modern philosophy, are not qualities in objects, but perceptions in the mind: And this discovery in morals, like that other in physics, is to be regarded as a considerable advancement of the speculative sciences; tho', like that too, it has little or no influence on practice. (T3.1.1.26: 468–9).

In this passage we can find the following claims:

1. You cannot find the vice until you examine your own reaction to the action, namely your own feeling of disapproval of it.
2. The matter of fact we are looking for is an object of feeling, not of reason; it lies in us, not in the object.
3. When we call an action vicious, we mean only that we are so constituted that we feel blame from considering it.
4. Vice and virtue are like sounds, colors, heat and cold which modern physics claims not to be properties or qualities of external objects, but only perceptions in the minds of observers.
5. Like the comparable claim in physics, this claim in morals is an important advance in science; but also like that claim in physics it has little or no effect on people's behavior.

Let us consider each of these claims in detail.

   1. What can Hume mean when he says that the vice lies in our reaction to the action? He certainly cannot mean that this reaction is vicious or that it constitutes vice. My condemning the murder or the murderer is not wrong! But then, in what sense could I have *found* the vice when I examine my own reaction to the action? Only in the sense that I now have an *explanation* of where my judgment of the vice or wrongness of the action comes from – namely my reaction to it.

2. Hume states that "the matter of fact" we have been looking for to account for the wrongness of the action is an "object of feeling, not of reason." If my interpretation of #1 is correct, he is looking for a matter of fact which *explains* our condemning the action of willful murder. But it is not a matter of fact which would *justify* our condemning the action. Why is willful murder wrong? If there is a justifying reason it would have to be something like the fact that it cuts off a productive life or, perhaps, that it goes against a general rule that is required for the public order. But the matter of fact that Hume says is "in yourself, not in the object" is not anything like these facts. It does not *justify* my moral condemnation of willful murder. Having denied that the vice is discoverable by reason, Hume now turns to an entirely different kind of question.

Think of a parallel example put forward by Hutcheson in his *Illustrations on the Moral Sense*. Hutcheson is concerned with the question whether the motivating reasons for an action can be derived solely from reason. He notes that when a person is asked why he pursues wealth he may answer that wealth is the means of obtaining pleasure or happiness. But Hutcheson says that if we then ask why the person desires happiness no answer is forthcoming. He writes: "One cannot imagine what Proposition he could assign as his *exciting* [motivating] *Reason*" (*Essay on the Passions*, p. 139–40). There must be an end to the answering of the question "why" when one is asking for a motivation for an action. Hutcheson cites the authority of Aristotle, who pointed out "that there are *ultimate Ends* desired without a view to anything else ..." However, and this is the point that makes the discussion relevant to Hume's discussion of willful murder, Hutcheson still acknowledges that the following proposition is true: "There is an *Instinct* or *Desire* fixed in his Nature, determining him to pursue his Happiness." But he adds that "it is not this *Reflexion* on his own Nature, or this *Proposition* which excites or determines him, but the *Instinct itself*." In other words, while the proposition about our psychology is supposed to *explain* why we pursue happiness, it is not itself a *reason or motive* for pursuing happiness. The nature of the question has changed.

Similarly, the matter of fact that Hume appeals to in order to explain why we condemn willful murder – the subjective disapproval of it which arises from "the constitution of your nature" – does not *justify* our condemnation of it. Just as motivating reasons come to an end, so do *justifying* reasons. All one can do when one has completed giving one's account of motivating or justifying reasons is to give an *explanation*. As we shall see in Chapter 9, unlike Hutcheson, Hume holds that there is more to these explanations than merely appealing to an instinct.[19] He seeks to explain the justificatory starting points. My point here is that both philosophers recognize the basic difference between motivation and justification on the one hand, and explanation on the other.

3. The crucial word in interpreting #3 is the word 'mean,' when Hume writes that when you make a moral judgment you "mean nothing, but that from the constitution of your nature you have a feeling or sentiment of blame from the contemplation of it." Clearly the moral judgment 'the killing of Sally by Annie was a vicious willful murder' does *not mean* the same as 'I am so constituted that I have a feeling of blame when I contemplate the killing of Sally by Annie.' That cannot be either the literal meaning of the moral judgment, nor what I intend to convey through my utterance of it. If Hume were giving such an account of the meaning of the first judgment then we could immediately dismiss his theory.

A more plausible interpretation is that he is identifying the impression which gives meaning to the term 'vicious' in the moral judgment that willful murder is vicious. Hume's point is that this impression is derived from the constitution of our nature, *not* from an external object. It is an *internal* impression, just like the impression of "power or efficacy" which he discussed in Book 1. Hume is not denying that we *ascribe* vice and virtue to actions and agents. He is giving a causal account of the origin of these impressions. It is our internal impressions of pain and pleasure which we *ascribe* to actions and agents.

7. THE ANALOGY BETWEEN VICE AND VIRTUE, AND SENSIBLE QUALITIES

4. This brings us to Hume's analogy between "vice and virtue" and "sounds, colours, heat and cold." The analogy was, no doubt, originally suggested to Hume by Section IV of Hutcheson's *Illustrations on*

---

[19] See pp. 261, 283 & 287–8.

the *Moral Sense* where he compared moral sense to "sensible Ideas" (*Essay on the Passions*, p. 177). Scholars dispute about what Hutcheson himself meant by the analogy, but it would take us beyond the topic of this book to enter into this discussion. We have already noted in Chapter 1 that Hume sent the passage we have been discussing to Hutcheson, asking him whether it was not too strong, and whether it did not have negative implications for religion.[20] We shall consider Hume's question to Hutcheson, and its implications for both their philosophies in the conclusion to this chapter. Here we shall focus on Hume's own use of the analogy.

Hume's claim that moral qualities should be compared to sensible qualities in that both are not "qualities in objects, but perceptions in the mind" takes us back to his explanation in Book 1 as to how certain sensible qualities are ascribed to external objects, what we there called his principle of projection.[21] The principle was first introduced in T1.3.14.25 as an explanation of why we ascribe the idea of necessary connection to objects. But, as we have seen, Hume went on to explain that we associate internal impressions such as "sounds and smells" with the spatially extended visual perceptions which are experienced together with them, and so think of them as located outside ourselves in space.[22] Similarly, we locate our feelings of moral pleasure and pain in actions and characters because these internal impressions are always experienced together with those actions or characters. The resulting associations of ideas cause us to ascribe those internal impressions of pain and pleasure to the objects which give rise to them, and are experienced along with them.

Hume's account of the ascription of sensible qualities to external objects is, as Peter Kail has shown, derived from Malebranche.[23] Malebranche had written that we mistakenly "attribute our own sensations to objects, and ... judge colors, odors, tastes, and other

---

[20] §8, pp. 35–6.   [21] Chapter 3 §8i, pp. 122–4.

[22] It is striking that in Book 1, colors, like shapes, are inherently spatial. In this passage in Book 3 he includes them among the internal sensible qualities.

[23] It is commonly assumed that Hume takes his account of the theory from Locke's *Essay Concerning Human Understanding*, Book 2, Chapter 8. But Kail has argued convincingly in Chapters 5 and 7 of his *Projection and Realism in Hume's Philosophy* (Oxford University Press, 2007) that the analogy is taken from Malebranche's *Search after Truth*, not from Locke. For Locke, *qualities* are powers in objects which cause perceptions in us; they are not themselves perceptions in our minds, as they are for Malebranche and Hume.

sensible qualities to be in the bodies we call colored, odiferous, and flavored," and that through the "natural judgments of the senses" the mind is disposed "to spread itself onto the objects it considers by clothing them with what it has stripped from itself," namely its own sensations or sensible qualities.[24] As we have seen above, Hume adopts this metaphor of the mind spreading itself on external objects in discussing necessity, as well as sensible qualities in Book 1 of the *Treatise*. As we shall see in a moment, he also explicitly uses the metaphor in relation to moral qualities in his *Enquiry Concerning the Principles of Morals*.

Hume also drew the analogy between sensible qualities and vice and virtue in his popular essay "The Sceptic," published two years after Book 3 of the *Treatise*. He wrote:

> Were I not afraid of appearing too philosophical, I should remind my reader of that famous doctrine, supposed to be proved in modern times, "That tastes and colours, and all other sensible qualities, lie not in the bodies, but merely in the senses." The case is the same with beauty and deformity, virtue and vice. (*Essays*, p. 166n).

As in Book 3, he follows Malebranche in referring to tastes and colors as qualities of the mind which we mistakenly ascribe to external bodies, and then argues that vice and virtue are also qualities of the mind which are ascribed in a similar way to actions and characters. Indeed, Hume's explanation in "The Sceptic" is even closer to that of Malebranche. He argues that in cases such as "vengeance," where the passion is very strong, we recognize that its object (to harm another person) derives its "value from the structure of human passions," not the object itself (p. 165). On the other hand, because of the calmness of our feelings of moral virtue or vice we fail to distinguish the feeling from "the perception of the object" and so ascribe the aesthetic or moral pain or pleasure to the external object itself.

5. Hume stresses that while the discovery of the subjectivity of both sensible and moral qualities is a considerable advance in "the speculative sciences ... it has little or no influence on practice" (T3.1.1.26: 469). We continue in practice to consider both sensible qualities and values as being in objects, in spite of our philosophical or scientific

---

[24] Nicholas Malebranche, *The Search after Truth*, trans. Thomas Lennon and Paul Olscamp (Cambridge University Press, 1997), p. 73 and p. 58.

reflections. The point he is making is familiar to us from his discussions of skepticism in Book 1: our natural common sense judgments will always prevail *in practice* in spite of the opposing view of our philosophical or scientific reflections.[25]

8. IS HUME A MORAL SKEPTIC?

The passage we have just considered suggests that the same basic Pyrrhonian dilemma appears in Hume's moral theory as in his theory of the external world. On the one hand we have our practical judgments which ascribe moral qualities to the agents. On the other hand our scientific analysis of human nature shows that these qualities are really in the spectator and only projected on to the agents. In practice we retain our natural common sense view of the objectivity of right and wrong, virtue and vice. But this does not show us that such a view is true.

It may be thought that Hume himself argues for the external reality of moral qualities in the sentence which follows our long quotation on page 246 above. The sentence reads as follows:

Nothing can be more *real*, or concern us more, than our own sentiments of pleasure and uneasiness; and if these be favourable to virtue, and unfavourable to vice, no more can be requisite to the regulation of our conduct and behaviour. (T3.1.1.26: 469; my emphasis)

Isn't Hume saying here that our moral sentiments of pleasure and pain are *real* in so far as they pick out actions which are independently virtuous and vicious? The correct answer is: no, he is not. A careful examination of the sentence shows that this is to read too much into his talk of the *reality* of our sentiments of pleasure and uneasiness. The *reality* of our moral sentiments is here tied up with the fact that "nothing can ... concern us more" than they do. They do not have their *reality* in picking out features of the world which already exist, but in their regulating "our conduct and behaviour."

This reading of the sentence is supported by Hume's discussion in "The Sceptic," where he again argues that his theory of value "takes off no more from the *reality* of" vice and virtue than the theory about colors, etc. takes away the reality of sensible qualities (*Essays*, p. 166n,

---

[25] Chapter 4, pp. 135 and 136.

my emphasis). Here his point in writing of the *reality* of vice and virtue is to argue that there is "sufficient uniformity in the senses and
feelings of mankind" that we can reach some agreement in moral
(and aesthetic) evaluations. Just as dyers and painters can practice
their trades in spite of the claim of modern physics that colors "lie
only in the eye," so we can continue to practice morality in the face
of the theoretical claim that value is purely subjective. Here again the
question of the *reality* of moral qualities is independent of the question of their subjectivity.

J. B. Schneewind has suggested that Hume escapes moral skepticism simply by making moral judgments subjective.[26] For the
subjectivity of moral qualities means that there is no independent
moral reality which they can fail to represent. Thus moral knowledge would be possible, unlike knowledge of the natural world.[27]
If this is right, it would seem that morals is the one area in which
Hume really does adopt Berkeley's famous strategy against skepticism. Berkeley had claimed to rescue knowledge from the skeptics
by arguing that there are no independent objects to which our ideas
must correspond.[28] Similarly, it may be argued, Hume thinks that
we gain moral knowledge by ridding ourselves of an independent
world of moral facts.

As we saw in Chapter 3, what Hume calls *knowledge* involves the
comparison of ideas, and adequate representation of independent
objects.[29] So Schneewind's Berkeley-like solution to the problem of
moral knowledge is not really open to him. Moreover, Hume argues
that in practice we continue to ascribe moral feelings to reality, even
though they really are mere perceptions of the mind. On Hume's
view we make an error in our everyday lives when we ascribe our
moral feelings of approval and disapproval to objects.

---

[26] "For Hume as for Pufendorf, the point of morality is not to inform us about the world, but
to move us. Hume's way of working this out gives him a way of bypassing moral skepticism
..." (J. B. Schneewind, *The Invention of Autonomy: A History of Modern Moral Philosophy*
(Cambridge University Press, 1998), 360–1.)

[27] This interpretation makes Hume's view on the possibility of moral knowledge like that of
Locke, in spite of their very different accounts of the foundations of morals. Moral knowledge for Locke is possible because the archetypes of moral terms (i.e. mixed modes) are in
some sense in us, and not in an independent reality; see ECHU 3.11.16; 4.3.18; 4.4.10.

[28] See Berkeley, *Principles of Human Knowledge*, esp. the Title Page, Introduction, and especially Part I, Sections 86–91.

[29] See Chapter 3 §1, esp. pp. 86–7.

9. THE ASYMMETRY BETWEEN SCIENCE AND MORALS: FACTS AND VALUES

It is important to recognize that, on Hume's view, there is a fundamental asymmetry between questions of morality on the one hand, and questions of science and matter of fact on the other. While this asymmetry is left implicit in Section 1 of Book 3 of the *Treatise*, it is explicitly laid out in both "The Sceptic" and the *Enquiry Concerning the Principles of Morals*. In "The Sceptic" Hume clearly contrasts our scientific judgments on the one hand, with those of aesthetics and morals, on the other. In science we assume "a real, though often an unknown standard, in the nature of things" and hold that truth is entirely independent of us (*Essays*, p. 164). He adopts a strong form of scientific realism: "Though all human race should for ever conclude, that the sun moves, and the earth remains at rest, the sun stirs not an inch from his place for all these reasonings; and such conclusions are eternally false and erroneous." Truth is entirely independent of human beliefs and even, perhaps, human concepts.[30] In contrast, he claims that our standards of beauty and moral worth are affixed to the object through our own feelings. In morals and aesthetics "the mind is not content with merely surveying its objects, as they stand in themselves: It also feels a sentiment of delight or uneasiness, approbation or blame, consequent to that survey; and this sentiment determines it to affix the epithet beautiful or deformed, desirable or odious."

While it could be argued that in "The Sceptic" Hume is not speaking in his own voice,[31] he was to make a similar contrast between our concerns for truth and for morality nearly a decade later in his *Enquiry Concerning the Principles of Morals* – where he clearly was. Here he writes that whereas through reason one "discovers objects, as they stand in nature, without addition or diminution," in the case of aesthetics and morals there is a "productive faculty ... gilding or

---

[30] For further discussion see my "Hume's Academic Scepticism," *Canadian Journal of Philosophy*, 16 (1986), 407–36.

[31] Though it would be hard to explain why he should feign to adopt such an uncompromising realism in an essay called "The Sceptic." On the question of Hume's commitment to the views expressed in "The Sceptic" see James Harris "Hume's Four Essays on Human Happiness and their Place in the Move from Morals to Politics" in *New Essays on David Hume*, eds. E. Ronchetti and E. Mazza (Milan: FrancoAngeli, 2007), pp. 223–36.

staining all natural objects with … colours, borrowed from internal sentiment … [producing] in a manner, a new creation."[32] According to Hume, moral and aesthetic values are projected on to an objective world by human beings. The world in itself, apart from human evaluators, is totally indifferent to our notions of right and wrong, beautiful and ugly.

That the world itself, including human actions and persons, is bereft of value is a profound and, for many, a frightening conclusion. It does no good, I think, to downplay the shocking quality of this conclusion, as many commentators attempt to do who insist on calling Hume a moral realist. It is true that Hume is not a complete moral relativist: he holds that there is a universal human response to actions such as those of intentional murder. In other cases such as homosexuality or adultery, he recognizes that there is a variation in our felt moral responses to actions and persons[33] – though at the same time he insists that there are general principles of human nature operating in our moral judgments, the general principles he examines in the rest of Book 3. But none of this mitigates Hume's *moral subjectivism*. Hume *denies* that morality exists in the nature of things apart from our human responses to the way things are – even though we naturally think it does.

The radical message of Hume's theory is, I think, clear from the famous final paragraph of Section 1 of Book 3 of the *Treatise*:

> In every system of morality, which I have hitherto met with, I have always remark'd, that the author proceeds for some time in the ordinary way of reasoning, and establishes the being of a God, or makes observations concerning human affairs; when of a sudden I am surpriz'd to find, that instead of the usual copulations of propositions, *is*, and *is not*, I meet with no proposition that is not connected with an *ought*, or an *ought not*. This change is imperceptible; but is, however, of the last consequence. For as this *ought*, or *ought not*, expresses some new relation or affirmation, 'tis necessary that it shou'd be observ'd and explain'd; and at the same time that a reason should be given, for what seems altogether inconceivable, how this new relation can be a deduction from others, which are entirely different from it. (T3.1.1.27: 469)

In this paragraph, Hume draws a fundamental distinction between descriptive statements and statements of value, between propositions

---

[32] EPM, Appendix I.21. [33] See "A Dialogue," EPM, pp. 110–23.

which describe *what is the case*, and propositions which tell us *what ought to be the case*. He tells us that it "seems inconceivable" that the latter kinds of proposition can be "a deduction" from the former, "which are entirely different from it."

It is true that there is a parallel here with Hume's skepticism about inductive inferences in Book 1, where he denies that reason can be the basis for these inferences (T1.3.6). There is no less a logical gap between *what is the case* and *what ought to be the case* than between *past regularities* and *what will exist in the future*. In the case of the latter inference, the gap is filled in by a principle of the imagination which Hume called 'custom or habit.' In case of the former inference, the gap is filled by a mechanism which projects our sentiments or feelings on to reality.

However, even though the logical gap is filled by psychological mechanisms in both cases, I believe that Hume thought those cases fundamentally different. In the case of morality, he believes there is no reality 'out there' which could, even in principle, fill the logical gap. On the other hand, if the interpretation I have given at the end of Chapter 3 is correct, in the case of induction he holds that there is an unknown reality which could close the gap, if we had better mental faculties.

10. CONCLUSION: "MORALITY . . . REGARDS ONLY HUMAN NATURE & HUMAN LIFE"

In this chapter I have considered the view which Hume shares with Hutcheson that moral distinctions do not exist in reality independently of a moral spectator or moral judge. However, in spite of his endorsement of this view, Hutcheson did not believe that the universe is indifferent to human conceptions of right and wrong. In his *Illustrations on the Moral Sense*, he argued that it is "highly probable ... that the DEITY also approves of *kind Affections*, otherwise he would not have implanted them in us, nor determined us by a *moral Sense* to approve of them" (*Essay on ... the Passions*, p. 176). As we saw in Chapter 1, Hume wrote to Hutcheson questioning this claim.[34] He reminded Hutcheson that in denying that morals were based on

---

[34] §8, pp. 35–6.

reason they were both raising doubts whether other rational beings would have the same morals as human beings. Given that moral sentiments function in order to help us adapt to the human world, why should we conclude that a rational being who created us would possess such sentiments himself? Why conclude that such a being would have feelings of any kind?

As a defender of the argument from design, Hutcheson would very likely have had a ready answer to Hume.[35] To gain experience of the beneficial and providential character of the Deity, one need only examine God's goodness as it manifests itself in the world we observe around us. In his *Inquiry into Beauty and Virtue*, he argued that the Deity has given human beings great "Evidences, thro the whole Earth, of his Art, Wisdom, Design, and Bounty" and He has shown "himself to them as Wise and Good, as well as Powerful."[36] Moreover, he held that "the Vice and Misery in the World are smaller than we sometimes in our melancholy Hours imagine" (*Essay on the Passions*, p. 121ff.) and do not detract from the goodness of the creator. While he allowed that an atheist could be moral, Hutcheson held that "belief in a DEITY, a PROVIDENCE, and a *future State*, are the only supports to a good Mind."[37]

Hume's detailed reply to Hutchesonian providentialism comes in his later publications, after the *Treatise*. In the Appendix which accompanied Book 3 of the *Treatise* he added a note in which he nominally accepted the argument from design.[38] But nowhere in the *Treatise* does Hume ever discuss the goodness of the Deity, an omission which would have been obvious to his contemporary readers. In his later writings he systematically showed the logical problems with the argument from design – though he does this in dialogues where he does not explicitly speak in his own voice.[39] In his *Dialogues Concerning Natural Religion*, his character Philo argues that the evil

[35] Remember that only Hume's side of this correspondence has survived.

[36] Hutcheson, *Inquiry into Beauty and Virtue*, I.VIII.III, p. 81.

[37] *Essay on the Passions*, VI.IV, p. 123. Hutcheson's arguments that an atheist can be moral are given in Illustrations VI, pp. 187ff; see the discussion in James Harris, "Answering Bayle's Question: Religious Belief in the Moral Philosophy of the Scottish Enlightenment," in *Oxford Studies in Early Modern Philosophy*, eds. Daniel Garber and Steven Nadler (Oxford: Clarendon Press, 2003), 229–53, esp. 233–4.

[38] T1.3.14.12App n; 633n.

[39] EHU, Sect. 11; *Dialogues Concerning Natural Religion*, esp. *Dialogues*, 2–8.

in the world outweighs the good, and that the most accurate inference from experience leaves us with the conclusion that the first
cause of the universe is entirely *indifferent* to human ideas of vice and
virtue.[40] He also argues that religion diverts a person's attention away
from her natural moral inclinations, because it proposes "a new and
frivolous species of merit."[41] Going to church, lighting candles, saying prayers, showing one's ability to quote a holy book, and appearing pious become more important than behaving morally. Hume
argues that religion by its very nature, far from supporting morality,
weakens a person's attachment "to the natural motives of justice and
humanity."

[40] *Dialogues*, 10–11. We now have good evidence that Hume had already reached this conclu-
sion around the time he wrote the *Treatise* (M. A. Stewart, "An Early Fragment on Evil," in
Hume and Hume's Connexions, eds. M. A. Stewart and John P. Wright (Edinburgh University
Press, 1994), 160–70).

[41] *Dialogues*, 12.16; cf. *Natural History of Religion*, Sect. 14.

CHAPTER 9

The foundations of morals

The overall problem which dominates Hume's discussion of morals in Book 3 of the *Treatise* is that of discovering the psychological principles which lie at the root of our moral evaluations. Like Hutcheson, he holds that these evaluations are based on feelings of pleasure and pain. We feel pleasure when we contemplate a "noble and generous action," and pain or uneasiness when we contemplate "one that is cruel and treacherous" (T3.1.2.2: 470). Our moral evaluations are not *inferred* from these feelings of pleasure and pain; rather the pleasures and pains *constitute* our moral evaluations.[1] At the same time, Hume follows Hutcheson in arguing that these pleasures and pains through which we judge characters and actions as moral or immoral are of a particular kind. To convince us that pleasures (and pains) come in different kinds, Hume asks us to reflect on the difference between the pleasure of a fine wine and that of a great piece of music, between that received from inanimate objects and from "the character or sentiments of any person," and finally the difference between the pleasure received from reflecting on the qualities of someone who serves our self-interest and those of someone who is actually morally virtuous (T3.1.2.4: 472). Moral pleasures and pains are the kind we receive when we consider a character "in general, without reference to our particular interest." Hume notes that while "the good qualities of an enemy are hurtful to us ... [he] may still command our esteem and respect." While it is clear that we often confuse self-interested

---

[1] "We do not infer a character to be virtuous, because it pleases: But in feeling that it pleases after such a particular manner, we in effect feel that it is virtuous" (T3.1.2.3: 471); "The pain or pleasure, which arises from the general survey or view of any action or quality of the *mind*, constitutes its vice or virtue ..." (T3.3.5.1: 614).

feelings with moral ones, they may still be distinguished by a person of keen moral sensibilities.

Hume holds that these disinterested pleasures and pains give rise to moral approval and disapproval, which on his theory are calm indirect passions – pride, humility, love, and hatred (T3.1.2.5: 473). He writes that moral approval and disapproval of others "is nothing but a fainter and more imperceptible love and hatred" (T3.3.5.1: 614) – or, to use words we would find more appropriate today, 'esteem' and 'contempt'. And as we saw in Chapter 6, moral self-approval is a form of pride.[2] And, for him, moral guilt is a form of humility – that is, shame.[3]

Hume states his problem concerning the psychological source of the pleasures and pains which constitute our moral judgments toward the end of Section 2 of Part 1 of Book 3. He asks "concerning this pain or pleasure, that distinguishes moral good and evil, *From what principles it is derived, and whence does it arise in the human mind?*" (T3.1.2.6: 473). He rejects the view that moral pleasure and pain are derived from an "*original* quality and *primary* constitution" like Hutcheson's moral sense which approves of benevolent characters and actions. Unlike Hutcheson, Hume thinks there are many different virtues besides benevolence, and it is implausible that we are hardwired to respond to each of them. Most significantly, as he goes on to explain in Part 2 of Book 3, there are certain "artificial virtues" which, unlike benevolence, could not be part of our original nature since they require that we first make discoveries about human nature and the physical world in which we live. Thus Hume sets out to find "some more general principles, upon which all our notions of morals are founded."

1. THE CONTROVERSY WHICH HAS EXCITED THE CURIOSITY OF THE PUBLIC

In Part 2 of Book 3 Hume takes up "the controversy" which, as he told us in Book 2, "of late years has so much excited the curiosity of

---

[2] §6, pp. 200ff.
[3] The connection between moral approval and disapproval and the indirect passions was stressed by Pall Ardal in *Passion and Value in Hume's Treatise* (Edinburgh University Press, 1966), though scholars still dispute the importance of this connection.

the publick," the controversy whether "*moral distinctions be founded on natural and original principles, or arise from interest and education.*"[4] The view that moral distinctions are based on "*interest and education*" was put forward by Bernard Mandeville in *The Fable of the Bees.* He argued that they were artificially inculcated by "skilful politicians [who] endeavour'd to restrain the turbulent passions of men, and make them operate to the public good, by the notions of honour and shame" (T3.3.1.11: 578). Mandeville wrote that these "skilful Politicians" gave "the Name of VIRTUE to every Performance, by which Man, contrary the impulse of Nature, should endeavour the Benefit of others, or the Conquest of his own Passions . . ."[5] The name vice was given to whatever gratified people's own appetites without any consideration of the public interest. In response, Hutcheson argued that "if Virtue be look'd upon as wholly Artificial" as Mandeville claimed, then even though it might contribute to the "greater Interest of *large Bodies or Societies* of Men ... a private Person may better find his *Interest,* or enjoy greater Pleasures in the Practices counted *vicious,* especially if he has any Probability of *Secrecy* in them" (*Essay on the Passions,* p. 9). In other words, it would still pay to be a free rider on the system, and cheat wherever possible. Hutcheson countered Mandeville's view by insisting that each person has "a *moral Sense* and *publick Affections*" which are "constituted by Nature" to form "our most intense and durable *Pleasures.*" This moral sense approves above all of "*universal calm Benevolence*" which limits and counteracts "not only the *selfish Passions,* but even the *particular kind Affections*" (p. 8). "*Universal calm Benevolence*" opposes not only our own selfish interests but also an overly narrow benevolence which favors our family and friends in opposition to the public good.

When Hume first takes up this controversy in Part 2 of Book 3 of the *Treatise,* entitled "Of Justice and Injustice," he appears to be taking the side of Mandeville.[6] He argues that the most important virtues, those on which the existence of an ordered society depends, are

---

[4] T2.1.7.2: 295; see Chapter 6, pp. 202ff.

[5] B. Mandeville, "An Enquiry into the Origin of Moral Virtue," in *The Fable of the Bees,* ed. F. B. Kaye (Oxford: Clarendon Press, 1924), 2 vols., Vol. I, p. 48–9.

[6] For the following analysis on Hume's relation to his predecessors I am indebted to Michael Gill's *The British Moralists on Human Nature and the Birth of Secular Ethics* (Cambridge University Press, 2006), Part 3, Chapter 18, "Hume's Progressive View of Human Nature," pp. 226–40. His analysis was first published in *Hume Studies,* 26 (2000), 87–108.

artificial. These virtues of justice serve the good of society and require the restraint of our natural passions. Hume differs from Mandeville in claiming that there is a gradual process by which human beings discover and follow these virtues, and that while they may be encouraged by skilful politicians, this is secondary to their natural development. He argues that the initial process by which the artificial virtues of justice are discovered is driven simply by men's self-interest, which comes to restrain itself through the adoption of general rules of justice.

But Hume also takes up Hutcheson's concerns with the free rider problem. While he rejects Hutcheson's notion of a universal calm benevolence which is approved by an instinctive moral sense, he argues that we naturally approve of the artificial virtues through sympathy with those who are affected by them. Artificial virtues are morally approved because of their *usefulness* to the public interest; this approval arises through *sympathy* with those affected by them, as well as sympathy with other moral judges. Our natural concern with what others think of us, as well as our ability to sympathize with others' pleasures and pains, allow the artificial virtues to be reinforced through education and the exhortations of skilful politicians. In this way, we come to take strong pleasure in being honest, and feel uneasy when we ourselves are tempted by dishonesty. All this arises without the need for any instinctive moral sense.

Hume summarizes his own two-part solution to the controversy between Mandeville and Hutcheson as follows: "*Self-interest* is the original motive to the *establishment* of justice: but a *sympathy* with *public* interest is the source of the *moral* approbation, which attends that virtue" (T3.2.2.24: 499–500). I shall consider this solution in detail in §§2–4 before returning in §5 to discuss the lessons he draws from it for his more general account of the foundations of morals.

2. HUME'S PRELIMINARY CONTRAST BETWEEN NATURAL AND ARTIFICIAL VIRTUES

Hume begins his account of the artificial virtues of justice in Part 2 of Book 3 by contrasting them with the natural virtues such as benevolence and love of children. He argues that we approve of the actions of giving to charity or looking after one's children because they result from certain natural passions. We approve of a father who looks after his children because this shows that he has the proper parental affection. On the other hand, "we blame a father for neglecting his child … because it shews a want [lack] of natural affection, which is the duty of every parent. Were not natural affection a duty, the care of children cou'd not be a duty" (T3.2.1.5: 478). Our primary moral duty lies in having the right feelings, in this case those of parental affection, which in turn result in the right actions. To make this clear, Hume considers an objection to his view. Couldn't one simply do the right thing – look after one's children – simply out of a "sense of morality or duty" (T3.2.1.8: 474)? Hume's answer is that one can, but only because there exists "in human nature some distinct principles, which are capable of producing the action" independently, and "whose moral beauty renders the action meritorious." He imagines a father who has no parental affection at all, and merely looks after his children out of shame, in order to "disguise to himself" (and, we might add, others) his lack of genuine parental affection. But, according to Hume, the father could not be motivated to act out of shame unless there were a motive such as love of children which is general in human beings, but which he happens to lack. Moreover, in the case of natural virtues, acting out of duty only has moral worth because there exists in human nature a natural inclination of which we morally approve.[7]

Hutcheson's fundamental virtue, benevolence or "humanity," is also for Hume, a natural virtue (T3.2.1.6: 478). Why, Hume asks, do we approve of the actions of a person who "relieves the distress'd, comforts the afflicted, and extends his bounty even to the greatest strangers"? His answer is that we approve of these actions because they are "proofs of the greatest humanity" and that it is that virtue which is the source of the rightness of the actions, and the motivation to perform them. A regard to the rightness of

---

[7] This remarkable discussion of moral duty can be directly contrasted with that found in Kant. See Immanuel Kant, *Groundwork of the Metaphysic of Morals*, ed. and trans. Mary Gregor (Cambridge University Press, 1998), Chapter 1, pp. 10–14. For Kant the true moral worth of the action is only apparent when there is a *lack* of natural inclination to perform the required action. Natural inclination is not the source of the moral worth of the action. However, if I am correct in my account below, Hume himself moves away from the position he takes here, though in a very different direction than later taken by Kant.

the actions can only be "a secondary consideration, and deriv'd from the antecedent principle of humanity, which is meritorious and laudable."

But what about duties such as repaying a loan or respecting someone else's property? Suppose I have borrowed $800 from you to pay my rent and promised to pay it back one month later. Hume asks: "*What reason or motive do I have to restore the money?*" (T3.2.1.9: 479). There may, of course, be a number of motives, including my friendship toward you and my concerns about my reputation. But one can also think of a number of plausible circumstances in which I would still have a duty to return the money, and these motives would no longer be operative. What if you and I have had a falling out in the intervening month, and have become enemies? What if I am now in desperate straits and my own family is in a great deal of financial difficulty? What if no one else knew about the loan, and you have very strong reasons to keep it secret? In these circumstances it will clearly be in my self-interest not to repay the loan, and yet it would still be my duty to do so.

Hume also considers and rejects a number of natural inclinations besides self-interest which could be the source of my duty or obligation to repay the loan (T3.2.1.10–13: 480–482). He rules out "private benevolence" because I am as much obligated to repay a loan to an enemy as a friend. What about concern with the "public interest," based on the recognition that if people regularly failed to repay loans then the whole system of commerce would break down? Hume points out that this is not a plausible motive, for "men, in the ordinary conduct of life, look not so far as the public interest, when they pay their creditors, perform their promises, and abstain from theft, and robbery, and injustice of every kind" (T3.2.1.11: 481). Besides, a concern for the public interest would not be strong enough to overcome men's self-interest in such cases. Finally, Hume denies that we could ever be motivated to perform such actions by a "universal affection to mankind," as Hutcheson thought (T3.2.1.12: 481–2): "There are no phænomena that point out any such kind affection to men, independent of their merit, and every other circumstance." Such a passion would have to be based on "love of mankind, merely as such, independent of personal qualities, of services, or of relation to ourself." But, as Hume argues in Book 2, love or esteem requires

"a double relation of impressions and ideas."[8] Without the consideration of particular pleasant qualities possessed by another person, love
and benevolence would never arise.

Impartiality is the mark of virtues, such as repaying debts, which
constitute justice. However, what Hume calls "our natural uncultivated ideas of morality" are *partial*, unlike the rules of justice
(T3.2.2.8: 488–9; cf. T3.2.1.18; 483). He says that in order to discover
the demands of natural morality we need to consider the "ordinary course" or "usual force" of the passions: "Every immorality is
deriv'd from some defect or unsoundness of the passions" and "this
defect must be judg'd of ... by considering ... the usual force of
... affections." By consulting the usual force of the passions we discover that people generally care more for their family members than
friends, and least of all for strangers. Thus, we blame a person whose
benevolent affections are focused on strangers, and who disregards
her own family – like Mrs. Jellyby in Charles Dickens' *Bleak House*.
In uncultivated natural morality we expect partiality to those most
closely related to us.

Thus it appears that we have no natural inclination or motive to
perform just actions. But why then do we have a duty to repay a loan
which we have promised to repay or, for that matter, refrain from
taking another's goods? Hume's answer is disputed by commentators
on his theory of justice. I shall argue that Hume *rejects* the requirement he seems to make at the beginning of Part 2 that for all virtues
there must exist some natural motive independent of our sense of
moral approval.[9] He writes that "we must allow, that the sense of justice and injustice is not deriv'd from nature" (T3.2.1.17: 483). In fact,
it seems reasonable to regard the account Hume gives of moral motivation and approval at T3.2.1 as in some sense *preliminary*. In the
final analysis, he argues that the morality of most natural virtues, as
well as all the artificial virtues, is not based on their being the object
of some natural passion – at least when society is fully developed.[10]
What Hume shows in the course of the development of his account

---

[8] Chapter 6 §4, pp. 196–8.
[9] Compare Rachel Cohon, "Hume's Difficulty with the Virtue of Honesty," *Hume Studies*, 21
     (1997), 91–112. Cohon, as I understand her, claims that in the case of artificial virtues Hume
     rejects what he calls the "undoubted maxim" at T3.2.1.7: 487.
[10] See §5, pp. 275–8 and §8, pp. 283–6 below.

of the origin of justice in Part 2 of Book 3 is that the "usual force" of the passions is not the basis of moral evaluation or, for that matter, of genuine moral motivation.

3. THE ORIGINS OF THE ARTIFICIAL VIRTUE OF JUSTICE

What Hume calls justice primarily concerns property, and rules concerning the disposition of external goods. His account of the origin of justice is an account of the origin of property, through the discovery of the rules which must regulate it. The basic problems which lead us to form such a virtue as justice are based on the problems which arise from the possession of external goods.

As Michael Gill has shown, following the general account given by Mandeville, Hume presents a conjectural history of how human beings originally came to develop any notion of property.[11] Hume argues that human beings were always social creatures. The natural appetite between the sexes and our natural and original generous feelings toward our offspring provides evidence that human beings have always lived in family groups. Moreover, human needs and the advantage which results from co-operation in working together in larger groups would have quickly led these family groups to band together. Nevertheless there were three basic circumstances which would have worked against the formation of these larger bands. The first is simply a matter of human psychology; the second of external circumstances; and the third a combination of the two. If any of these three circumstances had not existed there would be no problem of human beings living in larger social groups merely on the basis of natural morality. The first circumstance is the "*self-ishness* and *limited generosity*" of human beings (T3.2.2.16: 494). If each person had such a "tender regard for another" that he didn't care more for himself and his family than anyone else, then there would be no problem of having all goods in common. As we have seen, Hume rejects Hutcheson's universal calm benevolence which would, according to Hume, have precluded any need for division of external goods. The second problem arises from the "*easy change*"

---

11 Gill, *The British Moralists*, pp. 227–9.

of these goods which results in the fact that possessions can easily be transferred from one person to another. If property were fixed like attributes of our own bodies such as strength or beauty, so that no one could obtain them by taking them away from any one else, then there would be no conflict regarding who possessed what. The final circumstance, leading to social conflict is the "*scarcity*" of these goods "in comparison of the wants and desires of men." If there were not a scarcity of goods and everyone could have as much as she or he wanted or needed, we could live together without any social conflict. Hume reminds us that in the imaginary "*golden age*" invented by poets "the rivers flow'd with wine and milk: The oaks yielded honey; and nature spontaneously produc'd her greatest delicacies" (T3.2.2.15: 493–4). "Even the distinction of *mine* and *thine* was banish'd from that happy race of mortals" who lived in that age.

Hume elaborates on the "wants and desires" of human beings in order to show that our natural psychological state is ill suited to our living in groups beyond those of our immediate families. He attributes to them an insatiable greed to possess more and more external goods for ourselves and our families. Hume says that other passions which work against a social union "are either easily restrain'd, or are not of such pernicious consequence, when indulg'd" (T3.2.2.12: 491). "*Envy* and *revenge*, tho' pernicious ... operate only by intervals, and are directed against particular persons ..." However, greed or "avidity alone, of acquiring goods and possessions for ourselves and our nearest friends, is insatiable, perpetual, universal, and directly destructive of society" (T3.2.2.12: 491–2). The result, according to Hume, is a "solitary and forlorn condition, which must follow upon violence and an universal licence" (T3.2.2.13: 492). Many of Hume's readers would have recognized a strong echo here of Thomas Hobbes' description of the state of nature in Chapter 13 of *Leviathan*.[12] In fact, as James Moore has shown, in stressing the basic asocial characteristics of human nature which prevent us from forming into substantial societies, Hume is following a wider Epicurean tradition which

---

[12] Hobbes wrote that in the state of nature, there is "danger of violent death; and the life of man, solitary, poore, nasty, brutish, and short" (Thomas Hobbes, *Leviathan, or The Matter, Forme, & Power of a Common-wealth Ecclesiastical and Civill*, ed. C. B. Macpherson (London: Penguin, 1968), Chapter 13, 160–1.

was taken up in the early eighteenth century by skeptics such as Bayle and Mandeville – and which was strongly opposed by Francis Hutcheson.[13]

Even though, unlike Hobbes, Hume allows that people have genuine altruistic passions toward those closely related to them, the results for society of his analysis of the passions are much the same. Hume clearly lays out the philosophers' view of the "*state of nature*" as "full of war, violence and injustice" (T3.2.2.15: 493). This echoes Hobbes' claim that there is a "warre of every man against every man" which results from their natural passions – though Hobbes denied that there is injustice before the institution of a sovereign power.[14] Hume calls this state of nature a "philosophical fiction" (T3.2.2.14: 493) because he doubts whether human beings could ever have survived for any length of time "in that savage condition, which precedes society." Primitive humans would have quickly learned through "experience, that their selfishness and confin'd generosity, acting at their liberty, totally incapacitate them for society" (T3.2.2.24: 498–9). Nevertheless, he acknowledges the philosophical and methodological usefulness of considering the passions of human beings as independent of their understandings, and drawing what Hobbes had called an "Inference … from the Passions."[15]

Hume attributes the invention of the "artificial virtue" of justice to our "judgment and understanding" (T3.2.2.9: 489). Thus far, the solution, as well as the problem, sounds like that of Hobbes. However, Hume makes it clear that our faculty of judgment works in a purely unexceptional way, according to the principles he lays out in Book 1 of the *Treatise*. A convention or agreement to refrain from taking the property of others "arises gradually, and acquires force by a slow progression, and our repeated experience of the inconveniences of transgressing it" (T3.2.2.10: 490). While he does not use the terms here, it is clear that *custom and habit* are the principles which operate in teaching us to refrain from the goods of others. Through "repeated

---

[13] Moore, "Hume and Hutcheson," pp. 27ff.
[14] Hobbes, *Leviathan*, Chapter 13, p. 188. However, Hume points out in his *Enquiry Concerning the Principles of Morals* that this conception of the state of nature as a state of war is to be found in Plato's *Republic*, as well as Cicero's *De Republica* – where it is defended (EPM 3.15n).
[15] Hobbes, *Leviathan*, p. 186. Cf. T3.2.2.14.

experience" people come gradually to trust one another and develop the "expectation" of a restraint in one another's conduct. Through this expectation they develop "a general sense of common interest ... which induces them to regulate their conduct by certain rules" for the stability of possessions.

One might wonder whether Hume's account of the origin of the artificial virtue of justice does not go against his claim in Book 2 that "reason is, and ought only to be the slave of the passions, and can never pretend to any other office than to serve and obey them" (T2.3.3.4: 415). Is it not through reason or understanding that "the passions are restrain'd in their partial and contradictory motions" (T3.2.2.9: 489)? Is it not our understanding of the negative results of the instability of external goods which led us to invent rules for their stability to control our own behavior and passions? And has not reason become the master of our natural passion – our unrestrained greed – in order to prevent the disastrous consequences of letting it operate in a purely natural and unrestrained way?

Hume, however, regards the understanding as serving the fundamental goal of the passions, namely that of acquiring as many goods as possible for ourselves and those close to us. He writes that there is nothing "capable of controlling the interested affection, but the very affection itself, by an alteration of its direction" (T3.2.2.13: 492). The motive to change direction, that is to satisfy our self-interest by adopting a different form of behavior, comes from the passion itself. On Hume's view it is the self-interested passion which motivates reason or understanding to find the means to satisfy its goal of maximizing one's own possessions. Hume writes that "whatever restraint" the laws of nature devised by reason "may impose on the passions of men, they are ... only a more artful and more refin'd way of satisfying them" (T3.2.6.1: 526). The passion has, as it were, employed reason to find a way to satisfy itself. So truly, the proper role of reason is only to be the slave of passion, and to serve and obey it.

Motivated by the passion of self-interest, reason or understanding invents "the three fundamental laws of nature, *that of the stability of possession, of its transference by consent,* and *of the performance of promises*" or contract (T3.2.6.1: 526). These rules define *property:* "our property is nothing but those goods, whose constant possession is establish'd by the laws of society; that is, by the laws of justice"

(T3.2.2.11: 491). Property has no existence independent of these artificially constructed rules.

Above all, Hume is concerned to deny that the convention by
which men agree to abide by common rules to refrain from each
other's external goods takes the form of a *promise* (T3.2.2.10: 490) –
as it did in the case of writers like Hobbes and especially Locke, who
founded political society as an *original contract*.[16] Promises themselves rely on an independent convention and would make no sense
before the social union was formed. Hume uses a striking analogy to
explain how a convention or agreement can take hold without any
explicit act of will:[17]

> Two men, who pull the oars of a boat, do it by an agreement or convention,
> tho' they have never given promises to each other. Nor is the rule concern-
> ing the stability of possession the less deriv'd from human conventions,
> that it arises gradually, and acquires force by a slow progression, and by our
> repeated experience of the inconveniences of transgressing it.

He likens this process to the way languages were formed, or human
beings arrived at an agreement to use gold and silver as standards of
exchange for "payment for what is of a hundred times their value."

Hume stresses that while the rules of property were established
out of *self-interest*, nevertheless they serve the *public interest*. But this
public interest is an *unintended consequence* of the establishment of
these rules. Knud Haakonssen has called this ingenious idea "one of
the boldest moves in the history of the philosophy of law."[18] Hume
dispenses with Mandeville's claim that people were originally tricked
into serving the public interest by clever politicians. He writes that
the system of rules of justice is "advantageous to the public" even

---

[16] See John Locke, *Two Treatises of Government*, The Second Treatise, ed. Peter Laslett
(Cambridge University Press, 1988), esp. Sections 97–99 & 122. Hume's extended criticism
of the Lockean view, which formed the philosophical basis of Whig party politics of his day,
is to be found in his 1748 essay "Of the Original Contract" (*Essays*, pp. 465–87).

[17] When making the same point, using the same analogy, in his *Enquiry Concerning the
Principles of Morals* he says that his theory concerning the origin of property is "in the main,
the same with that hinted at and adopted by Grotius." He goes on to cite a passage from
Hugo Grotius's *The Law of War and Peace* where that author denied that private property
arose simply from a mental act (EPM, App. 3.8n, translated on pp. 179–80).

[18] Knud Haakonssen, *The Science of a Legislator: the Natural Jurisprudence of David Hume and
Adam Smith* (Cambridge University Press, 1981), p. 20.

though it was "not intended for that purpose by the inventors."[19] His account of the origin of justice does not require any extraordinary public concern on the part of the persons who devised it, nor does it require that people be tricked into adopting it. It is nothing but our own self-interest and limited generosity which lead us to devise the artificial virtue of justice, and what Hume calls our "*natural* obligation" to obey the rules of justice is based on no other passion (T3.2.2.23: 498).

However, Hume argues that this natural self-interested obligation to follow the rules of justice is only sufficient so long as social groups remain small; it is insufficient "when society has become numerous, and has encreas'd to a tribe or nation" (T3.2.2.24: 499). Self-interest is inadequate to account for the obligation which people feel in large societies to follow the laws of justice. It does not solve the free rider problem: for while one may realize that the whole system serves one's interests, one will still find many particular instances where it will be in one's own self-interest to opt out.

4. MORAL OBLIGATION TO BE JUST: MORAL JUDGMENT AND THE FIXING OF MORAL CHARACTER

Hume's account of the "*moral* obligation" to be just (T3.2.2.23: 498) consists of two stages: the first explains the "sentiment of right and wrong" in relation to just or unjust actions, and the second the source of the actual motive which causes us to perform just actions. Or more simply, the first stage explains our moral judgments, while the second explains moral motivation. Of course, Hume sees these two as intimately linked; but it is important to see just how.

Let me explain the first stage of Hume's account by returning to the example of the obligation to repay a loan. He begins his explanation of the sentiment-based moral judgment of artificial virtues by noting that when other people are dishonest we "never fail to observe" the harm, whether it directly affects ourselves or a third party (T3.2.2.24: 499). The harm caused by my unjust action of failing to repay your loan will be immediately obvious to you; but so

---

[19] T3.2.6.6: 529; cf. T3.2.2.21: 496. However, Hume says the opposite later in Book 3 where he writes that justice is "nothing but an artificial invention to that purpose" (T3.3.1.9: 577).

will the harm when you see me promising to repay a loan to another person. As a result of your *sympathy* with the feelings of the other person you will feel uneasiness and displeasure at me. Indeed, "when the injustice is so distant from us, as no way to affect our interest, it still displeases us" because we understand the tendency of such actions to cause harm to anyone who is affected by "the person guilty of it."[20] Hume now reminds us that "every thing, which gives uneasiness in human actions, upon the general survey, is call'd Vice, and whatever produces satisfaction, in the same manner, is denominated Virtue." You will feel disapproval of any action or character who causes harm to others, and consider him or her immoral. Finally, Hume says that because of our tendency to generalize or follow *general rules* "we naturally *sympathize* with others in the sentiments they entertain of us." I will feel your disapproval of me for my being a dishonest person.

This first stage of Hume's account of moral obligation may be summarized as follows. First, Hume stresses that moral sentiments of approval or disapproval are based on our consideration of the good or ill *consequences* of justice or injustice.[21] Secondly, these moral sentiments arise through our *sympathy* with those who experience these good or ill consequences. Finally, we *sympathize* with the judgments of moral approval or disapproval which others make of ourselves.

In the second stage of his account, Hume describes how these moral sentiments come to be as firmly fixed in people's characters as natural affections (such as parental love) and become the motivation for moral action. This comes about in the following way. Parents recognize that if their child follows the rules of justice, this will make his life "useful, both to himself and others" (T3.2.2.26: 500–1). Thus they inculcate these rules in their children through "custom and education." Think of when you were a child and your mother marched you back to the local grocer to return the cookie you stole. On Hume's view sympathy plays an essential role in this learning process. In order for the lesson to take hold you need to sympathize with the harm which results to the grocer when people steal from him, and

---

[20] It should be remembered that on Hume's account of sympathy we do not need to feel directly the victim's pain or pleasure, but only the causes of it (see Chapter 6 §9, pp. 211–12.).

[21] Other words he uses later in Book 3 to discuss this element of his theory are 'utility,' 'useful,' or simply 'tendency.'

with your mother's contempt for your action. In this way children come to feel dishonor in breaking the rules of justice, and honor in following them. Hume writes that the rules "take root in their tender minds, and acquire such firmness and solidity, that they may fall little short of those principles, which are the most essential to our natures, and the most deeply radicated [i.e. rooted] in our internal constitution." The artificial virtue of honesty becomes as firmly implanted in the minds of children as the natural or instinctive virtues.

It cannot be stressed enough that Hume thinks the artificial virtue of justice becomes part of our character. He writes that no qualities "go farther to the fixing the character, either as amiable or odious" than justice and injustice (T3.3.1.9: 577). The natural affection of parents leads them to inculcate the artificial virtue of honesty in their children though custom. However,

in a little time, custom and habit operating on the tender minds of the children, makes them sensible of the advantages, which they may reap from society, as well as fashions them by degrees for it, by rubbing off those rough corners and untoward affections, which prevent their coalition. (T3.2.2.4: 486)

As a child comes to practice the principles of justice for herself, they become for her a second nature, with the rough corners of the first – unregulated greed for more and more goods – rubbed off. We see here "the effects of custom" on character which Hume discusses in Book 2: as the newly civilized young people actively engage in the practices of justice, those regulated by the three fundamental laws of nature, they come to direct their own actions "without that opposition and emotion" which accompany original and natural unchecked greed (T2.3.4.1: 419).[22] In fact, as Hume went on to explain in his *Enquiry Concerning the Principles of Morals*, the "influence of education and acquired habits, by which we are so accustomed to blame injustice" becomes so strong that we are often no longer "in every instance conscious of ... the pernicious consequences of it" (EPM 3.47). He argues that this is the reason why, in spite of the fact that justice is a virtue recognized in all societies, we have such difficulty in

---

[22] Cf. Chapter 7 §7, pp. 228–31.

ascertaining its true origin in its social usefulness. Indeed, as Hume implies in the *Treatise*, we even come to think of justice as a natural virtue, originally built into the human mind.[23]

Hume also notes that the rules of justice are inculcated in people by politicians "who, in order to govern men more easily, and preserve peace in human society, have endeavour'd to produce an esteem for justice, and an abhorrence of injustice" (T3.2.2.25: 500). This was the point which Mandeville had insisted on. But according to Mandeville's theory, as we have seen, politicians tricked people into being virtuous by flattery, by appeal to their pride and shame. For Mandeville our sole reason for acting morally is rational self-interest.[24] Hume explicitly rejects Mandeville's view that this could be the *sole* source of the distinction between vice and virtue: for

if nature did not aid us … 'twou'd be in vain for politicians to talk of *honourable* or *dishonourable, praiseworthy* or *blameable. These words wou'd be perfectly unintelligible, and wou'd no more have any idea annex'd to them, than if they were of a tongue perfectly unknown to us.*

We need to have "a natural sentiment of approbation and blame" before we can ever understand what politicians – or parents – are saying to us when they praise us for just actions and blame us for unjust ones (T3.3.1.11: 579). Hume wrote in Book 2 that "*the pleasure, which we receive from praise, arises from a communication of sentiments*" through sympathy (T2.1.11.19: 324). As we have seen in the case of the teaching of morality to children, they must be able to sympathize with those who praise or blame them, as well as with the person affected by their actions, in order for the moral lesson to take hold.

It is sometimes said that Hume's moral theory focuses more on moral judgment than on moral agency.[25] He does sometimes point out that moral judgment may have little effect on action: while "my sympathy with another" may cause me to morally disapprove of a character who causes him harm, "I may not be willing to sacrifice any thing of my own interest, or cross any of my passions for his satisfaction" (T3.3.1.23: 586). I may well feel moral outrage when the

---

[23] In fact he drops the distinction between natural and artificial virtues in the *Enquiry Concerning the Principles of Morals*.
[24] See Chapter 6 §6, pp. 200–1.   [25] Schneewind, *The Invention of Autonomy*, p. 361.

leader of my country imprisons people without charging them with any crime in a court of law – or even has them tortured – but I might not do anything to endanger myself, or even put myself out in order to right such a wrong. On the other hand, Hume also states that while the interests of other people "touch us more faintly than our own, yet being more constant and universal, they counter-ballance the latter even in practice ..." (T3.3.1.30: 591). The constant reminder of the pains and sufferings of others may lead me on occasion to set aside my own interests and pleasures. In thinking about the effectiveness of moral judgment we also need to remember that in criticizing moral rationalism at the beginning of Book 3, Hume stresses that our judgments of morals *do* affect our actions, and that morality is a *practical* science (T3.1.1.5: 457).

There is no question that in his account of the moral obligation of justice Hume is concerned with moral motivation, as well as moral evaluation. In explaining how moral sentiments concerning just acts become firmly infixed in our characters through the processes of education, he is explaining how we become persons who perform moral actions as a matter of course, and so are not tempted to cheat on the system. While he does assert in Part 3 of Book 3 that it is "almost impossible for the mind to change its character in any considerable article" (T3.3.4.3: 608) when fully formed, he holds that the minds of children are malleable, and through education and sympathy with others they develop the basic virtues of justice which are required to live successfully in a civilized society.

In his discussions of *character* throughout Books 2 and 3 of the *Treatise*, Hume shows his concern for the psychological source of moral actions. We have already seen how in his discussion "Of Liberty and Necessity" in Book 2 Hume stresses that moral responsibility does not depend on transitory actions, but on those which derive from what is fixed and lasting in a person's character.[26] In Book 3 he stresses that "if any *action* be either virtuous or vicious, 'tis only as a sign of ... durable principles of the mind, which extend over the whole conduct, and enter into the personal character" (T3.3.1.4: 575; cf. T3.2.1.2: 477). Moral character is the most obvious source of feelings of pride and shame. Hume asserts that I will repay the loan

[26] See Chapter 5 §8, pp. 186–7.

as promised "if I have the least grain of honesty, or sense of duty and obligation" (T3.2.1.9: 479) – implying that I will feel shame and self-disapproval if I fail to repay it. Moreover, should I fail to repay, my dishonest character would cause hatred or contempt in others – which will be reflected back to me through my sympathy with their feelings.

5. THE REVISED DISTINCTION BETWEEN NATURAL AND ARTIFICIAL VIRTUES

When he revisits the question of the source of our moral judgments of natural virtues in Part 3 of Book 3 of the *Treatise*, Hume brings along with him the lessons he has learned from his study of the artificial virtue of justice in Part 2. It should be remembered that in the account of our "natural uncultivated … morality" at the beginning of Part 2, he argues that our primary moral duty lies in having the right feelings, such as parental affection. The man who fails to look after his children is blamed because he lacks that affection. Hume argues that this natural morality is based on the "usual force" of the passions.[27] But in studying the artificial virtues he concludes that moral approval and disapproval arise from considering the *consequences* of the action or character who performs it. Our moral judgments of people who violate the laws of justice arise from our sympathy with the persons they affect. When he revisits natural virtues in Part 3 he argues that moral judgments of benevolence and other so-called natural virtues are also based on a consideration of the consequences of the possession of the relevant trait on those who are affected by it. We now condemn the man who fails to look after his children because of the negative consequences of his lack of parental affection on his children. Our moral condemnation results from our sympathy with their suffering, not from the judgment that his affections are unnatural.

Thus, while Hume originally set out the artificial virtues as an anomaly, his analysis of their origin has given him the clue to the general principles which lie at the foundations of morals. In fact, it is some of the natural virtues which are now considered anomalous

---

[27] See pp. 261–2 above.

because they are not valued for their consequences (T3.3.4.11: 611–12; see p. 284 below). But, in general, we have the same reason to value most of the natural virtues as the artificial ones. In Part 3 of Book 3, Hume writes

> That many of the natural virtues have this tendency to the good of society, no one can doubt of. Meekness, beneficence, charity, generosity, clemency [forgiveness of others], moderation, equity, bear the greatest figure among the moral qualities, and are commonly denominated the *social* virtues, to mark their tendency to the good of society. (T3.3.1.11: 578)

Indeed, Hume argues that there is even more reason to think that our approval of these natural social virtues is based on sympathy with those affected by them, than is the case with artificial virtues. For "the imagination is more affected by what is particular, than by what is general" (T3.3.1.13: 580) and "every particular act of generosity, or relief of the industrious and indigent, is beneficial ... to a particular person." It is immediately apparent how the acts of a loving parent will benefit his children. In general, our sympathy with those particular persons affected by the person who possesses a natural virtue will lead to our moral approval or disapproval of her character. Hume writes that "we need no other explication of that esteem, which attends such of the natural virtues, as have a tendency to the public good" (T3.3.1.12: 580).

In the final analysis, Hume's distinction between the natural virtues and the artificial virtues is very different from his original formulation, and takes into account this difference between the generality of the consequences afforded by the artificial virtues and the particular and immediate consequences of the natural virtues:

> The only difference betwixt the natural virtues and justice lies in this, that the good, which results from the former, arises from every single act, and is the object of some natural passion: Whereas a single act of justice, consider'd in itself, may often be contrary to the public good; and 'tis only the concurrence of mankind, in a general scheme or system of action, which is advantageous. (T3.3.1.12: 579)

The historical importance of this distinction cannot be stressed enough.[28] Every individual act of justice does not benefit the

---

[28] Schneewind notes that "a series of post-Humean philosophical works has brought out the depth and importance of the distinction between acts that bring benefits only if there is a

individuals to which it is directed, nor does it always serve the public good. Hume gives the example of a just legal decision which awards damages to a dissolute rich person at the expense of an industrious poor one. Not only is the poor man a loser, but so is society as a whole. In fact, we don't have to go so far from our own everyday experience to think how little loss there would be to the general good if a poor man stole on occasion from a huge nationwide supermarket chain to feed his needy family. Nevertheless, Hume reminds us, that "the whole scheme ... of law and justice is advantageous to the society & to every individual; and it 'twas a view to this advantage, that men, by their voluntary conventions, establish'd it."[29] And, as we have seen, once it is "establish'd by these conventions, it is *naturally* attended with a strong sentiment of morals; which can proceed from nothing but our sympathy with the interests of society."

Hume's natural social virtues are no longer valued *because* they are natural; it is not the fact that they represent the "usual force" of the passions which gives them their value.[30] A careful reading of the end of Part 1 of Book 3, where Hume canvasses a number of meanings of the word *natural*, should have warned us that Hume's account of our "natural uncultivated ideas of morality" (T3.2.2.8: 489) would not be his final word on the subject. There he rejects the claim that "the character of natural and unnatural can ever, in any sense, mark the boundaries of vice and virtue" (T3.1.2.10: 475). He states that when '*natural*' is "oppos'd to what is unusual, perhaps virtue will be found to be the most unnatural." In other words, if natural means 'usual', virtue may well turn out to be unnatural. He added that this is certainly true of the heroic virtues which, of course, are rare and unusual. In any case, it is clear that he here rejected what he called the "usual force" of the passions as any mark of what is virtuous.

general practice with which all or most others comply, and acts that bring benefits even if no others do similar acts. Hume's introduction of it is one of his most brilliant achievements" (*The Invention of Autonomy*, p. 366).

[29] Hume added the words "& to every individual" in manuscript emendations he made to the *Treatise* after it was published. This is an important correction, for, as we have seen, those who established the rules of justice had in view only their own individual advantage – not the advantage of the society as a whole. The latter was an unintended result of their self-interested actions.

[30] See p. 264 above.

Hume holds that the sole mark of the natural virtues is that, unlike the artificial virtues, they produce (or, as we shall see in a moment, *tend to* produce) what is beneficial in every instance in which they are practiced.

6. REFINEMENTS OF SYMPATHY: ARRIVING AT A COMMON MORAL POINT OF VIEW

In Part 3 of Book 3 Hume considers two objections to his view that sympathy is the basis of our moral judgments. In answering these two objections Hume refines his account of moral judgment in crucial ways. The first refinement shows how we reach agreement in morals as a result of social interaction.[31] These corrections of our sympathetically biased moral judgments issue in impartial "calm judgments concerning the characters of men" which are easily mistaken for the operations of reason (T3.3.3.2: 603). The second refinement shows that we do not judge people morally according to the actual consequences they achieve, but rather according to the general tendency of their characters. The final result of both refinements is that the "judicious spectator" makes moral judgments from what Hume calls "*steady* and *general* points of view" (T3.3.1.15: 581–2).

The first objection which Hume considers is that sympathy cannot be the basis for moral judgments because it is itself biased in a way that moral judgments are not. As Hume explained when he introduced the concept of sympathy in Book 2, our sympathetic feelings vary in strength with our distance from the person being judged, as a result of the association of ideas.[32] For example, I feel far greater pleasure from the virtues of my son or daughter than I do from the same virtues in a stranger. However, I do not judge the stranger to be any less virtuous than my children. Does this not show that sympathy cannot be the basis of moral judgment? Hume tells us that he feels greater pleasure from considering the virtues of his servant, than those of the famous Roman senator Marcus Brutus whom he reads about in a history book. And yet he does not think that his servant is

---

[31] This is stressed in Jacqueline Taylor, "Virtue and the Evaluation of Character," in *The Blackwell Guide to Hume's Treatise*, ed. Saul Traiger (Oxford: Blackwell, 2006), pp. 276–95.
[32] Chapter 6, pp. 205–6.

more virtuous than Brutus (T3.3.1.16: 582). So how can our sympathetically based feelings be the basis of moral judgment?

In explaining how we maintain a common point of view in our moral judgments Hume draws an analogy with the apparent variations in the size of the objects of sight as we are more or less distant from them:

> All objects seem to diminish by their distance: But tho' the appearance of objects to our senses be the original standard, by which we judge of them, yet we do not say, that they actually diminish by the distance; but correcting the appearance by reflexion, arrive at a more constant and establish'd judgment concerning them. (T3.3.3.2: 603)

Just as we learn to correct for the reduction of the size of the image which appears to our sight as we move away from an object, so we learn to correct for the weakening of our feelings as we consider the moral characteristics of people at a greater distance from us. Analogous to one's changing distance from the physical objects in one's visual field is one's conversations with other moral evaluators. After listening to my friends and acquaintances describe the virtues of their own sons and daughters, I am led to put the virtues of my own children in perspective. I and my interlocutors are naturally led to find a common point of view by which we can correct for the contradictions in our feelings. Hume writes that "the only point of view, in which our sentiments concur with those of others, is, when we consider the tendency of any passion to the advantage or harm of those, who have any immediate connexion or intercourse with the person possess'd of it." We consider the characters of our own children as well as other people's children by their effects on their parents, friends, acquaintances and the wider social world around them. This is the common moral point of view at which we naturally arrive through "the intercourse of sentiments ... in society and conversation."

An expression which Hume uses in his account of justice may seem particularly appropriate here: There is a "progress of the sentiments" (T3.2.2.25: 500) as we arrive at a common moral point of view. Yet Hume notes that our actual feelings often do not follow the corrections we make in our moral judgments. "The *heart* does not always take part with those general notions, or regulate its love and hatred by them" (T3.3.3.2: 603). We will still be more sympathetic with the virtues – and vices – of our own relatives than those of other people. Still, Hume writes, "these variations we regard not in our general decisions, but still apply the terms expressive of our liking or dislike, in the same manner, as if we remain'd in one point of view" (T3.3.1.16: 582). Through experience of the world we learn to use a constant language of moral evaluation. We blame the actions of a tyrant who we read about in a history book as much as those of a contemporary tyrant whose actions cause the bloodshed we witness on the nightly evening news – even though our detest of the latter is much stronger than our dislike for the former. This is because we "know from reflexion" that the vicious action of the former "wou'd excite as strong sentiments of disapprobation as [that of] the latter, were it plac'd in the same position" (T3.3.1.18: 584).

However, the "reflexion" which Hume refers to should not be regarded as a self-conscious process, any more than the correction for distance in the case of sight. In both cases we end up judging the object from the point of view of those who are directly affected.[33] Concerning the corrections we make in the case of sight, John Locke wrote that "the *Ideas we receive by sensation, are often* in grown People *alter'd by the Judgment*, without our taking notice of it."[34] He attributes this to "an habitual custom." There is every reason to think that Hume is implying that the same mechanism is operating in the correction of our feelings when we make our moral judgments from a common point of view.

7. "VIRTUE IN RAGS" AND THE JUDGMENT OF CHARACTER

According to the account of moral judgment that we have arrived at thus far, our moral judgments are largely based on our sympathy

---

[33] One needs to interpret carefully what Hume means in Part 3 of Book 3 when he writes that in making moral judgments "we confine our view to that narrow circle, in which any person moves" (T3.3.3.2: 602). The "narrow circle" to which he is referring might take us beyond the limits of family and close friends which characterize "our natural uncultivated ideas of morality" (§2 above). It can include the effect of actions on one's "native country." It is quite clear that he thought that in making moral judgments of public figures we go well beyond natural morality: see Annette Baier's discussion of Hume's moral evaluation of Henry VIII in his *History of England* (*A Progress of Sentiments*, p. 190).

[34] ECHU, 2.9.8

with persons affected by the character we are judging. Virtue is largely considered a means to an end. However, we still admire people who are not able to achieve their ends. "Virtue in rags is still virtue; and the love, which it procures, attends a man into a dungeon or desart [i.e. desert], where the virtue can no longer be exerted in action, and is lost to all the world" (T3.3.1.19: 584). Think of jailed democracy advocates in a country under a brutal dictatorship. We do not withhold our moral admiration of them just because they are prevented from achieving their goal of defending political liberty. This is the second objection which Hume considers to his sympathy-based account of moral judgment. How can he claim that it is the non-moral consequences which are important in moral evaluation, when we morally approve of persons who are ineffective, and there are no consequences to be considered?

Hume's answer goes back to his distinction between "*power* and the *exercise* of it" in his discussion of the passions in Book 2 (T2.1.10.4: 311–12). While no such distinction is legitimate from a strictly scientific point of view, it is still made in our common way of thinking through the passions. We suppose that an object can have "power, independent of its actual exercise" and we are affected by that belief. Hume argues that "where any object … is fitted to attain any agreeable end, it naturally gives us pleasure … even tho' some external circumstances" are lacking "to render it altogether effectual" (T3.3.1.20: 584–5). In other words, we are affected by a partial or predisposing cause in cases where the complete cause which necessarily produces the effect is not yet in existence. "Where a character is, in every respect, fitted to be beneficial to society, the imagination passes easily from the cause to the effect, without considering that there are still some circumstances wanting to render the cause a compleat one." When we think of the character of the pro-democracy advocates our minds pass to the thought of the beneficial effects they would have on the lives of their fellow citizens, without considering the repressive governments which prevent them from acting. We go so far as to admire people who fail to achieve their goals, even when circumstances which they could have foreseen conspire against them. We admire Brutus and Cato, even though their actions to save Roman liberty had the opposite effect of hastening the onset of the empire and making the "convulsions and dying agonies" of the republic "more violent and painful."[35] Our admiration for them is based on our tendency to generalize beyond the particular historical reality in which they lived, and overlook the circumstances which made their characters work against the achievement of their goals.

In his own *History of England* Hume gives a striking example of "virtue in rags" or ineffective virtue in his controversial character study of the unlucky King Charles I. He begins his account of Charles with the claim that "the character of this prince, as that of most men ... was mixed; but his virtues predominated extremely above his vices."[36] He argues that Charles's "dignity was free from pride, his humanity from weakness, his bravery from rashness, his temperance from austerity, his frugality from avarice." He balances these virtues with a description of his vices: "his beneficent disposition was clouded by a manner not altogether gracious; his virtue was tinctured with superstition; his good sense was disfigured by a deference to persons of a capacity inferior to his own; and his moderate temper" did not prevent him from making overly hasty decisions. Summing up, Hume writes that Charles was "a good, rather than ... a great man." (For the distinction between *good* and *great*, see T3.3.3; in the *History* he describes Elizabeth I as *great*, and rather lacking in qualities of *goodness*.[37]) Hume goes on to explain how the circumstances of the day, particularly those which led Charles's subjects to demand more power for Parliament than had ever been demanded from any previous monarch, led to his downfall and execution. In other circumstances his virtues would have been ideal in maintaining "the authority of the crown," and in preventing the turmoil of civil war into which he and his subjects were thrown. However, the circumstances which prevailed in his day, circumstances which *ultimately* led to limited monarchy and balance of powers in the English constitution, conspired to the downfall of this good, but not great man.

---

[35] "That Politics may be Reduced to a Science," *Essays*, p. 30.

[36] David Hume, *The History of England from the Invasion of Julius Caesar to the Revolution of 1688*, 6 vols. (Liberty Classics: Indianapolis, 1983), Vol. V, pp. 542–3. This was the first volume of the *History* which Hume wrote and published; it was published in 1754, fourteen years after Book 3 of the *Treatise*.

[37] See his *History of England*, Vol. IV, pp. 351–3.

Thus our evaluation of a person's moral character is based on its *tendency* to produce beneficial or harmful effects, not on the actual effects the person succeeds in producing. The corrections we make to take account of "virtue in rags" are like the corrections we make to take account of the variations in our distance from the person being evaluated. It is true that we have stronger *feelings* of admiration for the person who is actually able to bring about improvements in the world, just as we do for members of our own families. However, a judicious moral spectator does not judge on the basis of her immediate feelings, but makes corrections in order to "pronounce in general concerning the degrees of vice and virtue" possessed by the character she is evaluating (T3.3.1.21: 585).

8. UTILITY, SYMPATHY, AND THE FOURFOLD SCHEME OF MORAL JUDGMENT

Thus we are left with the hypothesis that the social virtues, both natural and artificial, are morally approved on account of our *"extensive sympathy"* with those whom they have the tendency to benefit (T3.3.1.23: 586). We approve of a person who is kind, generous, humane, compassionate, grateful, and friendly, as well as honest, because these qualities benefit the people she affects (cf. T3.3.3.3: 603–4). These virtues correspond, at least roughly, to the virtues of benevolence which Hutcheson thought we approve of through an instinctive *moral sense*. Hume argues that his own alternative hypothesis that sympathy is the basis for our approval of such virtues receives added confirmation when we consider that there are other virtues which are admired simply on account of their usefulness to the person himself. He asks us to consider a businessman who is rather lacking in these "social qualities" but who shows a "dexterity in business" by which he has "extricated himself from … the most delicate affairs" (T3.3.1.25: 588). We admire him because he is clever and industrious, virtuous qualities which simply contribute to his own happiness. How can our admiration for these virtues be explained except by our sympathy for the man himself? We certainly don't approve of them because we ourselves can benefit in any way from them; for he is a perfect stranger.

Many of the qualities we admire because of their usefulness to a person himself are commonly called "natural abilities" rather than virtues because praise or blame can do little to alter them or their corresponding actions (T3.3.4.4: 609). People either do or do not have qualities such as prudence, common sense, sagacity, constancy, resoluteness – and parents and teachers can do little, even in younger children, to change these qualities. Nevertheless we admire a person for having such qualities and disapprove of her for not having them, and Hume thinks that this makes them sufficiently like other mental qualities to merit their being classified as virtues and vices.

Hume does appear to acknowledge that we are hardwired to approve of *some* of these natural abilities – although he stresses that they are in no way related to the virtues of benevolence which Hutcheson had ascribed to an innate *moral sense*. These are virtues which we simply find agreeable in another person such as "wit and eloquence" – and what we would now just call *charm* (T3.3.4.11: 612).[38] Hume writes that these virtues are approved of through "a certain sense, which acts without reflection," and that they have nothing to do with the beneficial "tendencies of qualities and characters." They "produce satisfaction in others by particular *original* principles of human nature, which cannot be accounted for" except by way of innate instincts (T3.3.1.27: 590). Ironically, Hume seems to allow a special Hutchesonian innate sense to explain our approval of such relatively trivial virtues – natural abilities which Hutcheson refused to count as virtues.[39]

Hume states that there are really only two systems of morality which "merit our attention" (T3.3.1.27: 589). Both of these systems recognize "that moral good and evil are ... distinguish'd by our *sentiments*, not by *reason*." The first system, the system of Hutcheson, maintains that these moral sentiments, arise simply "from the mere ... appearance of characters and passions" to an innate sense. The

---

[38] Hume writes here of "a certain *je-ne-sçai-quoi* of agreeable and handsome." He clearly had in mind a discussion of sympathy in Malebranche's *Search after Truth* where that author writes of "le je ne sçai quoi" in which reason has no part and which attaches us "to a trifle as if to the greatest of goods ..." This happens when "we see someone in a group whose appearance ... affects and penetrates us" and "we are led unreflectively to love him, and wish him well" (Nicolas Malebranche, *Recherche de la Vérité*, 3 vols., in *Oeuvres Complètes de Malebranche*, ed. G. Rodis-Lewis (Paris: Vrin, 1963), Vol. II, p. 242; compare *Search*, p. 407.

It would seem that the "je-ne-sais-quoi" appealed to by Hume in this passage does not require what *he* calls sympathy. One need not enter into the feelings of the other person when one approves of wit or eloquence. These qualities are immediately agreeable to the observer.

[39] Hume to Hutcheson, 17 September, 1739, HL I, pp. 33–4.

second system, he says, holds that moral sentiments arise "from reflexions on their tendency to the happiness of mankind, and of particular persons." This is the system of utility and sympathy which Hume favors. He is willing to acknowledge that an innate sense, as well as sympathy, plays a role in our moral judgments. But, as we have just seen, Hume thinks that this innate sense only approves of relatively trivial qualities such as a person's 'charm.' "Reflexions on the tendencies of actions have by far the greatest influence, and determine all the great lines of our duty." Our moral approval of just and humane actions arises from our sympathy with those they tend to affect. And this is the basis of our duty to perform such actions.

Taking these factors into account, Hume proposes a fourfold scheme for cataloguing moral virtues. They are either useful to others, useful to oneself, agreeable to others, or agreeable to oneself – though some are to be found in more than one category. We have already discussed virtues falling under each of the first three categories. Among the last set of virtues, those which are valued because they are *agreeable* to oneself, is a healthy pride or self-esteem – though Hume thinks that pride is also *useful* to ourselves in so far as it "capacitates us for business" (T3.3.2.14: 600). Having "good humour" or simply being an upbeat person is another virtue which is valued because it is agreeable to oneself. This was clearly a virtue which Hume himself possessed. Reflecting on his disappointment in the reception of the *Treatise* thirty-six years later, Hume wrote: "being naturally of a cheerful and sanguine Temper, I very soon recovered the Blow, and prosecuted with great Ardour my Studies."[40] His cheerful and hopeful disposition was both agreeable and useful to himself in so far as it led to his publication of his successful *Essays, Moral and Political* within the next two years.

In considering Hume's fourfold scheme of moral evaluation in general, there are three major points which one needs to keep in mind. First, what is primarily being morally judged are character traits, and only secondarily the actions which tend to flow from them. Secondly, our moral judgments of others, whether based on their usefulness or their agreeableness, are made from a point of view outside of ourselves – a point of view which we reach through

---

[40] "My Own Life," p. 2.

sympathy. Sympathy takes us entirely outside of our own concerns and lets us enter into the feelings and interests of those we are morally judging and – even more significantly – the pleasures and pains of those affected by them. Finally, it is, above all, the first two categories in Hume's fourfold scheme which are most important. It is a character's *usefulness* or *utility* to others and to herself which are primary in making moral judgments, and in determining what we ourselves ought to do. "These form the most considerable part of morality" (T3.3.6.2: 619).

9. CONCLUSION: HUME'S ANSWERS TO HUTCHESON AND MANDEVILLE

In conclusion, let me return to Hume's answer to the controversy *"whether ... moral distinctions be founded on natural and original principles, or arise from interest and education,"* the controversy between Hutcheson and Mandeville (T2.1.7.2: 295). Given what we have learned of his moral theory, are we to conclude that moral distinctions are based on "natural and original principles" as Hutcheson claimed, or in "interest and education" as Mandeville held?

As we have seen, Hume explicitly rejects the view of Hutcheson that morality rests on "original principles." Moral distinctions, for Hume, are not hardwired into us as they were for Hutcheson. In the first place, he argues that the fundamental virtues of justice, on which the peace and order of society depend, are invented by human beings. "Nature has ... trusted this affair entirely to the conduct of men, and not plac'd in the mind any peculiar original principles ..." (T3.2.6.1: 526). It is through experience and observation that we discover the contingent circumstances of external objects and human psychology which require us to invent the artificial virtues (T3.2.1.9: 474–5; see §4, above). In the second place, as we have seen, our moral esteem only depends on "particular *original* principles of human nature" in the *most trivial* of cases, such as our approval of another's charm, wit, or humor (T3.3.1.27: 590). Thirdly, as we saw in §5, it is wrong to think that Hume argues that genuine moral principles somehow "piggy-back" on our instinctive natural morality.[41]

---

[41] This expression is used by David Norton in his "Hume and Hutcheson: the Question of Influence," in *Oxford Studies in Early Modern Philosophy*, Vol. II, eds. D. Garber and

Our natural uncultivated partial morality actually makes us unfit to live in anything but the smallest social groups (3.2.2.6: 487). It stands in direct opposition to the principles of justice.

But sympathy is still a "natural principle" and in this respect Hume may be said to agree with Hutcheson, against Mandeville. We care about the feelings of others and we care about how they feel about us through the basic psychological principle of sympathy. Certainly Mandeville was right that morality largely depends upon the *interests* of other people and of society as a whole (though he did not take into account the relatively trivial virtues which do not have this tendency (T3.3.1.11: 578)). But he was wrong in thinking that there is no principle of human nature which causes us to care about those interests, independent of our self-interest. We form rules to serve those interests and subsequently approve of people who follow those rules because of our ability to *sympathize* with those affected by them. Secondly, Mandeville was right that education is necessary to inculcate a sense of morals in us. But, again, education is only able to operate on the tender minds of young children because of their ability to sympathize with those who praise and blame them for performing useful or harmful actions. Still, the basic psychological principle of custom and habit is required to infix the sense of right and wrong into a child's character.

Hume concludes Book 3 by reflecting that "those who resolve the sense of morals into original instincts of the human mind, may defend the cause of virtue with sufficient authority; but want [lack] the advantage, which those possess, who account for that sense by an extensive sympathy with mankind" (T3.3.6.3: 619). It is, of course, Hutcheson who resolves "the sense of morals into original instincts of the human mind" and defends it with authority. However, his theory lacks the advantage of Hume's. Hutcheson himself acknowledged that while the "moral sense" explains why we approve of particular virtues it cannot justify itself. He even conceived of the possibility of an evil moral sense which approves of qualities which harm others.

S. Nadler (Oxford: Clarendon Press, 2005), pp. 211–56), esp. p. 223. For criticisms of Norton's view of the relationship of the philosophies of Hume and Hutcheson, see James Moore, "The Eclectic Stoic, the Mitigated Skeptic," in *New Essays on David Hume*, eds. E. Ronchetti and E. Mazza (Milan: FrancoAngeli, 2007), pp.133–70 and Luigi Turco, "Hutcheson and Hume in a Recent Polemic," *ibid.*, pp. 171–98.

Hutcheson argued that one cannot "apply *moral Attributes* to the very *Faculty* of perceiving *moral Qualities*; or call his *moral Sense morally Good or Evil*, any more than he calls the Power of Tasting, sweet or bitter" (*Essay on the Passions*, p. 149).[42] But Hume argues that for this very reason Hutcheson's theory of the moral sense lacks the advantage of the theory that morality is founded in sympathy. Sympathy not only allows us to approve of particular virtues, but also of the sense of morals itself. When we reflect on this "principle inherent in the soul" we feel moral approval (T3.3.6.3: 619). We approve of our possession of a principle which is so useful to each of us and provides such benefit to society as whole. It is our ability to enter into the interests and feelings of other people which provides the source of morality. Hume writes that when we reflect on this principle "nothing is presented on any side, but what is laudable and good." The Conclusion to Book 3 of the *Treatise*, where Hume defends his theory against that of Hutcheson, must be considered his final word in answering the criticisms which Hutcheson sent to him after reading an earlier draft of his moral theory.[43]

---

[42] The problem is analogous to that of calling God good when one holds a Divine Command theory of moral goodness.

[43] Chapter 1 §8, pp. 32ff.

Bibliography and further reading

MODERN EDITIONS OF HUME'S OWN WRITINGS

Dialogues Concerning Natural Religion, edited by Norman Kemp Smith, second edition. Edinburgh: Nelson, 1947.

Dialogues Concerning Natural Religion, edited by Dorothy Coleman. Cambridge University Press, 2007.

A Dissertation on the Passions and The Natural History of Religion, edited by Tom L. Beauchamp. Oxford: Clarendon Press, 2007.

Enquiries Concerning Human Understanding and Concerning the Principles of Morals, edited by L. A. Selby-Bigge; third edition, revised by P. H. Nidditch. Oxford: Clarendon Press, 1975.

Enquiry Concerning the Principles of Morals, Oxford Philosophical Texts, edited by Tom L. Beauchamp. Oxford University Press, 1998.

Enquiry Concerning the Principles of Morals, A Critical Edition, edited by Tom L. Beauchamp. Oxford: Clarendon Press, 1998.

Enquiry Concerning Human Understanding, Oxford Philosophical Texts, edited by Tom L. Beauchamp. Oxford University Press, 1999.

Enquiry Concerning Human Understanding, A Critical Edition, edited by Tom L. Beauchamp. Oxford: Clarendon Press, 2000.

Enquiry Concerning Human Understanding and Other Writings, edited by Stephen Buckle. Cambridge University Press, 2007

Essays Moral, Political, and Literary. edited by E. F. Millar. rev. ed. Indianapolis: Liberty Classics, 1987.

The History of England from the Invasion of Julius Caesar to the Revolution of 1688, 6 vols. Liberty Classics: Indianapolis, 1983.

The Letters of David Hume, edited by J. Y. T. Greig. 2 vols. Oxford University Press, 1932.

New Letters of David Hume, edited by R. Kilbansky and E. C. Mossner. Oxford: Clarendon Press, 1954.

"The Natural History of Religion." In *A Dissertation on the Passions and The Natural History of Religion*, edited by Tom L. Beauchamp. Oxford: Clarendon Press, 2007.

A Treatise of Human Nature, edited by L. A. Selby-Bigge, second edition, revised by P. H. Nidditch. Oxford: Clarendon Press, 1978. [This edition includes *An Abstract of... A Treatise of Human Nature*. Hume's Appendix is intact as he had printed it in Volume 3 in 1740. Textual notes (pp. 663–73) record Hume's post-publication corrections and additions to the text.]

A Treatise of Human Nature, Oxford Philosophical Texts, edited by David Fate Norton and Mary Norton. Oxford University Press, 2000; reprinted with corrections beginning in 2001. [This text of the *Treatise* is the same as that of the Oxford Critical Edition: see the next item below. It incorporates into the text of Book 1 the insertions Hume listed in the Appendix to Book 3; also his post-publication manuscript amendments to Book 3. Changes are made to Hume's original published *Treatise* without any textual annotations. In addition to the *Treatise* the text includes *An Abstract of... A Treatise of Human Nature*. There is a 99-page interpretative Introduction by the editor, a glossary of difficult terms, and textual annotations including summaries of each part and section of the book (see pp. 421–2ff).]

A Treatise of Human Nature, A Critical Edition, edited by David Fate Norton and Mary Norton. 2 vols. Oxford: Clarendon Press, 2007. [Volume I presents a critical edition of the text of the *Treatise* and *Abstract* as described in the previous item, as well as *A Letter from a Gentleman to his Friend in Edinburgh* – Hume's defense of his book against criticisms made when he applied for the Edinburgh Chair of Moral Philosophy in 1745. *The index for this volume is contained in volume 2*. Volume 2 contains an account of the principles used in creating this critical edition of Hume's *Treatise*, "A Historical Account of *A Treatise of Human Nature* from its Beginnings to the Time of Hume's Death," and detailed annotations on the text meant to illuminate rather than interpret it (see pp. 685ff.).]

A Treatise of Human Nature (abridged), edited by John P. Wright, Gary Fuller and Robert Stecker. London: J. M. Dent, 2003. [Contains a chronology of Hume's life and times, as well as comments on the *Treatise* by philosophical critics from Hume's own day to our own.]

CLASSICAL AND EARLY MODERN BACKGROUND TO HUME'S THOUGHT

Addison, Joseph. *The Spectator*, Vol. III, edited by Donald F. Bond. Oxford: Clarendon Press, 1965.

Aristotle. "De Memoria et Reminiscentia." In *The Basic Works of Aristotle*, edited by Richard McKeon. New York: Random House, 1941: 607–17, 449^b–53^b.

Aristotle. *Nichomachean Ethics*, translated by H. Rackham. London: W. Heinemann, 1968.

Bacon, Francis. *The New Organon*, edited by Lisa Jardine and Michael Silverthorne. Cambridge University Press, 2000.

Bayle, Pierre. *The Dictionary Historical and Critical of Mr. Peter Bayle*, 5 vols., edited and translated by Pierre Des Maizeau, 2nd edn. London, 1735.

Bayle, Pierre. *Historical and Critical Dictionary: Selections*, edited by Richard H. Popkin and Craig Brush. Indianapolis: Bobbs-Merrill, 1965.

Baxter, Andrew. *An Enquiry into the Nature of the Human Soul*. London, 1733.

Berkeley, George. *An Essay towards a New Theory of Vision*. In *The Works of George Berkeley, Bishop of Cloyne*, Vol. II, edited by A. A. Luce and T. E. Jessop. London: Nelson, 1949

Berkeley, George. *A Treatise Concerning the Principles of Human Knowledge*. In *The Works of George Berkeley, Bishop of Cloyne*, Vol. II, edited by A. A. Luce and T. E. Jessop. London: Nelson, 1949.

Butler, Joseph. *Analogy of Religion, Natural and Revealed, to the Constitution and Course of nature*, second edition. London, 1736.

Butler, Joseph. *Analogy of Religion, Natural and Revealed, to the Constitution and Course of Nature*. In *The Works of Joseph Butler*, edited by W. E. Gladstone, 3 vols. Oxford: Clarendon Press, 1896.

Butler, Joseph. *Fifteen Sermons Preached at the Rolls Chapel*, in *The Works of Joseph Butler*, edited by W. E. Gladstone; with a new introduction by R. G. Frey, 3 vols. Bristol: Thoemmes Press, 1995.

Chambers, Ephraim. *Cyclopædia; or, An Universal Dictionary of Arts and Sciences...*, 2 vols. London, 1728.

Cheyne, George. *The English Malady: or a Treatise of Nervous Disease of all Kinds, as Spleen, Vapours, Lowness of Spirits, Hypochondriacal, and Hysterical Distempers &c.* London and Bath, 1733.

Cheyne, George. *Philosophical Principles of Natural Religion*, 5th edn. London, 1736.

Cicero. *Academica*. In *Denatura deorum. Academica*, translated by H. Rackham. Cambridge, Mass.: Harvard University Press, 1933.

Cicero. *Tusculan Disputations*. translated by J. E. King. London: Heinemann, 1966.

Clarke, Samuel. *A Discourse Concerning the Unchangeable Obligations of Natural Religion, and the Truth and Certainty of the Christian Revelation*, 3rd edn. London, 1711.

Clarke, Samuel. *Sermons on Several Subjects*, 7th ed., 11 vols. London, 1749.

Clarke, Samuel. *A Demonstration of the Being and Attributes of God and Other Writings*, edited by E. Vailati. Cambridge University Press, 1998. [first published 1705].

Descartes, Rene. *The Philosophical Writings of Descartes*, translated by John Cottingham, Robert Stoothoff, Dugald Murdoch, and Anthony Kenny, 3 vols. Cambridge University Press. 1985–1991.

Gay, John. "Preliminary Dissertation Concerning the Virtue and Morality," prefaced to William King's *An Essay on the Origin of Evil*. London, 1731.

Galileo Galilei. *The Discoveries and Opinions of Galileo*, edited and translated by Stillman Drake. New York: Anchor Books, 1957.

Haller, Albrecht von. *First Lines of Physiology*, edited by Wm. Cullen. Edinburgh, 1786.

Hartley, David. *Observations on Man, his Frame, his Duty, and his Expectations*. London, 1749.

Hobbes, Thomas. *Leviathan, or The Matter, Forme, & Power of a Commonwealth Ecclesiastical and Civill*, edited by C. B. Macpherson. London: Penguin, 1968.

Hutcheson, Francis. *Letters between the Late Mr. Gilbert, and Mr. Hutchinson on the True Foundation of Virtue or Moral Goodness*. London, 1735.

Hutcheson, Francis. *An Inquiry into the Original of Our Ideas of Beauty and Virtue*, 3rd edn., corrected. London, 1729.

Hutcheson, Francis. *An Inquiry into the Original of Our Ideas of Beauty and Virtue*, edited by Wolfgang Leidhold. Indianapolis: Liberty Fund, 2004.

Hutcheson, Francis. *An Essay on the Nature and Conduct of the Passions and Affections, with Illustrations on the Moral Sense*, edited by Aaron Garrett. Indianapolis: Liberty Fund, 2002.

Hutcheson, Francis. *Philosophiae Moralis Institutio Compendiaria, with A Short Introduction to Moral Philosophy*, edited with an Introduction by Luigi Turco. Indianapolis: Liberty Fund, 2008.

Locke, John. *An Essay Concerning Human Understanding*, edited by P. H. Nidditch. Oxford University Press, 1975.

Locke, John. *Two Treatises of Government*, edited by Peter Laslett. Cambridge University Press, 1988.

Malebranche, Nicolas. *Recherche de la Vérité*, 3 vols., edited by G. Rodis-Lewis, in *Oeuvres Complètes de Malebranche*. Paris: Vrin, 1963.

Malebranche, Nicolas. *The Search After Truth*, translated by Thomas M. Lennon and Paul J. Olscamp. Cambridge University Press, 1997.

Mandeville, Bernard. *A Treatise of the Hypochondriak and Hysterick Passions, Vulgarly call'd the HYPO in MEN and VAPOURS in WOMEN*. London, 1711.

Mandeville, Bernard. *Treatise of the Hypochondriack and Hysterick Diseases. In Three Dialogues*, 3rd edn. London, 1730.

Mandeville, Bernard. *The Fable of the Bees*, edited by F. B. Kaye. 2 vols. Oxford: Clarendon Press, 1924.

Newton, Isaac. *Opticks or a Treatise of the Reflections, Refractions, Inflections & Colours of Light*, based on the Fourth Edition London, 1730. New York: Dover, 1952.

Newton, Isaac. *Sir Isaac Newton's Mathematical Principles of Natural Philosophy and his System of the World*, translated by Andrew Motte (1729), revised by Florian Cajori, 2 vols. New York: Greenwood Press, 1969.

Plato. *Republic*, translated by Tom Griffith. Cambridge University Press, 2000.

Ramsay, Andrew Michael. *Les Voyages de Cyrus*, 2 vols. Amsterdam, 1732.

Ramsay, Andrew Michael. "Le Psychomètre ou Réflexions sur les différens caracteres de l'Esprit par un Mylord Anglois." *Mémoires pour l'Histoire des Sciences & des beaux Arts* , April, 1735.

Ramsay, Andrew Michael. *Philosophical Principles of Natural and Revealed Religion...*, 2 vols. Glasgow: Foulis, 1748–9.

Sextus Empiricus. *Outlines of Pyrrhonism*, Book I. In *Sextus Empiricus*, 4 vols., translated by R. G. Bury. Cambridge, Mass.: Harvard University Press, 1961.

Shaftesbury, Anthony Ashley Cooper, Third Earl of Shaftesbury. *Characteristicks of Men, Manners, Opinions, Times*, 3 vols. London, 1732; reprint, Indianapolis: Liberty Fund, 2001.

Voltaire. *Letters Concerning the English Nation*, edited by Nicholas Cronk. Oxford University Press, 1994.

Wollaston, William. *Religion of Nature Delineated*. London, 1724.

EIGHTEENTH-CENTURY RESPONSES TO HUME'S *TREATISE*

Beattie, James. *An Essay on the Nature and Immutability of Truth: In Opposition to Sophistry and Scepticism* (1770); reprinted New York: Garland Press, 1983.

Bentham, Jeremy. *A Fragment on Government* (1776). In *The Works of Jeremy Bentham*, edited by John Bowring, vols. 1–10. New York: Russell and Russell, 1962, Vol. I.

Bentham, Jeremy. *The Correspondence of Jeremy Bentham*, edited by Catherine Fuller. Oxford: Clarendon Press, 2000, Vol. XI.

Brown, Thomas. *Observations on the Nature and Tendency of the Doctrine of Mr. Hume Concerning the Relation of Cause and Effect* (1805); reprinted in James Fieser, *Early Responses to Hume*, Vol. IV (see below).

Kant, Immanuel. *Critique of Pure Reason* (1781); translated by Norman Kemp Smith. London: Macmillan, 1933.

Kant, Immanuel. *Groundwork of the Metaphysic of Morals*, edited and translated by Mary Gregor. Cambridge University Press, 1998.

Kant, Immanuel. *Prolegomena to any Future Metaphysics That Will Be Able to Come Forward as Science* (1783), second edition, edited and translated by Gary Hatfield. Cambridge University Press, 2004.

Oswald, James. *An Appeal to Common Sense on the Behalf of Religion*, 2 vols. (1766–72). Reprinted in James Fieser, *Early Responses to Hume*, Vol. IV (see below).

Reid, Thomas. *Essays on the Active Powers of the Human Mind* (1788), edited by Baruch Brody. Cambridge, Mass.: M.I.T. Press, 1969.

Reid, Thomas. *An Inquiry into the Human Mind on the Principles of Common Sense* (1764), edited by Derek R. Brookes. Edinburgh University Press, 1997.

Reid, Thomas. *Essays on the Intellectual Powers of Man* (1785), edited by Dereck R. Brookes. Edinburgh University Press, 2002.

Smith, Adam. *The Theory of Moral Sentiments* (1759), edited by D. D. Raphael and A. L. Macfie. Oxford University Press, 1999–2000.

A collection of early criticisms of Hume's writings, including the contemporary reviews of *A Treatise of Human Nature*, has been assembled in James Fieser (ed.), *Early Responses to Hume*, 4 vols. Bristol: Thoemmes Press, 1999–2000.

SELECTED SECONDARY SOURCES

Ainslie, Donald. "Scepticism about Persons in Book II of Hume's Treatise." *Journal of the History of Philosophy* **37** (1999): 469–92.

Allison, Henry E. "Hume's Philosophical Insouciance: A Reading of Treatise 1.4.7." *Hume Studies* **31** (2005): 317–46.

Anderson, Robert F. *Hume's First Principles*. Lincoln: University of Nebraska Press, 1966.

Anderson, Robert F. "The Location, Extension, Shape, and Size of Hume's Perceptions." In *Hume: A Re-evaluation*, edited by Donald W. Livingston and James T. King. New York: Fordham University Press, 1976.

Ardal, Pall. *Passion and Value in Hume's Treatise*. Edinburgh University Press, 1966.

Atwood, Margaret. *Negotiating with the Dead*. Cambridge University Press, 2002.

Baier, Annette. *A Progress of Sentiments: Reflections on Hume's Treatise*. Cambridge, Mass.: Harvard University Press, 1991.

Baier, Annette. *Death and Character: Further Reflections on Hume*. Cambridge, Mass.: Harvard University Press, 2008.

Baillie, James. *Routledge Philosophy Guidebook to Hume on Morality*. Routledge: London, 2000.

Barfoot, M. "Hume and the Culture of Science in the Early Eighteenth Century." In *Studies in the Philosophy of the Scottish Enlightenment*, edited by M. A. Stewart. Oxford: Clarendon Press, 1990, 151–90.

Baxter, Donald. "Identity, Continued Existence, and the External World." In *The Blackwell Guide to Hume's Treatise*, edited by Saul Traiger. Oxford: Blackwell, 2006, 114–32.

Baxter, Donald. *Time and Identity in the Treatise*. New York: Routledge, 2008.

Beebee, Helen. *Hume on Causation*. London: Routledge, 2006.

Beebee, Helen. "Does Anything Hold the World Together?" *Synthese* **149** (2006): 509–33.

Bell, Martin. "Sceptical Doubts Concerning Hume's Causal Realism." In *The New Hume Debate*, 2nd edn., edited by Rupert Read and Kenneth Richman. London: Routledge, 2007, 122–37.

Bell, Martin and Marie McGinn. "Naturalism and Scepticism." *Philosophy* **65** (1990): 399–418.

Blackburn, Simon. *Spreading the Word*. Oxford University Press, 1984.

Blackburn, Simon. "Hume and Thick Connexions." In *The New Hume Debate*, edited by R. Read and K. Richman, revised edition. Routledge: London, 2007, 100–12.

Brand, Walter. *Hume's Theory of Moral Judgment: A Study in the Unity of A Treatise of Human Nature*. Dordrecht, The Netherlands: Kluwer Academic Publishers, 1992.

Broadie, A. (ed.). *The Cambridge Companion to the Scottish Enlightenment*. Cambridge University Press, 2003.

Broughton, Janet. "Hume's Skepticism about Causal Inferences." *Pacific Philosophical Quarterly* **64** (1983), 3–18.

Broughton, Janet. "Impressions and Ideas." In *The Blackwell Guide to Hume's Treatise*, edited by Saul Traiger, Oxford: Blackwell, 2006, 43–58.

Buckle, Stephen. *Hume's Enlightenment Tract: The Unity and Purpose of An Enquiry Concerning Human Understanding*. Oxford: Clarendon Press, 2001.

Burton, John Hill. *Life and Correspondence of David Hume*, 2 vols. Edinburgh, 1846.

Cohon, Rachel. "Hume's Difficulty with the Virtue of Honesty." *Hume Studies* **21** (1997): 91–112.

Cohon, Rachel. "Hume's Artificial and Natural Virtues." In *The Blackwell Guide to Hume's Treatise*, edited by Saul Traiger. Oxford: Blackwell, 2006, 256–275.

Cohon, Rachel and David Owen. "Representation, Reason and Motivation." *Manuscrito* **20** (1997), 47–76.

Coventry, Angela. *Hume's Theory of Causation: A Quasi-Realist Interpretation*. London: Continuum, 2006.

Craig, Edward. "Hume on Causality: Projectivist *and* Realist." In *The New Hume Debate*, 2nd edn., edited by Rupert Read and Kenneth Richman. London: Routledge, 2007, 113–21.

Darwall, Stephen. "Hume and the Invention of Utilitarianism." In *Hume and Hume's Connexions*, edited by M. A. Stewart and John P. Wright. Edinburgh University Press, 1994, 58–82.

Dicker, George. *Hume's Epistemology and Metaphysics: An Introduction.* London: Routledge, 1998.

Downing, Lisa. "Occasionalism and Strict Mechanism: Malebranche, Berkeley, Fontenelle." In *Early Modern Philosophy: Mind, Matter, and Metaphysics*, edited by C. Mercer and E. O'Neill. Oxford University Press, 2005, 206–30.

Emerson, Roger. "The 'Affair' at Edinburgh and the 'Project' at Glasgow." In *Hume and Hume's Connexions*, edited by M. A. Stewart and John P. Wright. Edinburgh University Press, 1994: 1–22.

Falkenstein, Lorne. "Space and Time." In *The Blackwell Guide to Hume's Treatise of Human Nature*, edited by Saul Traiger. Oxford: Blackwell, 2006: 59–76.

Fogelin, Robert. *Hume's Skepticism in the Treatise of Human Nature.* London: Routledge, 1985.

Fogelin, Robert. "Hume's Scepticism." In *The Cambridge Companion to Hume*, edited by David Norton. Cambridge University Press, 1993.

Frasca-Spada, Marina. *Space and the Self in Hume's Treatise.* Cambridge University Press, 1998.

Frasca-Spada, Marina. "Simple Perceptions in Hume's *Treatise*." In *New Essays on David Hume*, edited by Emanuele Ronchetti and Emilio Mazza. Milan: FrancoAngeli, 2007, 37–54.

Frasca-Spada, Marina and Peter Kail (ed.). *Impressions of Hume.* Oxford: Clarendon Press, 2005.

Garrett, Don. *Cognition and Commitment in Hume's Philosophy.* Oxford University Press, 1997.

Garrett, Don. "A Small Tincture of Pyrrhonism: Skepticism and Naturalism in Hume's Science of Man." In *Pyrrhonian Skepticism*, edited by W. Sinnott-Armstrong. Oxford University Press, 2004, 68–98.

Garrett, Don. "Hume's Conclusions in 'Conclusions in Conclusion of this Book'." In *The Blackwell Guide to Hume's Treatise*, edited by Saul Traiger. Oxford: Blackwell, 2006, 151–76.

Gaskin, J. C. A. *Hume's Philosophy of Religion*, 2nd edn., New York: Macmillan, 1988.

Gay, Peter. *The Enlightenment: an Interpretation.* London: Weidenfeld and Nicolson, 1973.

Gill, Michael B. "Nature and Association in the Moral Theory of Francis Hutcheson." *History of Philosophy Quarterly* **12** (July 1995): 23–48.

Gill, Michael B. "Hume's Progressive View of Human Nature." *Hume Studies* **26** (2000): 87–108.

Gill, Michael B. *The British Moralists on Human Nature and the Birth of Secular Ethics.* Cambridge University Press, 2006.

Haakonssen, Knud. *The Science of a Legislator: the Natural Jursiprudence of David Hume and Adam Smith.* Cambridge University Press, 1981.

Hacking, Ian. "Hume's Species of Probability." *Philosophical Studies* **33** (1978): 21–37.

Hacking, Ian. *The Taming of Chance.* Cambridge University Press, 1990.

Hakkarainen, Jani. *Hume's Scepticism and Realism.* Tampere, Finland: Bookshop Tampere, 2007.

Harris, James. "Hume's Reconciling Project." *British Journal for the History of Philosophy* **11** (2003): 451–71.

Harris, James. "Answering Bayle's Question: Religious Belief in the Moral Philosophy of the Scottish Enlightenment." In *Oxford Studies in Early Modern Philosophy*, edited by Daniel Garber and Steven Nadler. Oxford: Clarendon Press, 2003, 229–53.

Harris, James. *Of Liberty and Necessity: The Free Will Debate in Eighteenth-century British Philosophy.* Oxford: Clarendon Press, 2005.

Harris, James. "Hume's Four Essays on Human Happiness and their Place in the Move from Morals to Politics." In *New Essays on David Hume*, edited by E. Ronchetti and E. Mazza. Milan: FrancoAngeli, 2007, 223–36.

Herdt, Jennifer. *Religion and Faction in Hume's Moral Philosophy.* Cambridge University Press, 1997.

Hurlbutt, Robert. *Hume, Newton, and the Design Argument.* Lincoln: University of Nebraska Press, 1965.

Jacob, Margaret. *The Radical Enlightenment: Pantheists, Freemasons, and Republicans.* London: George Allen and Unwin, 1981.

Jacquette, Dale. *David Hume's Critique of Infinity.* Leiden-Boston-Köln: Brill, 2001.

James, William. *Pragmatism.* London: Longmans, 1925.

Jones, Peter. *Hume's Sentiments: Their Ciceronian and French Context.* Edinburgh University Press, 1982.

Jones, Peter (ed.). *The Reception of David Hume in Europe.* London: Continuum, 2005.

Kail, Peter. "Hutcheson's Moral Sense: Skepticism, Realism, and Secondary Qualities." *History of Philosophy Quarterly* **18** (2001): 57–77.

Kail, Peter. *Projection and Realism in Hume's Philosophy.* Oxford University Press, 2007.

Kail, Peter. "Leibniz's Dog and Humean Reason." In *New Essays on David Hume*, edited by Emanuele Ronchetti and Emilio Mazza. Milan: FrancoAngeli, 2007: 65–80.

Kail, Peter. "How to Understand Hume's Realism." In *The New Hume Debate*, second edition, edited by Rupert Read and Kenneth Richman. London: Routledge, 2007, 253–69.

Kemp, Catherine. "Contrariety in Hume." In *New Essays on David Hume*, edited by Emanuele Ronchetti and Emilio Mazza. Milan: FrancoAngeli, 2007, 55–64.

Kemp Smith, Norman; see Smith, Norman Kemp.

Kozanecki, Tadeusz. "Dawida Hume'a Nieznane Listy W Zbiorach Muzeum Czartoryskich (Polska)." *Archiwum Historii Filozofii Spolecznej* **9** (1963): 127–41.

Kuehn, Manfred. "Kant's Critique of Hume's Theory of Faith." In *Hume and Hume's Connexions*, edited by M. A. Stewart and John P. Wright. Edinburgh University Press, 1994, 239–55.

Laird, John. *Hume's Philosophy of Human Nature*. London: Methuen, 1932.

Latimer, J. *Annals of Bristol in the Eighteenth Century*. Bristol, 1893.

Livingston, Donald. *Philosophical Melancholy and Delirium: Hume's Pathology of Philosophy*. University of Chicago Press, 1998.

Loeb, Louis. *Stability and Justification in Hume's Treatise*. Oxford University Press, 2002.

Mazza, Emilio. "In and Out of the Well: Flux and Reflux of Scepticism and Nature." In *New Essays on David Hume*, edited by Emanuele Ronchetti and Emilio Mazza. Milan: FrancoAngeli, 2007, 101–132.

McCosh, James. *The Scottish Philosophy*. New York, 1885.

McCracken, Charles. *Malebranche and British Philosophy*. Oxford: Clarendon Press, 1983.

McIntyre, Jane. "Personal Identity and the Passions." *Journal of the History of Philosophy* **27** (1989): 545–57.

McIntyre, Jane. "Character: A Humean Account." *History of Philosophy Quarterly* **7** (1990): 193–205.

Millican, Peter. "Hume's Sceptical Doubts Concerning Induction." In *Reading Hume on Human Understanding*. Oxford: Clarendon Press, 2002, 107–74.

Millican, Peter (ed.). *Reading Hume on Human Understanding*. Oxford: Clarendon Press, 2002.

Millican, Peter. "Hume's Determinism." Read to the 32nd meeting of the Hume Society in Toronto in August, 2005, forthcoming.

Millican, Peter. "Against the New Hume." In *The New Hume Debate*, 2nd edn., edited by Rupert Read and Kenneth Richman. London: Routledge, 2007, 211–52.

Moore, James. "Hume and Hutcheson." In *Hume and Hume's Connexions*, edited by M. A. Stewart and John P. Wright. Edinburgh University Press, 1994, 23–57.

Moore, James. "The Eclectic Stoic, the Mitigated Skeptic." In *New Essays on David Hume*, edited by Emanuele Ronchetti and Emilio Mazza. Milan: FrancoAngeli, 2007, 133–70.

Morris, William E. "Hume's Conclusions." *Philosophical Studies* **99** (2000): 89–110.

Mossner, Ernest C. "Hume at La Flèche, 1735: an Unpublished Letter." *The University of Texas Studies in English* **37** (1958): 30–3.

Mossner, Ernest C. *The Life of David Hume*, revised edition. Oxford: Clarendon Press, 1980.

Mource, H. O. *Hume's Naturalism*. London: Routledge, 1999.

Mullett, Charles. *The Letters of Doctor George Cheyne to Samuel Richardson (1733–1743)*. Columbia, Mo.: University of Missouri Press, 1943.

Noonan, Harold. *Routledge Philosophical Guidebook to Hume on Knowledge*. London: Routledge, 1999.

Norton, David F. *David Hume: Common Sense Moralist, Sceptical Metaphysician*. Princeton, N. J.: Princeton University Press, 1982.

Norton, David F. "Hutcheson's Moral Realism." *Journal of the History of Philosophy* **23** (1985): 397–418.

Norton, David F. (ed.). *The Cambridge Companion to Hume*. Cambridge University Press, 1993.

Norton, David F. "Hume and Hutcheson: the Question of Influence." In *Oxford Studies in Early Modern Philosophy*, Vol. II, edited by D. Garber and S. Nadler. Oxford: Clarendon Press, 2005, 211–56.

Norton, David F. and Mary Norton. *The David Hume Library*. Edinburgh Bibliographical Society, 1996.

Owen, David. *Hume's Reason*. Oxford University Press, 1999.

Pears, David. *Hume's System: An Examination of the First Book of his Treatise*. Oxford University Press, 1990.

Penelhum, Terence. *God and Skepticism*. Dordrecht: D. Reidel, 1983.

Penelhum, Terence. *David Hume: An Introduction to his Philosophical System*. West Lafayette, Ind.: Purdue University, 1992.

Penelhum, Terence. *Themes in Hume: The Self, The Will, Religion*. Oxford University Press, 2000.

Popkin, Richard. "Hume and Kierkegaard." *Journal of Religion* **31** (1951): 274–81.

Popkin, Richard. "So Hume did Read Berkeley." *Journal of Philosophy* **61** (1964): 773–8.

Price, H. H. *Hume's Theory of the External World*. Oxford: Clarendon Press, 1940.

Read, Rupert and Ken, Richman (eds.), *The New Hume Debate*, second edition. London: Routlege, 2007.

Rivers, Isabel. *Reason, Grace, and Sentiment*, II. Cambridge University Press, 2000.

Ronchetti, Emanuele and Emilio Mazza (eds.). *New Essays on David Hume*. Milan: FrancoAngeli, 2007.

Ross, Ian. "Hutcheson on Hume's Treatise: An Unnoticed Letter." *Journal of the History of Philosophy* 4 (1966): 69–72.

Ross, Ian. *Lord Kames and the Scotland of his Day*. Oxford: Clarendon Press, 1972.

Russell, Paul. "Dudgeon, William." In *Dictionary of Eighteenth-Century British Philosophers*, edited by J. W. Yolton, J. V. Price, and J. Stephens. Bristol: Thoemmes Press, 1999.

Russell, Paul. "Butler's 'Future State' and Hume's 'Guide to Life'." *Journal of the History of Philosophy*. **17** (2004): 425–48.

Russell, Paul. *The Riddle of Hume's Treatise: Skepticism, Naturalism, and Irreligion*. Oxford University Press, 2008.

Schneewind, J. B. *The Invention of Autonomy: A History of Modern Moral Philosophy*. Cambridge University Press, 1998.

Sher, Richard B. "Professors of Virtue: The Edinburgh Chair." In *Studies in the History of the Scottish Enlightenment*, edited by M. A. Stewart. Oxford: Clarendon Press, 1990: 87–126.

Singer, Ira. "Hume's Extreme Skepticism in Treatise I.IV.7." *Canadian Journal of Philosophy* **25** (1995): 595–622.

Smith, Norman Kemp. "The Naturalism of Hume." *Mind*, n.s. **14** (1905): 149–73, 335–47.

Smith, Norman Kemp. *The Philosophy of David Hume: A Study of its Origins and its Central Doctrines*. London: Macmillan, 1941.

Stewart, M. A. "The Stoic Legacy in the Early Scottish Enlightenment." In *Atoms, 'Pneuma', and Tranquility; Epicurean and Stoic Themes in European Thought*, edited by M. J. Osler. Cambridge University Press, 1991, 273–96.

Stewart, M. A. "An Early Fragment on Evil." In *Hume and Hume's Connexions,* edited by M. A. Stewart and John P. Wright. Edinburgh University Press, 1994, 160–70.

Stewart, M. A. *The Kirk and the Infidel*. Lancaster, England, 1994.

Stewart, M. A. "The Dating of Hume's Manuscripts." In *The Scottish Enlightenment: Essays in Reinterpretation*, edited by Paul Wood. University of Rochester Press, 2000, 267–314.

Stewart, M. A. "Religion and Rational Theology." In *The Cambridge Companion to the Scottish Enlightenment*, edited by A. Broadie. Cambridge University Press, 2003, 31–59.

Stewart, M. A. "Hume's Intellectual Development, 1711–1752." In *Impressions of Hume* edited by M. Frasca-Spada and P. J. E. Kail . Oxford: Clarendon Press, 2005, 11–58.

Stewart, M. A. and James Moore. "William Smith (1698–1741) and the Dissenters' Book Trade." *Bulletin of the Presbyterian Historical Society of Ireland* **22** (1993): 20–7.

Stewart, M. A. and John P. Wright (eds.). *Hume and Hume's Connexions.* Edinburgh University Press. 1994.

Strawson, Galen. *The Secret Connexion: Causation, Realism and David Hume.* Oxford: Clarendon Press, 1989.

Strawson, Galen. "David Hume: Objects and Power." In *The New Hume Debate,* second edition, edited by Rupert Read and Kenneth Richman. London: Routledge, 2007, 31–51.

Strawson, Galen. *The Evident Connexion: Mind, Self and David Hume,* Oxford University Press, forthcoming.

Stroud, Barry. *Hume.* London: Routledge, 1977.

Stroud, Barry. "Hume and the Idea of Causal Necessity." *Philosophical Studies* **33** (1978) 39–59.

Stroud, Barry. "'Guiding and Staining' the world with 'sentiments' and 'phantasms'." In *The New Hume Debate,* 2nd edn., edited by Rupert Read and Kenneth Richman. London: Routledge, 2007, 16–30.

Swain, Corliss. "Personal Identity." In *The Blackwell Guide to Hume's Treatise,* edited by Saul Traiger. Oxford: Blackwell, 2006, 132–50.

Taylor, Jacqueline. "Virtue and the Evaluation of Character." In *The Blackwell Guide to Hume's Treatise,* edited by Saul Traiger. Oxford: Blackwell, 2006, 276–95.

Traiger, Saul (ed.). *The Blackwell Guide to Hume's Treatise of Human Nature.* Oxford: Blackwell, 2006.

Turco, Luigi. "Sympathy and Moral Sense: 1725–1740." *British Journal for the History of Philosophy* **7** (1999): 79–101.

Turco, Luigi. "Moral Sense and the Foundations of Morals." In *The Cambridge Companion to the Scottish Enlightenment,* edited by A. Broadie. Cambridge University Press, 2003.

Turco, Luigi. "Le riposte di Hutcheson a Hume: Argomenti a favore e contro." In *Instruction and Amusement: Le ragioni dell'Illuminismo brittanico,* edited by Emanuele Ronchetti and Emilio Mazza. Padua: Il Poligrafo, 2005.

Turco, Luigi. "Hutcheson and Hume in a Recent Polemic." In *New Essays on David Hume,* edited by Emanuele Ronchetti and Emilio Mazza. Milan: FrancoAngeli, 2007, 171–98.

Underhill, Evelyn. *Mysticism,* 3rd edn. London: Methuen, 1912.

Warren, Howard C. *A History of the Association Psychology.* New York: Scribner's, 1921.

Williams, Bernard. *Shame and Necessity.* Berkeley: University of California Press, 1993.

Winkler, Kenneth P. "The New Hume." In *The New Hume Debate,* 2nd edn., edited by Rupert Read and Kenneth Richman. London: Routledge, 2007: 52–87.

Winkler, Kenneth P. "Hutcheson's Alleged Realism." *Journal of the History of Philosophy* **23** (1985): 179–94.

Wright, John P. *The Sceptical Realism of David Hume.* Manchester & Minneapolis: Manchester University Press & University of Minnesota Press, 1983.

Wright, John P. "Hume's Academic Scepticism." *Canadian Journal of Philosophy* **16** (1986): 407–36.

Wright, John P. "Association, Madness and the Measures of Probability in Locke and Hume." In *Psychology and Literature in the Eighteenth Century*, edited by Christopher Fox. New York: AMS Press, 1987, 103–27.

Wright, John P. "Metaphysics and Physiology: Mind, Body and the Animal Economy in Eighteenth-Century Scotland." In *Studies in the Philosophy of the Scottish Enlightenment*, edited by M. A. Stewart. Oxford: Clarendon Press, 1990, 251–301.

Wright, John P. "Butler and Hume on Habit and Moral Character." In *Hume and Hume's Connexions*, edited by M. A. Stewart and J. P. Wright. Edinburgh University Press, 1994, 105–18.

Wright, John P. "Hume, Descartes and the Materiality of the Soul." In *The Philosophical Canon in the 17th and 18th Centuries*, edited by G. A. J. Rogers and Sylvana Tomaselli. Rochester: University of Rochester Press, 1996, 175–90.

Wright, John P. "Dr. George Cheyne, Chevalier Ramsay, and Hume's Letter to a Physician" *Hume Studies* (April 2003): 125–41.

Wright, John P. "The Scientific Reception of Hume's Theory of Causation: Establishing the Positivist Interpretation." In *The Reception of David Hume in Europe*, edited by Peter Jones. London: Continuum, 2005, 327–47.

Wright, John P. "Reid's Answer to Hume's Scepticism: Turning Science into Common Sense." In E. Mazza and E. Ronchetti (eds.), *Instruction and Amusement: Le ragioni dell'Illuminismo brittanico*. Padua: Il Poligrafo, 2005, 143–63.

Wright, John P. "The Treatise: Composition, Reception and Response." In *The Blackwell Guide to Hume's Treatise of Human Nature*, edited by Saul Traiger. Oxford: Blackwell, 2006, 5–25.

Wright, John P. "Hume's Causal Realism: Recovering a Traditional Interpretation." In *The New Hume Debate*, 2nd edn., edited by Rupert Read and Kenneth Richman. London: Routledge, 2007, 88–99.

Wright, John P. "Kemp Smith and the Two Kinds of Naturalism in Hume's Philosophy." In *New Essays on David Hume*, edited by Emanuele Ronchetti and Emilio Mazza. Milan: FrancoAngeli, 2007, 17–36.

Wright, John P. "Hume on the Origin of 'Modern Honour': a Study in Hume's Philosophical Development." In *Philosophy and Religion in Enlightenment Britain*, edited by Ruth Savage. Oxford University Press, forthcoming.

Yolton, John. "Hume's Abstract in the Bibliothèque Raisonée." *Journal of the History of Ideas* **40** (1979): 157–8.

Yolton, John. *Perceptual Acquaintance from Descartes to Reid.* Minneapolis: University of Minnesota Press, 1984.

Yolton, John. *Realism and Appearances: An Essay in Ontology.* Cambridge University Press, 2000.

JOURNAL ARTICLES AND CONFERENCES ON HUME'S PHILOSOPHY

Articles on various topics in Hume's philosophy are to be found in many philosophical journals. These can be identified through the *Philosopher's Index* or the *Humanities Index.* Articles up to 1978 are listed by year and topic in Roland Hall, *Fifty Years of Hume Scholarship: A Bibliographical Guide* (Edinburgh University Press, 1978). These are supplemented by Hall's bibliographies which appear in the journal *Hume Studies* from 1977–85 and those of William Edward Morris from 1985 to the present.

Hume Studies, which began publication in 1975, is wholly devoted to articles on Hume's thought. There is unrestricted online access to articles in *Hume Studies* up to the last five years at www.humesociety.org/hs/browse.html Online access to articles in the most recent issues is restricted to members of the Hume Society: for details on membership (including student membership) go to www.humesociety.org/publications/index.html

The Hume Society sponsors an annual conference held at different locations throughout the globe, as well as at meetings of the three divisions of the American Philosophical Association. Periodic conferences on Hume are also sponsored by the British Society for the History of Philosophy, www.bshp.org.uk/ and the Eighteenth-Century Scottish Studies Society, www.ecsss.org/meetings.htm.

Index

justice, *see also artificial virtues*
  concerns property, 265
  distinguished from natural virtues, 276
  moral approval of, 261
  moral obligation of, 270–75
  moral sentiments of
    fixed by custom, 272, 275
    how formed, 271
  origin of
    3 sources of human conflict, 265
    convention arises through custom, 269
    from judgment/understanding, 267
    motivated by self-interest, 261, 265–70
    no natural motive of, 263–65
    not based on an original contract, 269
    serves the public interest, 269

Kail, Peter, 73, 89, 101, 113, 117, 124, 140, 249
Kant, Immanuel, 262
  on Hume on causation, 125
Kemp Smith, Norman, *see Smith, Norman Kemp*
knowledge, *see also insight*
  demonstrative, 43, 82–87
    degenerates to probability, 133
    involves necessity, 85
  distinguished from probability, 82
  implies necessity, 86
  intuitive, 84
  moral, whether possible, 252
  no knowledge of causation, 128
  reality of, 86
  relations are constant, 87
  requires adequate ideas, 86
  requires insight, x, 83
    into essences, 97
Kuehn, Manfred, 30

La Flèche
  Hume writes Treatise in, 19
  Jesuit college at, 25–26
Laird, John, 62
laws of nature, 268
libertarianism, *see free will; liberty, of indifference*
liberty, *see also will; free will*
  and voluntary actions, 171
  and necessity, xi–xii, 169–89
  of indifference, 171, 185, 189
    mistaken belief in, 182–86
    sensation of, 174
  of spontaneity, 170

Locke, John, 139, 154, 269
  and the experimental method, 27
  argument for the causal maxim, 94
  association of ideas in, 48–49, 56
  custom and habit, 56
  experimental method of, 44
  Hume's critque of
    on induction, 102–6
    insight into some causal connections, 105
  'natural' relations in, 49
  on abstract ideas, 66
  on causal reasoning, 88, 98
  on power, 4
  on the argument to design, 79
  on the existence of God, 3
  on thinking matter, 26, 80
Loeb, Louis, xv, 104, 132, 144, 145
love and hatred
  and moral approval and disapproval, 259
  have other persons as their objects, 198, 213
  produced by subjects related to others, 198

madmen, 181
Malebranche, Nicolas, 139, 249, 284
  calm desires vs. passions, 233
  imagination, theory of, 54–56
  influence on Hume's *Treatise*, 27, 56
  occasionalism of, 21, 56, 119, 127
  science of man and theory of natural relations, 56
Mandeville, Bernard, xiii, 201, 260
  experimental method of, 44
  Hume's reading of, 11
  influence on Hume, 13
  moral theory, 239, 260
    Hume's criticism of, 203, 261, 287
    Hutcheson's criticism of, 260
  on the Disease of the Learned, 8–9
  on virtue and vice, 201
  origin of virtue, 273
materialism, 80
mathematics, *see knowledge, demonstrative*
matter
  activity in, 5, 126
  modern conception of, 153–55
McCracken, Charles, 57, 127
Meditations of Descartes, 40–43, 129–30
melancholy, *see also Disease of the Learned*
  philosophical, 19
    and skepticism, 129, 130

For EU product safety concerns, contact us at Calle de José Abascal, 56–1°,
28003 Madrid, Spain or eugpsr@cambridge.org.

www.ingramcontent.com/pod-product-compliance
Ingram Content Group UK Ltd.
Pitfield, Milton Keynes, MK11 3LW, UK
UKHW020451240426
470322UK00016B/298